Economic Integration

Other International Economic Association publications

MONOPOLY AND COMPETITION AND THEIR REGULATION
THE BUSINESS CYCLE IN THE POST-WAR WORLD
THE THEORY OF WAGE DETERMINATION
THE ECONOMICS OF INTERNATIONAL MIGRATION
STABILITY AND PROGRESS IN THE WORLD ECONOMY
THE ECONOMIC CONSEQUENCES OF THE SIZE OF NATIONS
ECONOMIC DEVELOPMENT FOR LATIN AMERICA
THE THEORY OF CAPITAL
INFLATION
THE ECONOMICS OF TAKE-OFF INTO SUSTAINED GROWTH
INTERNATIONAL TRADE THEORY IN A DEVELOPING WORLD
ECONOMIC DEVELOPMENT WITH SPECIAL REFERENCE TO EAST ASIA
ECONOMIC DEVELOPMENT FOR AFRICA SOUTH OF THE SAHARA
THE THEORY OF INTEREST RATES
THE ECONOMICS OF EDUCATION
PROBLEMS IN ECONOMIC DEVELOPMENT
THE ECONOMIC PROBLEMS OF HOUSING
PRICE FORMATION IN VARIOUS ECONOMIES
THE DISTRIBUTION OF NATIONAL INCOME
ECONOMIC DEVELOPMENT FOR EASTERN EUROPE
RISK AND UNCERTAINTY
ECONOMIC PROBLEMS OF AGRICULTURE IN INDUSTRIAL SOCIETIES
INTERNATIONAL ECONOMIC RELATIONS
BACKWARD AREAS IN ADVANCED COUNTRIES
PUBLIC ECONOMICS
ECONOMIC DEVELOPMENT IN SOUTH ASIA
NORTH AMERICAN AND WESTERN EUROPEAN ECONOMIC POLICIES
PLANNING AND MARKET RELATIONS
THE GAP BETWEEN RICH AND POOR NATIONS
LATIN AMERICA IN THE INTERNATIONAL ECONOMY
MODELS OF ECONOMIC GROWTH
SCIENCE AND TECHNOLOGY IN ECONOMIC GROWTH
ALLOCATION UNDER UNCERTAINTY
TRANSPORT AND THE URBAN ENVIRONMENT
THE ECONOMICS OF HEALTH AND MEDICAL CARE
THE MANAGEMENT OF WATER QUALITY AND THE ENVIRONMENT
AGRICULTURE POLICY IN DEVELOPING COUNTRIES
THE ECONOMIC DEVELOPMENT OF BANGLADESH
ECONOMIC FACTORS IN POPULATION GROWTH
CLASSICS IN THE THEORY OF PUBLIC FINANCE
METHODS OF LONG-TERM PLANNING AND FORECASTING
THE MICROECONOMIC FOUNDATIONS OF MACROECONOMICS
THE ECONOMICS OF PUBLIC SERVICES
INFLATION THEORY AND ANTI-INFLATION POLICY
THE ORGANIZATION AND RETRIEVAL OF ECONOMIC KNOWLEDGE
ECONOMIC RELATIONS BETWEEN EAST AND WEST
ECONOMETRIC CONTRIBUTIONS TO PUBLIC POLICY
APPROPRIATE TECHNOLOGIES FOR DEVELOPING COUNTRIES

Economic Integration Worldwide, Regional, Sectoral

Proceedings of the Fourth Congress of the
International Economic Association
held in Budapest, Hungary

EDITED BY
FRITZ MACHLUP
President 1971–4

© The International Economic Association 1976

First edition 1976
Reprinted 1978

Published by
THE MACMILLAN PRESS LTD
London and Basingstoke
Associated companies in Delhi Dublin Hong Kong
Johannesburg Lagos Melbourne
New York Singapore Tokyo

Distributed in the United States
by Halsted Press, a Division of
John Wiley & Sons, Inc., New York

ISBN 0 333 18130 1

Text set in Great Britain at The Pitman Press, Bath
and printed in Hong Kong

Library of Congress Cataloging in Publication Data

Main entry under title:

Economic integration.

(International Economic Association publications)
"A Halsted Press book."
Includes index.
1.   International economic integration -- Con-
gresses. I.   Machlup, Fritz, 1902-   II. Inter-
national Economic Association.
HF1408.E34   1976   338.9   76–10281
ISBN 0–470–01381–8

Contents

Contents

Acknowledgements

The preparations for a large congress, the planning of its programme, its organisation and arrangements, the typing, translating, duplicating of the invited papers for distribution, the editing of the papers and reports for the volume of proceedings, countless other tasks during and after the congress, and, last not least, the financing of the entire undertaking, require the co-operation of many individuals, groups, institutions, agencies and foundations. An acknowledgement of their contributions is in order and may well take precedence over anything that is to go into this volume. The International Economic Association expresses its gratitude to

The Honorary Patron of the Congress, Jenö Fock, Prime Minister of the
    Hungarian People's Republic
The Presidium of the Hungarian Economic Association
The Hungarian National Bank
The Secretariat of the Congress in Budapest, including the charming ladies
    and gentlemen who acted as guides and advisers
The Hungarian hosts of the working groups
The interpreters operating the simultaneous translation of the speeches
The press covering the proceedings
The United Nations Educational, Scientific, and Cultural Organisation
    (UNESCO)
The Ford Foundation
The authors of papers, comments, and opening statements
The chairmen and vice-chairmen of plenary sessions and working groups
The Programme Committee for this congress
The Editor of Publications
The Secretariat of the Association

Executive Committees and Secretariat of the International Economic Association

The Programme Committee for this Congress

Professor Fritz Machlup (USA), Chairman
Professor Bela Balassa (USA)
Professor Raymond Barre (France)
Professor Oleg Bogomolov (USSR)
Professor Béla Csikós-Nagy (Hungary)
Dr Robert A. Gardiner (Ghana)
Professor Herbert Giersch (Federal Republic of Germany)
Professor Harry Johnson (UK)
Professor Ryutaro Komiya (Japan)
Professor Erik Lundberg (Sweden)
Professor Josef Pajestka (Poland)
Professor Raúl Prebisch (Argentine)

Authors of Invited Papers, Comments and Opening Statements, and Chairmen and Vice-Chairmen of Plenary Sessions and Working Groups

Note: affiliations and countries of residence are given as of the time of the invitations, without regard to later changes.

Professor Orlando d'Alauro (Italy), University of Genoa; General Secretary, Italian Economic Society. Chairman of Working Group D.

Professor Alexander I. Anchishkin (USSR), Central Economico-Mathematical Institute, Academy of Sciences of the USSR, Moscow. Vice-chairman of Working Group A.

Professor Åke Andersson (Sweden), University of Göteborg, and University of Pennsylvania (Philadelphia). Author of opening statement for Working Group A.

Professor Bela Balassa (USA), The Johns Hopkins University, Baltimore, Maryland. Author of main paper for First Plenary Session.

Professor Raymond Barre (France), Université de Paris. Chairman of Working Group F.

Professor Giorgio Basevi (Italy), Institute of Economics, University of Bologna. Author of discussion paper for Working Group D.

Professor Mamoun Beheiry (Sudan), Chairman, Development and Economic Affairs Committee, People's Council, Khartoum. Chairman of Third Plenary Session, first half.

Mr Raymond Bertrand (France), Organisation for Economic Co-operation and Development, Paris. Author of opening statement for Working Group E.

Professor József Bognár (Hungary), Chairman, Institute for World Economics, Hungarian Academy of Sciences, Budapest. Author of main paper for Third Plenary Session, first half, and Working Group G.

Professor Oleg T. Bogomolov (USSR), Director, Institute of Economics of the World Socialist System, Academy of Sciences of the USSR, Moscow. Author of main paper for Fourth Plenary Session, first half, and Working Group I.

Professor Henk C. Bos (Netherlands), Erasmus University, Rotterdam. Chairman of Working Group J.

Professor Richard N. Cooper (USA), Yale University, Connecticut. Author of main paper for Second Plenary Session, first half.

Professor João Cravinho (Portugal), Ministry of Economy, Lisbon. Vice-chairman of Working Group C.

Professor Béla Csikós-Nagy (Hungary), President, Board for Materials and Prices; President, Hungarian Economic Association, Budapest. Chairman of Working Group I.

Dr Victoria Curzon (Switzerland), Institut Universitaire des Hautes Études Internationales, Geneva. Author of opening statement for Working Group B.

Professor Roger Dehem (Canada), Université Laval, Quebec. Author of opening statement for Working Group G.

Professor Dimitrios Delivanis (Greece), University of Thessaloniki. Author of discussion paper for Fourth Plenary Session, second half, and Working Group B.

Mr Geoffrey R. Denton (United Kingdom), University of Reading. Author of discussion paper for Working Group H.

Professor Harry Eastman (Canada), University of Toronto, Ontario. Chairman of First Plenary Session.

Professor H. Edward English (Canada), Carleton University, Ottawa, Ontario. Author of opening statement for Working Group I.

Professor Ricardo Ffrench-Davis (Chile), Research Centre for National Planning, Catholic University of Chile, Santiago, Chile. Author of discussion paper for Third Plenary Session, second half, and Working Group A.

Professor Nuno Fidelino de Figueiredo (Brazil), President, Investment Bank, São Paulo. Author of discussion paper for Working Group C.

Professor Jenö Fock (Hungary), Prime Minister of Hungary. Address of welcome.

Professor Lev M. Gatovski (USSR), Institute of Economics, Academy of Sciences of the USSR, Moscow. Vice-chairman of Working Group C.

Mr Dharam P. Ghai (Kenya), Director, Institute for Development Studies, University of Nairobi. Author of discussion paper for Working Group H.

Professor Herbert Giersch (Federal Republic Germany), Director, Institut für Weltwirtschaft, Universität Kiel. Chairman of Working Group E.

Dr Igor E. Guryev (USSR), Academy of Sciences of the USSR, Moscow. Vice-chairman of Working Group D.

Professor Gottfried Haberler (USA), American Enterprise Institute for Public Policy Research, Washington, DC. Co-author with John P. Hardt of discussion paper for fourth Plenary Session, first half, and Working Group I.

Mr Mahbub ul Haq (Pakistan), International Bank for Reconstruction and Development, Washington, DC. Author of discussion paper for Working Group H.

Mr John P. Hardt (USA), Congressional Research Service, US Congress, Washington, DC. Co-author with Gottfried Haberler of discussion paper for Fourth Plenary Session, first half, and Working Group I.

Mr Rune Hellberg (Sweden), United Nations Conference on Trade and Development, Geneva. Vice-chairman of Working Group J.

Dr Helen Hughes (Australia), International Bank for Reconstruction and Development, Washington, DC. Author of opening statement for Working Group H.

Professor Harry G. Johnson (United Kingdom), London School of Economics. Chairman of Working Group G.

Professor Lord Nicholas Kaldor (United Kingdom), University of Cambridge. Chairman of Third Plenary Session, second half.

Mr Günal Kansu (Turkey), United Nations Conference on Trade and Development, Geneva. Author of discussion paper for Working Group H.

Mr Michael Kaser (United Kingdom), St Antony's College, Oxford. Vice-chairman of Working Group I.

Professor Peter Kenen (USA), Princeton University, New Jersey. Author of main paper for Working Group E.

Academician Tigran S. Khachaturov (USSR), Member, Academy of Sciences of The USSR; President, Association of Soviet Economic Institutions, Moscow. Chairman of Second Plenary Session, first half.

Professor Gunther Kohlmey (German Democratic Republic), Zentralinstitut für Wirtschaftswissenschaften, Akademie der Wissenschaften der DDR, Berlin. Author of main paper for Working Group J.

Professor Ryutaro Komiya (Japan), University of Tokyo. Author of discussion paper for Working Group C.

Professor Willi Kunz (German Democratic Republic), Nationalkomitee für Wirtschaftswissenschaften, Akademie der Wissenschaften der DDR, Berlin. Author of discussion paper for Third Plenary Session, second half, and Working Group A.

Dr Alexandre Lamfalussy (Belgium), Banque de Bruxelles. Author of main paper for Working Group F.

Dr Carlos Langoni (Brazil), Brazilian Institute of Economics, Rio de Janeiro. Reader of discussion paper by Germánico Salgado (absent) for Second Plenary Session, first half.

Professor Abba P. Lerner (USA), University of Tel Aviv (Israel), and Queens College, City University, New York. Author of discussion paper for Working Group J.

Professor Richard G. Lipsey (Canada), Queen's University, Kingston, Ontario. Author of discussion paper for First Plenary Session.

Professor Eduardo Lizano (Costa Rica), University of Costa Rica, San José. Author of main paper for Working Group H.

Professor Puntsagdashin Louvsandorzh (Mongolia), Director, Institute of Economics of the Mongolian Academy of Sciences, Mongolian People's Republic, Ulan Bator. Vice-chairman of Working Group H.

Professor Erik Lundberg (Sweden), Stockholm School of Economics. Chairman of Working Group A.

Professor Fritz Machlup (USA), New York University, and Princeton University, New Jersey. Presidential address in Second Plenary Session, second half.

Dr Margarita Maksimova (USSR), Institute of World Economics and International Relations, Academy of Sciences of the USSR, Moscow. Author of discussion paper for First Plenary Session.

Professor Edmond Malinvaud (France), Ministère de l'Economie et des Finances, Paris. Chairman of Second Plenary Session, second half.

Professor Robert Marjolin (France), Université de Paris. Author of discussion paper for Third Plenary Session, first half, and Working Group G.

Mr Carlos Massad (Chile), Executive Director, International Monetary Fund, Washington, DC. Author of discussion paper for Working Group F.

Academician Evgueni G. Mateëv (Bulgaria), Bulgarian Academy of Sciences, Sofia. Author of discussion paper for Second Plenary Session, first half.

Mr Madan Gopal Mathur (India), General Agreement on Tariffs and Trade, Geneva. Author of opening statement for Working Group J.

Professor Kosta Mihailović (Yugoslavia), Economic Institute, Belgrade. Author of main paper for Working Group D.

Professor Henk A. J. Misset (Netherlands), University of Amsterdam. Chairman of Fifth Plenary Session.

Professor Roman Moldovan (Romania), Vice President, Academy for Social and Political Sciences, Bucharest. Author of discussion paper for Third Plenary Session, first half, and Working Group G.

Professor Jan Mujzel (Poland), University of Lodz. Reader of summary report by Josef Pajestka (absent) on Working Group B.

Professor Robert A. Mundell (Canada), University of Waterloo, Ontario. Author of discussion paper for Working Group E.

Professor Preben Munthe (Norway), Oslo University. Author of opening statement for Working Group D.

Professor Jerzy Mycielski (Poland), Foreign Trade Research Institute, Warsaw, and Institute of Theoretical Physics, Warsaw University. Co-author with Witold Trzeciakowski of discussion paper for Fourth Plenary Session, first half, and Working Group I.

Professor Fritz Neumark (Federal Republic Germany), Universität Frankfurt. Chairman of Fourth Plenary Session, first half.

Professor Adolf Nussbaumer (Austria), Institut für Wirtschaftswissenschaften, Universität Wien. Vice chairman of Working Group B.

Dr Antonio del Olmo Parra (Spain), Permanent Representative, Ilustre Colegio Central de Economistas, Madrid. Vice Chairman of Working Group F.

Dr Zdeněk Orlíček (Czechoslovakia), Director, Institute for Research on Foreign Trade, Prague. Author of discussion paper for Fourth Plenary Session, second half, and Working Group B.

Professor Josef Pajestka (Poland), Vice-Chairman, Planning Commission of the Council of Ministers; President, Polish Economic Society, Warsaw, Chairman of Working Group B.

Mr Indraprasad G. Patel (India), Director, United Nations Development Programme, United Nations, New York. Chairman of Working Group H.

Professor Jouko J. Paunio (Finland), University of Helsinki. Vice-chairman of Working Group E.

Professor Garry Pursell (Australia), Development Research Center, International Bank for Reconstruction and Development, Washington, DC. Reader of discussion paper by Mahbub ul Haq (absent) for Working Group H.

Professor Stanislaw Raczkowski (Poland), Central School of Planning and Statistics, Warsaw. Vice-chairman of Working Group G.

Professor Poul Nørregaard Rasmussen, University of Copenhagen. Chairman of Sixth Plenary Session.

Professor Austin Robinson (United Kingdom), University of Cambridge. Chairman of Fourth Plenary Session, second half.

Mr Germánico Salgado (Ecuador), member of the Board of the Andean Group, Lima. Author of discussion paper for Second Plenary Session, first half.

Professor Mikhail V. Senin (USSR), Director, Council for Mutual Economic Assistance, International Institute of Economic Problems of the World Socialist System, Moscow. Author of discussion paper for Working Group J.

Professor Alexander K. Swoboda (Switzerland), Institut Universitaire des Hautes Études Internationales, Geneva. Author of discussion paper for Working Group E.

Professor Witold Trzeciakowski (Poland), Foreign Trade Research Institute, Warsaw. Co-author with Jerzy Mycielski of discussion paper for Fourth Plenary Session, first half, and Working Group I.

Professor Shigeto Tsuru (Japan), President, Hitotsubashi University, Tokyo. Chairman of Working Group G.

Mr Pierre Uri (France), Université de Paris. Author of main paper for Working Group C.

Mr Péter Veress (Hungary), Deputy Minister, Ministry of Foreign Trade, Budapest. Author of opening statement for Working Group C.

Professor Jean Waelbroeck (Belgium), Centre for Operations Research and Econometrics, Louvain, and University of British Columbia, Vancouver. Author of main paper for Third Plenary Session, second half, and Working Group A.

Dr Hilde Wander (Federal Republic Germany), Institut für Weltsirtschaft, Universität Kiel. Author of discussion paper for Working Group D.

Professor Marina von Neumann Whitman (USA), University of Pittsburgh, Pennsylvania. Author of opening statement for Working Group F.

Professor Hans Willgerodt (Federal Republic Germany), Universität Köln.

Author of main paper for Fourth Plenary Session, second half, and Working Group B.

Dr John H. Williamson (United Kingdom), International Monetary Fund, Washington, DC. Author of discussion paper for Working Group F.

Formal Opening of Congress
Address of Welcome
Fritz Machlup, President, International Economic Association

Mr Prime Minister, your Excellencies, dear colleagues, ladies and gentlemen
in this great hall and in the other rooms where our voices are being heard
and our pictures seen on screens, this is a moment of special significance for
some of us: the end of a period of almost three years of planning and
preparatory work, and the beginning of a week that will test whether our
plans have been sound and our preparations adequate. Will we fail or pass
this test? Most of us remember the feelings we had as young students before
an examination for which we had worked hard and conscientiously but
where we were still wondering what we might have missed in preparing for
it. Well, let us shed our tensions and be confident that we shall succeed; and
let us hope that this will be a week to which we all shall be able to look back
with pleasure and satisfaction.

Some of our tensions, I suspect will disappear only after a day or two. It
is for the first time that so many economists of different national background
and different ideological persuasion have gathered in one meeting. The largest
delegations are from socialist countries, but the numbers from nonsocialist
and mixed economies are not much smaller, and those from developing
countries are sizable. Will we all understand one another? Will there be
heated confrontations or cool scholarly argumentation of problematic
issues? Will we leave this congress feeling that we, each of us, delivered our
'message' but complaining that it fell on deaf ears and closed minds, or will
we instead depart with the firm resolution to think over with care what we
have heard here but may not have sufficiently appreciated at the moment?
The success of this congress shall be judged by the increase in our understanding of arguments and positions which we had been inclined to reject
or disregard.

One may say, without exaggeration, that this world congress of economists
opens a new phase in the history of the dialogue between East and West and
South: for, I repeat, never before have such large numbers of economists
from socialist, nonsocialist and developing countries participated in one
meeting. The International Economic Association has thereby in effect become
more international than it used to be. This is an achievement that should be
maintained in the future and, if possible, developed even further by steady
efforts by all concerned.

This congress will be honoured by an address of welcome from the Prime
Minister of our host country. Jenö Fock is not only the Patron of this
congress, but also a colleague of ours, who — as a political economist — has
dealt for more than a quarter of a century with the practical solution of the
great problems we study. The relationship between economic theory and
practice has often been compared to that between the theoretical medical
disciplines and the treatment of patients or the prevention of disease. This
does not mean that all economists are engaged in applied economics. There
are many whose chief interest lies in pure theory and who are motivated only
by intellectual curiosity, not by an urge to help humanity by offering
practical policy advice. Most economists, however, seem to be motivated by

the hope that the findings of their research and analysis may prove useful to policy makers. The man of the world of practical politics, on the other hand, does not believe everything the economists say, either as predictors of things to come or as prescribers of things to do. The man in charge of governmental decisions is well advised if he takes our advice with a few grains of salt. Nevertheless, again and again he turns to the professional economists with his timely questions. And he listens to one, and another, and a third, until he finds an economist who tells him just what he wanted to hear and advises him to do what he had wanted to do in the first place.

Prime Minister Jenö Fock has been engaged in practical economic policy in many fields: in microeconomics as well as macroeconomics, in domestic as well as international economic relations. As Prime Minister he has had to deal with all sorts of problems, but we understand that those of an economic character have always been closest to him. Thus we may regard him as a colleague. We are greatly honoured by his presence at the opening of this congress. Ladies and Gentlemen, the Chairman of the Council of Ministers of the Hungarian People's Republic.

Address of Welcome
Jenö Fock, Prime Minister of the Hungarian People's Republic

Mr Chairman, ladies and gentlemen, On behalf of the Government of the Hungarian People's Republic I want to greet the Fourth World Congress of the International Economic Association.

The venue of your meeting has, I think, been selected, not by chance, but deliberately on the basis of good reasons. The fact that you have chosen the capital of a country committed to building socialism as the place for your important world congress is evidence of a readiness to intensify the co-operation among economists of varying ideological persuasions. At the same time I consider your selection of the venue as expressing both your esteem for our People's Republic and your appreciation of the development of economic science in Hungary.

We know that the International Economic Association follows with great attention the events and processes taking place in international economic relations. The subjects of its scholarly deliberations are selected accordingly. It is gratifying that the present world congress has prepared an agenda for the discussion of an extremely important matter, the universal problems of economic integration.

The selection of this subject shows that the International Economic Association has correctly recognised the strongest tendency in the international development of our age, which is to an increasing extent characterised by the easing of tension and by the pursuit of the principles of peaceful coexistence. The efforts at liquidating the remnants of the cold war and at securing the universal irreversibility of the development towards peaceful coexistence seem to be increasingly successful. The deep-rooted changes taking place in international politics have opened up new possibilities and new vistas for economic co-operation.

Utilisation of existing opportunities for international division of labour has played an outstanding role among the factors in economic growth. The rate of growth of international trade since the end of the period of reconstruction following the Second World War has virtually everywhere exceeded the rate of growth of the countries' gross national products or national incomes. It is logical and absolutely justified that the attention of the economists of the world be concentrated on the economic problems of international division of labour.

The effects of the changes taking place in international economics will, to a lesser or greater extent, influence the economies of every country and promote, or possibly hinder, economic development. Positive and negative effects and tendencies may be enforced simultaneously. The governments of all countries must now in their policy decisions take account of the events that take place in international economic relations and must appraise their consequences.

In the socialist countries, which account for one sixth of our world, the national economy has been developing on the basis of plans founded on scientific results, without economic crises and recessions. This development has produced important successes that have influenced the shaping of the international economy in a positive way. The development of productive capacities, of systems of mass communication, of the supply of goods and services, and of the rate of scientific achievement has created significant reciprocal effects among countries and groups of countries.

The awareness of common problems has played an important part in strengthening relations among individual countries. The protection of the environment, for instance, can be solved less and less by any single country acting alone. There is no question that international co-operation is required for its promotion, and for the planned improvement of living conditions appropriate for human existence, as well as for the development of certain parts of the infrastructure, such as roads, waterways, or power systems.

All of these processes have created fresh obligations for the economists who are active in various countries; they have, at the same time, revealed new possibilities for the solution of the problems in a framework of international co-operation.

Based on economic and political considerations, various forms of international economic community, of plurinational, regional organisation, have been developed or are being developed in all parts of the world, irrespective of their level of economic development. The two most important ones are the CMEA, successfully comprising and co-ordinating the economic and scientific activities of the nine socialist countries, and the EEC, which includes nine of the Western European capitalist countries. Both these communities in their operations reflect and express the defined economic and political systems of their constituents. According to the principles adopted by the socialist countries belonging to the CMEA, this regional grouping will not lead to a policy of closed doors towards countries outside of the organisation. Such a policy would unfavourably influence the development of the countries participating in the regional integration and would simultaneously be disadvantageous to the economies of other countries. Efforts aimed at producing new ways for the international division of labour are gaining in strength in the countries or groups of countries on all five continents. Search in this direction in the developing countries of Latin America and Africa similarly indicates this process.

We desire that the development and intensification of the international division of labour should strengthen relations among peoples and countries. International trade and the creation of various forms of international economic co-operation should also serve as a bridge between countries. The economic communities and groupings, which are in varying stages of their development of integration, should produce and maintain relations with each other on the basis of equality and mutual advantage. This is an important conditions for the development of international economic co-operation founded on democratic principles, and it will correspond to the interests of all peoples.

The extremely widespread process of economic integration taking place in various forms will be realised under different social, political, and economic conditions and will therefore have different socio-economic consequences. The intensification of integration is a rather long process and, at the same time, the establishment of connections among many institutions in countries with different social and political systems requires considerable circumspection and tact. After all, it is not only a question of creating the required conditions and institutions, but also of re-establishing and strengthening mutual trust among governments. We, all of us, should work persistently for strengthening trust, and for counteracting those who stir up conflicts and misunderstandings. It is particularly you, the scholarly investigators of national economies and of international economic relations, who can do much for these good purposes.

In addressing this distinguished forum of international economists, I wish to emphasise that the social and political responsibility of those engaged in the practical application of economic sciences has gained special significance in our days. Economists are in a position to analyse the economic development of their respective countries in relation to the international economic processes and to judge the international impact of the decisions that are taken. The important activities of economists should find expression, first of all, in the utilisation of the achievements of the scientific–technical revolution to serve the interests and prosperity of mankind. This task may increasingly be performed through the international co-ordination of national objectives and the development and utilisation of available resources.

All I have said in connection with the activities of economists also indicates, of course, the recognition that some of the tasks exceed the framework of what is strictly defined as economics. It is necessary to take into consideration the international political factors that will affect the processes of world economic integration. The cultivators of economics should rely on the methods and results of the other social sciences as well. This aspiration is reflected in the fact that the agenda of this world congress includes the social and political relations of integration processes as well as the institutional analysis of the systems.

As the International Economic Association approaches the twenty-fifth anniversary of its establishment, I should like to refer to that part of its statutes that defines the object of the association as the widening of the personal contacts of economists working in different countries of the world and the strengthening of the spirit of mutual understanding. I think that the statement of this specification in your statutes has never been of more timely interest than it is in these days. It gives us pleasure that the association is increasingly able to fulfil this noble mission, as we find confirmed by the fact that we may welcome in Budapest more than 1600 economists coming from seventy-seven countries.

Permit me to speak with appreciation of those who have been engaged in the preparation of this congress: the Executive Committee of the International Economic Association, its President and its Secretary-General, who have repeatedly provided personal assistance to those engaged in the work of organising this large meeting.

I may state with pleasure that the Hungarian Economic Association has participated in the work of preparing this world congress and I hope that the results of their self-sacrificing work will be enjoyed by all of you who are attending. I trust that our visitors will be satisfied with the work of the Hungarian Economic Association.

In conclusion, I want to convey, on behalf of the Government of the Hungarian People's Republic as well as of myself, our best wishes for fruitful discussion to all of the participants in the congress. I hope that, in addition to the scholarly deliberations, you will also have the opportunity to get acquainted with our capital city and with the picturesque sights of our country.

Thank you for your attention.

Address of Welcome
Béla Csikós-Nagy, President, Hungarian Economic Association

Ladies and gentlemen, in the name of the Presidium of the Hungarian Economic Association, as well as of all the Hungarian economists, I greet all of the participants of the Fourth World Congress of Economists with respect and friendship. As it is well known to you, at the request of the International Economic Association the Hungarian Economic Association has taken charge of organising this Fourth World Congress of Economists.

The study of economics in our country has a long and successful history. Already in the last century the activity of our progressive economists led to outstanding achievements; several of them gained international reputations as well. Hungarian economists discovered very early the advantages of establishing associations; already in the last century an association of economists began to function. In its present form, the Hungarian Economic Association has existed since 1959. The reorganisation stemmed from the realisation that the improvement of economic theory and practice is a task requiring the collaboration of a large number of economists dealing with both theoretical and practical problems. The acquisition of knowledge and the exchange of ideas are well served by the organisation of economists into an association enhancing the opportunities for the development of their discipline.

The fundamental purpose of our Association is to further the study and the application of economics within a voluntary, progressive, Marxist-oriented framework that provides for the socialist development of the national economy, and to rally the Hungarian economists to achieve these targets. In order to realise the tasks put down in the statutes, the association organises lectures, conferences, inquiries and courses of lectures, engages in publishing, and conducts competitions.

The practical work of our association has been organised within the framework of sections in Budapest and county organisations in the country. The association has thirteen sections in Budapest and eighteen county organisations, with a total membership of 6000. In the last year our organisations, and sections have held 300 conferences.

We have put a heavy emphasis on dealing with young economists. Every year, we organise a nationwide meeting of them in order to maintain the necessary professional relationship with young graduates and even under-graduates.

In accordance with our purposes, the international relations activities of our association have expanded. Our association has been a member of the International Economic Association since 1962. The expansion of international relations is demonstrated by the increasing and active participation of Hungarian economists in international scientific conferences.

Speaking for them, we should like to hope that it was as a recognition of the activities of the Hungarian Economic Association that the International Economic Association assigned to us the honourable task of helping in the administrative work necessary to organise the Fourth World Congress of Economists and invited Hungary to be the host country of the congress. The preparations for the congress have been under way for a long time. It was in 1971 that the Executive Committee of the International Economic Association suggested to the Hungarian Economic Association that — after Rome, Vienna and Montreal — Budapest, the capital of Hungary, be the host city for the Fourth World Congress of Economists. The Presidium of our association started the preparatory planning work early in 1972. We created several committees, with the participation of experts in organising the congress and of economists working ardently for the cause of international economic integration and of international co-operation. The Presidium of the association is confident that this international congress will be an important contribution to the development of our discipline, both directly and indirectly.

When different views and approaches meet or differ with each other at our congress, we believe that we move nearer to a mutual learning and understanding of our respective thoughts. We hope and expect that the meeting will also be a contribution to international co-operation. During the preparatory planning, the Presidium considered (and we hope that this expectation will be fully proved by the congress) that we shall not only promote the development of economics, the co-operation of scholars and practical experts, but also that our congress will make a contribution to the great cause of international *détente*, of co-operation among countries and peoples of the world.

I welcome all the participants in the congress and members of their families who have accompanied them to Budapest, and wish them an enjoyable stay in our hospitable country. We are confident that the economists, our colleagues and friends who are here on the occasion of this congress will return to their countries not only with enriched professional experiences, but also even after such a short stay, with favourable impressions of our social and economic conditions.

Introduction

Fritz Machlup

The Fourth World Congress of the International Economic Association was held in Budapest from 19 to 24 August 1974 under the Presidency of the editor of this volume. It brought together almost 1800 economists from seventy-seven countries; over 500 persons participated actively in the discussions.

The theme of the congress had been chosen with several objectives in mind: it should be of general interest in virtually every part of the world and of professional interest to the largest possible number of economists; the subject should lend itself to a natural subdivision into separate problems for discussion in several working groups that would appear to and attract economists specialised in pure theory, in monetary and fiscal problems, in questions of industrial, agricultural, or labour economics, in the theory and policy of international trade, in socio-political and other institutional aspects, etc. Economic integration was just such a subject.

Among the objectives of our open congresses is that they combine an opportunity for all to hear a few selected speakers with an opportunity for as many as wish to participate in the discussion of problems falling under the theme selected. The technique of attaining these objectives is to provide for plenary sessions; for separate working groups with open discussion; and for final reports on the transactions of the working groups to give all participants an overview of the entire proceedings. Another goal of a world congress is to include in its programme representatives of as many countries as can possibly be accommodated. This goal was attained by the Congress of Budapest planning a programme that contained the names of eighty-one economists, 51 of these as authors or co-authors of main papers, discussion papers and opening statements, and another thirty as chairmen or vice-chairmen of six plenary sessions and ten working groups. The eighty-one economists on the programme came from forty-two different countries. In addition to the invited papers, there were contributed papers delivered by some who attended one of the ten working groups; many others spoke extemporaneously, addressing more directly the points raised during the discussion.

After preliminary explorations which the President had started in

November 1971, the Programme Committee was constituted in July 1972. Its first task was to formulate the topics for plenary sessions and working groups and select speakers to be invited for main and discussion papers. The most difficult problem faced by the committee was the conflict between two maximising or optimising objectives: to get the best specialist for each subject and to get the widest possible geographic distribution of speakers. Maximum efficiency (or proficiency) and optimum distribution cannot be attained at the same time; compromises have to be made. That the committee achieved a good compromise is attested to by an approximate balance of complaints: criticisms that not the most renowned specialist had been chosen for each topic, and protestations that several countries were not sufficiently represented on the programme balanced each other. The Programme Committee evidently had well succeeded in its balancing act; others may judge whether it should be compared to a balancing act of diplomats or to one of acrobats on the high trapeze in a good circus.

The programme, corrected for changes required by some last-minute cancellations and substitutions, is here reproduced:

PROGRAMME OF THE FOURTH WORLD CONGRESS OF ECONOMISTS
Monday, 19 August 1974

9.30–10.15am: FORMAL OPENING OF CONGRESS
Chairman: Fritz Machlup
Addresses of welcome by Fritz Machlup, President, International Economic
    Association; Jenö Fock, Prime Minister of the Hungarian People's
    Republic; and Béla Csikós-Nagy, President, Hungarian Economic
    Association

11.00am–12.30pm: FIRST PLENARY SESSION
Theme: 'Types of Integration'
Chairman: Harry Eastman (Canada)
Main paper: Bela Balassa (USA)
Discussion papers: (1) Margarita Maksimova (USSR); (2) Richard G. Lipsey
    (Canada)

3.00–4.30pm: SECOND PLENARY SESSION, FIRST HALF
Theme: 'Worldwide *versus* Regional Integration: Is there an Optimum Size of
    the Integrated Area?'
Chairman: Tigran S. Khachaturov (USSR)
Main paper: Richard N. Cooper (USA)
Discussion papers: (1) Germánico Salgado (Ecuador), read by Carlos
    Langoni (Brazil); (2) Evgueni Mateëv (Bulgaria)

5.00–6.00pm: SECOND PLENARY SESSION, SECOND HALF
Theme: 'A History of Thought on Economic Integration'
Chairman: Edmond Malinvaud (France)
Address: Fritz Machlup, President

Tuesday, 20 August 1974

9.00–10.30am: THIRD PLENARY SESSION, FIRST HALF
Theme: 'Socio-Political and Institutional Aspects of Integration'
Chairman: Mamown Beheiry (Sudan)
Main paper: József Bognár (Hungary)
Discussion papers: (1) Robert Marjolin (France); (2) Roman Moldovan
    (Romania)
Discussion continued in Working Group G

11.00am–12.30pm: THIRD PLENARY SESSION, SECOND HALF
Theme: 'Measuring the Degree or Progress of Integration'
Chairman: Nicholas Lord Kaldor (UK)
Main paper: Jean Waelbroeck (Belgium)
Discussion papers: (1) Willi Kunz (German Dem. Rep.); (2) Ricardo Ffrench-
    Davis (Chile)
Discussion continued in Working Group A

3.00–4.30pm: FOURTH PLENARY SESSION, FIRST HALF
Theme: 'Integration by Market Forces and through Planning'
Chairman: Fritz Neumark (Federal Republic Germany)
Main paper: Oleg T. Bogomolov (USSR)
Discussion papers; (1) Gottfried Haberler and John P. Hardt (USA);
        (2) Witold Trzeciakowski and Jerzy Mycielski (Poland)
Discussion continued in Working Group I

5.00–6.00pm: FOURTH PLENARY SESSION, SECOND HALF
Theme: 'Sectoral Integration: Agriculture, Transport, Energy and Selected
    Industries'
Chairman: Austin Robinson (UK)
Main paper: Hans Willgerodt (Federal Republic Germany)
Discussion papers: (1) Zdeněk Orlíček (Czechoslovakia); (2) Dimitrios
    Delivanis (Greece)
Discussion continued in Working Group B

Wednesday, 21 August 1974

9.00–12.00: Working groups, first session
3.00–6.00pm: Working groups, second session

Thursday, 22 August 1974

9.00am—12.00: Working groups, third session
3.00—6.00pm: Working groups, fourth session

Friday, 23 August 1974: Free

Saturday, 24 August 1974

9.00am—12.00: FIFTH PLENARY SESSION
Chairman: Henk A. J. Misset (Netherlands)
Reports by chairmen of working groups A, B, C, D and E

3.00—6.00pm: SIXTH PLENARY SESSION
Chairman: Poul Nørregaard Rasmussen (Denmark)
Reports by chairmen of working groups F, G, H, I and J

WORKING GROUPS: BASIC OUTLINE

Working Group A

Theme: 'Measuring the Degree or Progress of Economic Integration'
Chairman: Erik Lundberg (Sweden)
Vice-chairman: Alexander I. Anchishkin (USSR)
Main paper: see Third Plenary Session, second half
Discussion papers: see Third Plenary Session, second half
Opening statement: Åke Andersson (Sweden)

Working Group B

Theme: 'Sectoral Integration: Agriculture, Transport, Energy and Selected
    Industries'
Chairman: Josef Pajestka (Poland). Chairman's report read by Jan Mujzel
    (Poland)
Vice-chairman: Adolf Nussbaumer (Austria)
Main paper; see Fourth Plenary Session, second half
Discussion papers: see Fourth Plenary Session, second half
Opening statement: Victoria Curzon (Switzerland)

Working Group C

Theme: 'Industrial Policy: Location, Technology, Multinational Firms,
    Competition, and Integration of Product Markets'

Chairman: Harry G. Johnson (UK)
Vice-chairmen: João Cravinho (Portugal) and Lev M. Gatovski (USSR)
Main paper: Pierre Uri (France)
Discussion papers: (1) Ryutaro Komiya (Japan); (2) Nuno Fidelino de Figueiredo (Brazil)
Opening statement: Péter Veress (Hungary)

Working Group D

Theme: 'Migration and Integration of Labour Markets'
Chairman: Orlando d'Alauro (Italy)
Vice-chairman: Igor E. Guryev (USSR)
Main paper: Kosta Mihailović (Yugoslavia)
Discussion papers: (1) Hilde Wander (Federal Republic Germany);
(2) Giorgio Basevi (Italy)
Opening statement: Preben Munthe (Norway)

Working Group E

Theme: 'International Capital Movements and Integration of Capital Markets'
Chairman: Herbert Giersch (Federal Republic Germany)
Vice-chairman: Jouko J. Paunio (Finland)
Main paper: Peter B. Kenen (USA)
Discussion papers: (1) Robert A. Mundell (Canada); (2) Alexander K. Swoboda (Switzerland)
Opening statement: Raymond Bertrand (France)

Working Group F

Theme: 'Monetary and Fiscal Integration'
Chairman: Raymond Barre (France)
Vice-chairman: Antonio del Olmo Parra (Spain)
Main paper: Alexander Lamfalussy (Belgium)
Discussion papers: (1) Carlos Massad (Chile); (2) John H. Williamson (UK)
Opening statement: Marina von Neumann Whitman (USA)

Working Group G

Theme: 'Socio-Political and Institutional Aspects of Integration'
Chairman: Shigeto Tsuru (Japan)
Vice-chairman: Stanislaw Raczkowski (Poland)

Main paper: see Third Plenary Session first half
Discussion papers: see Third Plenary Session, first half
Opening statement: Roger Dehem (Canada)

Working Group H

Theme: 'Integration of Less Developed Areas and of Areas on Different
   Levels of Development'
Chairman: Indraprasad G. Patel (India)
Vice-chairman: Puntsagdasiin Luvsandorzh (Mongolia)
Main paper: Eduardo Lizano (Costa Rica)
Discussion papers: (1) Geoffrey R. Denton (UK); (2) Mahbub ul Haq
   (Pakistan), read by Garry Pursell (Australia); (3) Gunal Kansu (Turkey);
   (4) Gharam P. Ghai (Kenya)
Opening statement: Helen Hughes (Australia)

Working Group I

Theme: 'Integration by Market Forces and Through Planning'
Chairman: Béla Csikós-Nagy (Hungary)
Vice-chairman: Michael Kaser (UK)
Main paper: see Fourth Plenary Session, first half
Discussion papers: see Fourth Plenary Session
Opening statement: Harry E. English (Canada)

Working Group J

Theme: 'World Trade and Intraregional Trade: Trends and Structural
   Changes'
Chairman: Henk C. Bos (Netherlands)
Vice-chairman: Rune Hellberg (Sweden)
Main paper: Gunther Kohlmey (German Dem. Rep.)
Discussion papers: (1) Abba P. Lerner (Israel—USA) (2) Mikhail Senin (USSR)
Opening statement: Madan Gopal Mathur (India)

THE DESIGN OF THE PROGRAMME

A few asymmetries in the programme may call for explanation. The plenary
sessions on the first day were given to papers on general perspectives of the

theme of the Congress. The plenary sessions on the second day were given
to the presentation of the main papers and discussion papers on topics
assigned to four working groups; these four topics were of so general
interest, and of such bearing on all problems to be discussed on the following
days, that it was deemed desirable to have them presented to the plenum;
accessible to all, rather than only to the participants of the particular working
groups. This discrimination thus served a good purpose and was not, I hope,
resented by anybody. The papers prepared for the other working groups
were considered not less important but more suitable for presentation to
groups of specialists.

The rule for working groups was for each to have a chairman and a vice-
chairman to guide and moderate the discussions for two days; to hear a main
paper, two discussion papers, and an opening statement for the group
discussion; the chairman was to act also as rapporteur to tell the plenum
on the last day of the Congress about the discussions in his group. There
were only two departures from this rule: we had two vice-chairmen in one
very large working group, and in another we had four discussion papers. It
was thought desirable that Working Group H, on problems of integration
involving less developed areas, should have representatives from more
countries and continents. (Indeed, we had invited five discussion papers, but
one member of this panel failed to show up.) As it was, this working group
included eight economists from as many countries on five continents.

An overview of the topics can help us see in clearer relief the outline of
the theme of the congress. The first three topics, making up Part I of this
volume, present *general perspectives* ('Types of Economic Integration';
'Worldwide versus Regional Integration: Is there an Optimum Size of the
Integrated Area?'; and 'A History of Thought on Economic Integration').
Part II of this volume comprises the ten topics that were assigned to the
ten working groups as *special aspects* of the central theme.

The first of the special aspects is a technical problem: 'Measuring the
Degree or Progress of Integration'. It is followed by the controversial issue
whether 'Sectoral integration' promotes or hinders progress in general economic
integration. The next three topics may be seen as a triad: 'Integration of
Product Markets', 'Integration of Labour Markets', and 'Integration of
Capital Markets'. This trifocal exploration was probably clear to most
economic generalists but not always to the specialists who actually treated
the three subjects. The sixth of the special aspects is 'Monetary and Fiscal
Integration', appealing to a kind of specialist rather different from, say,
students of industrial policy or international migration. It is again another
bent of mind that concentrates on an examination of 'Socio-Political and
Institutional Aspects of Integration'. Analytical and other mathematical
theorists often refuse to view the socio-political and the 'purely' economic
as inseparably intertwined, let alone as a unit. A large contingent of
economists is interested, almost to the exclusion of other aspects, in the
integration processes involving 'Less Developed Areas' or countries; to arrange

a special working group for the discussion of the pertinent problems seemed imperative. But it was an issue of comparative economic systems, 'Integration by Market Forces and Through Planning', that appeared to evoke the greatest excitement (as one may well have expected in a meeting which, for the first time, brought together hundreds of economists from socialist and from nonsocialist countries). The last of the special aspects examined concerned the statistical record of performance and of observable trends in 'World Trade and Intraregional Trade'.

Even after the event the Programme Committee can be satisfied with the coherence and relevance of this outline. That in a few instances authors of main papers or comments may have done less than full justice to the designed division of intellectual labour was probably unavoidable. After all, the authors writing on the same topics had not had an opportunity for preliminary talks, joint seminars, previews or rehearsals; they came from different countries, indeed from ideologically different worlds, and thus it would be unrealistic to be disappointed with the degree of understanding achieved. At least this is the impression one receives from reading some of the reports on the discussions in the working groups.

THE SELECTION OF PERFORMERS

Having shown the rational design of the topical breakdown of the theme, I may attempt to support as perfectly reasonable the selection of authors for the main papers. The choice of Béla Balassa for the paper 'Types of Integration' was almost a foregone conclusion on the basis of his previously published work: the flow of publications of his untiring theoretical as well as empirical research in this field has been virtually unrivaled. Richard N. Cooper, after his seminal books and articles advancing most original ideas on economic interdependence and international coordination, was a perfect choice for the paper 'Worldwide versus Regional Integration'. That the President of the Association showed himself willing to hold forth on 'A History of Thought on Economic Integration' may indicate his over-reaching ambition, but no one could object to this assignment — at least not before the actual delivery.

The qualifications of the authors chosen for the main papers of the ten special aspects were never questioned by the Programme Committee: Jean Waelbroeck had done well-received empirical work on the problems of measurement. Hans Willgerodt had published studies on industrial organisation that marked him as a fine choice for the assignment on sectoral integration. Pierre Uri had for years headed an important research programme on industrial policy and European co-operation, which predestined him as author of the paper on industrial policy. The choice of Kosta Mihailović for the paper on migration was made on the basis of the recommendations by his colleagues in Yugoslavia, the country which probably has had the numerically largest international movement of labour. Peter B. Kenen, the author selected for the paper on international movements of capital, is currently the Director of the International Finance Section in Princeton and was known to be engaged in an empirical investigation of the very topic on which he was asked to perform for the congress. Alexandre Lamfalussy, a respected theoretical economist and president of a large bank, was a natural for the paper on monetary integration. For the difficult assignment on socio-political and institutional aspects, the Programme Committee was fortunate in obtaining acceptance by József Bognár, the Director of the Institute of World Economy and International Relations, of the Hungarian Academy of Sciences. It seemed imperative to find an economist from the developing world to author the paper on integration of less developed areas; Eduardo Lizano of the University of Costa Rica was the person tapped for this task. The delicate and ideologically sensitive issue of a comparative evaluation of market forces and planning in the process of economic integration called for an economist who could combine wisdom, tact, and analytical talent; Oleg Bogomolov, the Director of the Institute for World Socialist Economy of the Academy of Sciences of the USSR, was an almost obvious choice. Finally, the analysis of trends in world trade and intraregional trade was entrusted to Gunther Kohlmey, the respected member of the Academy of Sciences of the German Democratic Republic.

I might continue this presentation of the cast of eminent economists by introducing also the authors of the invited discussion papers – called 'comments' in this volume – and of the opening statements for group discussion. I shall not take the time and space to do this. The reader is invited to check the programme for the names of these authors and for the countries of their residence. I trust he will conclude that the standard of selection was not compromised by the desire to achieve wide geographic distribution.

It may, however, be desirable to review the cast of Chairmen of Working Groups, the ten economists who had the twofold task of organising a two-day discussion and of reporting on it to the plenum. These economists are among the most eminent in their respective countries, and, again, are named in the programme; their reports appear in this volume under the particular topics concerned and immediately following the opening statements for group discussion of each topic.

THE WORKING GROUPS

The chairmen of the ten working groups had two important responsibilities: to conduct a good discussion and, afterwards, to write a report about the discussion for delivery at plenary sessions on the last day of the congress. In both these tasks, they used rather different techniques, according to their habits or preferences. As to the conduct of group discussion, some of the chairmen proposed or imposed an agenda in order to attain a clearly structured discussion; other chairmen, more permissive, allowed unstructured talk or even the reading of lengthy papers prepared in advance. As to the reports on the transactions of the working groups, some chairmen used the report as a vehicle for expressing their own views, while others confined themselves to more objective accounts on what had gone on in their groups or rather on the highlights of the discussions.

The hope was that the invited main papers, discussion papers ('comments') and opening statements for group discussion would set the tone and determine the structure of the discussion. Besides these *invited* papers, the working groups would accept *contributed* papers, but only for distribution — by placing them on a table for participants to help themselves — not for oral delivery. Discussion should mean a sequence of brief interventions, either reacting to views of a previous speaker or, after the issues on the agenda had been sufficiently covered, raising new points and inviting reactions by others. A good discussion is not a succession of independent speeches on a variety of loosely related or unrelated issues; it is, instead, a succession of interdependent responses on an issue which the chairman has ruled to be open for discussion. Participants in a discussion ought to strive for a topical and logical integration of all the points made in addressing a specified issue. The imposition of time limits for interventions — say, five or six minutes — with priority given to brief interventions of, say, one minute only, is of great help in the conduct of group discussions. Some of the working groups had the advantage of having chairmen who enforced such rules. The President admits his failure to advise all chairmen of the desirability of this practice.

Some of the discussions suffered from another fault, perhaps inevitable at the first mass meeting of economists of different persuasion, different ideologies, different languages, and different conceptual systems. Too many of the participants felt morally obligated to praise the economic theory, system, institutions, and successes of their 'side'. There was a tendency to brag about the speed of progress, rates of growth, greater efficiency, superior performances on a variety of scores. This game of showing off and blowing one's trumpet is typical when children meet for the first time, and most adults retain some childlike attitudes when they meet strangers. This will improve as we learn to know each other better; indeed, I believe that the last days of the congress have shown much more mutual understanding and much less ideological ritualism. At future meetings adherents of different persuasions may more quickly proceed from preliminary recitations of articles of creed to discussions of established facts, plausible explanations, and open problems of theory and policy.

The President's inquiry about the attendance and active participation in discussions of the ten working groups elicited the following statistics compiled on the basis of responses from the chairmen and vice-chairmen of the groups:

Working Group	Topic	Attendance Max.	Attendance Min.	Discussion speakers (incl. contributed papers)
A	'Measuring the Degree or Progress of Economic Integration'	205	70	40
B	'Sectoral Integration: Agriculture, Transport, Energy and Selected Industries'	175	45	30
C	'Industrial Policy: Location, Technology, Multinational Firms, Competition and Integration of Product Markets'	220	130	150
D	'Migration and Integration of Labour Markets'	210	70	20
E	'International Capital Movements and Integration of Capital Markets'	180	160	40
F	'Monetary and Fiscal Integration'	220	140	45
G	'The Socio-Political and Institutional Aspects of Integration'	60	35	30
H	'Integration of Less Developed Areas and of Areas on Different Levels of Development	220	75	35
I	'Integration by Market Forces and through Planning'	300	100	35
J	'World Trade and Intra-regional Trade: Trends and Structural Changes'	120	40	25
		1910	865	450

These statistics may be questioned, especially because the sum of maxima of attendance exceeds the official registration figure for the congress. The divergence, however, is very small: within a ten per cent margin of error. Moreover, there was probably some migration from one working group to another, as not a few participants like to sample different discussions and thus attend more than one working group on the same day.

Some of us may be persuaded to take the statistics of attendance of the ten working groups as data indicating the demand for discussion of the various topics — or, at least showing the revealed preferences of the multitude of economists attending the congress. Let me discourage the reader from drawing such conclusions, for we cannot isolate the attractiveness of the topics from several other variables that influence the attendance. Some participants may care much less about the topic than about the announced speakers who were presenting the main paper and discussion papers; others may show their partiality to the chairman of a working group, who may be an especially renowned economist or who may have a reputation for his ability to run a good meeting and conduct an exciting discussion by keeping speakers from talking too long or from digressing from the subject. And there are also those who make their choice according to the location and environmental qualities of the meeting: distance, acoustics, and especially air-conditioning may have been the most important determining factors. Cool air was in short supply during these days of a record heat wave, aggravated by some hot air emanating from loquacious discussion speakers!

AN APPRAISAL

For enterprises which cannot render any profit-and-loss accounts it is now customary to attempt benefit- and-cost analyses, though the benefits are mostly subject to highly subjective evaluations. I would be inclined to suggest the following items in a list of benefits attributable to the Congress of Budapest.

(1) It was the first economic congress convened in a socialist country that was attended by over 800 economists from nonsocialist countries.

(2) It was, to the best of my knowledge, the first economic congress outside the USSR that was attended by almost 280 economists of the Soviet Union, including the most respected of the profession.

(3) It was therefore the first opportunity for an East—West dialogue on a large scale, and genuine efforts were made on the part of many participants to reach a better understanding of different points of view.

(4) According to numerous reports, a friendly atmosphere prevailed in almost all discussion groups and social gatherings, and many participants learned, perhaps to their surprise, that most economists 'on the other side' were neither fools nor knaves, neither mercenaries nor fanatics, but scholars engaged in serious scientific research.

(5) Many participants left with the firm conviction that co-operative as

well as parallel studies of certain economic problems could be promising and would be desirable. (I refer especially to Lundberg's report on Working Group A on problems of measuring, where periodic colloquia on the subject were proposed.)

(6) While it was clear that our common interests in the economics of integration has not brought about an integration of the economic thinking of different schools nor a close integration of economists working in different parts of the world, we were repeatedly reminded of the fact that integration can and should be understood as a process. An important step in this process has been made.

(7) Last not least, this congress has generated a fair number of scholarly papers, as the reader of this volume may verify. Thus, some progress in the economics of economic integration has been made.

A critical reader will surely find much to criticise in this volume; economists have traditionally cultivated the art of polemics and have developed sharp eyes for defects and errors in the writings of their professional colleagues. The editor has provided in this introduction detailed descriptions of the origin and the gestation processes of this volume because he hopes that an understanding of the background and of the intentions of those responsible for the proceedings of the congress may increase the reader's tolerance for concepts and ideas for which they ordinarily have little sympathy.

Part I
General Perspectives

1 Types of Economic Integration

Bela Balassa (USA)

I. CONCEPTS AND DEFINITIONS

In the Western economic literature, discussions of the types of economic integration of national states have customarily focused on the various stages of integration. From its lowest to its highest forms, integration has been said to progress through the freeing of barriers to trade ('trade integration'), the liberalisation of factor movements ('factor integration'), the harmonisation of national economic policies ('policy integration') and the complete unification of these policies ('total integration').[1]

These definitions have been criticised on the grounds that they conform to the principles of classical economic doctrines but do not apply to present-day market economies, which are characterised by a considerable degree of state intervention, and apply even less to developing and to socialist economies. As regards developing countries, the relevance of the proposed sequencing from the 'negative' measures of removing barriers to the 'positive' measures of policy co-ordination has been questioned by Kitamura, in whose opinion 'the attempt to co-ordinate and harmonise national economic policies will be an important instrument even in the earlier stages of the integration process' (1966, p. 45). Kitamura further claimed that 'in certain circumstances . . . integration may be accomplished to a considerable extent without lifting the existing trade barriers' (ibid.).

Pinder expressed the view that the co-ordination of policies is an important element of integration also in present-day developed market economies. He proposed to 'define economic integration as both the removal of discrimination as between the economic agents of the member countries, and the formation and application of co-ordinated and common policies on a sufficient scale to ensure that major economic and welfare objectives are fulfilled' (1968, p. 90).

While emphasising the need to consider policy co-ordination, the prominent Hungarian economist, Imre Vajda, criticised the definition put forward by

[1] For an early survey of proposed definitions of economic integration and the introduction of the described classification scheme, see Balassa, 1961.

Pinder for its excessive generality. Limiting himself, in the first place, to trade integration, Vajda introduced the distinction between 'market integration' and 'production and development integration'. The former is defined as 'the guarantee of unhindered sale of each other's products within the framework of the social system of participating countries', while the latter is said to involve 'raising to an international level and programming the production of those branches of industry which . . . cannot be developed to an optimum size within national boundaries' (Vajda, 1971, p. 35).[2]

Vajda's distinction between trade integration through the removal of barriers to trade and integration through industrial programming on the regional (plurinational) level is meant to apply to developed market, to socialist, and to developing economies as well. It will be used in the following discussion to evaluate the results of integration schemes in the three types of countries. Subsequently, the question of the optimal degree of market, production and development integration will be examined. In the final section, the relationship between economic integration and national sovereignty will be discussed.

II. INTEGRATION IN DEVELOPED MARKET ECONOMIES

The European Common Market or European Economic Community (EEC) is the dominant integration scheme in developed market economies. It has absorbed the United Kingdom, the major participant in its would-be competitor organisation, the European Free Trade Association, and now accounts for over four-fifths of the gross national product of Western Europe. Following the creation of the EEC, the existent quantitative restrictions on intra-area trade were soon abolished; tariffs on intra-area trade were reduced and, ahead of schedule, eliminated (1968); and a common tariff on extra-area imports was established.

The freeing of barriers to trade was accompanied by the rapid expansion of trade among the partner countries. Between 1959 and 1971, trade among the original member countries of the EEC (Belgium, France, Germany, Italy, Luxembourg, and the Netherlands) increased nearly sixfold, as against a four-fold increase in their total imports and exports. As a result, the share of intra-EEC trade in the total rose from one-third in 1959 to one-half in 1971.

The question arises of whether, and to what extent, the expansion of intra-EEC trade represents trade creation (the replacement of domestic by partner-country sources of supply) or trade diversion (the replacement of foreign by partner-country sources) and how these changes in trade flows affect the welfare of member and nonmember countries. Trade creation is considered beneficial as the elimination of protection for domestic production *vis-à-vis* pro-

---

[2] The definition of market integration is qualified by the clause 'as long as this is not obstructed by social-political interests or excluded by common production agreements'. In turn, the full statement on production and development integration refers to industries 'which, in view of their technological development, vertical integration, the size of their investments, and the shorter-than-average life of their capital equipment, cannot be developed to an optimum size within national boundaries without upsetting the internal equilibrium of the national economy' (Vajda, 1971, p. 35).

ducers in the partner countries permits the replacement of higher-cost domestic products with lower-cost partner-country products. In turn, trade diversion may be detrimental both to member and to nonmember countries. The elimination of barriers to intra-area trade entails discrimination against imports from nonmember countries that continue to pay a duty, thus providing inducements to replace the lower-cost products of nonmember countries by higher-cost products of the partner countries.[3]

In order to separate trade creation and trade diversion, one has to select a benchmark for evaluating changes in trade flows. Under the assumption that the historical relationship of imports to the gross national product would have remained unchanged in the absence of integration, the present author suggested that a rise in the ratio of the growth rate of total (intra-area and extra-area) imports to that of GNP be taken to represent trade creation, and a decrease in the corresponding ratio for extra-area imports to represent trade diversion (Balassa, 1963).[4]

The application of this method to the 1959—70 period shows the preponderance of trade creation in the EEC (Balassa, 1974). With growth rates of GNP increasing only slightly (5·5 per cent in 1959—70 as against 5·4 per cent in 1953—9), the growth of imports accelerated; the volume of total imports into the EEC countries rose at an average annual rate of 11·3 per cent, compared with 9·6 per cent in the pre-Common Market period. By 1970, total imports exceeded imports projected on the basis of the relationships observed in the preceding period by $11·3 billion. This increase accounts for over one-fifth of the imports of manufactured goods, where trade creation was concentrated.

While trade diversion has occurred in the case of foodstuffs, chemicals, and simple manufactured goods, it has been offset by increased imports of machinery and equipment, which have been associated with the expansion of investment activity and the trend towards the purchase of more sophisticated machinery in the EEC. Thus, the volume of extra-area imports rose at a rate of 8·9 per cent a year between 1959 and 1970, exceeding the rate of increase of 8·3 per cent in 1953—9.

It should, however, be added that the effects of the EEC on various groups of nonmember countries have been rather uneven. The main beneficiary has been the United States, which is the principal supplier of the sophisticated machinery and equipment demanded in the EEC countries. By contrast, developing and socialist countries have been adversely affected by trade diversion in food and in simple manufactured goods (Balassa, 1974). In particular,

---

[3] The decrease in demand for the imports of the nonmember countries may also lead to a deterioration in their terms of trade *vis-à-vis* the member countries. The latter may benefit, however, if integration permits the establishment of infant industries that eventually become competitive in the world market.

[4] The suggested method assumes that trade diversion would tend to depress imports from nonmember countries, as compared to their historical relationship with GNP in the importing countries. In turn, total imports, over and above the amount corresponding to their historical relationship with GNP, would indicate that purchases from partner countries have replaced domestic sources of supply. In the calculations, GNP as well as imports are expressed in constant prices.

by increasing barriers to food imports, the common agricultural policy has penalised foreign suppliers as well as domestic consumers. This contrasts with reductions in tariffs on the imports of industrial materials and manufactured goods in the framework of multilateral trade liberalisation that has proceeded since the Second World War.

Higher growth rates associated with the establishment of the EEC have also had beneficial effects on nonmember countries by increasing demand for their exports. These favourable effects, then, have counteracted the adverse repercussions due to trade diversion that some of these countries have experienced.

The described method is open to objections on the grounds that influences other than the creation of the EEC may have affected imports. However, the findings of other studies, which have used different methods, confirm the results. Although there is some evidence of trade diversion in manufactured goods, this is shown to be exceeded four to ten times by trade creation. At the same time, according to the various estimates, trade creation accounts for 15 to 30 per cent of the imports of manufactured goods by the EEC countries (Balassa, 1974).

Rapid increases of trade in manufactured goods indicate that firms in the member countries have made use of the possibilities offered by the abolition of tariffs and of quantitative restrictions. Increased trade has, in turn, contributed to the acceleration of economic growth in the EEC countries by permitting the exploitation of economies of scale and greater competition.[5] Economies of scale have been appropriated as increased specialisation has led to the construction of larger plants, the lengthening of production runs in the manufacture of particular products, and the use of specialised machinery and equipment. Gains have also been obtained through the rationalisation of production that has resulted from increased competition, especially in the previously highly protected economies of France and Italy.

Increased investment undertaken to exploit the possibilities for economies of scale has given a further boost to economic growth in the member countries, enabling them to maintain the rates of growth attained during the period of post-war reconstruction. Growth has been most rapid in Italy, with the result that differences in income levels among the individual countries have narrowed. Furthermore, all but one of the twenty-two regions that had income levels below four-fifths of the Community average have experienced higher-than-average growth rates. The most rapid increases have occurred in Southern Italian regions, where incomes per capita were the lowest (European Communities, Commission, 1971, pp. 312–14).

Rapid economic growth has also had beneficial effects on nonmember countries through higher extra-area imports. This should not disguise the fact, however, that the effects of the Common Market on various groups of nonmember countries have been rather uneven. The main beneficiary has been the

---

[5] In most industries, there has been no conflict between the exploitation of economies of scale and increased competition, as the integration of national markets has permitted both to occur simultaneously in the EEC. Thus, the predictions of those who feared the strengthening of monopolies have not been realised.

United States, which is the principal supplier of sophisticated machinery and equipment demanded in the EEC countries. By contrast, developing and socialist countries have been adversely affected by trade diversion in food and in simple manufactured goods (Balassa, 1974). In particular, the common agricultural policy has penalised foreign suppliers as well as domestic consumers by increasing barriers to food imports. This contrasts with reductions in tariffs on the imports of industrial materials and manufactured goods in the framework of multilateral trade liberalisation that has proceeded since the Second World War.

While the beneficial effects of integration on economic growth in the Common Market stem from 'market integration' in manufactured goods following the elimination of barriers to intra-area trade, little progress has been made with regard to 'production and development integration'. In technologically sophisticated industries, such as the aircraft, space, computer and electronics industries, where efficient operations are limited by the size of national markets, there is as yet no common policy at the EEC level. Rather, decisions on research and development and on public procurement are taken in the national framework,[6] thereby contributing to the establishment and the expansion of national firms that serve largely the country's own market.

As a result, certain agreements among national firms notwithstanding, production and research in these industries take place at less than optimum scale. This fact has retarded the development of technologically sophisticated industries in the EEC as compared with the United States, where firms have benefited from the existence of a large market and from governmental policies of research and development in particular industries (Balassa, 1973).

III. INTEGRATION IN SOCIALIST COUNTRIES

The Council for Mutual Economic Assistance (CMEA) was established in 1949, with the participation of the Soviet Union, Bulgaria, Czechoslovakia, Hungary, Poland and Romania, to provide a framework for the economic co-operation of these countries. Albania and the German Democratic Republic (GDR) joined shortly thereafter; subsequently, Mongolia and Cuba became full members, while Albania has ceased to participate in CMEA activities.

The following discussion will deal with the experience of the European member countries of the CMEA. In 1959 these countries signed the formal charter of the CMEA, which added to the original purpose of economic co-operation (as stated in the Founding Declaration of 1949) the objectives of 'speeding up economic and technical progress in [the member] countries' and 'raising the level of industrialization in industrially less developed countries' (Article 1).

In turn, the resolution on 'Basic Principles of the International Socialist Division of Labour', adopted in 1962, called for the rational division of labour

---

[6] It has been reported that, while 15 to 35 per cent of purchases by private industry are provided by the member countries, this share rarely exceeds 5 per cent in public purchases (European Communities, Commission, 1973, p. 4).

within the CMEA in the framework of long-term agreements based on the co-ordination of national plans. Reference was further made to the need for the increased multilateral co-ordination of plans, the working out of consolidated economic balances, and 'the future creation of a Communist world economy, directed according to a uniform plan' (1965, p. 379). The co-ordination of national plans remained one of the key objectives in the Comprehensive Programme, adopted in 1971. However, the document emphasised the primacy of national planning bodies in the process of co-operation and that of national interests in intra-CMEA specialisation; it made no mention of a common plan.[7]

To date, the main achievements of the CMEA include the exchange of technical information, the establishment of a multinational pipeline and electricity grid, and the creation of a common freight-car pool. Furthermore, differences in income levels have been reduced, as growth has been more rapid in countries at lower levels of development (for instance, Bulgaria and Romania). Finally, long-term bilateral trade agreements between CMEA member countries have provided assured markets for the products of the partner countries.

With the availability of assured market outlets, the trade of the CMEA countries has continued to grow. However, the rate of expansion has slowed down, and the share of intra-area trade has declined since the CMEA charter was signed. The average annual rate of growth of imports by the CMEA countries, taken together, was 8·5 per cent in the period 1959–71 as against 10·7 per cent in 1953–9.[8] The differences become larger if calculations are made in terms of constant prices and they cannot be fully accounted for by reference to the slowdown in the rate of economic growth. Thus, while the annual average rate of growth of the combined net material product of the CMEA countries fell from 10·3 per cent in 1953–9 to 7·2 per cent in 1959–70, the rate of growth on the volume of total imports declined from 12·3 to 8·2 per cent.[9]

It would appear, then, that by comparison with the EEC there has been a decline in the extent to which the CMEA countries have utilised their trade potential. This result represents a continuation of trends observed in the period following the Second World War. On the basis of trade, GNP and population figures, Pryor concluded that in the years 1956 and 1962 the volume of trade

[7] This apparent change reflects the rejection of Khrushchev's proposal (*Kommunist,* Aug 1962) for 'establishing a unified planning organ' and of the idea of planning on the CMEA level. Thus, in reporting on a symposium of CMEA specialists held in January 1969, Jozef Pajestka, Deputy Chairman of the Polish Planning Commission, noted that 'the symposium assessed as unjustified concepts involving the introduction of planning on the scale of the entire socialist community – that is supranational planning' (*Zycie Warszavy,* Jan 12–13 1969, cited in Shaefer, 1972, p. 21).

[8] Parallel developments are observed in the Soviet Union as well as in the other CMEA countries, although increases in imports were somewhat greater in the latter case. The relevant data for 1953–9 and 1959–71 are: Soviet Union 10·1 and 7·8 per cent; other CMEA countries, 11·2 and 9·0 per cent.

[9] Growth rates of net material product for the individual countries were averaged, using 1971 values estimated by the International Bank for Reconstruction and Development (1973); current values of trade were deflated by the use of price indices computed by Marer (1972).

of the CMEA countries was only 50–60 per cent of that of comparable West
European countries, while such differences had not been observed in the inter-
war period (1968, p. 164).

Also, the share of intra-area trade in the CMEA has decreased since 1959.
Excluding trade with China, which fell precipitously during the 1960s, we
find that the share of intra-CMEA trade in the total declined from 71 per cent
in 1959 to 63 per cent in 1971, involving mainly a shift to trade with developed
market economies. Whereas, in the period 1953–9, developed market economies accounted for 21 per cent of CMEA imports (excluding imports from
China), their share in the total reached 27 per cent in 1971.[10] In turn, the rate
of expansion of imports from developing countries slowed down during the
1960s. The share of these countries in CMEA imports increased from 3·6 per
cent in 1953 to 7·4 per cent in 1959 and reached 8·7 per cent in 1971.

Various factors account for the lack of full utilisation of the trade potential of the CMEA countries and for the trend towards increased imports from
developed market economies. To begin with, the centralisation of economic
decision making, reflected in the planners' desire to lessen the uncertainty
associated with foreign trade, as well as in the absence of direct trade relationships between firms, tends to limit the volume of trade.

Opportunities for trade may also be foregone because of the lack of appropriate price signals. Despite improvements in pricing with the introduction of
charges for capital, domestic prices in the CMEA countries do not adequately
express resource scarcities and are divorced from prices in foreign trade. In
turn, foreign-trade prices show considerable variations in bilateral relationships,[11] while exchange rates do not appropriately reflect inter-country differences in commodity values. Under these circumstances, there is a risk that
trade in particular commodities may involve a loss, rather than a gain, for the
countries concerned, and this risk tends to discourage trade among them.[12]

Although several of these factors discourage trade with developed market

[10] In this connection, note that in the 1953–9 period the effects of relaxing the embargo that had been applied by the NATO countries on the export of a variety of products to the CMEA were already observable.

[11] It has been shown that 'in the framework of bilateral clearings which regulate the
trade between CMEA countries, the differences in the prices of identical products sold
to various partners are much greater than those having ever occurred in the history of
clearing agreements' (Ausch, 1972, p. 79). Also, despite the fact that the prices in intra-
CMEA trade are supposed to be based on world market prices, considerable differences
have been observed between the two sets of prices. In 1962, the only year for which
detailed information is available, average prices in intra-CMEA trade exceeded prices in
the world market by 25·9 per cent in the case of machinery, 15·4 per cent for raw
materials, and 1·7 per cent for agricultural products (Ausch and Bartha, 1959, p. 109).
The authors of the calculations note that the differences are even greater if one takes
into account the lower quality of machinery in intra-CMEA trade and the considerable
dispersion that is shown within particular commodity groups (ibid.).

[12] It has been reported that in some instances the foreign-exchange value of imported
inputs exceeded that of exports in Hungary during the 1950s (Balazsy, 1957). While
such cases can be detected by the use of efficiency coefficients in foreign trade that compare domestic labour and capital costs to foreign exchange (Shagalov, 1965, p. 58), the
lack of appropriate scarcity prices for labour and capital reduces the practical usefulness

economies as well, the prices used in trade with them tend to reflect scarcity relationships in the world market. Furthermore, the need for sophisticated machinery, materials and other intermediate products that are not available, or are available in limited quantities, in CMEA countries has given a boost to imports from developed market economies. These imports are paid for largely through exports of food, raw materials, fuel, and simple processed goods.

With regard to Hungary, Vajda speaks of a duality of trade, as the 'intermediary goods imported from the West are absorbed in the production of finished goods, which are not sufficiently competitive in Western markets' (Vajda, 1971, p. 53). Such products, sold within the CMEA, are regarded as 'soft goods', while food, raw materials, and fuels that find ready markets in the developed market economies are considered 'hard goods'.

At the same time, in bilateral relationships between CMEA countries there is the attempt to attain trade balance for individual commodity groups, in particular for 'hard goods' and for 'soft goods'.[13] Moreover, countries at lower levels of industrial development increasingly demand that CMEA partner countries accept their machinery products in exchange for imported machinery (Montias, 1967, p. 168).

These developments have reinforced the practice of bilateralism, which tends to restrict the volume of trade and to reduce its efficiency. This is mainly because the requirements of bilateral balancing of trade induce countries to limit imports and to purchase from nations with which the country has an export surplus, rather than from the lowest-cost source.

The practice of bilateralism is reflected in estimates of the extent of multilateral balancing of trade. In 1954–8, the years preceding the signature of the CMEA Charter, the five CMEA countries for which data are available had the lowest index of multilateral balancing among sixty-five countries studied by Michaely (1962). The relevant values for the 1954–8 period were: Soviet Union, 12·7; Hungary, 11·5; Poland, 9·8; Czechoslovakia, 7·3; and Bulgaria, 6·4. This compares with an average of 29·2 for all other countries taken together.[14]

The tendency towards bilateralism has not been offset by the operation of the International Bank for Economic Co-operation (IBEC), which has been

---

of these coefficients. Thus, despite their formal identity, they are not equivalent to the domestic resource cost of foreign exchange introduced in the Western economic literature by Michael Bruno (1967). It should be added that some authors speak of 'commodity inconvertibility' in reference to the fact that the CMEA countries tend to discourage trade outside of quota arrangements, in particular purchases by tourists, partially because such purchases reduce the availability of goods in domestic markets and partially because they may entail losses to the national economy due to distortions in price relationships (Holzman, 1966).

[13] Tibor Kiss notes that 'the practice of distinguishing "hard" and "soft" commodities has become general; "hard" commodities would be exchanged only for "hard" ones and "soft" commodities only for "soft" ones' (1971, p. 223).

[14] The index of multilateral balancing for a particular country is derived as the sum of the absolute differences between each trading partner's export and import shares, expressed in percentage terms, so that the index assumes values from zero to 100 (Michaely, 1962, p. 688).

established for the purpose of carrying out clearing operations and providing credit in intra-CMEA trade. Available data indicate that the weighted average of the index of multilateral balancing in intra-CMEA trade was highest in 1963 (5·5), the year of IBEC's establishment, and declined to 4·2 by 1970 (McMillan, 1973, p. 32).

The limited impact of IBEC is explained by the lack of automatic clearing of bilateral balances and the low level of credits.[15] With creditor and debtor countries having different interest rates, the practice of bilateral negotiations on yearly settlements has not been conducive to multilateral balancing within the CMEA. By contrast, the use of convertible currencies in much CMEA trade with other countries allows for compensating surpluses and deficits among them.

This explains why the degree of bilateralism is far greater in trade among the CMEA countries than in their trade with other nations. For the Soviet Union in 1970, the index of multilateral balancing was 4·7 in trade with the CMEA partner countries and averaged 22·2 in trade with market economies (McMillan, 1973, p. 21). Given the restrictive effects of bilateral balancing, this difference in the *modus operandi* of trade has contributed to an increase in the share of CMEA trade with developed countries where convertible currencies are in general use.

In turn, efforts have been made in intra-CMEA trade to exploit the advantages provided by economies of scale in the framework of specialisation agreements that correspond to 'production and development integration', in Vajda's terminology. The report on the first twenty years of the operation of the CMEA provides information on progress made with regard to specialisation agreements in various industries. It is added, however, that 'so far only the first steps have been made in this complex and important field and the advantages of socialist division of labour have not yet been fully utilized' (1969, p. 54). Moreover, according to one author, 'these agreements did not induce substantial changes in export patterns since they were based on the existing division of labour' (Simai, p. 117). The same author further notes that in 1964 the share of products traded under specialisation agreements in the total exports of machinery and equipment to other CMEA countries ranged between 4·5 per cent in Czechoslovakia and 20·7 per cent in the GDR.[16]

While specialisation agreements have assumed importance with regard to products such as machine tools, ball-bearings, and trucks, their growth has be been limited by much the same factors as have restricted the expansion of intra-CMEA trade in general. The lack of direct contact among firms in the

[15] According to the *Bulletin* of the IBEC, credit transactions in 1970 accounted for 6 per cent of the total transactions on clearing-rouble accounts.

[16] The validity of higher figures reported for 1967 has been questioned on the grounds that the sudden increases shown may be due to a reclassification of trade and may conflict with the figures used in projections for 1970−5 (Brabant, 1974, p. 274). Also, specialisation agreements are often disregarded in practice. Thus, it has been reported that Poland exported 22 out of 29 items subject to such agreements in 1963; 24 out of 40 in 1964; 15 out of 34 in 1966; 48 out of 68 in 1967; and none out of 79 in 1969 (Gora and Knyziak, 1971, p. 55).

CMEA countries reduces information flows, and tends to exclude some promising forms of co-operation. Thus, there are few agreements on the division of the production process through the exchange of parts, components and accessories, or through common ventures by industrial firms in the CMEA countries. Considerations of the availability of goods according to appropriate specifications and at the desired time also have a restraining influence, as does the fact that in the absence of scarcity prices it is difficult to evaluate the gains from specialisation. According to one author, actual or perceived conflicts in national interests manifest themselves 'in an insufficient specialization and inadequate international co-operation of the engineering industries' (Kiss, 1971, p. 169).[17]

IV. INTEGRATION IN DEVELOPING COUNTRIES

During the post-war period, various attempts have been made at economic integration among developing countries. Integration schemes in the individual regions include the Latin American Free Trade Association (LAFTA), the Central American Common Market (CACM), the Andean Common Market (ACM), the Caribbean Community (CARICOM), the East African Community (EAC), the Central African Customs and Economic Union (Union Douanière et Economique de l'Afrique Centrale, or UDEAC), the West African Economic Community (Communauté Economique de l'Afrique de l'Ouest, or CEAO), the Regional Co-operation for Development (RCD), the Maghreb, and the Arab Common Market.[18]

These integration schemes have generally not lived up to expectations.[19] The CACM provides the only case where tariffs on intra-area trade were abolished and a common external tariff was adopted. As a result, trade among these countries increased rapidly, with the average annual rate of growth exceeding 30 per cent between 1961 and 1968. However, following the unilateral introduction of fiscal incentives by member countries and the withdrawal of Honduras from the CACM, the rate of increase of intra-area trade among the remaining member countries declined also.

[17] The same author offers some general remarks on the factors adversely affecting intra-CMEA trade. In his opinion, 'exaggerated centralization of export and import activities, adherence to a strict licence system even in the trade between CMEA countries, and the great divergences between domestic and foreign-trade prices, together with an excessive protectionism, have resulted in so high a degree of isolation of the national markets as to nearly frustrate the projects of economic integration' (p. 170).

[18] The member countries of the various integration schemes are as follows: LAFTA: Argentina, Bolivia, Brazil, Chile, Colombia, Ecuador, Mexico, Paraguay, Peru, Uruguay and Venezuela. CACM: Costa Rica, El Salvador, Guatemala, Honduras and Nicaragua. ACM: Bolivia, Chile, Colombia, Ecuador, Peru and Venezuela. CARICOM: Antigua, Barbados, Belize, Dominica, Grenada, Guyana, Jamaica, Montserrat, St Kitts–Nevis–Anguilla, St Lucia, St Vincent, and Trinidad and Tobago. EAC: Kenya, Tanzania and Uganda. UDEAC: Cameroon, Central African Republic, Congo-Brazzaville and Gabon. CEAO: Ivory Coast, Mali, Mauretania, Niger, Senegal and Upper Volta. RCD: Iran, Pakistan and Turkey. Maghreb: Algeria, Morocco and Tunisia. Arab Common Market: Egypt, Iraq and Jordan.

[19] For a detailed discussion, see Balassa and Stoutjesdijk (1974).

In LAFTA, the target date for completely freeing trade was repeatedly post-poned and the annual negotiations on tariff reductions, carried out on an item-by-item basis, slowed down after a few years and have made practically no progress in recent years. In the ACM, tariff reductions are proceeding according to schedule but quantitative restrictions on intra-area trade have been largely retained and the establishment of the common tariff has been postponed. Finally, in CARICOM, duties on much intra-area trade have been eliminated, but, given similarities in production patterns and high transportation costs among the small islands participating in it, the prospects for the expansion of intra-area trade are not very favourable.

In Africa south of the Sahara there has been disintegration rather than in-tegration in recent years. With the establishment of independent states, free-trade relations existing in colonial times have not been continued. In the EAC, the common tariff has been preserved although member countries follow different policies with regard to duty drawbacks on machinery and equipment. Also, the EAC Treaty of 1967 permits countries with a deficit in intra-area trade in manufactures to impose transfer taxes on such trade, and quantitative restrictions have also been applied.

The UDEAC has a common external tariff, but additional taxes may be im-posed by the individual member countries, and differences in tax rates provide a protective element in intra-area trade. In the CEAO, agricultural trade has been freed, but tariff reductions on manufactured goods will be subject to future negotiations on an item-by-item basis.

The RCD group did not envisage general trade liberalisation, but only the freeing of trade on items produced by common enterprises. Among the Maghreb countries, economic co-operation is limited to a few fields, including standardisation, telecommunications and transport. Finally, while there is free trade in agricultural products in the Arab Common Market, the proposed pre-ferential agreements in industry have not yet materialised.

Various factors account for the limited progress made in efforts at 'market integration' in developing countries. First, item-by-item negotiations on tariff reductions encounter considerable difficulties because of the power of special interests. Second, differences in the level of industrial development have made agreements on trade liberalisation difficult. Third, in view of the distortions in relative prices due to protection, it has been difficult to determine the benefits to be derived from integration and there has been a tendency to consider changes in the trade balance as a sign of gains or losses. Last but not least, the governments of the individual countries have been reluctant to proceed with integration because they are anxious to safeguard their sovereignty.

Considerations of national sovereignty, the difficulties of estimating bene-fits and costs, uncertainty as regards future changes in prices and costs, and the problems encountered in intergovernmental negotiations also explain the virtual lack of success in 'production and development integration' in the manufacturing sector. While several agreements have been reached with regard to transportation, communications and water resources, where bene-fits are relatively easily quantifiable, there are few cases of so-called 'integration industries' in the developing countries.

In LAFTA, there are twenty agreements on product specialisation among private firms, none of which are in basic industries such as metals and metal transformation, petrochemicals and fertilisers, pulp and paper, and heavy equipment. In the ACM, a sectoral programme has been established in the metal transformation industries but technical obstacles have so far impeded the establishment of firms in the branches allocated to several of the countries. There are no integration industries in CARICOM, while in the CACM only three plants are operating under the integration-industry regime that provides exclusive rights to the CACM market.

In East Africa, proposals made for the allocation of industries among the member countries have not been put into effect and duplication in new industries continues. Duplication of facilities is also observed in the UDEAC and the CEAO. Finally, among fifty-six joint-purpose enterprises identified in the RCD only three have been set up and only one of these (a plant producing banknotes) has free access to the regional market.

V. TRADE INTEGRATION: AN EVALUATION

The preceding review of the experience of developed market, socialist, and developing economies suggests certain conclusions regarding the possibilities for, and the preconditions of, 'market integration' and 'production and development integration'. First of all, the use of prices reflecting resource scarcities will clarify the available choices and reduce uncertainty with regard to possible gains and losses from integration. As a result, there will be less resistance to the elimination of barriers on intra-area trade and decisions on production and trade can be decentralised.

These conclusions apply irrespective of social system. As the experience of Hungary since 1968 indicates, markets and prices can be used to advantage in socialist countries too.[20] At the same time, the experience of that country points to the fact that decision making at the firm level will give desirable results only in the absence of monopoly positions, since otherwise the interests of the firm and those of the national economy would differ. In such instances, and where infant-industry considerations limit the reliance that can be placed on foreign competition as an anti-monopoly device, intervention by central authorities would be required in order to avoid possible distortions.

It further appears that the optimal degree of market, as against production and development, integration will depend on the size of the market of the integrated area: the larger this market, the fewer will be the industries where

[20] In summarising the conclusion of the conference on the establishment of a system of prices in intra-CMEA trade, held with the participation of economists from the member countries, Béla Csikós-Nagy noted that 'it has been accepted, almost unequivocally, that co-operation has to be developed in the direction of activating the commodity and money relationships' (1971, p. 204) in the CMEA. Djachenko also noted that 'socially necessary expenditures of labor cannot be established administratively; they are developing and taking shape through commodity–monetary relationships' (1958, p. 44).

monopoly positions may emerge, because the full exploitation of economies of scale requires only a single firm. In the EEC, the aircraft, space, computer and electronics industries come into this category; in LAFTA, economies of scale may be appropriated in the framework of a single firm in, for instance, fertilisers and automobiles; and in the EAC the case will be the same in the production of steel or paper. Thus, the desirable scope of production and development integration will vary inversely with the combined market size of the countries participating in an integration scheme.

Interference with allocation patterns brought about by the market mechanism will also be desirable in cases when participating countries are at different levels of industrial development, lest such disparities be perpetuated. This conclusion represents the application of the infant-industry argument to the integration of nation states and will apply irrespective of social system, as is shown by the cases of Romania in the CMEA, Ireland in the EEC, and Honduras in the CACM.

However, production and development integration and the need to safeguard the interests of countries at lower levels of development require joint decisions. The taking of such decisions in turn entails a diminution of the national sovereignty of the individual countries. The existence of a trade-off between the (uncertain) benefits of integration and the (partial) loss of national sovereignty leads to the conclusion that the chances of success of integration schemes increase with their size and the homogeneity of the would-be partner countries.

VI. ECONOMIC UNION AND NATIONAL SOVEREIGNTY

The issue of national sovereignty is put in an even sharper focus in the case of an economic union that involves, in addition to trade integration, the co-ordination of economic policy making. The co-ordination of economic policies in turn requires political decisions that would necessitate establishing a common decision-making apparatus. In this connection one may again cite Vajda, according to whom 'Economic union is not a stage on the path leading towards political union, but a possible and desirable consequence of the latter' (1971, p. 41).

The experience of the EEC confirms this conclusion. Recent efforts to achieve monetary integration without the co-ordination of economic policies have proved to be a failure. And, as noted elsewhere,

> . . . progress in policy co-ordination, and in transforming the Common Market into an economic union, is hampered by the present institutional structure. At the same time, changes in this structure would necessitate political decisions and a degree of political integration that is not presently acceptable to the national governments. (Balassa et al., 1974, p. 7.)

In Vajda's view, the lack of progress towards economic union in the Euro-

pean Common Market is an expression of the fact that economic interest is
not in itself sufficient to moderate the nation states' concern about their
sovereignty. For the same reason, he believes that 'today the development of
the Council of Mutual Economic Assistance into an economic union would be
a no more realistic aim than in the case of the European Economic Community' (1971, p. 43).

Rather than attempt to make a prediction about the likelihood that one or
another integration scheme will be transformed into an economic union, it is
better to emphasise, in conclusion, that the conflict between national
sovereignty and economic self-interest can be resolved only if there is a political
interest and the political will to do so. Economic integration thus appears as
part of a political process the final outcome of which is determined by essentially political factors.

REFERENCES

Ausch, S., and Bartha, F., 'Theoretical Problems of CMEA Intratrade Prices', in *Socialist
    World Market Prices*, ed. T. Földi and T. Kiss (Leyden and Budapest: A. W. Sijthoff
    and Akadémiai Kiadó, 1969), pp. 101–27).
Ausch, Sandor, *Theory and Practice of CMEA Co-operation* (Budapest: Akadémiai Kiadó,
    1972).
Balassa, Béla, 'Towards a Theory of Economic Integration', in *Kyklos, XIV* (1961),
    pp. 1–14.
Balassa, Béla, 'European Integration: Problems and Issues', in *American Economic Review,
    Papers and Proceedings*, May 1963, pp. 175–84.
Balassa, Béla, 'Industrial Policy in the European Common Market', in *Banca Nazionale
    del Lavoro Quarterly Review*, Dec 1973, pp. 311–27.
Balassa, Béla, 'Trade Creation and Trade Diversion in the European Common Market: An
    Appraisal of the Evidence', in *Manchester School*, May 1974.
Balassa, Béla, et al., *European Economic Integration* (Amsterdam: North Holland, 1974).
Balassa, Béla, and Stoutjesdijk, E. J., 'Economic Integration among Developing Countries'
    (International Bank for Reconstruction and Development: 1974), mimeo.
Balázsy, Sándor, 'A külkereskedelem gazdaságosságához' ('On the Economic Efficiency
    of Foreign Trade'), in *Közgazdasagi Szemle*, Mar 1957, pp. 303–20.
Brabant, J. M. P. van, *Bilateralism and Structural Bilateralism in Intra-CMEA Trade*
    (Rotterdam: Rotterdam University Press, 1973).
Brabant, J. M. P. van, *Essays in Planning, Trade, and Integration in Eastern Europe*
    (Rotterdam: Rotterdam University Press, 1974).
Bruno, Michael, 'The Optimal Selection of Export-Promoting and Import-Substituting
    Projects', in *Planning the External Sector: Techniques, Problems and Policies* (New
    York: United Nations, 1967).
Council for Mutual Economic Assistance, 'Basic Principles of the International Socialist
    Division of Labor', (original published in Moscow, 1962). English translation in Heinz
    Köhler, *Economic Integration in the Soviet Bloc* (New York: Praeger, 1965).
Council for Mutual Economic Assistance, *A Survey of 20 Years of the Council for
    Mutual Economic Assistance* (Moscow, 1969).
Council for Mutual Economic Assistance, *Comprehensive Programme for the Further
    Extension and Improvement of Co-operation and the Development of Socialist
    Economic Integration by the CMEA Member Countries* (Moscow, 1971).
Csikós-Nagy, Béla, 'Concluding Address', in *Socialist World Market Prices*, ed. T. Földi
    and T. Kiss (Budapest and Leyden: A. W. Sijthoff and Akadémiai Kiadó, 1969),
    pp. 101–27.

Djachenko, V., 'Osnovnye napravleniya sovershenstovovaniya tsen vo vzaimnoj torgovle stran—chlenov SEV' ('Main Trends in Improving Prices in Trade among CMEA Members'), in *Voprosy ekonomiki,* no. 12, 1967. English translation in *Problems of Economics,* June 1968, pp. 40—9)

European Communities, Commission, *L'Evolution régionale de la Communauté* (Brussels, 1971).

European Communities, Commission, *Memorandum from the Commission on the Technological and Industry Policy Programme* (Brussels, 3 May 1973).

Gora, S., and Knyziak, Z., *Miedzynarodowa specjalizacja produkcji krajow RWPG* ('International Specialisation of Production of the CMEA Countries') (Warsaw: PWE, 1971). Cited in Z. M. Fallenbuchl, 'Comecon Integration', in *Problems of Communism,* Mar—Apr 1973, pp. 25—39.

Holzman, F. D., 'Foreign Trade Behavior of Centrally Planned Economies', in *Industrialization in Two Systems: Essays in Honor of Alexander Gerschenkron*, ed. Henry Rosovsky (New York: Wiley, 1966), pp. 237—65.

International Bank for Reconstruction and Development, *World Bank Atlas,* (1973).

Kiss, Tibor, *International Division of Labour in Open Economies, with Special Regard to the CMEA* (Budapest: Akadémiai Kiadó, 1971).

Kitamura, Hiroshi, 'Economic Theory and the Economic Integration of Underdeveloped Regions', in *Latin American Economic Integration,* ed. Miguel S. Wioczek (New York: Praeger, 1966). pp. 42—63.

Marer, Paul, 'Postwar Pricing and Price Patterns in Socialist Foreign Trade (1946—1971)', *International Development Research Center Report no. 1* (Bloomington: Indiana University, 1972).

McMillan, C. H., 'The Bilateral Character of Soviet and Eastern European Foreign Trade', in *Carleton Economic Papers,* 73—12, Apr 1973.

Michaely, Michael, 'Multilateral Balancing in International Trade', in *American Economic Review,* Sep 1962, pp. 685—702.

Montias, J. M., *Economic Development in Communist Rumania* (Cambridge, Mass.: MIT Press, 1967).

Pinder, John, 'Positive Integration and Negative Integration', in *The World Today,* Mar 1968, pp. 88—110.

Pryor, F. L., 'Socialist Industrialization and Trade in Machinery Products: Discussion', in *International Trade and Central Planning,* ed. A. A. Brown and E. Neuberger (Berkeley: University of California Press, 1968), pp. 159—64.

Shaefer, H. W., *Comecon and the Politics of Integration* (New York: Praeger, 1972).

Shagalov, G., 'Ekonomicheskaya effektivnost vneshnej torgovli sotsialisticheskikh stran' ('The Economic Efficiency of the Socialist Countries' Foreign Trade'), in *Voprosy ekonomiki,* no. 6, 1965: English translation in *Problems of Economics,* Dec 1965, pp. 49—60.

Simai, Mihály, 'Exports and Export Performance', in *Foreign Trade in a Planned Economy,* ed. I. Vajda and M. Simai (Cambridge: Cambridge University Press, 1971), pp. 113—31.

Vajda, Imre, 'External Equilibrium and Economic Reform', ibid., pp. 45—60.

Vajda, Imre, 'Integration, Economic Union, and the National State', ibid., pp. 28—44.

Comments
Margarita Maksimova (USSR)

Our congress is devoted to the discussion of problems the significance of which is growing steadily in world economics and politics. This is borne out by the obvious fact that processes of integration are becoming widespread in various regions of the world and embrace different groups of states — socialist, capitalist and developing ones. It is further confirmed by the fact that economic integration exercises an increasing influence on both the domestic economy and the policy of individual countries, as well as on relations between countries. The character, extent and scale of integration processes in the world, within the framework of each social system, also have a certain effect on international economic relations. And we see in broad and truly international economic co-operation, a vital factor for peace and the security of nations.

Now, turning to the paper by Balassa, I should like to make the point that it is mainly concerned with the results of economic integration in the EEC, CMEA and a number of groupings of developing countries. Acknowledging the work done by Balassa, I think he should have begun differently and first posed a more general question: what is meant by economic integration, what content is given to this term? To establish points of departure on this very complicated question and perhaps to come to a more or less common view seems to be a useful effort. It depends to a considerable extent not only on our understanding of the principal types of integration — primarily integration of socialist countries, and integration of capitalist countries — but also on the choice of criteria for, and consequently the evaluation of, various aspects of so dynamic a phenomenon of international life as the various integration processes with their so different consequences.

I regard integration as a trend in world development that has objective foundations and that has been called into existence by the needs of the productive developments and international division of labour. In the light of the contemporary scientific and technological revolution, effective development — not only of individual enterprises and branches, but also of the national economies of many countries as a whole — increasingly depends on the degree and extent of economic ties with other national economies. The share of the national product sold by most countries on external markets now reaches 10, 20, or even more per cent.

It is not only a matter of quantitative growth. Fundamental qualitative changes are taking place in the character of international economic exchange. Its sphere involves not only a growing mass of commodities, but also capital investment, manpower and a variety of specialists. There is an intensification of scientific and technical contacts and a growth of industrial co-operation. And, significantly, the durability and stability of ties between national economies of the countries involved are assuming increasing importance. All this, I repeat, is a reflection of the general requirements of the process of development of productive forces and the internationalisation of economic life.[1]

[1] For more detail see M. M. Maksimova, *Ekonomicheskiye problemy imperialisticheskoi integratsii: Ekonomicheskii aspekt* ('Economic problems of imperialist integration: the economic aspect') (Moscow: Mysl, 1971), section I.

Economic integration is a specific manifestation of this process. We think that it differs from earlier forms of international economic co-operation in the more complicated and universal character of the ties between countries that are included in appropriate regional groupings, as well as by the greatly increased role of the state in regulating such ties on a collective basis. The most general features of economic integration that distinguish it from other phenomena in the world economy are, in my opinion, the following.

First, integration is a process of the development of stable and deep ties, and of the division of labour between national economies, that is accompanied by the mutual complementing and adjustment of individual enterprises, branches and economic areas of various countries, and leads to the formation of international economic complexes initially within the framework of groups of countries close to each other on the level of economic development.

Second, integration is an adjustable process, in the sense that it demands conscious co-ordinated efforts on the part of subjects (economic organisations, states) in shaping and effectively regulating economic ties between national economies and between their corresponding spheres, branches and enterprises. The state machinery of individual countries and international institutions has an active role to play here.

Third, processes of integration are of a predominantly regional character and tend to develop most fully in those parts of the world that have the appropriate economic and political prerequisites.

Fourth, as integration proceeds, deep structural changes occur in the economies of the countries involved and new economic proportions are established, leading ultimately to the higher social productivity of labour and to savings in time.

Fifth, in its essence, integration is closely connected with class and social relations and with politics, and therefore can (and does) take place (as distinct from international economic co-operation in general) only between countries with the same type of socio-economic system and mode of production. This sets limits to integration groupings.

In view of all this, economic integration can, in my opinion, be generally defined as the objective process of development of deep and stable relationships and of division of labour between national economies, a process of formation of international economic complexes within the framework of groups of countries with the same type of socio-economic system — a process consciously regulated in the interests of the dominating classes of these countries.[2]

Hence, there exist different types of economic integration — if we give to the definition of 'type of integration' the broadest content, reflecting both the economic and political essence of appropriate integration groupings, the totality of instruments and measures that serve to carry out integration processes, and so on. The main criterion is the socio-economic system of integrated countries. Consequently, in present-day life we distinctly discern three main types of integration: integration of socialist countries, integration

---

[2] For more detail see *World Marxist Review*, no. 7, July 1973, pp. 14—18; and M. M. Maksimova, *Ekonomicheskiye problemy*, chapter 7.

of capitalist countries, and integration of developing countries.[3] Each of these types of integration has its characteristic features and regularities, an integration mechanism of its own.

Furthermore, it is essential to distinguish — as is done by many — between types of integration and different stages, because the latter are not identical with integration processes that take place under a planned economy or a market economy. A confusion of concepts as regards types of integration and stages, or phases, of development leads (as I believe is to be found in Balassa's paper) to a wrong comparison of the results of the development of the integration processes. Thus, in effect, Balassa is automatically applying the stages of development that were passed through by the EEC, as well as its mechanism of activity, to the work of the CMEA; and this preconditions a number of erroneous assessments of the results of CMEA activity in the sphere of integration.

It is a matter of common knowledge that for a long time the integration measures of the EEC's agencies have dealt chiefly with trade relations and customs policy. In fact, certain progress has been achieved in this field. But, as Balassa admits, grave complications and problems have arisen in connection with the currency and energy crises and with mounting inflation, as well as with the Six becoming the Nine.

It is only in recent years that the EEC has raised the question of a new stage — the transition to a joint scientific, technical, and industrial policy, and to the establishment of an economic and monetary alliance. This stage, in the common belief of Western economists and Common Market officials,[4] involves far greater difficulties. Understandably so, because it deeply affects the basic interests of the countries, the private companies, the different classes and the social groups.

The mechanism of capitalist integration is based on a combination of competition and state monopoly regulation, principles of planned development within individual corporations — national, transnational, and international — and spontaneous development on the scale of the world capitalist market. This, I think, is one of the main sources of the grave difficulties and contradictions that are being experienced by the European Community and by other West European groupings.

A different character, different stages of development and a different mechanism are inherent in socialist integration. It is not at all obligatory, for example, for socialist countries to make use of such methods as the establishment of customs unions or free-trade zones, since these do not have

[3] The integration of the developing countries has its own pronounced specific features that are connected both with the comparatively low level of economic development of these countries and with their position in the world economy. It is characterised by the existence of two opposite tendencies. On the one hand, it is the striving of the democratic forces of these countries to strengthen their economic independence and overcome their backwardness through joint action within the appropriate regional groupings. On the other, it is the striving of reactionary forces relying on outside support to consolidate the positions of foreign capital in integration complexes and to bar the development of countries along the democratic road.

[4] See, among others, works and contributions by W. M. Corden, J. C. Ingram, E. Salin, F. X. Ortoli and R. Dahrendorf.

for them the role they play in Western countries. On the other hand, the existence of social ownership of the means of production allows the introduction of such forms of integration as are based on the planned development of socialist economy, on the planned activity of socialist state and economic organisations.

It is therefore quite natural that integration in the CMEA should have started with higher and more complex forms — co-ordination of economic plans, and the creation of a mechanism for scientific, technical and production co-operation that, through the joint efforts of the participating countries, would undertake to tackle major problems in the energetics sphere, including atomic energy, the production of raw materials, the establishment of electronic computer systems, and a number of other advanced branches of industry and co-operation of production on an international basis.[5] The facts show that substantial progress has been made in these and other spheres.[6]

This progress also made itself felt in such key synthetic indices of economic development as rates of growth of national income and of the industrial output of the CMEA countries. In the twenty-five years from the CMEA's foundation (1949—73), the combined national income of the member countries has increased eightfold, and industrial production more than twelvefold. For comparison's sake, it can be pointed out that the corresponding indices for the EEC Six over the same years were 3·6-fold and 5·5-fold (for the EEC Nine it was threefold and fourfold respectively.[7]

While paying particular attention to the co-ordination of plans and joint production, scientific and technical activity, the CMEA member countries also attach much importance to commodity and money relations, to the development of trade, to the improvement of the price system, and to monetary-financial and credit relations.[8]

The economic integration of socialist countries is a complex process. Like any new process, it involves certain difficulties of both an objective and a subjective nature and presupposes that certain views and methods of economic management need to be brought up to date to cope with new demands. This process presupposes a comprehensive approach to many economic problems and calls for the ability to find the most effective and

[5] See CMEA, *Comprehensive Programme.*

[6] In more detail see *Narodnoye khozyaistvo stran-chlenov Soveta ekonomicheskoi vazimopomoshchi, p. 3; Narodnoye khozyaistvo SSR v 1972* (Moscow; TSU, 1973; 1974); O. Bogomolov, Integration by Market Forces and through Planning' (Chapter 12 below).

[7] Calculated from: *Narodnoye khozyaistvo stran-chlenov Soveta ekonomicheskoi vzaimopomoschchi, p. 3; Narodnoye khozyaistvo SSR v 1972* (Moscow; TSU, 1973); *Monthly Bulletin of Statistics*, May 1974; *The Growth of World Industry* (1970).

[8] In 1950—73 reciprocal trade of the CMEA countries grew by a multiple of 10·5 to reach 47,500 million roubles in 1973, or 63 per cent of their aggregate foreign-trade turnover. For the years indicated, this percentage on the whole remained stable and was far in excess of the corresponding index for the EEC countries (some 50 per cent in 1973). It is characteristic that, in the pre-war period, reciprocal trade among the present CMEA countries accounted for only 10 to 15 per cent of their foreign trade. (See *Narodnoye khozyaistvo stranchlenov Soveta ekonomicheskoi vzaimopomoshchi; Vneshnaya torgovlya*, no. 6, 1974; and *Aussenhandel Monatsstatistik*, no. 1, 1974.)

most rational solutions to meet the interests not only of a given country, but also of all the members of the community. This is precisely the line that the Communist and Worker's Parties of the socialist countries, their governments and their scientific communities have been following.

The experience of the CMEA and its economic bodies and, especially, the current Comprehensive Programme for socialist integration, testify to the huge possibilities offered by the joint activities of the CMEA countries in many diverse spheres of their mutual contacts and relations.

It is obvious that socialist integration will go through a number of stages in its development. These will not repeat the stages of capitalist integration, but will be governed by their own laws. It is equally obvious that it would be absurd to demand that the socialist countries should employ methods and mechanisms typical of capitalist integration, just as it would be absurd to try to apply the distinctive features of socialist integration to relations dominating in the capitalist world. This position is dictated by commonsense, and I am sure that the problem is understood by participants in this congress.

The differences between socialist and capitalist integration are indeed very profound and it would be an illusion to underestimate their depth. But are the differences between the types of integration an insurmountable obstacle to ties between appropriate integration groupings? I am sure they are not.

In the modern world there are tasks demanding collective effort — those of developing to the utmost international economic ties, of promoting genuinely equal and mutually advantageous co-operation among all countries, irrespective of socio-economic system. This task applies equally to the socialist, the capitalist and the developing countries, whether within integration groupings or outside them. It presupposes joint action both on a bilateral and a multilateral basis, and many diverse forms of ties and co-operation between countries and integration groups of countries in the common interests of all peoples. I am referring, above all, to the interests of ensuring peaceful life all over the world, of raising the material and cultural standards of the broad masses of people in all countries, the successful solution of problems facing mankind in the fields of energy, natural resources, environmental protection, the wiping out of famine and disease, the exploration of outer space and the oceans, and the full development of the forces of production.

As regards the problem of possible co-operation between integration groupings of countries with different socio-economic systems — notably, the CMEA and the EEC, and all the indications point this way now — I should like to stress that this co-operation will require the elaboration of a largely novel and original mechanism. Such a mechanism must, in my view, reflect the specific features of the different groupings and the requirements of ties between them, and must be based on the principles of genuine equality of the rights of all partners.

It is the honourable duty of scientists and, of course, economists to promote in every way the development of international co-operation and the fruitful solution of the complex problems of mankind.

Comments
Richard Lipsey (Canada)

Balassa has admirably summarised (1) views on types of integration; (2) much of the existing evidence on the apparent success and failure of different schemes of integration in developed market economies, socialist countries, and developing countries; and (3) some possible reasons for some obvious, and some alleged, lacks of success in these schemes. I shall discuss his paper under these three headings.

I. DEFINITIONS OF INTEGRATION

His introductory discussion shows how difficult it is (a) to get a common definition of integration that applies to all types of economies ('applies' in the sense of outlining a relevant area of interest), and (b) to separate the question of definition from the question of choosing the appropriate tools for achieving integration. Possibly a search for a single definition is inappropriate. Possibly in mainly-market economies, such as those of the United States and Canada, trade and factor integration *is* the most important objective, while in mixed economies, such as those of France and the United Kingdom, a substantial amount of policy integration is needed in order to reap the benefits of regional specialisation. In socialist economies, the main emphasis may need to be on policy integration.

II. MEASURES OF SUCCESS

To attempt any measure at all of the successes and failures of integration schemes is a heroic task. I greatly admire the work of Balassa and of others that is briefly summarised in the present paper. But the task of a critic is to criticise, and I do so not just to find fault, but with the basic idea that an iterative process is possible: measurement — criticism — better measurement — better criticism, and so on. I presume that one of our major tasks at this conference is to ask if we can get better measures than we now have of the successes and failures of integration schemes.

The main measure used by Balassa is based on changes in trade patterns. Trade diversion is assumed to cause a fall in the ratio of *trade with the outside world* to GNP, while trade creation is assumed to cause a rise in the ratio of *total trade* to GNP.

The main problems here, it seems to me, lie with the basic concept of trade creation and trade diversion. They are static concepts. Their effects are once-for-all changes in the allocation of resources. At any date in the future their effects must be measured against *what would otherwise have been*, not by what is happening to trade at that time. In the economic theorist's model without adjustment lags, the introduction of a scheme for regional integration causes a once-for-all shift to more intra-integrated area trade and less trade with the outside world, and the forces that *subsequently* influence the allocation of resources become once again cost changes due to technological advance, and demand changes due to differing income elasticities of demand as real income rises as a result of growth. We shall call the first set of forces affecting the allocation of resources *integration induced* and the second set *growth induced*.

Adjustment, however, does not occur instantaneously. The two sets of forces, integration induced and growth induced, are intermixed.[1] The more sudden the integration, the more likely it is that integration-induced effects will dominate, at least for the first few years; but the longer the time lapse the more would normal growth-induced effects dominate. The morals are: (1) the longer the time since a relatively sudden move towards integration, the harder is it to discern the effects by studying changes in the patterns of trade; and (2) the more gradually the integration measures are introduced, the more will the effects be mixed up, even in the short term, with growth-induced effects.[2] No one, for example, would expect current changes in intra-United States trade to be explained by the concepts of trade diversion and trade creation caused by the introduction of a free-trade area almost two centuries ago. The effects are there, of course, but they are measured by what might have been, not by what is changing now.

One way of illustrating these problems is to note that the static theory of customs unions has no place for an increase in the volume of trade with the outside world; it remains constant or it falls. Yet in his paper Balassa notes the increase in imports of high-technology-based products from the United States into both the EEC and the CMEA countries. This, of course, is no mystery. Economic growth, whether or not caused by regional integration, will lead, through a high income elasticity of demand, to imports from countries providing high-technology-based products. But this suggests that, over any extended period of time, (1) the effects of trade diversion in reducing trade with the outside world could be masked by a high income elasticity of demand for the products of the outside world, and/or (2) the favourable effects of trade creation could be masked by a low income elasticity of demand for the products of other countries in a regional grouping.

All this does not mean to say that the measures are useless, nor does it deny the dramatic nature of the comparison between the shifts that have occurred in intra-EEC trade and those that have occurred in intra-CMEA trade — but by themselves they are not conclusive. Furthermore, the change in the volume of trade should be measured against the potential for intra-integrated area trade. As the debates of twenty years ago about unions between 'complementary' and 'competitive' economies showed, this potential can vary greatly among different regional groups.[3]

---

[1] The problem becomes even more complex conceptually if integration itself affects the growth rate.

[2] Income elasticities vary as income varies (because various sectors of the economy rise and fall in relative importance as growth proceeds). Thus, what might have been cannot simply be measured by projecting the pre-integration income elasticities into the post-integration period.

[3] I have focused attention on the volume of trade. Balassa makes frequent references to percentages. For example, he writes 'we find that the share of intra-CMEA trade in the total declined from 71 per cent in 1959 to 63 per cent in 1971, involving mainly a shift to trade with developed market economies'. The percentage is a hard taskmaster

Could we get some other measure as a substitute or as a cross check? To illustrate the difficulties, let us consider an alternative. One measure of the success of regional integration is the absence of duplicated industries producing the same product in various member countries. This suggests that we look at production rather than trade. In the neo-neoclassical model used by many Western economists, products are distinct from each other, and each is homogeneous. In such a world, specialisation of production and growth of trade go hand in hand, and they become alternative measures of the same thing. But consumer goods industries in Western economies abound with the production of similar but not identical products.

Consider an example. Before a customs union is formed, countries A and B each have a car industry producing solely for its domestic market. After integration, both car industries survive, but A's industry exports half its production to B, as does B's industry to A. There has been a large increase in the volume of trade but no increase in regional specialisation in production.

A Western economist who accepts consumer sovereignty will regard this change as a gain because it increases the range of consumer choice. A Western economist who is critical of the tendency of capitalist economies to proliferate the production of very similar commodities — and there are many who are — will not regard this as a significant gain. But, however we may value the change, we get very different answers if we look at changes in the patterns of trade and at changes in the location of production.[4] Which is more relevant?

Whatever may be the problems of measurement, I find it hard not to be impressed by the differences pointed to by Balassa between the development of intra-EEC trade and that of intra-CMEA trade. (I have said nothing about his report on the developing countries, because I cannot in any way disagree with his depressing conclusion that, with one or two notable exceptions, the movements for regional integration have made little or no headway there.)

III. EXPLANATIONS

I should like here just to note, and briefly comment upon, the main points made by Balassa in his conclusion.

(1) *There is a need for a better system of prices to reflect relative scarcities.* Surely one does not have to accept the Western subjective theory of value to agree that it is desirable to know real opportunity costs: how many nuts and bolts must we export to get the quantity of imports we want (a) for one of our regional partners and (b) from the outside world?

---

since it insists on adding to the constant total of 100! To illustrate the problem, note that the figures quoted are consistent with an absolute trade-creating increase in intra-CMEA trade from 71 to 126, which itself caused economic growth, which, in turn, operating through a high income elasticity of demand for high-technology goods, increased trade with developed countries in real terms from 29 to 74. (Trade with the developing nations has been ignored for purposes of this illustration.)

[4] In view of some of the changes in EEC trade I think this illustration is a relevant, although an extreme, example. I can think of no examples of the opposite extreme case: an increase in the specialisation of production *without* an increase in the volume of trade.

There is one interesting point worth noting here. Once one has decided to satisfy needs for a particular commodity by importing rather than by domestic production, all one has to know is quoted prices abroad. It does not matter how prices in foreign countries were arrived at; the raw prices give one opportunity costs and allow one to calculate which foreign country demands the lowest real sacrifice in exports for a given quantity of imports. Uncertainty about what prices in different foreign countries reflect should not, therefore, contrary to what Balassa seems to imply, lead a country to favour trade with one foreign country over another. Where this uncertainty does cause trouble is in the decision between importing and producing at home. To decide whether to export nuts and bolts and import cheese and crackers, or to produce cheese and crackers and, hence, fewer nuts and bolts at home, one wants prices that reflect the real opportunity costs in domestic production. Arbitrary prices will lead to mistaken decisions (mistaken in the sense of preventing the maximising of production).

(2) *'[D]ecision making at the firm level will give desirable results only in the absence of monopoly positions'*, and, *where monopolies occur, product and development integration are needed.* Possibly. But it is important to note that where the EEC has had least success is in high-technology-based industries (such as aircraft and computers) where governments play a large part in supporting often inefficient local industries. The fear of monopoly should not blind us to the fact that it is more efficient, in terms of resource use, to have one huge monopoly serving the whole integrated area than a series of government-protected monopolies serving the markets in each individual country. Government co-operation is required to create the efficient super-monopoly. It may afterwards be desirable to control the monopoly's pricing policy, but the resource gain is there, whether or not this is done. Government co-operation is required where governments exert a strong influence on resource allocation (for instance, by subsidising a local industry). Whether the end result is a monopoly or a series of competing firms is beside the point. It is interesting to note that the EEC has had least success in promoting integration in areas where the production of high-technology products are being encouraged by individual governments.

(3) *Interference may be justified for the aid of less developed regions.* This is particularly important when we realise that many comparative advantages are acquired rather than dictated by nature. (The importance given in recent years in Western economies to the concept of human capital reflects this point.)

It seems to me that in the ensuing discussion we should not spend too much time trying to find a single definition of integration, but should concentrate our attention on measuring its effects, on evaluating successes and failures and, where there are failures, in trying to identify causes. These are the themes set by Balassa in his own paper.

2 Worldwide *versus* Regional Integration: Is there an Optimum Size of the Integrated Area?

Richard N. Cooper (USA[1])

I. INTRODUCTORY

A skilful programme committee chooses for its conference papers titles that deceive in their simplicity but that on close inspection turn out not to be simple at all and that raise more questions than an author can hope to answer in the 5000 words allotted him. They thus lay the groundwork for future research and for future conferences. Certainly the title of this paper is deceptively simple, yet it cloaks a problem that goes to the heart of political theory: how should human beings organise their collective endeavours, especially those that require governmental action, so as to achieve best their diverse and often conflicting objectives?

The recent historical origins of the question posed in the title are clear enough. There has been a running debate since the Second World War (with antecedents in the 1930s) over whether the world economy would be better served by full multilateralism or by regional groupings that 'discriminate' in favour of members and against nonmembers. This question arose especially with respect to customs unions and free-trade areas, where the principal instrument of discrimination was the import tariff. But it also arose with respect to balance-of-payments policy (with the Sterling Area and the European Payments Union as the leading examples of regional groupings) and, more recently and more hypothetically, with respect to the range of common currencies — what is the optimal area for a single currency? As usually posed, these questions concern groupings of nations. But similar questions, deriving from a different starting point, have been asked with increasing force about the optimal provision of public goods and services *within* nations, particularly those with a federal structure, which have shown increasing strain in recent years in trying to provide public goods both efficiently and with sufficient regard for local variations in public desires.

Thus, from a theoretical point of view, the issue posed in the title goes

---

[1] The author is grateful to George von der Muhll for comments on an early draft of this paper.

beyond possible regional relationships among nations. Put more generally, we can ask: what is the optimal combination of communities, or regions, for an integrated area? In some cases the answer may involve regional groupings of existing nations; in others it may involve several regions within existing nations. But, before proceeding further, we should make a few distinctions about the meaning of 'integrated area'.

II. SOME IMPORTANT DISTINCTIONS CONCERNING 'INTEGRATION'

Although a detailed discussion of alternative forms of integration will be covered elsewhere, several distinctions are necessary here before proceeding to a discussion of optimal integrated areas. First, 'integration' can refer to the legal and institutional relationships within a region in which economic transactions take place. Second, it can refer to the market relationships among goods and factors within the region. This distinction becomes clear when we imagine a nineteenth-century *laissez faire* economy with no government barriers to interregional transactions, but with markets not linked because of ignorance or high transportation costs. The region would be integrated in the first sense but not in the second. This would remain true even where there is a high degree of intergovernmental co-ordination between the countries comprising the region. If, on the other hand, there are institutional or legal barriers to trade and capital movements, then, obviously, markets cannot be fully integrated either, at least in the sense of equal product and factor prices. But these prices may move in parallel with one another, indicating market integration at the margin — that is, high sensitivity to developments elsewhere in the region.

Before we return to this distinction between institutional and market integration, it is useful to draw a second distinction, between integration as a state of affairs and integration as a process. Much of the post-war debate on regionalism *versus* globalism was concerned with process rather than with state of affairs. The advocates of economic regionalism saw it as an effective route to attain some other objective, either economic globalism or regional political unification. The universalism of the Bretton Woods Agreement and of the General Agreement on Tariffs and Trade, both laid down in the 1940s, stood in sharp contrast to the regionalism of the Sterling Area, the European Payments Union, the European Coal and Steel Community and the European Economic Community. Each of the latter institutions was hotly resisted, in the early stages, as an undesirable retreat from the universalism that the architects of the post-war international economic system hoped to achieve. The regional institutions, for their part, were rarely justified as ends in themselves, although occasionally that strand of thought was present. Rather, they were regarded as superior means to achieve more far-reaching ends. Thus, Robert Triffin argued persistently that the European Payments Union, with its implied discrimination against the US dollar, represented by far the most effective way to achieve currency convertibility and to restore a truly multilateral system of international payments.[2] Like-minded countries with similar problems would move more quickly together than they could either separately or when grouped with countries facing very different problems. To try everything at once would impede progress, as the failure of the International Trade Organisation seemed to suggest. On this formulation, the objective of both parties to the debate is the same, namely a multilateral world economy, with judgements differing only on the best way to achieve it.

Unfortunately for clarity in the debate, another group, associated with the name of Jean Monnet, had quite different objectives, and sought to use the same instruments of economic regionalism to attain its objective of regional political unification. A confusion was thus introduced: the probability that economic regionalism would eventually lead to economic universalism was reduced to the extent that it would lead to regional political integration.

Integration as a process involves establishing a situation that is not in long-run equilibrium: partial integration creates new problems that, in turn, call for further integrative measures, and so on.[3] One thing leads to another, and eventually political integration captures the minds of the people. In the first version of integration as process, success among a limited group of countries breeds a willingness by others to join in, and eventually the regional approach becomes global. In the second version, it creates durable political bonds within the region. In either of these frames of reference, the 'optimal' region for integration is that that best achieves the desired objective rapidly and securely.

We return to integration as a state of affairs. Markets are integrated if one price prevails for each product or factor, after allowance for transportation costs. On this market formulation, the optimum integrated area is the world as a whole, for any artificial interference with price equilibration (except that designed to eliminate market imperfections) will, *ipso facto*, represent a source of inefficiency in the allocation of resources. What, then, is the case for regionalism? It lies, I believe, not in the realm of private goods, but in the realm of public or collective goods, where these are defined broadly to include the nature of the economic regime itself — that is, the system of property ownership, of contract, of risk-bearing, and the like. Some individuals may not want an economic regime based on markets, and are willing to pay the economic price for that decision. Viewed from the perspective of public goods, 'regions' really means governmental jurisdictions, and the inquiry must begin with the functions of government. The standard list calls on governments to provide public goods, to stabilise the level and growth of

---

[2] For a selection of Triffin's numerous articles and memoranda written in the early post-war era, see his *The World Money Maze* (New Haven: Yale University Press, 1966), especially pp. 376–405.

[3] On the theory underlying the neo-functionalist approach to political integration, see Ernest B. Haas, *The Uniting of Europe* (Stanford: Stanford University Press, 1958); and Joseph S. Nye, *Peace in Parts* (Boston: Little, Brown and Co., 1971), especially pp. 48–54.

income, to redistribute income and, above all, to provide a regulatory framework for economic and social transactions. Whether a region is 'optimal', then, depends on its optimal suitability for performing these various functions. 'Optimal' means 'best able to serve the various social objectives', where 'best' is in the Pareto sense of not permitting closer achievement of one objective without compromise the attainment of some other objective.

The perspective adopted here thus renders irrelevant the classic distinction by Viner between trade-creating and trade-diverting customs unions, and their analogues in the monetary arena. As Cooper and Massell showed a decade ago, in terms of straight national income a unilateral tariff reduction dominates the formation of a discriminatory trading bloc; the formation of customs unions must therefore be rationalised along different lines.[4] Harry Johnson has provided a more general framework for regarding protection in general and customs unions in particular as devices (perhaps inefficient ones) for the attainment of public goods – that is, features from which the public at large derives some satisfaction, whether these be nationalism, redistribution of income, or a level of industrial production above what could be sustained by the operation of unimpeded market forces.[5] In this context the formation of regional groupings on a discriminatory basis may represent the most efficient method for attaining a proven objective; but the results would have to be shown in each specific case, for the general optimality of discriminatory trade or payments arrangements cannot be assumed.

THE OPTIMAL PROVISION OF COLLECTIVE GOODS

The optimal provision of public goods involves both technological considerations and the accommodation of public preferences. We shall first consider the technological side, where considerations generally (but not always) press for enlargement of governmental jurisdiction, while accommodation of public preferences generally (but not always) presses for relatively small governmental jurisdictions.

Three technical factors have a bearing on the provision of public goods: economies of scale, the presence of externalities (including the important special case in which some of the objects of regulation are mobile), and the possibilities for reducing economic disturbances through integrating markets. We shall take up each of these considerations in turn, the last especially in the context of economic stabilisation.

[4] Charles A. Cooper and B. F. Massell, 'A New Look at Customs Union Theory', in *Economic Journal*, LXXV (Dec 1965), pp. 742–7, and 'Toward a General Theory of Customs Unions for Developing Countries', in *Journal of Political Economy*, LXXIII (Oct 1965), pp. 46–76.
[5] Harry G. Johnson, 'An Economic Theory of Protectionism, Tariff Bargaining, and the Formation of Customs Unions', in *Journal of Political Economy*, LXXIII (June 1965), pp. 256–83.

ECONOMIES OF SCALE

Scale economies offer a traditional argument for increasing the size of jurisdictions, at least up to a point. Certain public goods, especially those that for efficiency require a high degree of specialisation, experience strong economies of scale. Examples would be certain forms of scientific research, public health, police investigatory work, the penal system, some aspects of national defence, and flood control and irrigation. Where scale economies are substantial, the governmental jurisdiction (or its functional equivalent in facilities shared among jurisdictions) must be large enough to encompass the scale required, or else its residents will either enjoy lower quality services or pay more than is technically necessary for those services.

The optimum scale for governmental jurisdiction will vary, of course, from public good to public good. Where jurisdictions can be effectively separated along functional lines, they can be tailored to the requirements of each different good. (Los Angeles and London both offer examples of urban areas with many overlapping jurisdictions, drawn, in part, along functional lines.) Where, as a practical matter, that is not possible, the choice of scale of a jurisdiction should be governed (other things being equal) by the minimum cost of the package of public goods that is to be offered. Because of organisational, managerial, and informational costs, the optimal jurisdiction will be well below the global level.

EXTERNAL EFFECTS

External effects arise when activities within one jurisdiction directly affect the welfare of residents of another jurisdiction, other than through market prices. External effects can be either positive, as in the case of malarial control, or negative, as in the case of downstream water pollution. In one respect, external effects can be thought of as a more general case of economies (or diseconomies) of scale: once a service (for instance, malarial control) is provided, the marginal cost of additional consumption (enjoyment) of that service is low or zero; and, therefore, the *average* cost to citizens is lower, the larger the jurisdiction in terms of taxable population. It is, however, worthwhile to preserve the distinction between the two considerations, since economies of scale normally refer to technical input-output relationships in the production of a well-defined good or service, and not to the consumption effects.

A special kind of externality arises from the mobility of the objects of policy action. Here the problem is that the 'public good' by community preference may involve unwelcome restraints on certain elements of the community — for instance, its business firms or its radio stations or its high-income members. Activation of these regulatory or redistributional policies will then drive the adversely affected parties out of a jurisdiction that is too small relative to their domain of mobility. They will escape the onerous

action by leaving the jurisdiction in question.[6] To prevent this, the jurisdiction must either inhibit the mobility of its residents or become large
enough to encompass their entire domain of mobility. The latter course does
not necessarily involve enlargement to the global level, because, as a practical
matter, persons and firms are not globally mobile. Considerations of
economics, geography, language and culture all limit the actual domain of
mobility.

The mobility of factors beyond a government jurisdiction limits the
capacity of that jurisdiction to redistribute income. The heavily taxed will
move out, and those who are subsidised will move in, both of which movements undercut the fiscal viability of redistributional policies. It is true that
even trade in goods and services will affect the rewards to factors of
production, as underlined in strong form by the Heckscher—Ohlin—Samuelson
theorem concerning factor-price equalisation. But the imposition of tariffs
can alter the free-trade distribution of income; and, in any case, the resulting
factor rewards are *before* allowance for income taxes, which can serve
redistributive objectives. It is factor mobility, not commodity movement,
that really limits the possibilities for redistribution.

Similar considerations apply to attempts by jurisdictions to regulate
business activity — for instance, capital structure, financial disclosure, safety
and pollution. Once the regulations go beyond what is acceptable to the
mobile firm, where 'acceptability' will be influenced by the competitive
environment in which the firm operates, it will depart for a jurisdiction with
less onerous regulations.[7]

ECONOMIC STABILISATION

A third consideration for the optimal size of an integrated region concerns
the objective of economic stabilisation. If policy measures to stabilise the
level of income or employment are uncertain in effect or costly to use, as
they typically are, any arrangement that reduces the macro-economic
disturbances to the region in question will be beneficial. For a given region,
macro-economic disturbances (that is, disturbances that in the absence of
countervailing action would perceptibly alter the level of aggregate income or
employment) can arise either within the region or from outside it. Its
economy will respond to these disturbances in some well-defined way,
depending on, among other things, the openness of the region, and it can

---

[6] A recent example of this process was the proposal by the new Labour government
in Britain in 1974 to tax the total income of foreign residents in Britain. The proposal
was greeted with howls of protest, some foreign residents made plans to leave, and the
British government backed away from its initial position.

[7] For a further discussion of these issues, and of the influence of mobility on the
formulation of government policy, see Richard N. Cooper, *Economic Mobility and
National Economic Policy*, The Wiksell Lectures 1973 (Stockholm: Almqvist and
Wiksell, 1974).

take steps to compensate for the disturbance with various regional instruments of policy, the impact of which depends also on the structure of the regional economy.

How, then, should the boundaries of a region be drawn from the viewpoint of maximising the stability of the regional economy? By boundaries is meant here the limits of application of tariffs or direct controls on interregional transactions and/or of a single currency or fixed exchange rates between currencies within the region.

First, consider the disturbances that create economic instability. If internal disturbances are low compared with disturbances emanating from outside the region, the region should perhaps insulate itself from other regions, using the devices indicated above. This is analogous to risk-splitting in the writing of insurance: a low-risk group can gain by separating itself from the rest. By contrast, if internal disturbances are large relative to disturbances emanating from outside the region, the region may gain by amalgamating with other regions and thus, in effect, exporting some of its disturbances to the larger area. Finally, if the relative importance of disturbances originating inside the region is about the same as those originating outside, but the disturbances have different patterns (that is, are less than perfectly correlated), then the interests of each of two regions will generally be well served by joining, since the distrubances will partially offset one another and produce a lower *net* disturbance in both regions; that is, the regions will engage in risk-spreading rather than in risk-splitting by joining one another and forming a single region, analogous to enlarging an insurance pool.[8]

If we now take the net disturbance as given, reduced as it may have been through export or through import of partially offsetting disturbances, we can ask how much damage it will do to the region in which we are interested, and how the region may take policy action to mitigate the remaining damage. Mundell has pointed out that if factor mobility is high within a region, adjustment to some disturbances can take place quite smoothly, as shifts in demand among goods lead to prompt re-employment of any redundant factors. Kenen has made a related point in emphasising the importance of diversity in an economy, both to reduce the net disturbance through the mutual offsetting of uncorrelated disturbances, and to spread the impact widely throughout an economy, thereby reducing the social cost.[9] In Mundell's formulation, stabilisation requirements alone imply as small an area as possible (each with its own floating currency), for that leads as close as possible to a regime of

[8] For a more formal analysis of the impact of disturbances on the income levels of different regions, see Cooper, *Economic Mobility*, mathematical appendix.

[9] Robert A. Mundell, 'A Theory of Optimum Currency Areas', in *American Economic Review*, LI (Sep 1961), pp. 657–64; and Peter B. Kenen, 'The Theory of Optimum Currency Areas: An Eclectic View', in R. A. Mundell and A. K. Swoboda (eds), *Monetary Problems of the International Economy* (Chicago: University of Chicago Press, 1969), pp. 41–60.

complete price flexibility, and the market will always clear. Efficiency in the use of money leads Mundell's optimum currency area to stop far short of this atomism. Kenen's emphasis on disturbances suggests that even in the realm of stabilisation alone the optimum area may be far larger than Mundell's argument implies.[10]

Moreover, extremely open (small) economies may find themselves bereft of useful instruments of policy to deal with disturbances. McKinnon has suggested that money illusion in an open economy may diminish to the point at which fluctuations in the exchange rate of the region's currency may cease to be effective in influencing patterns of demand and, indeed, may simply induce residents to hold 'foreign' currencies.[11] Also, a region may be so open that standard macro-economic fiscal action ceases to be an effective instrument of demand management, because the great leakages abroad vitiate its domestic impact.[12] This vitiation of policy is a more complicated question than at first meets the eye, because, of course, the disturbances are also strongly attenuated in these very open economies; and we must therefore ask whether, on balance, the region is worse off in terms of macro-economic management than it would be with more effective instruments of policy but also with larger net disturbances.[13]

[10] The contrary pulls on regional size of these two factors can be set down in informal mathematical terms as follows:

$$U - U^* = H(d, f),$$

where U is the regional unemployment rate, U^* is the unemployment rate that is sustainable over time in the absence of disturbances, d represents the average level of net disturbances over a period of time, and f represents the friction in the factor market that inhibits the immediate absorption of any unemployed labour. It seems reasonable to assume that

$$\frac{\partial H}{\partial d} > 0. \qquad \frac{\partial H}{\partial f} > 0. \quad H(0, f) = H(d, 0) = 0.$$

Suppose, then, that we want to minimise H by a judicious choice of size, s, for the region, within which trade is free and one currency prevails, but beyond which trade is subject to tariffs and where other currencies exist with flexible exchange rates between those currencies and that of our region.

$$\underset{s}{\text{Min }} H \rightarrow \frac{\partial H}{\partial d} \cdot \frac{\partial d}{\partial s} + \frac{\partial H}{\partial f} \cdot \frac{\partial f}{\partial s} = 0.$$

By the arguments in the text, $\dfrac{\partial d}{\partial s} < 0$ and $\dfrac{\partial f}{\partial s} > 0$

so that a minimum may be assumed to exist. The resulting region would be 'optimal' in this dimension only.

[11] Ronald I. McKinnon, 'Optimum Currency Areas', in *American Economic Review*, LIII (Sep 1963), pp. 717–24.

[12] Cooper, *Economic Mobility*; R. I. McKinnon and W. E. Oates, *The Implications of International Economic Integration for Monetary, Fiscal, and Exchange-Rate Policy*, (International Finance Section, Princeton University, 1966), pp. 16–17.

[13] For a discussion of this issue, see R. N. Cooper, 'The Relevance of International Liquidity to Developed Countries', in *American Economic Review*, LVIII (May 1968), p. 636.

But the reduced effectiveness of policy instruments limits the region's capacity to compensate for disturbances arising outside the region, at least so long as some social cost is associated with their exercise at more intensive levels.[14]

Most of the considerations discussed above — economies of scale, external effects, escape from regulation and redistribtuion, effective economic stabilisation — argue for increasing the size of jurisdictions. The entire globe would be the logical limit to this process. Only increasing difficulties of management (diseconomies of scale associated with management and bureaucracy) and, for those regions that can profit by it, risk-splitting, cut in the other direction, toward the smaller scale of the optimal jurisdiction. But we have not yet made allowance for the diversity of preferences for collective goods.

DIVERSITY OF PREFERENCES

Individuals differ greatly in their preferences for collective goods, both of the systemic type (that is, the fundamental nature of the regime, capitalist or socialist; strong preference for order *versus* high respect for individualism; etc.) and for specific public goods (for instance, provision for flood control, parks or scientific research). These strong differences are conditioned by differences in cultural background and in income level. Obviously the greater the diversity of preferences within a given jurisdiction, the more difficult it will be to satisfy, even approximately, all the demands of residents for public goods, as public goods are by their very nature provided in roughly equal amount to all residents of the relevant area. There are thus large consumption losses in jurisdictions with a wide diversity of tastes, relative to what would be possible with different jurisdictions each catering more precisely to the preferences of its residents. This consideration thus pushes strongly toward relatively small communities that are homogeneous in their preferences for collective goods; it underlies much of the pressure for greater decentralisation of government and for more local control.

In a recent book, *Size and Democracy*, two political scientists pose the trade-off in a slightly different way. They present the conflict between 'system capacity' and 'citizen effectiveness'; that is, the capacity of the governmental system to deliver the (public) goods efficiently, as against the ability of its citizens to participate effectively in making governmental decisions affecting the level and composition of public goods to be provided. At one point, however, these authors seem to suggest that, particularly on the grounds that it may provide an environment favourable to the dissenting

---

[14] This last qualification is necessary because, in its absence, an instrument of policy could simply be worked at a sufficiently high level of intensity to deal with the problem, so long as it has any impact at all. But, in fact, there are limits to how hard the use of each particular policy measure can be pushed.

citizen (which may be everyone on some issue or other), there is a positive value to diversity among the citizenship and to pluralism as such. This would suggest enlarging the jurisdiction despite the advantages cited above for having communities with homogeneity of tastes. The authors do not, however, attempt to weigh this desire for pluralism against the necessary consumption loss of other public goods as a result of diversity in tastes.[15]

Considerations of liberty, however, may press for smaller, more numerous jurisdictions rather than large diverse ones if individuals are mobile. Breton has put the point strongly: 'The number of levels and sizes of units [of government] should be such that for any level of costs, the power of politicians − defined as their capacity to depart from the preferences of citizens − should be minimized.'[16] Those fearful of the coercive powers of the state would set the scale of jurisdictions at a low level, even if that meant sacrificing some economic efficiency, for the sake of keeping politicians under check through competition with other jurisdictions.

CONCLUSION: WHAT IS THE OPTIMAL AREA?

How are these conflicting considerations to be weighed against one another? That itself is an issue involving the diversity of preferences, for different individuals may be willing to sacrifice differing amounts of income (as taxes) in the form of less efficient provision of conventional public goods in order to purchase some given amount of liberty, or national prestige, or sense of cultural identity. It is necessary, as Samuelson has told us all along, to have a social welfare function that weights not only the provision of goods and services but also the individuals who make up the community. But to say that we need a social welfare function is, while formally correct, merely to pass the question to the agent who specifies that function.

FUNCTIONAL FEDERALISM

Compromise among the various considerations is possible. Under a system of functional federalism, the trade-off between scale economies and diversity of tastes is made for each public good separately, leading to many overlapping governmental jurisdictions, each dealing with its own set of highly specialised and closely related problems (for instance, police protection, weather forecasting and control, and flood control). Each has its own autonomous decision-making structure and its own citizenry, which may differ from issue to issue. This, in a way, is the method of specialised international organisations, each established by separate treaties, and it can also be seen in federal

[15] Robert A. Dahl and Edward R. Tufte, *Size and Democracy* (Stanford: Stanford University Press, 1973), especially pp. 22−5 and 138.
[16] Albert Breton, 'Theoretical Problems of Federalism', in *Recherches Economiques de Louvain*, XXXII (Sep 1970), p. 114.

countries.[17] It is an attractive idea, and in practice it will be necessary, at least in some degree. The notion of sovereignty inevitably becomes ambiguous under a system of functional federalism, for there is no sovereign, only a series of partial sovereignties. But that ambiguity is necessary to achieve the objective of the optimal provision of public goods, unless, of course, the existence of an unambiguous sovereignty is itself regarded as the overriding public good.

However, a system of functional federalism with partial sovereignties has its disadvantages as well. In the first place, both technology and tastes are in flux. A pattern of organisation that is optimal now will probably not be optimal ten years from now. Yet an ongoing bureaucracy develops vested interests of its own and is very difficult to change. Every country is living with outdated but durable – not to say tenacious – governmental institutions. Flexibility would be lost through a proliferation of jurisdictions, none with overriding authority.

In the second place, a system of functional federalism would, in the absence of a higher authority willing and able to sacrifice its vested interests in particular jurisdictions, inhibit bargaining and political compromise *across* functional, jurisdictional boundaries. For much of the time it is useful to have each issue operate on its own track, with its own set of conventions and sanctions to influence behaviour. But from time to time the inability to bargain across issue areas would prevent communities from reaching an optimal configuration of public goods.

CONTEMPORARY RELEVANCE

I shall close with some comments on the contemporary relevance of what are otherwise broad and largely inconclusive generalisations.

The pressures for enlargement of governmental jurisdictions are strong and growing in the modern world. Activities in each jurisdiction have impacts on other jurisdictions in an increasing number of areas. Economies of scale and externalities in some activities have been growing as well, so that, to the extent that those activities are desired as public goods, the jurisdiction required to carry them with any efficiency has also increased in size. Not the least of the sources of 'spillouts' in the modern world is the fact that governments have become active in the pursuit of a variety of social objectives, and these pursuits often vary from country to country, setting up strains, including those arising from the mobility of firms and persons between different jurisdictions. Even when factor mobility is not present, one hears charges of 'unfair' competition from a country that pursues practices

[17] For a stimulating discussion of the division of labour among different levels of government, see Mancur Olson Jr, 'The Principle of "Fiscal Equivalence": The Division of Responsibilities among Different Levels of Government', in *American Economic Review*, LIX (May 1969), pp. 479–87.

somewhat different from one's own. Economic stabilisation and income redistribution have become more difficult to achieve for countries acting alone. On all of these grounds, therefore, an argument can be made for increasing the size of jurisdictions — for forming regional groupings of nations.

The EEC is one response to these pressures. The motivations behind the formation of the Community were many, and mainly political; but at their root was a preception that European nations acting singly would have a diminishing influence on the course of world events and, hence, even on their own welfare. They joined together, therefore, to pool their influence and to try to restore some autonomy to their evolution.

The Community is relatively homogeneous by global standards, so that the welfare loss associated with 'harmonising' various policies will be less than it would be for a larger and more diverse group of countries. Other successful attempts at economic integration — The Central American Common Market and, on a more limited basis, the Andean group of countries — also reflect a high degree of homogeneity relative to the world at large — although we should keep in mind that homogeneity always looks greater from a distance than it really is. The United States has been relatively successful, in part because, while very large, it is relatively homogeneous in taste and outlook, and it has a system of decentralised government capable of catering to variations in local preferences. Indeed, the greatest internal difficulties within the United States have arisen when local preferences — for instance, on racial discrimination — offend a national norm.

Growing centralisation and bureaucraticisation in response to pressures for enlargement have created counter-pressures for greater decentralisation in governmental decision making. These arise partly out of psychological revulsion at the growing distance between the average citizen and his government, partly out of the perception that centralisation really reduces responsiveness to local preferences.

The communist countries are committed to such a fundamentally different conception of the basic economic regime that it is difficult to contemplate meaningful integration between them and other countries except along highly specialised and functional lines. Many less developed countries are still groping for the appropriate underlying regime for themselves, trying to adapt a colonial legacy to new needs and to indigenous preferences, and until this process is completed it will be difficult to integrate such countries with others whose basic regime is settled and is generally regarded as satisfactory. Once again, integration along specialised functional lines is about all one should reasonably try at this stage, and even there such attempts as have been made are often plagued by difficulties because some countries question the fundamental propositions that others take for granted.

For these various reasons, therefore, regional integration regarding public goods seems to be a more promising route than does global integration. Indeed, there should be no objection to groups of countries getting together to pursue their common interests, so long as neither their intent nor their effect is gain at the expense of other countries. There are numerous opportunities to form such 'clubs' such that their activities are not at the expense of, but may be beneficial to, other countries.

I conclude, therefore, in the same way as Alec Cairncross did in his recent discussion of the optimal firm: there is no such thing.[18] Nor is there such a thing as an optimal region, at least at the high level of generality that has been considered here. Not the least of the difficulties is that close co-operation among nations, or within regions, *builds* close ties and more homogeneous preferences as well as reflecting them, a point well perceived by the advocates of the economic route to political unification of Europe. Rather, optimality calls for a much more complex array of jurisdictions, compromising between the desire for greater decentralisation and the technical need for greater centralisation in decision making.

---

[18] A. K. Cairncross, 'The Optimal Firm Reconsidered', in *Economic Journal*, LXXXII (Mar 1972), supplement, pp. 312–20.

Comments
Germánico Salgado (Ecuador)

The subject of Cooper's paper does, as he says, touch upon the heart of political theory, and it would not be to the point to analyse the paper solely in terms of any one given objective among all the many objectives of collective endeavour. He rightfully emphasises the possible conflict among objectives and the necessity of posing the problem of the scope of governmental jurisdictions as the search for a conciliation among these objectives, given certain technological, economic and political parameters. In reality, this is the only suitable way of analysing the motivations and the scope of integration among societies, and it has been most stimulating to see these phenomena examined in all their complexity, without the extreme simplification of the 'classic' theory of the customs union. This theory, in spite of its limitations, continues to be the conceptual scheme by which various integration efforts are frequently evaluated, even those being made among developing countries, whence the applicability of this theory is even more questionable than it is in the case of integration among more developed countries.

The conclusions of Cooper's paper, which centres on the provision of public or collective goods, point out the almost always opposing forces that are exerted, on the one hand, by technological factors (economies of scale, externalities, and the need for economic stabilisation), which in general induce a broadening of governmental jurisdictions; and, on the other hand, by the diversity of preferences, which generally tends to limit such jurisdictions to groups that are more homogeneous in their social preferences.

In the specific case of relationships among countries, the net result of the interaction of these forces is the growing tendency to constitute regional groupings — that is, integration efforts limited in scope to societies in which there exists a relative homogeneity of social preferences with regard to certain high-priority objectives — as opposed to global integration with worldwide jurisdiction, the actual possibility of which is now more remote than ever. This is especially the case with the economic integration efforts among developing countries, motivated by the technological factors already mentioned, as well as by profound differences in objectives and interests relative to those of the richer countries of the world.

The fundamental element of motivation of these efforts is a preference for industrialisation and technological development, which would be, in that sense, a public good in exchange for which the participants are willing to accept certain sacrifices with respect to other social objectives. The type of industrialisation that the developing nations are seeking requires a broadening of the dimensions of the economy, combined with a policy that is protective, or, in a more general sense, discriminatory towards other governmental jurisdictions having more advanced industrialisation. This need for discrimination affects their dealings not only with industrialised nations, but also with the many developing countries that, because of a relatively greater economic dimension or because of having gained a head start in their processes of industrialisation, have attained relatively higher levels of industrial development and technology.

To the preference for industrialisation, which is a motivating element in

the formation of economic groupings among developing countries, there can
be added another preference that, in the future, will be a great stimulus to
the establishment of new regional groupings, whether these be undertakings
of thoroughgoing economic integration or the results of joint endeavours in
limited spheres of action. This new factor is the preference for greater
autonomy of decision, brought about by a greater bargaining capacity in the
context of the world economy. As Cooper notes, this motivation played a
role in the constitution of the EEC, but, in the case of groupings of developing
countries, either it did not exist or it was not considered important enough
to help shape the tools of integration. It is well known that some of the first
attempts at integration had their origins in efforts towards economic rationalisation induced by the colonial powers. This state of affairs has undergone a
very pronounced change. The sheer economic and political weight of the
industrialised world — states and multinational companies — is now being
more strongly felt and also more determinedly resisted by the poor countries
than ever before. Recognition of this fact is one of the determining factors of
the present political context of developing countries. The formation of
groupings in an effort at least to reduce the great differences in bargaining
capacity is clearly, then, an objective that reinforces the already existing
tendencies towards the creation of regional groupings. This is a special case
of an external effect, brought about by the enlargement of governmental
jurisdiction, that tends to segregate further the weak countries from the
powerful ones, and to diminish still more the possibility of world integration.

Taking these factors into consideration, we can then very reasonably
expect a still greater effort on the part of the developing countries to constitute regional groupings. The term 'groupings' is used here in its broadest
sense: associations formed among countries in order to serve common
purposes that require what Cooper would call a broadening of 'governmental
jurisdictions'. This term comprehends a vast range of possibilities of
association or co-operation: starting at the top with the functionally complex
association that implies voluntary subjection to formulas of economic
integration the purpose of which is to constitute one single economic space,
on down the list to the functionally more limited relationships that are the
result of agreements for conjoint action in specific areas of common interest.
To this second group belong such associations as the Organisation of
Petroleum Exporting Countries (OPEC), the Intergovernmental Council of
Copper Exporting Countries, those that could be established to promote
collective action to facilitate, say, the transference of technology, and so on.
The Andean group is a typical example of the first kind of relationship. The
objectives pursued by associations like the Andean group — that is, the
establishment of an industrial base and the adoption of common policies in
relation to the centres of world economic power — are difficult to attain and
their success depends on the careful inclusion of only those societies that are
relatively homogeneous in their social preferences. For this reason it is
probable that this type of grouping will limit the number of its members, as
well as its geographical area, in order to ensure a thoroughgoing and efficient
association. Logically, this is not the case with other less comprehensive
formulas of co-operation, in which there can exist a much greater flexibility
in the relationship owing to the limited nature of its objectives. As is already

becoming evident, there will among the countries of the Third World be an ever-greater inclination to constitute this type of association in the interest of fulfilling concrete political and economic objectives. From this point of view as well, then, the near future does not appear to hold in store a state of affairs conducive to worldwide integration, with the freedom of movement of goods and factors of production that this implies.

It would be well to examine briefly the possible structure and scope of the groupings of the first type: regional economic integration associations among developing countries. It has already been noted that one of their fundamental motivating forces is industrialisation. The question here is not to evaluate the rationale behind this 'preference for industrialisation'. What is important is to recognise the fact that, in every modern integration attempt among developing countries, the fundamental political reason for accepting the limitations of sovereignty implied by integration is the possibility of the joint construction of a broader and more efficient industrial base. This still holds true in spite of the fact that some of these integration projects may have found their original inspiration in other factors. In some cases the initial impetus may have been found in a desire to enjoy the benefits that would stem from an expansion of trade, making fuller use of existing complement-arities, as was the case, in effect, with the Latin American Free Trade Associ-ation (LAFTA) and the Central American Common Market. For other groupings, the original motivation may have been the possibility of realising savings through the establishment of common services (this was, in large part, the reason for the creation of the East African Community). Be this as it may, all these groupings have sooner or later had to come to grips with what is now their common fundamental objective: making use of the technological advantages of their greater economic space in order to create an interdependent industrial structure — based largely on the newer industrial activities — which will be of greater economic scale and greater technological complexity. The lack of adequate instruments and policies for co-operative endeavour in this very important area has led these associations to a state of stagnation and, in some cases, to the very real danger of rupture or dissolution.

On the basis of experience, it can be safely said that industrial development is the 'public or collective good' *par excellence* that is sought after by the developing countries in their integration efforts. It is a fact well recognised by the more recent regional groupings such as the Andean group or the Caribbean Community, which have placed great emphasis on the drawing up of policies to allow for the joint construction of that industrial base. This is, without a doubt, one of the most complex problems faced by those who design the policies for economic integration, since they have to consider not only the need for efficiency, but also the legitimate aspiration of all the member countries to participate to a 'satisfactory' degree in the benefits that derive from that 'public good' — that is, industrialisation. This in turn implies the necessity of interfering to a certain extent with the market forces in order to avoid concentration of industrial activity in countries that are or appear to be better endowed. If there results a loss of efficiency, it is offset by the resulting greater stability of the integrated society and, consequently, by the increased possibility for all of the members to satisfy their preferences for industrialisation.

In 1965, Charles A. Cooper and B. F. Massell[1] found, upon examining the case of customs unions among developing countries in terms of static efficiency, that there exists a potential gain for all participants in a system of joint industrial development the elements of which are basically the same as the ones that have been mentioned here as characteristic of the new directions that economic integration is actually pursuing among these countries today. In theoretical terms, I can add nothing further to this analysis. But it would be interesting to refer to the general reply that Richard Cooper gives to the question of the optimal size of the integrated area. There is not, he says, 'such a thing . . . , at least at the high level of generality that has been considered here'. I am in complete agreement with him, and to substantiate this judgement it will be useful here to consider briefly certain characteristics that will most likely be common to regional groupings among developing countries as a result of the emphasis they give to industrialisation.

It is clear that the greater the degree of homogeneity among the member countries with respect to their levels of industrial development, the greater will be the possibility that all will be able to gain from integration and that the process will be less conflictive and easier to conduct from the technical and political points of view.

With respect to the countries of Latin America, in which I have had firsthand experience and which for the past twenty or thirty years have all taken a similar stance in the policy of important substitution, I can simplify and say that fundamentally, the concept of homogeneity has come to mean, a similar economic dimension or size, measured in terms of national income as a market indicator. By virtue of this definition, then, regional groupings that include countries with acknowledged differences in economic dimension will be faced with many more difficulties in neutralising the tendencies towards concentration of economic activity. In point of fact, this is what has happened with LAFTA, which seeks to bring together countries like Brazil with Paraguay or Bolivia. Even direct allocation of industries according to the dictates of detailed industrial programming would stand little chance of ultimate success if one or more of the participating countries were to have an industrial sector substantially more efficient and diversified than those of the other countries. Furthermore, even if industrial programming were technically possible, there can be no doubt that it would be comparatively more conflictive here than in the case of a more homogeneous grouping of countries.

If the stability of the integrated society is one of the objectives that should be considered in the determination of the optimal size, as indeed it must be, then there can be little doubt that, *ceteris paribus*, the grouping formed by more homogeneous countries will come closer to fulfilling that objective. The enlargement of the integrated area serves, of course, some of the objectives pursued by the grouping, but the internal structure of the association itself influences the attainment of other and, *a priori*, equally important objectives.

In summary, it is impossible to formulate a serious answer except with regard to a specific case and the evaluation of its various objectives.

[1] 'Toward a General Theory of Customs Unions for Developing Countries', in *Journal of Political Economy*, 1965.

Comments
Evgueni G. Mateëv (Bulgaria)

At the beginning of his paper, Cooper makes a distinction between institutional integration and market integration. An illustration: it is possible in a 'nineteenth-century *laissez-faire* economy with no government barriers to interregional transactions' that the markets may nevertheless remain unintegrated.

Had this distinction been conducted in a sufficiently consistent manner, it would have served as a starting point for raising essential questions. What does determine the degree to which markets are linked under some, or under other, institutional relationships? This question will lead us far beyond the framework of the 'ignorance or high transportation costs' by which Cooper, *passim*, limits his explanation, and will show us the trends towards internationalisation of production under the contemporary highly developed technology. In addition, it becomes possible and necessary to analyse the various forms and manifestations of the international division of labour and to establish an adequately broad content of the concept of 'integration', without restricting it to any one market institution. Again, following this path, it is possible to find an explanation for, and make an assessment of, the different legal and institutional relationships that favour or impede integration.

Cooper has preferred another way of developing the theme. He restricts the concept of 'integration' it to its direct manifestations in market relationships and, so far as they are concerned, links the differentiation of the individual regions to governmental interference, as a manifestation of particular preferences. His logical pattern is thus as follows.

First step. Economic integration is considered from the angle of the integrated markets: 'On this market formulation, the optimum integrated area is the world as a whole'.

Second step. Regions arise when, in this integrated market, an 'artificial interference with price equilibrium' is carried out.

Third step. The artificial interference is performed by the state organs. Their considerations? I quote: 'It lies, I believe, not in the realm of private goods but in the realm of public or collective goods, where these are defined broadly to include the nature of the economic regime itself'. In other words, political considerations prevail or play a decisive role in the differentiation of regions.

Fourth step (and, at the same time, an inference). 'The communist countries, are committed to such a fundamentally different conception of the basic economic regime that it is difficult to contemplate meaningful integration between them and other countries except along highly specialised and functional lines.'

The further inferences from Cooper's thesis can be, as is seen, only in the direction that the prospects for economic co-operation are extremely limited. This train of thoughts gives rise to essential objections.

To reduce economic integration to the conditions of a market in which 'artificial interference' is absent is a purely formal approach that does not take into account the content of the process. There is no need to point out that this definition is unsuitable for integration in the economic system of the socialist countries, an integration that is an incontrovertible fact. It is inadequate, however, to explain integration even in the capitalist system. Let us recall the circumstance, noted also by Cooper, where artificial interference may be lacking and yet there can be no integration.

The essence of integration and the need of its development are deeply embedded in the internationalisation of production processes. The national product becomes ever more complex in the sense that it embodies an increasing number of different products with an ever more complex technology. Modern technology requires a high concentration of production and scientific research. Under these conditions, the national framework, not only of the small and medium but even of the large states, proves narrow. Of necessity, the division of labour assumes an ever greater scale. For the realisation of this process, a wide system of measures, both in connection with the market and in many other fields, becomes necessary. All this, as a whole, characterises the degree of economic integration.

This definition is as obvious as it is essential from the viewpoint of the further inferences.

Above all, on this basis the factors that influence measures with respect to the market become understandable. Cooper claims that 'regions really mean governmental jurisdictions, and the inquiry must begin with the functions of government'. If we remain with this definition we shall have to regard 'the governmental jurisdiction' as a free result of certain preferences and the scales of integration as a passive consequence of these free preferences. Conversely, if we take into account the deep factors of the internationalisation of modern production, we shall open for ourselves the way to those powerful forces that have an effect on governmental jurisdiction itself. It will become clear that not all and any preferences in this field may count on success. Some individuals may, for instance, prefer that the two parts of Europe should remain economically divided by a Chinese wall and even — let us paraphrase one of Cooper's thoughts — may be inclined to pay the economic price for such a policy. The point is that the price for their preferences will be paid not by them but by the national economy, which would hardly agree to pay such a price for a long period of time when the expansion of economic co-operation represents a necessary consequence of, and is at the same time a factor in, its very development.

If we look for the essence of integration in the factors that lead to an expansion of the international division of labour, it will become clear that measures regarding the market are not the sole form in which integration is expressed. This concept of integration is excessively narrow, even for the capitalist economy, because it leaves out of the field of vision such factors as the complex relationships connected with the international corporations. It is, further, utterly unsuitable as regards the socialist countries, in which integration is expressed not only in a marked increase in their mutual trade (it rises nearly twice as rapidly as their GNP), but also in more profound ways. It leads to ever closer co-operation in working out the short- and long-term plans as a basis for this trade.

Cooper's approach also puts the question of the relationship between the regions on a very narrow base. He limits his attention to the classical instruments of market policy, which are inadequate to explain the relationships between the different regions in the capitalist economy and are quite unsuitable to explain economic co-operation between socialist countries, and the countries of other regions.

As regards third countries, integration within the socialist system does not, to any degree, raise obstacles to co-operation — neither to imports and exports nor to some greater forms of co-operation. In this respect, the integration in the CMEA differs very markedly from the governmental jurisdictions in the EEC, which, as Cooper claims, exhaust the characteristics of integration in this system. This particular feature is closely connected with public ownership — that is, with the fact that in the socialist countries the centre of a jurisdication can be simultaneously an importer and exporter.

The prejudice continues to exist in the West that the planning of the socialist economy is a factor that restricts opportunities for economic co-operation with third countries. In all probability, Cooper has planning, among other things, in mind when he notes 'the fundamentally different conception of the basic economic regime'.

It is true that planning is a particularly powerful factor in deepening integration within the system of the socialist countries, owing to which it differs essentially from their relations with third countries. Public ownership and planning are, however, no obstacles to the development of the widest possible co-operation with third countries. The plan is a process and not Moses's tablets, and allows the prompt utilisation of all newly emerging possibilities for the expansion of exchanges. Every socialist country is limited in its imports from third countries by one factor only: by the possibility to export — that is, by this artificial interference of the third country about which Cooper speaks. What is more, the planned character of the economy also ensures considerable advantages for the contracting party from third countries: first, stability of the economic ties; second, a large volume of transactions — as large as the contracting party, in its turn, may take.

The inference we may draw from this is sufficiently clear. Unlike Cooper, I believe that there are sufficient grounds to make economic co-operation between the socialist system and third countries possible, and that this co-operation is not only possible but also of mutual interest. Objective factors do exist for its expansion, irrespective of the preferences of some who may impede this objectively necessary process.

3 A History of Thought on Economic Integration (Presidential Address)

Fritz Machlup

The Chairman of the Programme Committee imposed on the President of this association an unduly hard task. Perhaps he felt some hostility towards him and wanted to be nasty; or he did not realise how difficult his assignment was! Anyway, I found myself saddled with the commitment to produce for this Presidential Address a history of thought on economic integration.

In painstaking library research I have amassed a large amount of material, so much that I cannot possibly present it within the limits of a paper. I decided to publish the promised *History of Thought on Economic Integration* as a separate book and to offer today merely a report on it with some extracts and some excerpts. A major deficiency of both the book and this report is that my search of the literature is limited to publications in English, French and German, with a few items in Italian. I must ask for your understanding and forgiveness of my disregard of the literature in other languages.

Like Gaul and many other things, my study is divided into three parts. The first deals with the term, its history, and its meaning; the second with the idea and its strands; the third with the authors and their main contributions. The reason for separating the first and the second parts will be immediately obvious. Words are supposed to convey ideas, but neither words nor concepts remain forever unchanged. New terms are introduced to convey old concepts, and old concepts are modified, enlarged or restricted without change in the terms employed. The history of an idea must therefore be distinguished from the history of the word attached to it at present or at any one time.

The separation of the third part from the second will allow me to present a more plastic picture of the ideas than could be done in a history where each author has to be exhibited with his particular contributions to the literature.

I. THE TERM, ITS HISTORY AND ITS MEANING

The word 'integration', taken from the Latin, is of course very old. In Latin, *integratio* was mostly used in the sense of 'renovation'. The *Oxford English Dictionary* gives 1620 as the date for the first use in print of integration in the sense of 'combining parts into a whole'.

THE USE OF THE TERM IN ECONOMICS

In economics the word was first employed in industrial organisation to refer to *combinations of business firms* through agreements, cartels, concerns, trusts and mergers — horizontal integration referring to combinations of competitors, vertical integration to combinations of suppliers with customers.[1] In the sense of *combining separate economies* into larger economic regions the word integration has a very short history.

The word had not been so used anywhere in the old, chiefly historical literature on the economic amalgamation of the nation state, nor in the literature on customs unions, including the *Zollverein*, nor in the literature on international trade before the 1940s. No subject index of any book that I know on international economics prior to 1953 contains the entry 'integration'.

The Encyclopaedia of the Social Sciences, published in 1937, did have in its index the entry 'integration', but it was 'Integration, industrial — see Combinations, industrial' (XV, p. 629) and the cited article began with the distinction of horizontal and vertical combinations through mergers, concerns, and cartels (III, p. 664). The new *International Encyclopedia of the Social Sciences*, published in 1968, does include 'International Integration', and indeed has four articles on the subject. Three of them — those entitled 'Regional Integration', 'Global Integration', and 'Functional Integration' — were written by political scientists.[2] Only the fourth article, 'Economic Unions', was by an economist (VII, pp. 541–6).

A large family of words — ranging from economic *rapprochement* via co-operation and solidarity, to federation, amalgamation, fusion, and unification — had been given a new name: economic integration. But who did it? Who were the terminological innovators?

My search for the first user or users has had all the characteristics of a detective story. There were several suspects, wrong clues, vain efforts, surprising discoveries, and much suspense. A few times the search seemed successfully completed, but then a still earlier source was found and possible links had to be investigated. Indeed, I cannot be sure that I have tracked down all writers responsible for the novel use of the old term.

My detective story is too long to be included in this paper. To abbreviate

---

[1] I have dealt in detail with the differences between the integration of enterprises or industries and the integration of economies in my essay 'Integrationshemmende Integrationspolitik', in *Bernhard-Harms Vorlesungen 5/6*, ed. Herbert Giersch (Kiel: Institut für Weltwirtschaft, 1974).

[2] In political science, the term 'political integration' (meaning integration within and among countries) has been used at least since the late 1920s. The following statement may be quoted in support of this opinion: 'the "appearance of political integration" which the League has already produced in some measure, is to find its economic complement'. The complement, however, was still called 'European economic solidarity'. See Harry D. Gideonse, 'Economic Foundations of Pan-Europeanism', in *The Annals of the American Academy of Political and Social Science*, CXLIX (May 1930), p. 155.

a detective story, perhaps to tell 'who done it' but not to convey the suspense of the search, would be to ruin the story. I shall therefore give here neither the whole nor the partial story. I confine myself to the disclosure that the term in question in its new economic meaning made its appearance between 1939 and 1942. For the rest I simply refer you to my book.

Having found out who were the first users of the term in its new economic meaning, I turned to the question of when and how the term invaded the official languages of Washington, London, Paris and other centres of government. This was another search, again with many wrong clues and disappointed expectations. The earliest evidence I found of an official use of the term in its new economic meaning was dated 1947; two years later the term was firmly established in America as well as Europe.

THE MEANING OF THE TERM

Now that I know (or believe I know) the history of the term in its new meaning, I must admit that this meaning is by no means clear. We find a few bits of unanimity, a fair amount of consensus, but also much divergence among the users of it.

Users are virtually unanimous on one question: that integration can be understood either as a process or as a state of affairs reached by that process. Whether that state has to be the terminal point or an intermediate point in the process is not always clear, but this ambiguity can be taken care of by distinguishing between *complete* and *incomplete* integration. More difficult is the question of what it is that is to be integrated: people, areas, markets, production, goods, resources, policies, or what? The most important questions, however, ask (1) what is the substance, what are the essential criteria, of such integration; and (2) by what indications or symptoms can one decide whether there is or is not a process at work, or a state of affairs attained? These are very different questions. Users of the term may agree on what the substance is and yet disagree on how one can find out or what one should observe; conversely, some might agree on possible indicators without agreeing on the essentials, on what it is all about. Just to give one example, there is fundamental disagreement on the relation between economic integration and equalisation of incomes (or of the prices of productive services) in different areas, some writers regarding equalisation as the essence of integration, others as a possible consequence, others as the main target, others as an indicator, and others as merely incidental or even unrelated to economic integration.

A wide consensus exists on three issues: (1) that economic integration refers basically to division of labour; (2) that it involves mobility of goods or factors or both; and (3) that it is related to discrimination or nondiscrimination in the treatment of goods and factors (for example, with regard to origin or destination). This consensus does not imply agreement on a definition. We shall have to discuss all three issues before we can decide on their comparative significance.

Many disagreements about the most appropriate definition can be disposed of by the use of adjectives modifying the noun. When Balassa presented us with a very helpful review of definitions,[3] he proposed the rejection of some definitions as being too wide. Yet, one does not have to reject a definition on these grounds as long as the concept can be narrowed through the use of a qualifying adjective with the term. For example, Balassa wanted the definition of economic integration to restrict the process or state of affairs to different *nations* joining in a *regional group* or bloc. This is an unnecessary restriction (and an uneconomical one) because the economics of the matter is the same whether it is different provinces of a state that become 'more integrated', or different nations within a bloc, or different blocs in the world as a whole. One can easily differentiate by speaking of *national* (interprovincial, intranational), *regional* (multinational), and *worldwide* (global, universal) integration.

Similarly, instead of arguing whether certain arrangements for co-ordination or unified management of particular sectors of two or more economies deserve to be called economic integration, one may agree to speak of such arrangements as *sectoral* integration, as distinguished from *general* economic integration. Again, instead of arguing whether a very small increase in the division of labour deserves or does not deserve to be regarded as economic integration (seen as a process), one may agree to speak of attaining higher and lower *degrees* of integration.

Balassa proposes that we distinguish *trade* integration, *factor* integration, *policy* integration, and *total* integration. One wonders, however, to what extent factor integration presupposes trade *and* factor integration. Moreover, one may ask whether factor integration refers to all types of factors of production and to what extent it would coexist with unrestricted movement of goods. Perhaps one had better speak of common or integrated product markets, labour markets, and capital markets.[4]

Complete integration of markets implies adequate mobility of whatever it is that is supplied in the markets in question and nondiscrimination in the sense that neither sellers nor buyers are influenced by the origin or destination of the thing bought or sold. Mobility need only be adequate (rather than perfect); it suffices for all practical purposes if a certain part of the total supply can be moved without undue cost or trouble.

Can we take division of labour to be an essential part of the definition of economic integration? If we do, we carry out, I believe, the intentions of

[3] Balassa, 'Towards a Theory of Economic Integration', *Kyklos*, XIV (1961), pp. 1–17, and *The Theory of Economic Integration* (Homewood, Ill.: Irwin, 1961), pp. 1–3.

[4] The term '*market* integration' was proposed by Vajda. See his 'Integration, Economic Union and the National State', in *Foreign Trade in a Planned Economy*, ed. Vajda and M. Simai (Cambridge: Cambridge University Press, 1971), p. 33. Vajda wanted 'market integration' to be supplemented by 'production and development integration' (pp. 35ff).

most, perhaps all, users of the term; I believe also that we thereby conform
to the ideas of socialist as well as of free-enterprise economists. A very neat
formulation in terms of an analogy helpful in explaining the essence of
general economic integration has recently been offered by a Polish economist,
Stanislaw Chelstowski. As he puts it, in an article on 'CMEA and Integration'
(*Polish Perspectives*, XV, Dec 1972), it means 'tailoring the economic fabric
of each country to the requirements of an international division of labour'
(p. 10). But how much international division of labour has to be arranged
for? Is there a minimum and/or a maximum of exchange of products that
makes it economic integration?

I submit that the idea of complete integration implies the *actual* utilisation
of all *potential* opportunities of efficient division of labour. The notion of
taking advantage of an existing but hitherto unused opportunity relegates
the entire conception from the domain of recorded observations to the
domain of delicate calculations.

The calculations relevant for the evaluation of actual and potential
exchange are so delicate and complex because they involve an indefinite
number of inputs and outputs indirectly related to one another by alternative
employment and alternative production. General economic integration of the
economies under consideration does not refer to particular industries or
sectors, nor to particular factors or products, intermediate or final, but
rather to the *entirety of economic activities* of the region (country, bloc, or
world). It is an integration of all productive resources available anywhere in
the region for the production of all the many goods and services demanded
under actually or potentially realised conditions. It is constituted by a
complete interweaving and interdependence of *all* economic sectors,
industries, branches, and any activities whatsoever, in the closest possible
approximation to the theoretical model of general equilibrium in a system
with unrestricted mobility of all movable factors and products, intermediate
and finished.[5]

The essential criterion of complete general economic integration is
commonly seen in equality of prices of equal goods and equal services. That
is to say that all means of production (original or intermediate) in the
integrated economic region that are both perfectly mobile and perfectly
substitutable for one another (hence, genuinely equal) will receive the same
prices and will have the same marginal net-value productivity in all their uses.

The economically optimal relationships among all costs and prices in the
completely integrated area can be determined only in a system of perfect
interdependence. This presupposes that all enterprises and all agencies in
charge of planning and allocation have to make their calculations on the basis
of opportunity cost. Every means of production, wherever actually used, has
to be valued according to the social utility that could potentially be derived
from alternative uses. Such alternative uses may be anywhere in the

[5] Machlup, in *Bernard-Harms-Vorlesungen* 5/6, p. 43.

(supposedly) integrated region and in any sector, industry or branch, however remote. All means of production have to 'compete' for all possible uses, and all branches of production have to 'compete' for all possibly usable means of production. In market economies this competition includes effective competition among enterprises; in comprehensively planned economies in involves competition among all conceivable alternatives in the considerations of the decision-making agencies or boards. Expressed in a slightly modified way: all inputs are considered eligible to compete for uses in the production of all conceivable outputs, and all outputs are considered eligible to compete for allocations of all conceivable inputs. In this interrelatedness and interdependence among all economic activities I see the essence of general economic integration. This is the principle, and it applies equally to a single country, a group of countries, or the whole world.[6]

Certain 'positive measures' are needed even in free-enterprise economies to supplement what Tinbergen chose to call the 'negative measures' of eliminating all restrictions on trade, travel, migration, capital movements and payments. There is need for a monetary system that facilitates foreign payments by securing the interchangeability of different currencies or, still better, by replacing the separate national currencies with an international one. Tax harmonisation would avoid some distortions in resource allocation and consumption if indirect taxes, such as sales taxes or value-added taxes, were made uniform for all goods and services throughout the area to be economically integrated. Yet I have a strong suspicion that the actions recommended to or adopted by several governments in the name of monetary integration and fiscal harmonisation are counterproductive. Let me state my reasons for saying so.

The most urgent prescription that the money doctors (or money quacks) gave to governments desiring *monetary* integration was fixed exchange rates with the smallest possible bands for permissible oscillations around parities. This prescription would be fine if the countries were prepared to give up their autonomy over credit policy. Fixed exchange rates were possible so long as governments did not pursue monetary policies designed to aim at other targets, such as maintaining full employment, accelerating economic growth, counteracting fluctuations in business activity, or keeping price levels more stable than they are abroad. With other targets proclaimed as national goals, a system of fixed exchange rates became inoperable. Yet the advocates of fixed rates stubbornly stuck to their prescription and, in order to avoid or postpone adjusting them, resorted to foreign-exchange restrictions, to controls of capital movements, and even to outright impediments of trade. Thus, a policy advertised as instrumental to the achievement of monetary integration and as conducive to greater economic integration became in effect a 'positive' obstacle to integration, setting back general integration by many years.

What should we, then, make of the term 'monetary integration'? I

---

[6] Ibid., pp. 44–5.

propose that this term be used only for measures, policies, or processes that facilitate monetary transactions by anybody or for any purpose. Absence of restrictions is the minimum meaning of the term; the maximum is the use of a single, uniform currency. Somewhere in the spectrum is co-ordination of national monetary policies, which, however, is a practical–political impossibility under present-day ideologies concerning the functions of national central banks. It does not now qualify as a practical instrument of monetary integration.[7]

Harmonisation of *fiscal* institutions, particularly the tax system, has been an important subject of analysis, discussion, and positive government action in recent years. It is firmly believed that equalisation of indirect taxes in all member countries of a common market is an important step on the way to higher degrees of general economic integration. That this is wrong, at least if the tax rates are not different for different goods, has been known since Ricardo and has been repeatedly restated, most recently by Gottfried Haberler.[8] Yet, in deference to the practitioners' beliefs and pressures, the member countries of the EEC, although they have abolished customs duties on intra-community trade, make border-tax adjustments, collecting from importers and refunding to exporters. These import taxes and export premiums have been established and maintained as compensatory adjustments in line with the principles of harmonisation and integration. What these 'positive' measures imply is the maintenance of checkpoints at the frontiers between the countries of the presumably integrated group.

Would it be unreasonable to suggest that a highly significant trait or probe of economic integration may be the nonexistence of any checkpoints at the frontiers between member countries? What the authors of the Constitution of the United States of America recognised almost 200 years ago is far from being realised by the architects of the Common Market: that a shipment from Germany to France must not be treated differently from a shipment from Bavaria to Baden-Württemberg, or from Burgundy to Normandy. Perhaps one may go even farther and say that full economic integration between two or more countries with market economies is not

---

[7] If a group of countries is determined to give strongest possible support to economic integration for the region, the member countries will have to abolish their independent national central banks and adopt a uniform currency, issued by a community central bank. If they are not prepared to do so without a lengthy transition period, they can speed up the process toward a uniform currency by adopting a parallel standard, with both national and regional (or international) currencies circulating side by side, not linked by fixed exchange rates, and with no restrictions on the use of the regional (or international) currency in payments, contracts and settlements, foreign or domestic. If the members of the group of countries are not prepared to follow such a plan of gradual substitution of an international currency for their own, the only contribution they can make, through monetary arrangements, to the attainment of general economic integration is to continue to let their currencies float but to remove all restrictions on payments and financial transactions.

[8] Gottfried Haberler, 'Probleme der wirtschaftlichen Integration Europas', in *Bernhard-Harms-Vorlesungen 5/6*, pp. 23–6.

reached as long as they still know the volume of trade between them. No statistic tells us what the trade volume is between Pennsylvania and Ohio.

With so many different conditions helpful or harmful to the progress of economic integration, it is difficult, or perhaps impossible, to find any comprehensive description, let alone any short formula, to express the combined effects to be expected. I look forward to studying the papers of Working Group A of this congress, which may give us new insights into the problem of 'measuring the progress or degree of economic integration' or, more likely, of devising separate indices of different conditions and different effects that seem to be sufficiently relevant to give meaning to the confident assertions as to how far the existing regional blocs have progressed towards their professed objectives.

One of the most widely used tests consists in comparisons of various trade ratios: what portion of total purchases in any part of a region that is supposed to be, or is intended to become, integrated is of goods and services produced in that same part (province, state, country); what portion is of goods and services produced in other parts of the region; and what portion is of things produced in the rest of the world? Analogous tests are made for total sales of output: what portion is sold to residents of the same part of the region (province, state, country), what portion to other parts of the region, and what portion to the rest of the world? Numerous studies of this sort have been made, with most surprising results. Yet none of the tests proposed or applied can be admitted as conclusive in an attempt to measure the degree of economic integration attained. The main reason for this scepsis lies in the fact that integration is essentially, as I have said before, a *relative* achievement, a ratio of actually realised to potentially realisable opportunities for effective division of labour. We may have learned how to measure actual trade, actual migration, actual capital movements, but we have not yet learned how to measure the unused potential.

Additional difficulties of a conceptual nature arise from the fact that economic integration is relative not only to unknown potentials but also to the area under consideration. We must distinguish the *degree* of integration achieved within a *given territory* from the *extension of the territory* to be integrated.

If new territory is added to a region with the intent of having the resources and activities in the new territory integrated with those of the 'old' area, one must expect a reorganisation of activities and a reallocation of resources in both parts of the extended region, and, of course, more trade between them. Any increased division of labour between the old and the new parts of the extended region should express itself in new trade flows that increase the share of intraregional trade in total world trade. Of course, the combined shares of domestic trade and of what was previously counted as intraregional trade within the old region would then be lower. As the network of trade widens and the relative share of trade among the closest neighbours is reduced in the process, it would surely be erroneous to infer from this that the extension of external trade and the smaller relative share of internal trade mean a lower degree of general economic integration of the original 'home area'.

Let us then affirm that the notion 'degree of integration' calls for a specification of the area or combination of areas to which it is supposed to apply. We should note that different degrees of integration may have been reached (a) within the old region; (b) between the old region and one newly joined with it; (c) between the old region and the rest of the world; and (d) between the extended region (the combined area) and the rest of the world. If other regional blocs exist, even more combinations would be interesting, especially the degree of integration (e) between the extended region and the other regional blocs.

If we thus accept the idea that the degree of integration may be estimated (or at least a rough impression formed) separately for each area and for each combination of areas, we shall find it possible to speak of a relatively high degree of integration within area A, a lower degree within area $A + B$, a still lower one within $A + B + C$, and so on until we have the entire world. This is not inconsistent with expressed policy statements of several governments. They are, as a rule, determined to take advantage of all efficient opportunities for division of labour within their own country; they very much want to utilise many such opportunities within the regional group of which they are a member; they hold that considerable gains could be derived from trade with other regional blocs (for example, East–West trade); and they are not prepared to forgo promising opportunities for trade with the rest of the world. It would be unnecessarily confining to estimate the degree of integration just for the economic activities within the regional bloc. The concept makes sense for any and all combinations of territories, even if we are still far from knowing how to measure it.

II. THE IDEA AND ITS DIFFERENT STRANDS

After some brief reflections on economic thought and analysis and on political and economic objectives, I shall make it my main task in this part of my paper to dissect the complex idea of general economic integration or, using another metaphor, to disentangle some of the many different strands out of which the conceptual yarn has been spun.

ECONOMIC THOUGHT, ECONOMIC ANALYSIS AND POLITICAL AIMS

In distinguishing economic thought and analysis I follow the example of Joseph Schumpeter. There had been many comprehensive works on the history of economic thought or economic doctrines, but Schumpeter found their scope too wide for careful theoretical dissecting.

In a history of the idea of general economic integration it would, however, be too restrictive and too pretentious to limit oneself to pure economic analysis. However, one may still recognise Schumpeter's distinction by sorting

the contributions into different categories, one of which is labelled
'economic theory'. It will contain economic analyses of the abstract issues
raised in the theory of economic integration, ranging roughly from the theory
of division of labour and comparative costs via the theory of factor movements and factor prices to the theory of the economic effects of customs
unions.

Just as economic analysis wants to be segregated from broader economic
thought, so economic thought often wants to be separated from social and
political thought. This separation, however, is difficult to carry through in a
history of the idea of national and international economic integration,
because social and political issues are inseparably linked with economic ones.

THE MAIN STRANDS OF THE IDEA

Every serious discussion of economic integration, national, multinational or
worldwide, is based on concepts and issues of international-trade theory.
Movements of goods, services, ideas, people, capital funds and monies across
natural or political frontiers are what interregional and international
economic relations are all about — and all of these movements are part and
parcel of economic integration. Trade is usually regarded as the quintessence
of economic integration, and division of labour in several of its aspects as its
underlying principle. This holds for intranational as well as international trade.

I shall try to disentangle the strands of which the theory of international
and interregional trade and the idea of economic integration have been spun
and woven. Again, I must refer my audience to my book for a more detailed
description and explanation of these strands; in this paper I can offer only a
sort of inventory, a bare listing of the concepts and issues pertaining to the
subject.

'Division of labour' is the key term. It looks simpler than it proves to be:
one has to make some seemingly pedantic distinctions if confusions are to be
avoided. There are different types of intra-plant, intra-firm and intra-industry
division of labour, apart from the more general division of labour referring to
the production of different goods without any technological links or interrelations.

That the extent of the market limits the degree to which division of labour
is practicable is easy to comprehend. Likewise it is easy to see that the
efficiency of division of labour is largely attributable to the advantages of
specialisation, though one has to warn again that the connotations of specialisation are not as plain and unambiguous as many may have thought.

One of the greatest stumbling blocks on the way to a full understanding
of trade theory is the distinction between absolute and comparative
advantage. Many a student has never fully grasped how a country can have a
comparative advantage *vis-à-vis* its trading partners in producing a certain good
when its cost of producing it (in terms of labour and other required factors
of production) is clearly higher than the cost in other countries; yet, all it

takes for the comparative advantage to exist is that the cost disadvantage in producing other goods is even greater.

Partly because of endemic misunderstandings, partly because of understandable disbelief in the conclusions derived from largely unrealistic assumptions, the implications of the law of comparative advantage for commercial policy have not always been accepted. 'Free-Trade Doctrine: Adherence and Dissent' is the heading under which I discuss in my book how the advocates of free trade justify taking the theory with its idealised assumptions as an adequate support for their precepts, and how the dissenters justify their penchant for protective tariffs and other trade restrictions.

If efficient division of labour is conducive to increased output, how is this increase divided among the trading partners? Dividing the gains from trade, or figuring out how the market mechanism operates to apportion the gains from trade among the countries involved, has been a brain-twister for generations. After much fumbling the problem was solved by intuitive comprehension as well as rigorous demonstration. However, the solution yielded another argument for protective tariffs, since it showed that the terms of trade could be influenced by clever tariff setting: the optimum tariff to capture more of the gains was designed to change the reciprocal offers of the trading nations in such a fashion that any clear monopolistic or monopsonistic position in foreign trade could be exploited to secure for one country a gain at the expense of the others and, in addition, at the expense of the total (combined) gain from international trade.

A less unethical set of arguments against free trade was formulated on the basis of widely recognised market failures. The most general characterisation of market failure is in terms of divergencies between social and private marginal costs and marginal benefits. However, the proof that externalities exist does not constitute a proof that a tariff would 'internalise' and correctly take account of the existing difference.

The existence of infant industries and developing countries has long been the strongest argument for protection of domestic production against imports, although it has been clear to many that temporary subsidies to the 'promising' industries, rather than tariffs and other import barriers, would be the policy justifiable by the argument. The argument, though theoretically tenable, suffers from the practical difficulty that the selection of the industries that would have the greatest promise of acquiring in due course the comparative advantage they lack for the time being is quite arbitrary: no sound operational criteria for the selection are available. Other pleas for prohibitions or restrictions of imports have been made in the name of national or regional self-sufficiency, independence, and (military or political) power. The underlying arguments are usually beyond the reach of economic analysis and not seldom beyond the reach of commonsense.

On a very different plane are arguments for tariff protection for the purpose of influencing the distribution of income in favour of particular groups, especially of workers in countries where labour is relatively scarce. The idea is that countries ordinarily import products for which, in domestic production, relatively large inputs of scarce (dear) factors are used, and that these imports make these factors less dear. Where labour is relatively dear, shutting out imports will keep labour dear by protecting it from the competition of cheap labour abroad. The theory is based on a set of strong assumptions, some of which are widely regarded as unacceptable. One of the grounds of rejection is that raising labour income and improving the terms of trade may be two incompatible objectives of tariff protection. If tariffs improve the terms of trade for the country that imposes them, its imports become cheaper relative to exports; and, if imports are thus made cheaper rather than dearer (in real terms), the incomes of the dear factors employed in the domestic production of import substitutes will not be improved — indeed, the dear factors (labour) may be worse off.

The theories thus applied in the argument for tariff protection rest on a theorem that demonstrates that, even without any international movements of labour or capital, free trade of goods must, under specified conditions, succeed in equalising the earnings of equal factors in the trading countries. The trouble with this theorem is that it lacks empirical relevance, because some of the underlying assumptions, though serviceable for other purposes, are quite untenable in the context of the theory in point. The 'equilibrium' at which all original abundances and scarcities of productive factors in the trading countries will supposedly have disappeared (as all factors are used in the same proportions everywhere and receive the same prices everywhere) will never be reached if — as some of the most unrealistic assumptions are dropped — the process of equalisation is stopped. It is not difficult to see why, in a more realistic model of the world, stopping the equalisation process is the rule rather than the exception.

The theorem of the international equalisation of the prices of factors of production under free trade was first demonstrated for excessively simple cases: for only two factors, two products, two countries. The theorem expanded and refined, however, is no longer confined to these simple cases; yet its empirical relevance is not any greater. In the discussions of the deviation of observed reality from the conclusions derived from the theorem, it has been attempted to find which of the assumptions can be regarded as the most vulnerable, the most responsible for the variance. While there are several candidates for rejection, the charge of being most manifestly contrary to fact is placed on the assumption that all traded goods are produced in all countries and with exactly the same technique, employing exactly the same proportions of productive factors. Another serious objection is to the basic lemma of the argument that the factors in different occupations, industries, and countries are actually equal. Just as land differs in fertility and location, labour differs in many respects and can surely not be regarded as homogeneous. The theorem of the equalisation of the prices of the same factors in different countries, and the theory derived from it, can surely not apply to heterogeneous factors.

If free trade alone cannot, for several reasons, succeed in having equal factors receive equal prices in all activities in all trading countries, free trade of products combined with free international movement of factors might be expected to reduce and eventually remove international differences in factor prices. Yet, international mobility of factors cannot be counted upon to eliminate all wage differentials even for really equal labour. For one thing, the objective and subjective costs of migration are usually too high, and, moreover, the lags in the responses to the stimuli — differences in earnings — may be too long ever to allow equalisation of real wage rates to be fully realised. According to one view, free mobility may even increase existing inequalities. The so-called 'backwash effect' would drain cheap-labour countries of their best workers; and countries or regions that promise the biggest returns would attract not only the best workers but also most capital; thus the rich would become richer, and the poor poorer.

Before we leave this subject we ought to recall that early writers on international trade had assumed that neither labour nor capital was able to move abroad. The modern theorist knows full well that international migration of labour and international movements of capital have become facts of life. However, he knows also that the effects of trade and the effects of factor movements have to be studied separately before one can proceed to study them in combination. Thus, 'trade integration' without international movements of factors remains a subject of analysis.

One type of economic integration that has often been emphasised is the international transfer of technology and enterprise. In recent discussions this problem has been dealt with in connection with multinational companies and with governmentally organised co-operation in industrial projects. The problem, however, is not of recent origin; the classical writers did neither overlook nor disregard it. Nor did they fail to stress the significance of transport and communication. That cheap transportation and speedy communication are among the most fundamental conditions of economic integration is one of the oldest insights. No wonder that historians have assigned to the successive revolutions of transport technology a major role. No wonder, also, that theorists analysing the effects of tariffs were wont to simplify their models for purposes of comparative statics by assuming transport costs to be zero. No wonder, too, that at least one economist (Bastiat) tried to elucidate the effects of tariffs on prices and production by speaking of them as 'negative railways'.

Equal to cheap transport as a precondition of economic integration ranks cheapness and reliability of transfers of money. This requires a monetary system that allows people to remit funds abroad with a minimum of bother, risk, and other costs. Needless to say, the oldest literature dealt chiefly with easy payments in foreign trade; the freedom and ease of capital movements entered the discussion only later. The importance of easy payments has been extensively discussed in mercantilist writings about unification of the nation state, prior to which a wide variety of gold and silver coins, differing from each other in weight and fineness, circulated within the provinces, principalities and splinter states. After the establishment of nation states, the formation of monetary unions to guarantee the interconvertibility of national currencies became an object of public discussion, governmental negotiations and actual agreements (none of which has proved a lasting success). The discussion continues. No economist will question that monetary integration in the sense of unification may make a significant contribution to general economic integration, but many will disagree on the best sequence of steps to bring it about. Questions such as the stability or rigidity of foreign-exchange rates, the autonomy of national monetary authorities, the co-ordination of national monetary policies, the use of governmental restrictions and controls of foreign payments and transfers of capital, and the eventual replacement of national currencies by a uniform money for the entire economic union have all remained controversial. A good many economists hold that the existence of free markets for currencies, unencumbered by controls and restrictions, can secure all the monetary integration that is needed to achieve a very high degree of general economic integration.

Emphasis on the absence of restrictions and controls of transfers of money is particularly important in connection with the integration of capital markets. One would expect that within a regional economic union mobility of capital funds would be given one of the highest priorities. By some strange quirk in official thinking, capital movements into and out of countries in the EEC have been regarded with great suspicion and apprehension, and consequently have been subjected to governmental controls of increasing strictness. No agreement is in sight on the question of whether 'speculative' movements of funds are gravely disturbing (or even inimical) to trade integration or whether the prohibitions and restrictions imposed to avoid these 'undesirable' flows of funds are even more injurious to the progress of economic integration.

That arrangements to promote economic integration can be intranational (to create an integrated national economy), multinational (to create an integrated regional economy), or worldwide (to create an integrated world economy) has often been said. There has been disagreement on the question of whether regional integration would be a help or a hindrance in the progress toward worldwide integration. The answers often depended on tacit assumptions regarding the forms of regional arrangements. With respect to trade, it will make a difference (a) whether it is a customs union or a free-trade area that is being established, (b) whether the tariffs of the countries before they enter into these arrangements were high or low, and (c) whether the common external tariff of a customs union is high or low. Assuming that some of the countries had very low tariffs but that the external tariff of the union is high, the new regional integration would involve economic disintegration from the point of view of the world as a whole. If, on the other hand, the pre-union tariffs of the countries had been high but the external tariff of the union is low, the new arrangement would promote regional and worldwide integration at the same time. As to the comparison between a customs union and a free-trade area, it is often said that, because in a free-trade area the member countries retain their own, possibly quite different, tariffs on imports from nonmenber countries, it constitutes a lower form of integration. Whether this verdict is correct depends on the level of the tariffs; if the separate and different tariffs on imports from outside the area are low but the common external tariff of an alternatively established customs union would be high, the free-trade area would be more favourable to worldwide integration than the customs union would.

Considerations in this vein arc best clarified by comparing the levels of abolished and erected tariffs, provided that tariffs are the only man-made obstacles to trade. Comparisons of this sort, however, make little sense where trade is directed by central trading agencies ('state trading') on principles other than market-price guides or shadow prices calculated on the basis of opportunity costs. Neither trade/income ratios nor time series showing the growth of intraregional trade would indicate the degree of trade integration achieved — simply because actual trade is no proof that the potential is being fully realised. The question is whether advantage is taken of all opportunities for efficient division of labour. This cannot be ascertained except by reference to market prices or shadow prices.

Market prices are not always reliable guides in selecting the 'right' products for export or import: as mentioned before, even if competition were pure (atomistic), entry free, and all markets perfect, when differences exist between private and social marginal benefits or costs, resource allocation solely on the basis of free-market prices will not be optimal. But matters may be worse as a result of imperfect competition, monopoly, and oligopoly. Many economists, recognising the imperfections of competition in domestic markets, have seen one of the greatest benefits of free (or freer) trade in the competition from foreign producers, which could end the oligopolistic sinecures of domestic firms and force them the work with greater efficiency.

The probability of forced efficiency under the pressure of foreign competition has become one of the weightiest arguments for the formation and extension of customs unions. Not that worldwide free trade would not be far more effective in removing domestic restrictions on competition; but political resistance to it seems insuperable. But the same vested interests as are fiercely opposed to global free trade are willing to 'cope' with regional free trade, and some loosening of monopoly positions can be expected also from a regional common market. It is not forgotten, however, that many politically influential industrial groups have accepted the establishment of the common market only in the hope that cartels and mergers will succeed in averting the outbreak of unlimited competition among producers. Several plans for European customs union were quite explicit in this respect.

Whether union between weaker and stronger nations is likely to retard, if not thwart, the economic development of the weaker partners is a controversial question. It has been argued that the less developed countries will be held back, not helped, by such integration, especially because industrialisation will be concentrated in places or areas already most industrialised. To avoid such concentration, positive measures for regional development have been prescribed.

An essential argument in the welfare economics of regional economic integration concerns the choice between nondiscriminatory protection and discriminatory liberalisation. The first point to be settled is whose welfare should count: that of an individual country joining with one or more others in a customs union (or mutual-preference bloc), or that of all union or bloc members combined, or that of all countries taken together, nonmembers as well as members. From a cosmopolitan point of view — that is, from a free-trade point of view — discrimination and, therefore, tariff preferences have always been suspect. Depending on circumstances, including the level of duties (before and after), tariff preferences can conceivably cause greater divergences from the ideal free-trade pattern than uniform protection would.

Customs unions and free-trade areas, with all duties on trade among the members abolished, represent the highest degree of tariff preference (though international law has exempted this maximum preference from the application of the most-favoured-nation clause). The economic effects of this discrimination in favour of bloc members have been difficult to analyse. One of the most important distinctions made for such analysis is that between trade creation and trade diversion. If countries A and B form a union by removing the tariffs on imports from each other but retain a tariff on imports from C, a new import from B, no longer subject to duty, may displace in A either a home-made product of A's or an import from C. If it displaces A's domestic product, new foreign trade (though it is intra-union trade) is created. If it displaces a previous import from C, no new trade is created, but trade is diverted from a cheaper source of supply to a more expensive one, which (thanks only to the tariff discrimination) becomes more competitive. From the point of view of greatest possible economy in production, a customs union will increase combined economic welfare only to the extent that the effects of trade creation outweigh those of trade diversion.

This statement disregards the effects of possible economies of scale that the extension of the market (through removal of tariffs between A and B) may permit to be realised. If national markets were too small for 'optimum-sized' plants or most efficient types of organisation to be used, larger plants and larger firms could, in multinational markets, produce at lower unit cost. But should one attribute to the customs union effects that could be realised even better by generally freer trade? It is the abolition of tariffs, not the maintenance of tariffs on imports from nonmember countries, that affords the benefits in question. Incidentally, after years of experience with common markets, the empirical evidence of the existence of substantial economies of scale is still held to be inconclusive. If they exist, however, they can give rise to the phenomenon of 'trade suppression' – the opposite of trade creation – in cases where the more economical production of an enlarged output in one of the union countries results in an elimination of both some dutiable imports from a nonmember country and some duty-free imports from a member country.

The analysis of the welfare effects of a customs union in terms of creation and diversion of trade was incomplete, and new strands were added to the theory in quick succession. The first was the consumption effects of price reductions due to the removal of the duties on imports from members countries. Even with no shifts in resource allocation to make better or worse uses of opportunities for comparatively more advantageous production – indeed, even if production remained unchanged everywhere – the changes in relative prices charged to consumers would induce them to rearrange the pattern of their consumption in line with their preferences. Favourable consumption effects may conceivably outweigh any adverse production effects of trade diversion from lower-cost to higher-cost sources of supply. (Incidentally, it was in the analysis of comparisons of this sort that the 'theory of second-best' was developed.)

Instead of comparing the separate magnitudes of production effects and consumption effects in order to appraise the net effect upon welfare, a novel way to look at the two effects together has recently been proposed. It specifies that trade diversion be defined as the substitution of an unchanged physical volume of tax-free imports from the favoured trade partner for taxed imports from the previous (lower-cost) source of supply. If the definition thus limits trade diversion to the physical quantities of goods previously imported from countries now excluded by the discriminatory tariff, any increase in consumption induced by the price reduction effected by the removal of the duty on imports from the favoured source constitutes new trade – that is, trade creation – as consumers substitute imports for some domestic products. Looking at the results in this fashion, one comes back to the simple verdict that trade diversion reduces, and trade creation raises, the economic welfare of the integrated countries.

Another two-step analysis has been proposed to facilitate appraisals of the effects of the creation of customs unions or free-trade areas. Instead of sorting out the various positive and negative effects of the discriminatory reduction or removal of import tariffs while the tariffs on imports from nonmember countries are left unchanged or unified at agreed levels, one can analyse the results in two simple steps: the first step is a general abolition of tariffs on all imports from anywhere, the second the selective and discriminatory imposition of duties on imports from particular countries (with a uniform tariff in the case of a customs union, different tariffs in the case of a free-trade area, and more complicated arrangements in the case of other preferential schemes). All trade creation will be the result of the tariff abolition, and all trade diversion (plus some trade suppression) will be attributable to the discriminatory reimposition of tariffs.

A customs union may be seen as a compromise between free-traders and protectionists. The former are happy about the abolition of barriers in intra-union trade, the latter about the continuation of barriers against extra-union imports. (The height of these barriers determines who has made the greater concession.) Some of the free-traders were counting on a gradual lowering and pushing outward of the walls: more countries would join the union and a continuing growth of world trade would be admitted or even promoted.

The two groups of friends of the customs union, those aiming at regional protection and those aiming at eventual worldwide trade integration, have been greatly aided by a third group: those who cared far less about economic integration as an objective but saw it as a catalyst of political integration. They were hoping that closer economic relations among the members of a customs union would lead to closer political ties and eventually to political unification.

Limitations of time and space compel me to stop this exercise of pointing out some of the most important strands in the idea of general economic integration. Among the issues omitted here but designated for treatment in my book are the following: investment creation and investment diversion; degrees or intensity of integration within a given area; intensity *versus* extension; the significance of trade/income ratios; methodological distinctions regarding the effects of integration; positive and welfare economics; estimates of benefits; and the inclusion of public goods.

III. THE CONTRIBUTORS

I propose five labels for my files of contributors:

(1) *historians* reporting on the formation of nation states, customs unions and unification projects;
(2) *political economists* proposing, promoting or opposing various integration projects;
(3) *statesmen, men of affairs, and men of letters* promoting or rejecting customs unions and other projects for economic integration, regional or worldwide;
(4) *committee members and Organization staff* studying, promoting, and reporting on integration projects; and
(5) *economic theorists* analysing essential issues of international trade and economic integration.

These classes may in many instances be overlapping. An economist writing on the history of the making of a nation state or on the history of customs unions would be classified here as a historian; he may at the same time be a theorist, classified in group (5), if he has contributed to the economic analysis of the effects of customs unions. In addition, he may belong to group (4) as one of the members of staff of an international organisation who (generally anonymously) collaborated on drafting a public statement or report issued by that organisation. The distinction between groups (2) and (3) may be somewhat arbitrary, since a statesman, a man of affairs or a man of letters may on the basis of his studies or insights qualify as a political economist. The decision in a doubtful case will be guided by the character of the man's main activities or major publications.

I shall make several double entries. For example, Eli Heckscher, Jean Marchal, and Jacob Viner will appear as historians and as theorists; Friedrich List, Lionel Robbins, Gottfried Haberler, Charles Kindleberger, Maurice Allais, Nicholas Kaldor and others will be entered both as political and as theoretical economists. Many more double entries could be justified, especially in the categories of economists arguing for or against a particular cause or programme, and those engaged in theoretical analysis.

HISTORIANS OF CUSTOMS UNIONS AND INTEGRATION PROJECTS

Perhaps I should justify why I include historians in a history of thought on the subjects on which they report. Historians select the events and circumstances, which they research according to the importance they attach to them; and these implicit valuations of relative importance are necessarily based on some general thoughts and insights. If historians report, for example, on Colbert's efforts to remove interprovincial trade barriers in France, they evidently imply that such a policy has had some significance for the economic and political development of France and that Colbert may have been aware of that significance, although perhaps – as some try to show – for reasons not tenable on the ground of present economic theory. If historians report on the free-trade and protectionist debates among the American colonies before the Confederation, on the development of the British system of Imperial Preference, on the creation of the EEC or the CMEA, they cannot help having some point of view – sometimes perhaps a little vague or even naïve, but sometimes very clear and explicitly stated – from which they judge the course of events. The views of historians, or their concealed value judgements, may be as important for a history of thought on economic integration as the views of 'pure' economic theorists. Representatives of the historical school of economics may attach even more importance to the historians' accounts than to the theorists' speculations.

In my book I begin with a listing of the subjects of historical research that are likely to have elicited relevant thoughts on economic integration, and then proceed to a list of the publications that I came across or consulted as I prepared the survey of historical events. In this necessarily brief address, I must refrain from doing either. I shall confine myself to presenting the headings under which I arrange the historians' subjects:

(a)   customs associations and discriminatory import prohibitions in the
       Holy Roman Empire of the German Nation from the sixteenth to
       the eighteenth century;
(b)   unification of Great Britain;
(c)   unification of France;
(d)   British colonies and Commonwealth;
(e)   United States of America;
(f)   German *Zollverein*;
(g)   other European customs unions;
(h)   trade agreements and most-favoured-nation clause;
(i)   European projects that failed to come off;
(j)   worldwide arrangements on payments, credits, and trade;
(k)   West European economic co-operation;
(l)   East European economic co-operation;
(m)   Latin American regional arrangements;
(n)   African regional arrangements;
(o)   Asian regional arrangements;
(p)   Australian regional arrangements.

    The bibliography of historical writings on the events recorded under these
headings will be far from complete and yet too long to allow me to offer any
annotations on the books and articles cited. From my reading of the
historical literature I came away with some strong impressions, two of which
– with regard to historians' predictions and explanations – I shall mention
here.
    Some of the historians of customs unions have entertained very firm ideas
on economic or political prerequisites or consequences, and some of these
ideas sound a bit odd to us, who have the benefit of the hindsight. In a fine
study by Pentmann published in 1917 we can read that any customs union
beyond that of a single nation state – for example, a European customs
union – would be impossible as well as undesirable. Why should a historian
stick his neck out on statements of this sort, especially in an otherwise
excellent piece of historical research?
    More than a few historians were infected with the mercantilistic belief in
the blessings of exports and, especially, an export surplus. In the papers left
by the late Jacob Viner I found a little handwritten note with a delightful
quotation. No reference or author, unfortunately, was written on the note,
so that I do not know whether it was an authentic quotation or perhaps
Viner's invention. (Viner may have composed the fictitious quotation as
an examination question.) Here is the statement, which may be given the
title 'Beware of worldwide integration': 'There is a story told of a German
professor, who is said to have explained the decline of the Roman Empire
by the fact that, as the Empire grew and grew, in the end it comprised all the
known world – and therefore its foreign trade shrank to nothing.'

POLITICAL ECONOMISTS AS PROPONENTS, PROMOTERS, AND OPPONENTS

I shall present here an abbreviated list of political economists who have been proponents, architects or promoters of schemes of economic integration, and a few who have been dissenters. For some of them the advocacy or opposition that they expressed was a major concern, a cause to which they were deeply committed; for others it was just an incidental comment, a casual statement of opinion.

I mention only three names in connection with proposals for national integration before 1814: John Digby, Earl of Bristol, arguing (in 1641) for reunification of England and Scotland; Johann Joachim Becher, an Austrian mercantilist, arguing (in 1668) for and against a variety of causes, including economic unification of the German Empire; and Alexander Hamilton, arguing (in 1778) for American union.

I have a long list in connection with proposals for various European trade arrangements, 1814–1914: Michael Alexander Lips, Carl Friedrich Nebenius, Friedrich List, Adam Müller, Johannes Scharrer – all five concerned with the formation of the policies of the German *Zollverein*; Léon Faucher, Michèl Chevalier, Gustave de Molinari, Pierre Paul Leroy-Beaulieu – four French economists, arguing for or against customs unions, free-trade areas, and other trade arrangements; Richard Cobden and Sir Robert Giffen – both British, the former stressing the benefits from general or even unilateral free trade, the other arguing against a 'British *Zollverein*'; John Prince-Smith, Alexander von Peez, Lujo Brentano, Albert Schäffle, Sandor von Matlekovits, Sartorius von Waltershausen, Josef Gruntzel, Gerhard Hildebrand, Gustav Schmoller – nine economists, German, Austrian or Hungarian, discussing, advocating or opposing a variety of trade alliances or commercial policies for their own or other European countries; and, finally, Vilfredo Pareto – an Italian who advocated customs unions and other closer economic relations as means for the maintenance of peace.

As advocates or opponents of *proposals for European customs union*, 1918–39, I list Wladimir Woytinsky, Franz Eulenburg, Gustav Stolper, Alfred Weber, Elemer Hantos, William Rappard, Paul van Zeeland, Sir Arthur Salter, and Barbara Wootton – representing a variety of countries and discussing the pros and cons of a variety of plans between the two world wars.

The discussion of proposals for economic integration, 1945–74 brings us to the period after World War II and up to the present, with all of the participating economists still alive and active: Ralph G. Hawtrey,[9] Willard Thorp, Harold Van B. Cleveland, Charles Kindleberger, Adam Marris, Robert Marjolin, Robert Triffin, Gottfried Haberler, Alfred Müller-Armack, Kiyishi Kojima, Heinz Arndt, Nicholas Kaldor. Some of these economists have been rather sceptical regarding the alleged advantages of regional integration, and others have questioned the benefits of proposed extensions of the region in question.

[9] Hawtrey died, at the age of 95, while this volume was being prepared for publication.

STATESMEN, MEN OF AFFAIRS, AND MEN OF LETTERS

Inclusion in this group of men need not imply a judgement that the person
here named cannot be regarded as a political economist. Persons are listed as
statesmen, men of affairs and men of letters because it is chiefly in these
capacities or because of their achievements in these fields that they have
become known to the world.[10] I shall again group the selected contributors
to the idea of economic integration according to the period in which they
lived and worked for this cause.

In the three centuries from Erasmus to Fichte, 1521—1808, we find
chiefly philosophers, statesmen and publicists writing or acting to promote
national economic unification or multinational economic association
or federation. Erasmus of Rotterdam was the earliest promoter of German
economic unification; the Duc de Sully wanted a political and economic
unification of Europe on a federal basis; Jean Baptiste Colbert tried hard,
but in vain, to end the economic particularism of the provinces and local
authorities of France; Bishop Royas y Spinola proposed to the Hapsburg
Emperor a large economic union as a means for achieving a political union;
the Abbé de Saint Pierre and Jean-Jacques Rousseau advocated a permanent
association of European states for the sake of lasting peace; Immanuel Kant
had similar plans; William Penn was influential and, almost a century later,
Alexander Hamilton was successful in bringing about a federal union in
America with complete economic unification; and two Germans, Justus
Möser and Johann Gottlieb Fichte, argued for economic unification of
Germany.

In the period from Napoleon to World War I, 1812—1914 we find,
apart from Napoleon himself — who sought economic integration by
conquest — chiefly Germans and Austrians busily arguing or compaigning for
or against the formation and expansion of the German *Zollverein*: the
Freiherr von Stein, Johannes von Görres, Johann Benzenberg, Prince
Metternich, the Freiherr von Bruck, von Delbrück and Prince Bismarck.
We also find Sir Robert Peel, John Bright and Sir William Gladstone
espousing the cause of free trade for Britain and the world, and, near the
end of the century, two other British statesmen, Joseph Chamberlain and
Cecil Rhodes, dreaming and scheming for a greater Britain, an imperial
customs union, or a world federation under British rule. The same period
saw the Frenchman Tanneguy Duchatel propose a Franco—Belgian customs
union, and his compatriots Émile de Girardin and Paul de Leusse promote
plans for customs unions in Western Europe and Central Europe, respectively.
The American statesman James Blaine proposed a pan-American union, and
the Italian statesman Camillo Cavour stipulated the precise criteria for a

---

[10] One cannot help being arbitrary in such matters. Thus I listed Cobden as an
economist while Bright will be shown here as a statesman and man of affairs; and I
entered van Zeeland among the economists while Hendrik Brugmans will be included
here as a humanist and educator.

customs union that would not be in violation of the most-favoured-nation rights of countries outside the union. Finally, early in the twentieth century, a German politician, Hans von Schwerin-Löwitz pleaded for the establishment of a United States of Europe with high tariffs agianst imports from overseas, especially for the protection of agriculture. The mid-nineteenth century had heard Victor Hugo's voice of hope: 'The day will come. . . . '

The period between the two world wars, 1915–39 produced many champions of economic integration. There was a plan for 'Mitteleuropa' (Central Europe), proposed by Friedrich Naumann, another for 'Pan-Europa', proposed by Count Coudenhove-Kalergi, and one for a North Atlantic union, proposed by Clarence Streit. In addition, the French statesmen Aristide Briand, Edouard Herriot, Louis Loucheur and André Tardieu, the German statesman Georg Gothein, Walther Rathenau and Gustav Stresemann, and an English lawyer, William Ivor Jennings, proposed and promoted various kinds of customs unions and federations. A few of these champions of economic integration continued after World War II to work for their ideas.

World War II and after, 1940–74, is the period during which several of the plans for regional economic integration materialised and worldwide integration also progressed. The list of statesmen, officials and writers who played a role in this movement includes Winston Churchill, Franklin D. Roosevelt, Cordell Hull, Paul Reynaud, Léon Blum, Raoul Dautry, Alcide de Gasperi, Hendrik Brugmans, Harry Truman, George C. Marshall, Dean Acheson, William Clayton, Benjamin Cohen, Charles Bohlen, Walter Lippmann, Arthur Vandenberg, Ernest Bevin, Georges Bidault, Paul Ramadier, Count Carlo Sforza, Paul Hoffman, Paul-Henri Spaak, Robert Schuman, Jean Monnet, Duncan Sandys, Edmond Giscard d'Estaing, Walter Hallstein, Charles de Gaulle.

COMMITTEE MEMBERS AND ORGANISATION STAFF

The fourth of my categories of sources of economic thought on economic integration consists of groups of persons who did their talking, arguing, agreeing and writing for the most part anonymously, as members of committees or staffs of a large variety of organisations. In some instances the chairman, executive director or secretary of the organisation, committee or staff was so prominent that the group report was officially or inofficially given that person's name. (Examples include the 'Harriman Committee Report' of 1947, the 'Spaak Report' of 1956, and the 'Mansholt Report' of 1968). Some of the persons active in producing, or even responsible for, the reports were probably well-known economists or statesmen included in the lists of contributors under one of the other headings.

I cannot in this paper furnish a catalogue of even the most important reports relevant to my subject. But it may be worthwhile making a few significant distinctions about the groups from which the reports have emanated. These groups may be national or international, official or private, temporary or permanent. These three pairs of differences allow eight combinations, and specimens of every one of these can be found in well-equipped library collections. Most numerous have been the reports from official bodies or committees, national and international; and of greatest historical importance have been the reports of temporary (*ad hoc*) official international committees.

ECONOMIC THEORISTS

The survey of the contributions of economic theorists has been the biggest undertaking of my research project, especially because virtually all economic propositions about international economic integration are part and parcel of the theory of international trade and finance, and, obversely, because most of this body of theory is directly relevant to issues of economic integration. In my book – the by-product of my research for this Presidential Address – I review over 200 works (articles and books) by more than a hundred economists. Here I must confine myself to a mere enumeration of the writers in a roughly chronological order under five broad headings.

Among the early writers who expounded the advantages of extending the area of trade during the period 1691–1879 are Sir William Petty, Charles Davenant, Isaac Gervaise, Patrick Lindsay, David Hume, Adam Smith, Robert Torrens, David Ricardo, James Mill, John Stuart Mill, William Ellis, Mountifort Longfield, John Elliot Cairnes, Hans von Mangoldt and Alfred Marshall.

As eloquent advocates of protection or free trade during the period 1837–61 may be counted three writers somewhat outside the mainstream of trade theory: Friedrich List, Henry C. Carey and Frédéric Bastiat.

'Factor Prices and Incomes, Factor Endowment and Mobility, 1887–1974' is the heading I give in my book to a review of the writings of Charles Bastable, Frank W. Taussig, Francis Y. Edgeworth, Eli Heckscher, Gustavo del Vecchio, Frank Graham, Jacob Viner, Mihail Manoïlescu, Gottfried Haberler, Bertil Ohlin, Wolfgang Stolper, Tibor Scitovsky, Joan Robinson, Richard Kahn, Ian Little, James Meade, Lloyd Metzler, Raul Prebisch, Paul Samuelson, Abba Lerner, J. de Graaff, Ivor Pearce, Svend Laursen, Wassily Leontief, Victor Morgan, Ronald Jones, Harry Johnson, Robert Mundell, Subimal Mookerjee, Roy Harrod, Max Corden, Kelvin Lancaster, Jagdish Bhagwati, Donald MacDougall, Murray Kemp, John Chipman, James Melvin and Robert Baldwin.

Some of these writers appear also under my fourth heading, 'The Effects of Customs Unions and Other Forms of Economic Integration, 1892–1974', because they contributed both to the general theory of international trade and to the more specific theory of regional economic integration. The authors I include here are: Frank W. Taussig, Jean Marchal, Gottfried Haberler, Lionel Robbins, Wilhelm Röpke, John de Beers, Kurt Rothschild, Jan Tinbergen, Luigi Einaudi, Herbert Giersch, Jacob Viner, Helen Makower, George Morton, James Meade, Charles Kindleberger, Maurice Allais, Jean

Weiller, François Perroux, Robert Marjolin, Petrus Verdoorn, Franz Gehrels, Bruce Johnston, Gunnar Myrdal, Richard Lipsey, Kelvin Lancaster, Erich Schneider, Harry Johnson, Fritz W. Meyer, Tibor Scitovsky, Sidney Dell, Béla Balassa, Alexandre Lamfalussy, Hans Liesner, Raymond Mikesell, Mordechai Kreinin, Michael Michaely, Charles Cooper, Benton Massell, Jaroslav Vanek, Hirofumi Shibata, Lawrence Krause, Richard Cooper, Murray Kemp, Jagdish Bhagwati, Nicholas Kaldor, Imre Vajda, Kiyoshi Kojima, Max Corden, Erik Thorbecke, Paul Streeten, Pierre Uri, John Spraos, Jean Waelbroeck, André Marchal, Edward Mishan, James Melvin, Melvyn Krauss and Edwin Truman.

Under the fifth and last heading, 'Monetary and Fiscal Integration', writings by the following authors are annotated: John Maynard Keynes, Dåg Hammarskjöld, Robert Triffin, James Meade, Fritz Neumark, Carl Shoup, Robert Marjolin, Gottfried Haberler, Tibor Scitovsky, James Ingram, Robert Mundell, Gottfried Bombach, Hans Möller, Peter Kenen, Ronald McKinnon, Clara Sullivan, Douglas Dosser, John Williamson, Stephen Marris, Herbert Grubel, Harry Johnson, Marcus Fleming, Fred Hirsch, Robert Hawkins, Max Corden, Bela Balassa, Peter Oppenheimer, Victor Morgan and Raymond Barre.

I cannot claim that my search has been exhaustive. There are surely many omissions, and some of them may make my survey seriously deficient. None of the omissions, however, is *mala fide* and I hope that both those left out and those who feel that the annotations in my book fail to do them full justice will forgive me. My intentions have been good.

Part II
Special Aspects

4 Measuring the Degree or Progress of Economic Integration (Main Paper, Working Group A)

Jean Waelbroeck (BELGIUM)

This paper presents leading ideas in post-war research on integration. In the spirit of Tinbergen (1952), the goal is understood to be the clarification of the connection between the instruments and objectives of economic policy. In the present context, the instruments are the tariff and nontariff barriers that hamper integration. Trade and capital flows are, in Tinbergen's terminology, 'irrelevant variables', interesting only because of their impact on the objectives of policy makers. The latter are variables that affect welfare and its distribution to consumers.

I. INSTRUMENTS OF INTEGRATION POLICY: ELIMINATION OF IMPEDIMENTS TO TRADE

TARIFFS

As has long been known, the level of tariffs is more difficult to measure than it would seem at first sight. Tariff schedules are public, but their interpretation is often made difficult by peculiar institutional clauses. Furthermore, it is difficult to obtain a good measure of the restrictive impact of tariffs. Average tariff rates will not do, for, if the rate is zero on one good and prohibitive on another, the average tariff is zero. It is necessary to use *a priori* weights, which inevitably are arbitrary.

Balassa (1965), Basevi (1966), Corden (1966) and Johnson (1965) have raised a more subtle issue by proposing to use input–output analysis to measure the effective *rates of protection* achieved by tariffs on value added. This approach raises a host or problems. The assumptions of fixed technical coefficients and of perfectly competitive price adjustment are both debatable. It is clear that the concept of effective protection, like many tools of analysis, relies on oversimplified assumptions. Applications of this tool have drawn attention, however, to two important policy problems. The first is that, because tariff rates in developed countries rise with the degree of manufacture, effective protection rates are substantially higher than are nominal tariff rates. The other is that the system of protection erected by developing countries is so haphazard that it may well be a major cause of inefficiency.

NONTARIFF BARRIERS

The effect of nontariff barriers on trade is difficult to measure. A key concept is the tariff equivalent of a quota, equal to the difference between the world price of a product and its price in the protected market. Interesting applications of this idea have been made by Baldwin (1960) and Holzman (1969). As noted by Bhagwati (1966), the concept is valid only if there is pure and perfect competition in domestic markets.

II. IMPACT OF INTEGRATION ON IRRELEVANT VARIABLES: TRADE AND FACTOR MOVEMENTS
TRADE EFFECTS

The novelist P. Doninos proposed the fiction that in addition to our own world there are several 'anti-mondes': alternative worlds in which all events except one are identical to those in our own history. Measuring the effect of integration necessitates the construction of such a fictitious anti-monde, which represents what the world economy would be like if obstacles to trade had not been removed.

Measures of the effect of integration on trade may be distinguished according to method or according to time. The first method is to use a fully specified structural model of domestic and international trade. Such calculations may be made *ex ante* – the appropriate position for decision making – or *ex post*. Regarding calculations *ex post*, a number of observers have resorted to what Verdoorn and von Bochove (1972) called 'residual imputation'. Here the anti-monde is constructed by projecting pre-integration flows, and the impact of integration is taken to be the residual obtained by subtracting projected flows from actual flows.

EX ANTE CALCULATIONS: STRUCTURAL MODELS

The accuracy of *ex ante* forecasts of trade effects depends on the reliability of the price elasticities that are used. In addition to this general problem, a key issue is whether the effect of a tariff is the same as that of an equivalent price change. The thorough investigations by Kreinin (1961) and Krause (1962) have established the fact that tariff elasticities substantially exceed the usual import-demand elasticities. The elimination of a tariff is perceived by business as irreversible; there may be nonlinearities due to threshold effects that cause the import response to a large price cut to be proportionately larger than the response to a small cut.

Another way to predict the effect of integration is to use linear programming. This is valid if economic agents behave like pure competitors. As pointed out by Negishi (1972, p. 35) in his criticism of Kemp, the use of programming to simulate general-equilibrium behaviour implies that, unless international prices are fixed, the programming model is solved jointly with a complex fixed point problem.

EX POST CALCULATIONS: RESIDUAL IMPUTATION

Under the residual-imputation approach, the effect of integration is computed by comparing actual trade to an anti-monde that is constructed by projecting trade flows on the assumption that no integration would take place. All studies use the familiar assumption that market shares tend to be rather stable in the absence of integration. They also use the common sense idea that the validity of this assumption can be increased by disaggregating markets by products and by commodities. Similarly, and here many studies are deficient, the analysis should cover domestic as well as foreign trade. Perhaps the chief goal of studies of integration is to discover whether there has been trade creation. This can be verified only by observing trade matrices that cover both domestic and foreign sales.

The next idea is less orthodox. Authors of residual-imputation studies often take it for granted that a country's growth has a roughly symmetrical effect on its exports and imports. Except in Linder's book (1961), this 'gravity model' has received little recognition in economic theory, even though it is much more firmly established empirically than are most of the conclusions of orthodox trade theory.

A generally overlooked point is that projections that do not take into account changes in competitive strength lead to misleading results. In theoretical work, trade diversion is defined by comparing situations where balances of payments are in equilibrium. There is an obvious danger of confusing trade diversions so defined with the loss of markets that third countries may suffer as a result of an overvalued exchange rate.

Finally, it remains necessary to find ways of accounting for what Lipsey called 'growth effects': the impact of changes in taste and technology. The method used is to look for a 'control group' that is subject to the same growth effects but is not influenced by integration. The control group can be the pre-integration period; or it can be represented by trade flows outside the integrating area that are little affected by integration effects.

EX POST ESTIMATES: STRUCTURAL MODELS

In principle, the estimation of a fully specified model of production and trade can give a firmer grip on the data than the residual-imputation method does. In early studies, integration effects are represented by dummies representing changes in trends or in income elasticities. The specification of these models is too crude to exploit the inherent power of the structural method. The recent work by Verdoorn and Schwarz (1972) and by Resnick and Truman (1974) goes further by attempting to take account of all the forces that influence trade and production.

RESULTS

These studies confirm that the formation of EFTA and the EEC has been a considerable event in the history of international trade. The impact of eliminating tariffs has been considerable, implying trade responses consistent with tariff elasticities of −4 or more. There seems to have been only a minor amount of trade diversion, even for agriculture (Thorbecke, 1974). Perhaps a third, or a half, of intra-EEC trade is the result of net trade creation; for EFTA, trade creation is approximately one-third smaller.

EFFECT OF INTEGRATION ON FACTOR MOVEMENTS

Both the theoretical work by Mundell (1957) and the survey of the views of businessmen as reported by Kreinin (1965) suggest that tariffs influence direct investment. Most of the work on this subject is, unfortunately, superficial: it is difficult to do better, because of the unsatisfactory level of accuracy of the data and the constant changes of restrictions on capital exports.

In his paper at this congress, Mihailović reviewed the effect of integration on movement of labour. This effect has been very small in both the EEC and EFTA.

III. THE OBJECTIVES OF INTEGRATED POLICY: EFFECTS ON WELFARE

The most interesting effect of integration is on the objectives of economic policy; unfortunately it is in this area that the empirical results are the most disappointing. We survey, in succession, the effect on welfare and on income distribution.

EFFECT ON WELFARE ACCORDING TO CLASSICAL TRADE THEORY

There has sprung up an enormous amount of literature based on a classical trade model that assumes given techniques, nonincreasing returns in production, convex social-welfare functions for countries, and perfect competition. This literature bypasses the study of the effect of trade on income distribution, assuming it to be cancelled by lump-sum transfers, which are costless and have no effect on incentives. (See, for example, Samuelson 1962.) Although this assumption is highly unrealistic, I shall find it convenient to retain it in this section.

This theory leads to an elegant method of estimating the welfare effects of integration. The first step is to show that a small reduction of a tariff brings a gain that is proportional to the level of the tariff. The magnitude of this efficiency gain can be measured by a lump-sum transfer abroad that would exactly offset it, leaving the country on its initial level of utility; this turns out to be equal to the level of the tariff, multiplied by the change in imports. As the tariff drops, the gain gradually vanishes. It is natural to measure the welfare gain by the area of a 'welfare triangle' of base Δm and height t, where Δm is the increase in imports brought about by the adoption of free trade and t is the initial level of the tariff.

Viner (1950) has drawn attention to the fact that this simple analysis does not apply to customs unions. The preference granted to customs-union partners may be a cause of waste by causing a switch from cheap imports from outside the union to more expensive suppliers within it. Because of such 'trade diversion' the customs-union avenue to integration involves costs that do not arise if integration is worldwide.

WELFARE GAINS UNDER MORE GENERAL ASSUMPTIONS

But all this discussion is counting angels on the point of a needle. Welfare triangles are minute. Pre-EEC tariffs averaged at some 12 per cent, and the more optimistic estimates of trade creation suggest orders of magnitude of some $10 billion: the area of the welfare triangle is $12 billion x 0·12 x 1/2 = 0·6; a $600 million gain, from which it is necessary to subtract the costs of trade diversion in industry and agriculture. The welfare significance of the EEC appears less than that of the Concorde aeroplane. The assumptions that underlie such calculations are, however, unrealistic. In fact, as Bhagwati (1965) and, more recently, Stern (1973b) have noted, attempts to verify empirically the predictions of the classical model have on the whole been unsuccessful.

A realistic analysis of international trade in manufactures has to start from the realisation that manufactures are sold in imperfect markets and produced under conditions of increasing returns; that comparative advantage in manufactures is due to the hazards of invention and to the heritage of externalities and scale economies; and that there is not a finite number of goods but a continuous range of more or less substitutable products, most of which are not actually produced. Important contributions to this more realistic view of international trade are Vernon's product-cycle hypothesis (1966), Linder's monography (1961), and the promising start made by Negishi (1972) in working out its implications rigorously; it seems appropriate, therefore, to christen it the VLN model. This model, unfortunately, does not lead to an elegant method comparable to the welfare-triangle formula. It is mainly useful in providing guideposts, which may prevent gross errors in estimating the welfare gains from integration. It is wrong to assume that the change of assumptions will drastically change the conclusions that are reached.

The VLN model assumes profit maximisation. This means that, unless demand is very inelastic, firms will find ways of exploiting scale economies. Unless externalities are very diffuse, they will find ways to internalise them – for example, by using discriminatory prices to capture a consumer surplus arising from production of a good. It is hard to believe that large-scale economies are left unexploited in developed countries today, with their large levels of demand and their openness to foreign trade.

Integration may, however, prevent the elimination of other, less visible obstacles to trade. The first is the riskiness of exporting, which is such an obvious element to business decision making. Since, as Koopmans has noted (1967), scale economies are strongly linked to indivisibilities, producers may find that they must choose between the present output and a much higher one, the sale of which may require costly investment in developing foreign markets. If a risk of discrimination is perceived as the new market is suddenly invaded, the larger output will seem attractive only if the foreign price hoped for covers not only the tariff, but also a risk premium justified by the risks involved.

A second idea is that markets become more perfect as the number of participants increases. One of the significant effects hoped for from integration is an increase in the number of firms able to compete effectively in each market. If this increases the elasticity of demand, as perceived by firms, there will be a double gain: a narrowed gap between marginal cost and price and, if firms are in equilibrium at a point of decreasing average cost, a reduction in costs. It is easy to see that the resulting increase in production could be large, and the gain in efficiency substantial.

There exists no theoretically well-grounded formula for computing gains from integration under VLN assumptions. Enough is known, however, about returns to scale and the connection between productivity and learning to make informed guesses possible. Balassa (1974) estimates various effects of integration on the welfare of EEC countries, taking into account returns to scale, an effect of integration on investment, a secondary effect due to the reinvestment of the extra growth, and finally also welfare triangles. Estimates such as this suggest that the total gain may be three or four times greater than is implied by calculations of welfare triangles, but that it is still less than 1 per cent of GNP. Are such figures trustworthy? There has been such a lack of research on equilibrium under increasing returns that there are perhaps mechanisms under which larger gains could be predicted. However, until a credible example is constructed, there is no choice but to accept these pessimistic estimates.

We are left, therefore, to search for other reasons if we wish to believe that integration has as large a welfare effect as is usually supposed. One possibility is the vague concept that Leibenstein (1966) has christened X-efficiency. As Leibenstein has shown, there is much evidence that different producers do not operate at the same efficiency levels. As technology is, on the whole, freely available, this finding suggests that productivity may be strongly affected by psychological and sociological obstacles.

Integration may perhaps help to erode the psychological and sociological bars to greater productivity. But the spectacle of the British shipbuilding industry dying on its feet without eliminating the restrictive labour practices that hamper its modernisation does not encourage optimism. In Italy, industry has continued to find it worthwhile to offer high wages to migrants to the north, rather than to move capital to the south and take advantage of the lower wages that could be accepted by the migrants' brothers. The arguments for a large X-efficiency effect are therefore not strong either.

WELFARE EFFECT OF INTEGRATION IN DEVELOPING COUNTRIES

Something ought to be said about the possible effects of integration on the growth of developing countries. There has been little research on this subject, because integration experiments in these countries have been rather unsuccessful. Yet it may be that it is in developing countries that integration would have the greatest welfare effect.

Developing countries have been called fractured economies, in that the productivity of factors in alternative uses is not correctly reflected by market prices. Chenery has formalised, as the two-gaps hypothesis, the idea that shortage of foreign exchange limits the growth of many developing countries. Balassa's research on the growth of semi-industralised countries has uncovered evidence that, as countries reach a certain stage of development, an outward-oriented pattern of development becomes far more effective than are the autarkic strategies that many developing countries have adopted. It will be worthwhile to develop a theory of integration adapted to such an economic context. While this is a controversial area of research, it appears that differences of several per cent in growth rates may hinge on the adoption of correct trade strategies by developing countries. This is much more than the welfare effects of integration for developed countries, and suggests that integration between developing, and between developing and developed, countries is one of the most important areas for policy experiment and research today.

IV. THE OBJECTIVE OF INTEGRATION POLICY: EFFECTS ON INCOME DISTRIBUTION

INTERNATIONAL DISTRIBUTION OF INCOME

The classical argument that a country gains from adopting free trade is based on the assumption that world prices are fixed. The empirical literature on international trade suggests overwhelmingly that this is not true, even for small countries. Demand for exports is not perfectly elastic. There is also some evidence (for example, Kreinin, 1961) that foreign supply is price-inelastic, so that cutting tariffs increases import prices. The adoption of free trade leads to a deterioration of the terms of trade, which in turn offsets the efficiency gains made possible by free trade. Basevi (1968) has shown that, for the United States, the loss from worse terms of trade is large relative to the welfare-triangle measure of the gain from greater efficiency.

Such results are not strange. A well-known theorem shows that a country that has monopoly power in trade can always gain from imposing a tariff, unless this brings about retaliation (Kemp, 1964). The implication is that trade negotiators are right when, in international negotiations, they try to minimise their own tariff concessions and maximise those of their partners.

Indeed, post-war progress in integration has crucially depended on the techniques of *quid pro quo* bargaining, which offer scope for offsetting the effect of trade liberalisation on the international income distribution. It is, of course, the outstanding advantage of the customs-union formula that the offsetting tends to occur automatically. Thus, the criticism of customs unions by James Cooper and Massel (1965), who argue that, if world prices are given, a country gains more from reducing tariffs than from joining a customs union, has no practical relevance.

The classical theoretical reasoning is not adequate for appraising the effect of integration on the welfare of developing countries. The main issue there is economies of scale, which are assumed away by classical theory. Integration between countries at different stages of industrialisation is apt to work to the advantage of the more advanced countries, whose industries benefit from economies of scale, and to stifle their less advanced competitors. It is because no way has yet been found to overcome this difficulty that developing countries have had so little success in integration experiments.

DISTRIBUTION OF INCOME WITHIN COUNTRIES

Here the relevant results of the classical theory of international trade are not useful for understanding empirical facts. The main results are the factor-price equalisation theorem, which asserts that, under appropriate assumptions, specialisation (though not complete specialisation) by countries in exports of goods that are produced with relatively large quantities of the countries' abundant resources will equalise the rewards of factors of production between countries; and the Stolper–Samuelson theorem, which asserts that protection of industries employing predominantly a relatively scarce factor will increase the reward of the factor. In a celebrated article, Leontief (1954) suggested that, contrary to the predictions of the first theorem, American trade involves a net import of capital services. Much has been written on the subject since then, but criticism has had greater success in casting doubt on Leontief's conclusion than in proving that the opposite conclusion is true. Concerning the second theorem, computations by Baldwin (1971) suggest that the American tariff has no strong bias against labour-intensive imports, so that the problem examined is not important in practice.

What is unrealistic in the classical theory is the assumption that capital and labour are homogeneous. For policy purposes, the income-distribution implicacations of integration must be considered in a world where capital cannot be shifted at will and where labour is tied to enterprises and industries by acquired skills, seniority, and even by sentiments of pride in the continuation of a tradition.

From this point of view, the dominant fact is that integration has a large effect on production and trade. Since factors of production are not very mobile, integration potentially involves a sweeping redistribution of income among individuals. It is not the rewards of 'labour' and 'capital' that are at stake, but workers who fear for their jobs and employers who fear bankruptcy.

Governments will engage in integration policies only if they feel that these will not inflict substantial losses on parts of the population. Obstacles to trade in manufactures among developed countries have been reduced rapidly only because experience has shown that the result was largely what Balassa (1966) has called intra-industry (as opposed to inter-industry) specialisation. Enterprises have been able to replace, by products made and sold at a profit, products that could not be sold profitably in the absence of protection. The ability of farmers to adapt to sudden changes in market conditions is less than that of industrial firms; it was the desire to avoid harm to groups of farmers that led EEC governments to align protection rates on the highest prevailing levels when the common agricultural policy was formed.

The only real experiment in integration involving developing and developed countries has been the Commonwealth Preference Scheme. The evidence is strong that this led to inter-industry (rather than intra-industry) specialisation in the United Kingdom. The fear of similar effects on income distribution has led governments to hedge the generalised preference schemes that have been introduced in recent years with so many escape clauses that their impact is likely to be small. Major progress in integration among developed and developing countries will take place only when it appears that this will not have a marked effect on the inter-industry distribution of incomes in developed countries. Perhaps the substantial broadening of the range of exports of developing countries, which has occurred recently, will facilitate the removal of obstacles to trade in this area.

V. CONCLUSIONS

This discussion of studies on the measurement of the effects of integration reveals a broad consensus on three facts. The post-war integration among developed countries has brought about considerable changes in trade and has led to substantial progress in international specialisation. The resulting gain in efficiency seems to be a surprisingly small fraction of the GNP of these countries. Apart from the common agricultural policy of the EEC, this integration has not led to marked changes in the distribution of incomes among individuals or among countries. These conclusions apply to integration among developed countries. For developing countries, there is much less agreement, and the scant success of the experiments that have so far been undertaken has made it difficult to tell which of the conflicting views about integration effects was correct.

From the policy maker's point of view, perhaps the most important effect of integration is on the distribution of incomes within and among countries. In fact, success of future experiments in integration seems to depend on the ability of their proponents to devise ways of cancelling their effects on the distribution of incomes. It seems that this is an area of research that would merit more attention from empirical research than it has received in the past.

98   *Economic Integration*

REFERENCES

Balassa, B., *The Theory of Economic Integration* (Homewood, Ill.: Irwin, 1961).
Balassa, B., 'Tariff Protection in Industrial Countries. An Evaluation', in *Journal of Political Economy,* Dec 1965.
Balassa, B., 'Tariff Reductions and Trade Among the Industrial Countries', in *American Economic Review,* June 1966.
Balassa, B., *Trade Liberalization Among Industrialized Countries, Objectives and Alternatives,* Council for Foreign Relations, Atlantic Policy Studies (New York: McGraw-Hill, 1967).
Balassa, B., and Kreinin, M., 'Trade Liberalization Under the Kennedy Round: The Static Effects', in *Review of Economics and Statistics,* May 1967.
Balassa, B., *The Structure of Protection in Industrial Countries and its Effect on Exports of Processed Goods from Developing Countries, in the Kennedy Round, Estimated Effects of Tariff Barriers,* part II (New York: UNCTAD, 1968).
Balassa, B., et al., *European Economic Integration* (Amsterdam: North Holland, 1974).
Baldwin, R. E., *Non-Tariff Distortions in International Trade* (Washington: The Brookings Institute, 1970).
Baldwin, R. E., 'Determinants of the Commodity Structure of U.S. Trade', in *American Economic Review,* Mar 1971.
Basevi, G., 'The U.S. Tariff Structure: Estimates of Effective Rates of Protection of U.S. Industries and Industrial Labour', in *Review of Economics and Statistics,* May 1966, pp. 147–60.
Basevi, G., 'The Restrictive Effect of the U.S. Tariff and its Welfare Value', in *American Economic Review,* Sep 1968.
Bhagwati, J., 'The Pure Theory of International Trade, A Survey', in *Surveys of Economic Theory* (Macmillan and St Martin, 1965).
Bhagwati, J., 'The Equivalence of Tariffs and Quotas', in *Trade, Growth, and the Balance of Payments,* Essays in Honour of G. Haberler, ed. R. E. Baldwin (Chicago: Rand McNally, 1966).
Chenery, J., and Raduchel, W., 'Substitution in Planning Models', in *Studies in Development Policy,* ed. H. Chenery, (1971).
Cooper, C. A., and Massell, B. F., 'A New Look at Customs Union Theory', in *Economic Journal,* Dec 1965.
Corden, W. M., 'The Structure of a Tariff System and the Effective Rate of Protection', in *Journal of Political Economy,* June 1966.
Corden, M., *The Theory of Protection* (Oxford: The Clarendon Press, 1971).
Denison, E. F., *Why Growth Rates Differ: Postwar Experience in Nine Western Countries* (Washington: The Brookings Institute, 1967).
Evans, H. D., *A General Equilibrium Analysis of Protection: The Effects of Protection in Australia* (Amsterdam: North Holland, 1972).
Glejser, H., 'The Effects of EEC on US Direct Investment and Trade', forthcoming in *Quantitative Analysis of International Trade,* ed. H. Glejser.
Johnson, H. G., 'The Gains from Freer Trade in Western Europe, An Estimate', in *Manchester School,* Sep 1958.
Johnson, H. G., 'The Theory of the Tariff Structure, with Special Reference to Development', in *Trade and Development* (Geneva: Institut Universitaire des Hautes Études Internationales, 1965).
Holzman, F. D., 'On the Technique of Comparing Trade Barriers of Products Imported by Capitalist and Communist Nations', in *European Economic Review,* Autumn 1970.
Kemp, M., *The Theory of International Trade* (Prentice Hall, 1964).
Kemp, M., *A Contribution to the General Equilibrium Theory of Preferential Trading* (Amsterdam: North Holland, 1969).
Koopmans, T., *Three Essays on the State of Economic Science,* Cowles Monograph (1957).

Krause, L. B., 'United States Imports 1947–1958', in *Econometrica,* Apr 1962.

Kreinin, M. E., 'Effects of Tariff Changes on the Price and Volume of Imports', in *American Economic Review,* June 1961.

Kreinin, M. E., 'Freedom of Trade and Capital Movement – Some Empirical Evidence', in *Economic Journal,* Dec 1965.

Kreinin, M. E., 'Price *vs.* Tariff Elasticities in International Trade, A Suggested Reconciliation', in *American Economic Review,* Sep 1967.

Leibenstein, H., 'Allocative Efficiency and X Efficiency', in *American Economic Review,* June 1966.

Leontief, W., 'Domestic Production and Foreign Trade, The American Capital Position Reexamined', in *Economia Internazionale,* Feb 1954.

Linder, S., *An Essay on Trade and Transformation* (New York: Wiley, 1961).

Linneman, H., *An Econometric Study of International Trade Flows* (Amsterdam: North Holland, 1966).

Lipsey, R. G., 'The Theory of Customs Unions, A General Survey', in *Economic Journal,* Sep 1960.

Little, I. M. D., Scitovsky, I. T., and Scott, M., *Industry and Trade in Some Developing Countries* (OECD, 1970).

Meade, J. E., *The Theory of Customs Unions* (Amsterdam: North Holland, 1955).

Mundell, R., 'International Trade and Factor Mobility', in *American Economic Review,* June 1957.

Negishi, T., *General Equilibrium Theory and International Trade* (Amsterdam: North Holland, 1955).

Resnick, S. A., and Truman, E. M., 'An Empirical Examination of Bilateral Trade in Western Europe', in Balassa, 1974.

Samuelson, P. A., 'The Gains from International Trade', in *Canadian Journal of Economics and Political Science,* 1939.

Samuelson, P. A., 'Prices of Factors and Goods in General Equilibrium', in *Review of Economic Studies,* 1953.

Samuelson, P. A., 'The Gains from International Trade Once Again', in *Economic Journal,* 1962, pp. 820–9.

Schmitz, A., and Bieri, J., 'EEC Tariffs and US Direct Investment', in *European Economic Review,* Nov 1972.

Scitovsky, I. T., *Economic Theory and Western European Integration* (Stanford: Stanford University Press, 1958).

Stern, R. M., 'Testing Trade Theories', Research Seminar in International Economics, DP 48 (June 1973).

Stern, R. M., 'Tariffs and Other Methods of Trade Control, A Survey of Current Developments', in *Journal of Economic Literature,* Sep 1973.

Stolper, W. F., and Samuelson, P. A., 'Protection and Real Wages', in *Review of Economic Studies,* Nov 1941.

Thorbecke, E., 'The Effects of European Integration on Agriculture', in Balassa, 1974.

Tinbergen, J., *On the Theory of Economic Policy* (Amsterdam: North Holland, 1952).

Verdoorn, P. J., and von Bochove, C. A., 'Measuring Integration Effects, A Survey', in *European Economic Review,* Nov 1972.

Verdoorn, P. J., and Schwarz, A. R. N., 'Two Alternative Estimates of the Effects of EEC and EFTA on the Pattern of Trade', in *European Economic Review,* Nov 1972.

Vernon, R., 'International Investment and International Trade in the Product Cycle', in *Quarterly Journal of Economics,* May 1966.

Viner, J., *The Customs Union Issue* (New York: Carnegie Endowment for International Peace, 1950).

Comments
Ricardo Ffrench-Davis (Chile)

I. INTRODUCTORY

Waelbroeck has presented a useful survey of several aspects related to the measurement of the degree of integration and of the benefits and costs implied. He has told us about some of the different and divergent approaches, and of their shortcomings. Because of their wide number and variety it is difficult to discuss each one in only a few minutes, and the working group seems the place appropriate to do it. I have chosen, therefore, to concentrate on some extensions or different approaches, dealing with assumptions especially relevant for developing countries.

One can think of at least two reasons for evaluating the degree or progress of economic integration: one, to judge the dynamism and net benefits of processes that have taken, or are taking, place; the other, to contribute to the design of strategies and policies that most efficiently promote integration in each particular political and economic framework.

The degree and progress of economic integration can be measured by several alternative indicators. Frequently, the unity (merging into one) of each of the member countries' commodities, capital and labour markets is mentioned as the basic requirement for achieving economic integration. This implies the intraregional mobility of resources, unified public policies, and a unique currency, with a common price system for goods and factors as an outcome. Various quantitative indicators are commonly used in measuring the degree of integration in factor and commodity markets, as reviewed by Waelbroeck. These indicators give a limited view of the *size of the benefits accrued and of the integrating forces built into the process.* This is because: (1) a comprehensive view of the progress of an integration process requires the consideration of other, less measurable aspects and the assignment to each indicator of weights (probably ordinal or qualitative) that vary according to the characteristics of the member countries and the stage of integration in question;[1] and (2) during the process of moving toward full integration, direct 'progress' (whether it is harmonisation, unity or mobility) in one specific field may imply either a regressive move in other aspects or greater difficulty in making further progress. These side, or indirect, effects seem to be extremely important in the case of processes involving countries with heterogeneous levels of underdevelopment and diverse political regimes. Both characteristics will probably be present in most integration schemes covering developing countries.

I should like to deal with these two points in this short note, adopting an approach that rests on examples derived from experience of the Latin American efforts toward integration and, particularly, those of the six countries belonging to the Andean Common Market.

[1] We must recall, for example, that the *formal* process of integration of the EEC was initiated at a much more advanced stage than has been attained by developing countries such as those in Latin America.

II. THE FRAMEWORK OF DEVELOPING COUNTRIES

The incidence and efficiency of economic policies depend on the framework where they are applied, and on their timing and mix. A schematic description of some developing countries may be useful to clear up the exposition. Let us suppose that our member countries have different political regimes, with only some of them promoting social change. All have small markets; dual trade policies, consisting of subsidised imports of some raw materials and capital goods and sizable restrictions (including quantitative obstacles such as import quotas and prohibitions) on the remainder of trade; poorly defined but generous policies toward foreign investment; industries that duplicate industries in other countries of the group, and that are being developed geared to a highly protected domestic market; and different degrees of industrialisation.[2]

The overall framework, and the timing and mix of policies determine, among other things, their effect on the degree of national integration within each country, on the distribution of benefits and costs among members, and on the rationality or efficiency of economic policies. For example, some steps may promote the integration of specific sectors or regions of each country, while at the same time increasing the duality of each economy (regional integration with national disintegration); others may concentrate the benefits on only some of the members, because of the attraction of the most dynamic industries and of scarce factors by the countries providing already acquired external economies (unequal distribution of the benefits of integration); yet offers may weaken the bargaining position of member countries towards foreign capital (with the result that integration of commodity markets is accompanied by the denationalisation of economic decisions and influence); and premature harmonisation of certain policies may impose restrictions on the co-ordination of other policies.

When designing the policies and sequences of steps to be taken, it then quite obviously becomes necessary to look for the direct and indirect effects of any move in order to evaluate whether it means progress, and, if so, whether it is progress of a major or a minor kind. It can be asserted that the farther a group of countries is from full integration, the more probable it is that certain forms of harmonisation, promotion of mobility, or market unification (especially those involving indiscriminate liberlisation) will have a number of major negative effects. This assertion can be labelled as a further extension of the 'Second-best' to integration theory. Its implication is that the frequent view that integration is enhanced by any freeing of reciprocal trade or by unity of institutions and policies is oversimplified: the overall framework, and the mix and timing of steps are crucial for the political and economic consequences of any action.

The framework outlined above is, I believe, the general rule in all processes of integration involving developing countries, and the strategy employed must be adapted to it. Let us briefly consider three aspects: capital markets, commodity markets, and the harmonisation and rationalisation of trade policies.

---

[2] Other important features, such as large, open or disguised unemployment and income concentration, and their interrelation with trade policies, will be omitted for lack of space.

III. CAPITAL FLOWS

The freedom of capital flows is frequently mentioned as a priority component of integration. However, in most, if not all, stages short of full integration, it appears that the benefits brought by free capital movements are scarce, while the costs are sizable. We can mention three undesirable types of flows that would be brought by such an 'integration' of capital markets. Funds would tend to flow (a) away from the less developed members (this is supported by most of the available empirical data on market movements within countries with backward regions); (b) towards the countries with less propensity to introduce social changes (social change encourages flights of capital and these are best checked by controls on the movements of capital); and (c) out of the countries with greater restrictions on trade (that is, while these restrictions are being replaced by higher exchange rates as all member gradually adopt a common external tariff). All of these capital movements are destabilising. On the other hand, those flows that are desirable, and are a positive ingredient of integration, can be channelled via a regulated market. If they are thus channelled, there is neither need nor convenience in reverting to the politically biased search for free capital movements. Furthermore, an original and positive form of capital-markets integration would be to devise a common set of selective rules regulating foreign investment in all member countries.

Consequently, in measuring the progress of integration in the framework sketched above, it appears that a low or negative priority ought to be assigned to what is traditionally called capital-markets integration. I believe that this low priority holds, though with less emphasis, even if all members impose common restrictions on movements from or to third countries.

IV. COMMODITY MARKETS

The situation with respect to commodity 'markets' is different. Its integration obviously must have priority. But the real problem is how. Some choices are: (a) a uniform liberlisation of reciprocal trade for the universe of commodities, or (b) a slower, or delayed, liberalisation of some of the already existing industries, and an abrupt freeing of the output of new industries. The second alternative means lesser trade creation, in the static sense. But in the type of economies that we are dealing with (and Waelbroeck seems to imply that the same holds true for developed economies) that sort of trade creation (if tied to inter-industry specialisation) is doubtfully beneficial in the short-run, and the political obstacles that it tends to promote may be an important deterrent at the outset of an integration agreement. On the other hand, the rapid liberalisation of reciprocal trade in new industries is a strong, positive impediment to the traditional outcome of duplicating productive capacity in each of the small, isolated, domestic markets. This policy, accompanied by a *relative* price protection with respect to third countries (as opposed to either absolute or quantitative forms of protection) means a significant step forward in improving the allocation of resources. In the common wording of integration theory, instead of the costly trade diversion we would have dynamic trade creation.

But there are additional points worth recalling relative to the integration of commodity markets. The isolated removal of trade restrictions opens the way to some crucial problems in the framework described above. One is related to foreign investment and another to the distribution among member countries of the benefits and costs of integration.

V. A CODE FOR FOREIGN INVESTMENT

Let us deal with the first problem. Merging several domestic markets of one given product into a single market, while retaining the various autonomous political authorities, enlarges the bargaining power of foreign investors; now they can count on all domestic demand investing only in the country that provides more favourable conditions. An integration scheme, then, makes necessary some common selective treatment toward foreign capital by all member countries, so as to avoid a detrimental competition to attract foreign investment. A wisely designed code can only improve the position of developing countries, which have frequently granted enormous protection to the output of foreign enterprises that assemble luxury goods for the small domestic market. Moreover, this is a field where an integration process offers a good opportunity for rationalising poorly defined economic policies. The imaginative effort started a few years ago by the Andean countries provides a good example of trends toward policy improvements.

VI. INDUSTRIAL PLANNING AND THE DISTRIBUTION OF GAINS

The other point relates to the distribution of the benefits among nations, which, as Waelbroeck suggests, tends to be unequal when developing countries with different degrees of industrialisation begin an integration process. This inequality stems mainly from the importance of larger existing external economies in the more developed countries.

A large proportion of the economic activities that would benefit from the integrated market tend to concentrate in the more developed countries. From a short-run and narrow economic point of view, that might be an adequate outcome; but it has at least one important shortcoming: partner countries would want to remain within the integration process and contribute to its strength only so long as they obtained a 'fair' share of the benefits. One way to deal with this problem, is, as the Andean countries are doing, to centralise at the supranational level the responsibility for allocating the main productive activities among the countries concerned. In such a scheme, for distributive purposes, the decision about where a given family of products or an industrial complex is to be located is taken out of the market; the remaining decisions on the techniques and volume of production continue, in most cases, to be made at the level of the enterprise or of national authorities,[3] within the framework of the price relations influenced by the common external tariff.[4] This scheme, for which experiments are being conducted in theory or in practice in some other regional groupings of developing countries, is an alternative to

[3] The scheme classifies decisions in three categories: macro-economic from the regional point of view, macro-economic at the national level, and micro-economic. The first are assigned to the supranational centre, the second to national authorities, and the last to the enterprise.

[4] This policy ought to prevail whether the decisions are centralised at the government, or decentralised at public or private enterprises.

lump-sum financial transfers. The former, I believe, takes care more efficiently
and permanently than the latter does of the distributive problem I have
described.

The implication with respect to the progress indicators is that the exclusion
of a number of items from the general automatic liberalisation of reciprocal
trade can be viewed as a prerequisite for the introduction of a distributive
scheme that strengthens the political will of member countries, rather than as
a slowing of market integration.

VII. TRADE POLICIES

To conclude this discussion, I should like to refer briefly to policy harmonisation and progress in integration.

Yesterday it was mentioned, correctly, that the temporal reintroduction of
quantitative restrictions on reciprocal trade (in regional groupings) means a step
back. I believe that the most damaging effects of such actions can be avoided
if the emphasis allotted to the harmonisation of different trade policies is
changed. Frequently the most inflexible agreements on common policies are
on tariffs, while provisions are more flexible for nontariff restrictions. This,
to some degree, encourages countries that face balance-of-payments difficulties
to make use of nontariff restrictions, since these afford them a greater degree
of freedom. If one believes that tariffs are, in most cases, more efficient than
quantitative restrictions for allocating resources and redistributing income,
then greater freedom should be allowed in their adjustment. In other words,
some greater flexibility in the harmonisation of tariffs (or other *price* restrictions on reciprocal trade), and in the adoption of the common external tariff,
may facilitate the permanent elimination of those *unwanted* nontariff restrictions, especially in countries that for decades have been using import quotas.

A word about nontariff barriers. Among these restrictions have been mentioned those related to road safety, product standards and control of diseases.
Properly speaking, these are not quantitative restrictions but *qualitative* regulations. We can have other important forms of intervention of the same sort,
such as controls on the prices of imports and exports, and on the imports of
subsidiaries of multinational enterprises. An efficient tariff policy seems to require the complementary coexistence of several qualitative restrictions. Hence,
they should subsist and be harmonised. This is another case in which an integration process, rather than freeing markets, ought to impose trade regulations
that are suited to the specific nature of, and objectives being pursued by, the
member countries.

I believe it is by taking into account the kind of problems and assumptions
that I have sketched that research on integration strategies and policies would
make present theory more relevant for developing countries.

Comments
Willi Kunz (German Democratic Republic)

I. SOME INTRODUCTORY CONSIDERATIONS

The tremendous dynamics of the productive forces in the past few decades have led to processes of international economic integration, both in socialism and in capitalism. Barriers impeding the further development of these forces are being removed. Integration is leading to greater concentration and a higher potential of science and production, to higher dynamics and efficiency, and to equally strong interdependencies within the community in which integration processes are taking place.

According to a widely held opinion, forcefully expressed in Marxist literature, economic integration is a stage in the internationalisation of economic life and will in the long term lead to the formation of comprehensive international economic complexes and to the gradual fusion of various national economies. This process is taking place through the union of several countries of identical socio-political structure. The aim is to create optimal scientific, technical, economic and political conditions for the development of the productive forces in the interest of the ruling class in the group of countries concerned. A certain governmental mechanism of management with the corresponding economic and legal instrumentation is employed for the achievement of this goal.

A union for the purpose of *integration always takes place only between countries of the same social order.* Hence, an awareness of the aims, tasks and conditions of the social order concerned is a prerequisite for the assessment of the degree and progress of economic integration.

II. THE COMPARISON
SOCIALIST ECONOMIC INTEGRATION

We deduce the meaning and progress of economic integration in the CMEA primarily by reference to the basic interests of socialism.

The efforts of the CMEA countries towards the fulfilment of the aims of socialist production, and for developing and deepening socialist economic integration, have already led to significant results that have a direct influence on the working and living standards of the people.

Increases in production and its efficiency, a growing national income with increasing net incomes per capita, high rates of growth in retail sales at stable prices, acceleration of housing construction, social rents and the exchange of consumer goods all are important goals for the improvement of the standard of living of the working people in the CMEA countries.

With national income growing at an average of 8 per cent per annum in the period 1951–72, the CMEA has been experiencing a much higher growth rate than have the industrial capitalist countries, for which the corresponding average was 4·5 per cent per annum.[1]

[1] Computed from to the following sources: UN, *Statistical Yearbook*; CMEA, *Statistical Yearbook* (Moscow, 1973); and *Sodrushestvo Sozialistitsheskoe* (Moscow:

The CMEA countries have also shown a higher rate of increase in the development of industrial productivity. Over the period 1958–69 this rose by 180 per cent, as against 166 per cent for the EEC countries.[2]

In the field of agricultural production, where development was particularly complicated for a few years, an increase of 138 per cent was recorded over the period 1963–71. This compares with an increase of 116 per cent for North America and 120 per cent for Western Europe, and is in excess of the increase registered by any other group of countries in the world.[3]

The volume of foreign trade of the CMEA countries has likewise developed very rapidly; it rose over elevenfold in the period 1950–73. Inter-CMEA trade rose from 4·5 thousand million roubles in 1950 to 47·5 thousand million roubles in 1973;[4] that is, more than tenfold in terms of value. The share of inter-CMEA trade over this period has remained constant, at about 60 per cent.

The changes that have taken place in the pattern of the foreign trade of the CMEA countries are remarkable. A considerable and above-average increase is noticeable in the output of engineering goods and industrial consumer goods. In particular, those CMEA countries that were formerly economically less developed were able to increase their exports of machines, industrial equipment and transport vehicles at a much faster rate than their total exports. Thus, Bulgaria increased the share of these products in its total exports from 2·6 per cent in 1955 to 38·8 per cent in 1973, and in Poland the share of these products increased from 13·1 to 38·8 per cent over the same period.

In economically developed countries, such as Czechoslovakia and the GDR, the share of machines, industrial equipment and transport vehicles in total exports has been more or less constant at between 46 and 52 per cent for the last thirteen years. However, imports in this category rose, over the same period, from 21·7 to 36·3 per cent (Czechoslovakia) and from 12·7 to 33·0 per cent (GDR).[5]

The rise of the economic potential of the CMEA is expressed by a continuously more modern and highly productive economic and industrial structure, by the high capacity of its science and technology, and by the steadily rising share of the CMEA countries in important global index figures of production, productivity and consumption. This applies, for example, also to the production of energy and to the most important industrial raw materials. Thus, as opposed to the EEC countries, the CMEA is in a position to cover its demands for energy. The CMEA generated 1063

International Institute for Economic Problems of the Socialist World System and of the CMEA Secretariat, 1973), appendix: See, also Juraj Vigas, 'The Economic Development of the National Economies of the CMEA countries', in *Plànovanè Hospodarstivi*, no 2, 1974, pp. 9–10.

[2]*IPW Reports*, no. 1 (Berlin, 1972), p. 75..

[3]UN, *Statistical Yearbook, 1972*, p. 11.

[4]N. S. Patolitshev, 'Co-operation of the CMEA Countries in Foreign Trade is Growing', in *Foreign Trade of the USSR*, no. 5, 1974.

[5]All figures from: *The National Economy of the CMEA Countries* (Moscow: CMEA Secretariat, 1974; and *Sodrushestvo Sozialistitsheskoe*, pp. 146ff.

thousand million kilowatt hours of electric energy in 1971, as against 615 thousand million in the EEC. In 1950, the level was nearly the same, with 135 thousand million and 123 thousand million kilowatt hours, respectively. The production figures for hard coal and anthracite in the CMEA and the EEC are 692 million and 159 million tonnes, respectively: here, too, the production level was nearly balanced in 1950. The CMEA has also increased its share in the world's output of steel from 18·9 per cent in 1950 to 28·6 per cent in 1972.

This development underlines the fact that the CMEA countries have been pursuing a long-range, planned raw-material and energy policy. This has been co-ordinated within the community, with the result that a sound foundation has been created for their economic success and corresponding stability.

The results obtained by the CMEA could not have been achieved except under the conditions of a planned socialist economy, on the basis of social ownership of the means of production.

The planning of the international economic relations and the development of integration within the CMEA is related to such important fields as: joint development of raw-material deposits and sources of energy; increasing the division of labour, specialisation and co-operation in the processing industry to concentrate and intensify production processes; and rapid growth of inter-CMEA trade. International co-operation in the field of planning within the CMEA, in conformity with the stipulations of the Comprehensive Programme, is increasingly characterised by the fact that the time horizons, scales and interdependencies are continuously being extended, and that the stages preceding production are increasingly becoming the object of co-operation, particularly in research, development and project planning, as well as in the drawing up of new technologies.

On this basis, the CMEA countries have created a standard system of communication engineering, the Unified Computer System (consisting of third-generation computers), and a joint space programme. They have also been working together very successfully for many years in the Nuclear Research Institute of Dubna (USSR). The greatest progress in the planning of the joint scientific and technical work has been made in the CMEA plan for the co-ordination of the principal trends of scientific and technical research. This plan specified fifty problems for the years 1966 to 1970; for 1971 to 1975 the plan listed 260 problems for multilateral co-operation, and some 2400 problems for bilateral co-operation. This is the basis for the formation of co-ordination centres, international research teams, design offices and scientific—technical councils.

The CMEA countries are starting to open up tremendous development resources by adopting a joint raw-material and energy policy. Joint development concepts for important branches of industry such as metallurgy, machine-tool production and farm machinery manufacture are in preparation.

In this connection, the directives concerning joint prognostics among the CMEA countries must also be considered. These prognostic activities go as far ahead as the year 2000 in some cases, and they are an essential starting point for working out standard programmes that can be generally accepted and put into practice in the CMEA countries.

CAPITALIST ECONOMIC INTEGRATION

Economic integration in capitalism is subject to the profit efforts of the ruling class as a result of existing capitalist ownership of the means of production.

The foreign economic relations among the industrial capitalist countries are characterised by far-reaching internationalisation and many elements of integration, yet they are also marked by growing internal contradictions. Powerful concerns are operating in many countries through international production and a corresponding market organisation, particularly in branches involving intensive scientific work and research.

Spontaneous price and inflation development, as well as the unchecked flow of international capital, greatly upset the balance of payments. As a reaction to this development, governments employ whatever means they have at their disposal in an endeavour to maintain a proper equilibrium of economic growth, the development of prices and currency, the balance of payment and employment. This equilibrium is becoming increasingly unstable, with the result that more and more countries are being forced to intervene to the detriment of others, either globally or in certain fields of foreign economic relations.

But in spite of the indisputable growth effects of integration within the EEC countries over a prolonged period, the years 1973 and 1974 indicate a clear downward trend of economic growth. With the exception of Italy, the growth rates of industrial production in the EEC countries have been declining since the last quarter of 1973, whereas consumer prices in these countries increased by between 6 and 12 per cent in 1973.[6]

The EEC Commission[7] expects that GNP within its economic area will grow by an average of only 2 per cent in 1974, that the previous surplus in the balance of payments will be replaced by a deficit of the order of $10 thousand million, and that there will be more short-time work and higher unemployment.

It is obvious that the EEC mechanism does not function for the entire process of reproduction. Competition, as well as parallel development work and production, have not been reduced in any way. On the contrary, they have been intensified, because the mechanism within the EEC is still mainly determined by capitalist market laws, in spite of certain regulatory measures.

Undoubtedly, centripetal as well as centrifugal forces, tendencies both of integration and of disintegration, are operating in Western Europe. The current crisis in the EEC is thus only part of the general crisis of the imperialist system.

III. SOME CONCLUSIONS AND PERSPECTIVES

As a result of socialist planned economy and plan co-ordination, economic integration within the CMEA has increased in stability and effectiveness with each passing year. This is expressed by the continuous growth rates of the overall economic development of the CMEA, and by the CMEA countries'

---

[6] According to figures given in OECD, *Main Economic Indicators* (Paris).
[7] See *The Times*, 2 Feb 1974, and *Frankfurter Allgemeine*, 4 Feb 1974.

increasing harmony on the economic level of development, particularly since the approval of the Comprehensive Programme. New forms of the mechanism of co-operation are being successfully employed; for instance, joint prognostics, planned co-ordination of long-term time horizons, and the formation of international economic organisations and associations in order to integrate entire industries, to start adopting forms of joint planning, and to embark upon joint investments within the framework of a co-ordinated raw-material, fuel and energy policy. International specialisation and co-operation in the fields of machine building, chemistry and consumer goods production are being intensified, combined with a rapidly growing exchange of goods.

An appraisal of the EEC shows that there is currently a definite decline in all fields and relations within it. The mechanism of the EEC is not functioning. Separate measures taken by individual countries are directed against the Community.

It is self-evident that the process of integration within the EEC is stagnating, that severe contradictions are arising, and that significant setbacks are taking place in certain fields. Serious disintegration trends are becoming evident. EEC practice will continue to be marked by integration and dis-integration tendencies in the future.

Two forms of economic integration, with their institutional organisations, which differ completely from each other in their socio-economic character, stand opposite one another. They are competing economically, are co-existing, and are gradually beginning to establish practical economic relations with one another.

In the economic field, the course from confrontation to co-operation among states of differing social order, and, also, among integrating communities, presupposes, however, that all discriminations are eliminated and that mutually advantageous relations are promoted. This is the only way to intensify co-operation, and thereby contribute to the further international-isation of economic life, without attempting an integration of the two socio-economic systems.

Opening Statement for Group Discussion
Ake E. Andersson (Sweden)

In this opening statement to the discussion, I should like to introduce some complementary points that have not been discussed in the main paper presented.

In most studies of the development of international integration, and also in Waelbroeck's paper, the focus is mainly on the international development of relative prices of products and factors of production. This is of course a legitimate principle as long as the countries under comparison are to a significant extent market economies. If, however, any of the countries under comparison are planned with quantitative instruments or have price distortions for internal political reasons, the comparisons have to be performed directly in the primal or quantitative side of the economies. Before discussing the problem of measurement of integration, I should like to question the 'nation' as a primary building block in the study of integration.

I. INTEGRATION AND THE CONCEPT OF THE NATION

The existence, constancy and economic relevance of bordered nations are major postulates of international-trade analysis. These fundamental elements of the analysis are mostly assumed to be homogeneous inwards to such an extent that they can be treated as *points in space.*

This is, of course, a very helpful construct in the analysis of the consequences of tariff barriers, mainly because these barriers are always based on the existence, constancy and relevance of bordered 'point-markets'. Nowadays most of us want to include all kinds of nontariff barriers, and at this point we may get into analytical problems with the postulated relevance of the point nations.

Some of the nontariff barriers that are influential with respect to trade cannot be analysed with regard to their consequences for integration unless we divide the large nations into regions. One artificial but simple example is enough to clarify the issue. Let us assume that the government of a large country wants to protect its manufacturing from international competition by levying a tax on all inland expenditures for the transport of foreign-produced goods and services. This would, of course, mean a tariff-equivalent reduction of the country's imports from other countries. The more important reactions in this case would be intranational; that is, between different nonjurisdictional sub-areas in the large country. Manufacturing near the borders would be practically unaffected directly, while manufacturing far away from the borders would be protected from foreign competition in direct correspondence to the transportation distance from the borders. The repercussions on the patterns of relocation, investment, trade, migration and, finally, welfare would in this case be spread over the whole spatial system, both intra- and internationally.

This brings me to the second point, where I shall use a model in order to be as brief as possible.

II. THE PROBLEM OF INTEGRATION MEASUREMENT

In measurements of integration we want to compare a multidimensional situation in the world before and after changes in a number of parameters, the values of which are controlled by nations. In order to make these comparisons comprehensible, we ordinarily want one single measure of the degree of integration or of its counterpart, segregation. To make the issue clear I shall use a simple measurement model:

$$S = (\underbrace{\sum_{c,r} a_{cr}|X_{cr}^0 - X_{cr}|^p}_{\text{Disequilibrium effect}} + \underbrace{\sum_{c,r} a_{cr}|X_{cr} - X_{cr}^*|^p}_{\text{Barrier effect}})^{1/p},$$

where S = degree of segregation (which goes to zero at full equilibrium and all barriers at minimal levels);

X_{cr}^0 = actual level of production of product c in region r;

X_{cr} = level of production at full equilibrium with unchanged barriers;

X_{cr}^* = level of production with full equilibrium and all barriers to trade at minimal levels; and

$a_{cr_1 p}$ = are valuation coefficients.

I shall not discuss the valuation problem, which has been covered by Waelbrock. Instead, I shall focus on the problem of determining the X and X^* vectors.

III. THE INTERRELATIONS BETWEEN TRANSACTION COSTS, TRADE, AND LOCATION OF PRODUCTION

One empirically very successful school makes trade a function of imposed barriers, on the one hand, and of the distance-related transaction costs, on the other. This school has had its main proponents in Finland and the Netherlands. Similar analyses of trade in services have been reflected in the large number of empirical works on travel behaviour in the United States.

The most popular estimation form has been the following:

$$X_{ij} = X_1^{\alpha 1} \ X_j^{\alpha 2} \ D_{ij}^{\alpha 3} \ T_{ij}^{\alpha 4} \ K, \tag{1}$$

where X_{ij} = the value (or volume) of trade between area i and j;

X_i = production in area i;

D_{ij} = distance between area i and j; and

T_{ij} = imposed barrier between area i and j.

Normal estimates for trade in goods have been: $\alpha_1 = \alpha_2 = 1$ and $\alpha_3 = -0.7$. For trade in services, $\alpha_3 = \leqslant -2$.

These results are important for political decisions on the changes in imposed barriers in response to a sudden change in distance-related costs. But the estimated forms have a much deeper implication in a number of problem areas, only reflected in minor ways in the paper by Waelbroeck.

The model shows that trade is a function of location. I shall now show that location is a function of trade. Let us introduce sectors into our analysis and define $_{rs}X_{ij}$ = trade between sectors r and s and areas i and j, and

$$_{rs}a_{ij} = {_{rs}X_{ij}}/{_sX_j}, \tag{2}$$

where $_sX_j$ = production in sector s and area j.

In accordance with (1) we can now make the coefficients (2) *functions* of the location of production, distances, and imposed barriers to trade:

$$_{rs}a_{ij} = {_{rs}f(\overline{X}, \overline{D}, \overline{T})}, \tag{3}$$

where $\overline{X}$ = production in areas and sectors (a vector);
$\quad\ \ \overline{D}$ = distances between areas (a matrix); and
$\quad\ \ \overline{T}$ = imposed barriers between areas (a matrix).

These results are important for political decisions on the relevant changes in imposed barriers in response to a change in distance-related costs (that is, transaction costs). But these estimates have a much deeper implication. The model shows that trade is a function of location (X_i, X_j). It is also possible to show that *location* is a function of trade.

Seeing the world as an endogenous static system, we can get the simultaneous equilibrium allocation of trade *and* production in areas and sectors:

$$\lambda X = A(X, \overline{D}, \overline{T})X. \tag{4}$$

This is a nonlinear eigen-equation, where trade, location and efficiency (measured by the maximal λ) are *simultaneously* determined. Sectors with distance elasticities that are high (in absolute values) will be located more to the centre of the communication system than will sectors with low distance elasticities. This explains why certain areas where possibilities for personal communication are favourable get large shares of advanced service production.

In this model a change in any tariff or nontariff barrier could be traced all the way to its consequences for trade and efficiency after full recognition of relocation.

IV. GROWTH AND INTEGRATION

Model (4) is deficient in one important respect. It disregards growth and changes. Growth can be introduced by assuming the existence of stock co-efficients, $_{rs}b_{ij}$, which must also be functions of location, distances (although to a lesser extent), and imposed barriers. We consequently have

$$X = A(X, \bar{T}, \bar{D})X + \mu B(X, \bar{T}, \bar{D}) X, \tag{5}$$

where μ = growth (assumed proportional) of the irreducible (or indecomposable) parts of the world economy.

A decrease in any element of A or B, whether induced by a change in an imposed barrier or in distance would mean an increased growth of the world economy and a relocation of production. Technological advances could either be represented as trend changes in the coefficients of A and B or be treated as produced by a research and development sector with its own, presumably high, distance elasticity.

V. INTEGRATION, UNEMPLOYMENT AND TRADE

The model used above shows that the structure of production in different areas and the trade between areas are simultaneously determined by imposed and nonimposed barriers to trade. This implies that, if any single barrier is changed, there will be a shift in the location of production. This shift induces a need for reallocation of labour between sectors and areas. Such a reallocation of factors, due to changes in A or B, often goes slowly, implying excess demand and supply (that is, disequilibrium). These disequilibrium situations are characterised by unemployment and inflation occurring simultaneously in different areas. In order to separate these disequilibrium costs of integration from the integration advantages – that is, to perform a correct measurement of the *progress* of integration and its welfare effects – we must have a theory of behaviour in disequilibrium states. This is not presented by Waelbroeck nor by me in model (5). The analysis of integration needs an adjustment theory with or without *tâtonnement*, and this is not yet available. When it is, it should provide a good basis for measurement of both the degree *and* progress of integration.

Report on Group Discussion
Erik Lundberg (Sweden)

In order to measure the degree of integration we first need a definition of integration that is as clear and exact as possible. That is self-evident. For any kind of description of the progress of integration we should like to have some kind of model of how an integration process works.

Our discussions have shown clearly that there are many dimensions to the concept of integration. The concept refers to some kind of unification of parts into a whole system; for example, the economies of a group of nations. The integration process can refer to various aspects of economic life. Thus, we may speak of trade integration or factor integration (in the form of liberalisation of movements of capital and labour). Policy integration would be a more generalised concept not necessarily referring to any specific item. We can, furthermore, use the term 'selective integration' in order to mark out a specific area of policy; for example, referring to technical development and co-operation in research.

Relative to the process of integration we can distinguish spontaneous integration from an integration process following specific policy measures (as reducing barriers to trade). It was stressed in the discussion that integration is a more narrow concept than internalisation. When Yugoslavia and Finland increase their trade with the Soviet Union that hardly means an integration process but, rather, a bit of internationalisation.

A good deal of our discussion has dealt with the problem of whether there is, or is not, a fundamental difference between the integration processes of socialist countries and those of capitalist countries — using these simple distinctions. Many economists from the socialist camp maintained that there was such a fundamental distinction, and that it was therefore necessary to speak of two different types of integration. To justify this view, reasons were given that referred both to the separate integration *aims* as well as to quite different mechanisms and policies of integration. Therefore, the measure of integration or the use of indicators of integration could not be the same for both economic systems.

In the West — the capitalist sphere — integration nearly always implies some kind of *market orientation*. Therefore, such measures as international trade development, share of integrated trade, price dispersion or differences and similarities in price structures are meaningful. Examples were presented of an indicator of the degree of capital market integration by using a dispersion measure of relevant interest rates. Several formulas along that line were proposed and applied for comparing degrees of integration of groups of countries and over periods of time.

The definition of integration — and, therefore, also the measures — for CMEA countries should rather refer directly to indicators of 'production and development', to use Imre Vajda's term. Market and trade developments should be regarded as secondary phenomena and, therefore, not so useful as for the West. Definitions and measures should thus refer to indicators of co-ordination of five-year and longer-term plans for the development of production structure and investment. Such measures could refer to the total economy, to industry and to specific branches of industry (machine tools and electric power were mentioned as examples).

In this connection, we had an interesting discussion about how and to what extent actual market prices or prices used in the planning operations (or eventually coming out as 'shadow prices') could be used as a basis for studying degrees of integration among socialist economies. Questions were raised – but not answered – as to the significance of these kinds of prices for judging degrees of integration.

In fact, there was a lively discussion on the relative validity of price statistics as an eventual basis for measuring degrees of integration among the economies. Although the economists from socialist countries were doubtful about the usefulness of price dispersion measures for this purpose, they still maintained that prices and price relations in their countries were more reliable and more significant for relevant analysis than were prices under present conditions in Western non-socialist countries. Although partly derived from world market prices, the price relationships in socialist economies were given a high degree of long-term stability. In the West, inflation, business cycles, monopoly positions, and so on, would tend to make current price measures doubtful, not least from the point of view of measuring degree and development of integration. Economists from the West did not fully share this view. On this point we had a confrontation of views and very little meeting of minds.

In other respects there was more agreement on possibilities of measurement – integration being a multidimensional concept. One group of measures discussed referred to the structure of production and its development within the countries of integration. One could, for example, look at the development towards concentration of production, comparing it with the consumption pattern, and thereby find indicators. The underlying theory is that an integration process would imply division of work under economies of scale and from that would follow concentration of production in the various integrating countries.

The types of measures discussed so far are similar in that they all refer to indications of integration processes. It was also suggested that the degree of integration could be measured with regard to the *deviations* from *the aims* of the integration process. Increased trade, equalisation of prices, and so on, are not the ultimate aims of integration, but only secondary consequences or indicators. It was suggested that the *equalisation of living standards* within a country or a group of integrating countries is an end result and an aim of 'complete' integration. From this point of view, the dispersion of living standards could be used as a measure of integration.

There was a significant difference in views between economists from socialist and those from non-socialist countries as regards both the process or mechanism of integration and the role of integration policy. In the CMEA countries, integration occurs mainly under government direction by means of the co-ordination of plans on different levels. In the West, the idea of a relatively free integration process is in the foreground, and the role of governments is limited to the creation of economic policy conditions for a more or less spontaneous process. The importance of the multinational corporations in this process was pointed out and discussed.

On a very abstract level of reasoning, a mathematical model of an integration process was presented. This model was constructed to show how the structure of production in different areas, changes in efficiency, and trade between them are determined by various factors, including barriers to trade. The underlying assumptions of the model were so generally formulated that the model could be used for clarifying the properties of integration processes in both socialist and capitalist systems. There was a lively discussion of the assumptions and of the intricate properties of the model presented. There was general agreement that this type of approach could be helpful and that much research along this line would be needed. However, some members of the group expressed scepticism regarding the usefulness of a large mathematical model. Nevertheless, there was undoubtedly an interest in finding ways of exact reasoning with the support of mathematical stringency and that attitude could be found in both camps.

It should be added that there were also present economists who were sceptical even of the usefulness of measurement and quantification of integration. 'Life is so rich and varied, we should not be martyrs of thinking in quantitative'terms', was a view expressed. Much can be done by means of broad historical research, by describing lines of development and current tendencies. There was a general agreement that different types of approaches are complemenatry and should all be tried.

This general attitude can be given some concreteness by means of the following very tentative programme of research fields that was presented.

(1) Measuring and analysing dispersion in prices and interest rates over time and among groups of countries, both for CMEA countries and Western groups of countries.

(2) Studies of how, and to what extent, investments in various branches in individual countries are dependent on production development in the whole area of integration.

(3) Studies of trends in industrial concentration within the group — with special reference to increasing returns (as gains from integration).

(4) Research in effects of integration on income distribution; consequent studies of equalisation of living standards as measures of integration.

(5) Analysis of various aspects of policy integration on the basis of mathematical models of integration processes.

5 Sectoral Integration: Agriculture, Transport, Energy and Selected Industries (Main Paper, Working Group B)

Hans Willgerodt (FED. REP. GERMANY)

I. INTRODUCTORY

When general integration of different economies is not attainable within an acceptable time span, policy makers frequently turn to international economic integration of individual branches of production. This sectoral integration is sometimes intended to be an indirect way of accomplishing general economic integration: by successive steps one economic section after another is to be included in a scheme of integration. It is hoped that total integration will eventually result from this piecemeal procedure.

On the other hand, sectoral integration is often treated as an end in itself. This approach abstracts from the general repercussions on the national economies. Nevertheless, no sectoral integration can be examined for its effects without taking into account its implications for the other parts of the economies involved.

II. SECTORAL INTEGRATION AS A WAY TO ECONOMIC UNION

Some twenty years ago, many proposals were made to integrate various sectors of the West European economies. The hope was that, when sectoral integration proved successful, governments would then go further towards general integration. Most of these proposals were not accepted, but at least the European Coal and Steel Community (ECSC) was put into operation. Was it really a pacemaker for the EEC? It is open to doubt whether the ECSC had any influence on the speed with which the EEC was founded. Probably both are the outcome of a general political reconciliation among the participating countries. But the establishment of the ECSC certainly did have some additional integrating effects on other sectors. For instance, discriminatory railway charges (broken charges at the frontier, etc.) were abolished, the sectoral labour market was unified, and the efforts to harmonise indirect taxes and to adopt the more neutral system of taxes on value added were perhaps reinforced by the famous tax dispute in the ECSC.

Another example of sectoral integration to which pacemaking abilities were ascribed is the so-called common agricultural market of the EEC. In many publications it is praised as the cornerstone of European economic and political unification. This agricultural market of the EEC was designed on the implicit assumption that the exchange rate parities among the member states would remain stable. Agricultural prices in the EEC are determined in terms of European units of account, and the corresponding national prices are calculated by applying a declared parity or some other official exchange rate (for instance, central rate) to the common prices in European units of account. Changing parities or exchange rates in the EEC therefore involve proportional changes of agricultural prices in domestic currencies. Since such variations of prices were regarded as politically intolerable, it was hoped that governments would abstain from altering the exchange rates. Instead, they were expected to accomplish monetary integration with fixed parities, narrow bands of exchange-rate deviations from parity, and, as the final stage, the establishment of a common European currency.[1] But, despite the agricultural regulations of the EEC, the stability of exchange rates among most of the member states has disappeared. The 'common agricultural market' was fragmented into several (now six) areas with different prices; in order to separate these areas from one another, a system of compensations was introduced to offset the effects of changes in exchange rates on national prices of agricultural products. Agricultural prices have been renationalised and, in this respect, the common market of the EEC no longer exists. The expected leverage of this sectoral integration failed to materialise and the underlying theory failed with it.

Some elements of the sectoral approach to economic unification can also be found in most plans to dismantle tariff barriers and quantitative restrictions to trade. The former Organisation for European Economic Co-operation provided that quantitative restrictions had to be removed gradually. For each commodity the import values were calculated as a percentage of the total imports of a country in a year of reference preceding the period of liberalisation. These percentages were summed and taken as a measure of the status of liberalisation that the countries should reach within a prescribed period. For commodities that were liberalised the quotas were abolished entirely. Thus, some branches of industry were integrated earlier than others.

Many of the economic integration schemes of the last twenty years have used the same procedure of gradually lowering the barriers to international trade. In the case of customs unions or free-trade areas, the lowering of import duties by uniform percentages seems to avoid differential treatment of particular sectors of the economies. But such a procedure of uniform tariff reduction can have quite different effects on different industries, especially when the tariffs are not uniform at the outset.

[1] Cf. Hans Willgerodt, Alexander Domsch, Rolf Hasse and Volker Merx, *Wege und Irrwege zur europäischen Währungsunion* (Freiburg im Breisgau, 1972).

Integration by successive steps can be subjected to the following principal criticisms.[2]

(1) The increased integration of one sector can cause a disintegration of other sectors, if the sectoral balance of trade runs into a deficit. The sum of foreign exchange available to pay for imports may be given, or it may be impossible to increase it sufficiently to cover the additional expenditure for imports in the integrated sector. In either case, imports of other commodities must be diminished, by means of higher import barriers (quotas, tariffs, and so on) or the adjustment mechanisms of the balance of payments (that is, deflation or devaluation). Whether under such conditions a net gain for integration and trade can be achieved will depend on the relevant elasticities of demand and supply and the measures taken to correct the balance of payments. The probability that one country incurs a deficit in its balance of trade and services is much lower when many sectors are integrated simultaneously, because increases in exports may compensate for increases in imports.

(2) Even if the sectoral balance of trade remains in equilibrium, a disintegration of other less integrated sectors may result if factors of production are attracted by the integrated sector from other export industries.

(3) Even if disturbances of the balance of payments can be minimised, each additional step of sectoral integration means uncertainties and changing conditions for investment and production. The competitive position of industries is altered not only by adaptations of the balance of payments, but also by changes in the effective rates of protection for the home market or in the degree of discrimination in foreign markets. These rates depend on many items, including the general competitive position in the factor markets. On the whole, there are numerous indirect effects of sectoral integrations on sectors that are not yet integrated.

It may be that governments are unwilling to accept the more appropriate medicine of immediate general integration and that sectoral integration becomes a second-best solution with the disadvantages mentioned above. One might add, however, that these disadvantages must not be overrated.

(1) The balance of trade and payments can remain relatively undisturbed if different sectors are integrated at the same time and the resulting changes in exports and imports offset one another.

(2) Similar offsets may occur if integration leads to more intra-industry specialisation than inter-industry specialisation, as has been demonstrated by Balassa, Grubel and others for the integration of countries on similar levels of development.[3] This is so because different commodities are included

---

[2] Cf. Fritz W. Meyer, 'Die europäische Agrargemeinschaft und ihre Auswirkungen auf die gegenwärtige und zukünftige Handelspolitik und das Transferproblem', in *Gutachten zu Fragen einer europäischen Agrargemeinschaft* (Bonn: Auswärtiges Amt, 1953), pp. 225–53.

[3] Cf. Herbert G. Grubel, 'Intra-Industry Specialisation and the Pattern of Trade', in *The Canadian Journal of Economics*, XXXIII (1967), pp. 374–88.

in the same category in the international trade classification, although their supply and demand conditions differ widely in the integrating countries. No wonder that after integration a country's imports and exports of commodities belonging to the same category can expand simultaneously. But trade of close substitutes (for instance, many finished industrial products or hotel and travel services) may also increase in both directions, because producers of differentiated goods can gain a share of the market in other countries even if similar products are already produced there.

(3) Increased exports of integrated sectors can lead to a transfer of factors of production from nonintegrated but import-competing industries to the integrated sector. Consequently, imports may also increase in the non-integrated sectors.

A more political argument in favour of sectoral integration as a way to general economic integration runs as follows: most governments are reluctant to accept the results of unrestricted worldwide or even regional free trade; they try, therefore, to maximise the advantages of integration without losing too much of their economic sovereignty. There are several reasons for this attitude.

(1) The gains from integration may be unequally distributed among the participating countries. According to the traditional doctrine of comparative costs, small countries tend to gain relatively more by freer trade than do large countries, because the latter may already have realised most of the advantages of the division of labour through trade inside their own territory. This argument, however, overlooks a possible accumulation of growth in industrial centres, which are more likely to exist in the larger countries. Small countries cannot always be sure that they will be able to develop such centres after integration. The larger countries may have a better competitive position from the outset because of their already existing industrial agglomerations.

(2) A regional integration among countries with a small economic base can lead to a common market that is, at first, not large enough to allow the installation of a broad spectrum of industries with optimum-size plants in all of the participating countries. External economies and advantages of agglomerations may bring about a concentration of industries in some of the member states. This leads other member countries to feel that they are not getting a fair portion of total industrialisation, the magnitude of which is often supposed to be given.[4]

(3) Sometimes small countries can gain more by integration, but they can also lose much more by the disintegration that a dominant member of an

[4] Cf. Miguel S. Wionczek, 'Introduction: Requisites for Viable Integration', in *Latin American Economic Integration*, ed. M. S. Wionczek (New York, Washington and London, 1966), p. 11; Carlos M. Castillo, *Growth and Integration in Central America* (New York, Washington and London, 1966), chapter 13 and literature quoted there; and Sven Heldt, 'The Andean Group: An Answer to Some Problems of LAFTA', *Kiel Discussion Paper no. 18* (Feb 1972).

integrated area could bring about without too much damage to itself. Small countries may therefore be reluctant to become integrated into a regional bloc without strong political guarantees that the large partner will not use its potential against it. In this case, the smaller countries may turn to greater self-sufficiency, combined with some regulated integration of special sectors. Alternatively, they may choose more general free trade with the outside world, thereby neutralising the influences of dominant economies through competition.

These arguments have led to proposals for controlled integration of individual industries. To avoid possible concentration of industrial activity in some of the participating countries, international regulation of industrial investments has been proposed. According to these proposals, one country after another is entitled to establish certain industries with a capacity sufficiently large to supply the whole integrated market or, at least, a large part of it. Such schemes were applied in Central America and the Andean group. The complementarity agreements of LAFTA (these are a form of government-sponsored international specialisation cartel) also include the principle of reciprocity, that is, of sharing the advantages from specialised investment: one country suspends its production of a product and opens its market to a specialised producer of another country, who can benefit from economies of scale and may hope to realise monopoly profit. The second country is supposed to reciprocate with another product.

In an economic order with dominant private enterprise and flexible market prices, there has to be a solution to the problem of centralised government planning of the investments being put into practice, if market signals point in another direction. The Central American 'integration industries'[5] should have had the privilege of internal free trade for their products over a period of ten years, during which competitors in the same industry, but without the status of 'integration industry', were excluded from this advantage. Actually, the free movement of goods in the Central American Common Market was generalised much earlier. If such rationing of freer trade inside a region is used as an instrument to develop new industries with plants of optimum size, it cannot continue to work in this direction once sectoral integration has been completed.

After integration has been achieved, new industries can be protected against internal newcomers only by a system of monopolistic privileges such as licences, tax exemptions, subsidies, and the like. The currently dominant approach to industrial development therefore excludes competition from the outside world by higher import duties or restrictive import quotas. This serves to promote import substitution and to avoid idle capacities, which may come into being if the planners have taken the whole demand of the integrating countries as the relevant market for the new plants without

[5] Cf. *Economic Cooperation in Latin America, Africa and Asia. A Handbook of Documents*, ed. S. Wionczek (Cambridge Mass. and London, 1969), p. 121.

considering the attitudes of the consumers, who may prefer products from
the world market. On the other hand, high tariff walls around such a
common market not only exclude imports, but also create an incentive for
direct investment from other countries, thus stimulating competition inside
again. To avoid this new competition, it is a common practice to discriminate
against foreign capital by means of taxes, licences, requirements to sell a
majority percentage of shares to national residents, restraints on the transfer
of capital and dividends, nationalisations, and so on. Elements of this chain
of interventions are found in the procedures of the Andean group. The
social costs of these controls can be high, and the prevailing optimism, the
hope that monopolies resulting from industrial planning will easily and
effectively be kept under public control,[6] has not been justified empirically.

There is only one way out of this dilemma: to lower the barriers to
imports from third countries. But the transition to more general free trade
brings forth another difficulty for centralised investment planning in market
economies. The distribution of industries among the integrating countries is
not necessarily in accordance with the long-run relations of comparative
costs and advantages. It is highly unlikely that the government officials who
negotiate the allotment of industries to the member states will be able and
willing to accept the locations that would allow the industries to be competitive in the long run. Officials think in terms of equitable industrialisation
and political opportunities that can be influenced and even determined by
pressure groups within the countries involved. Tinbergen's argument that
'industrial activities can be carried out in many places, provided only that the
transportation facilities are adequate'[7] is no answer to this problem. It does
not follow that investment planning by political negotiations does not come
into conflict with the market forces. Moreover, the location of industries is
far from being irrelevant for their competitive position, especially in the case
of heavy industries as discussed by Tinbergen. Otherwise, the movement of
the German steel industry to the North Sea and the relocation of the steel
industry in the United States cannot be explained.[8] As soon as the transition
to general free trade and general integration is under way, the sectoral
investment planning will be put to the test of economic efficiency. And
then the promotors of sectoral integration may not be willing to sacrifice
their vested interests. For that reason, sectoral integration by international
investment planning may become an obstacle to, rather than a vehicle for,
economic unification.

Fortunately, the alternative to heavy interventionism by international
concerted investment control is not *laissez faire*, but some sort of market-

---

[6] Cf. Sidney Dell, *A Latin American Common Market?* (London, New York and
Toronto, 1966), p. 138.
[7] Jan Tinbergen, 'Heavy Industry in the Latin American Common Market', in
Latin American Economic Integration, p. 174.
[8] Cf. Friedrich Hertle, *Standortprobleme der amerikanischen Eisen- und
Stahlindustrie* (Tübingen, 1959).

oriented interventionism. Within a customs union, a transfer of funds from the centres of growth to the less developed regions can be organised, as is normal in most West European countries and in the EEC, in order to decentralise economic activity to some extent. Government decisions regarding public utilities are an unavoidable indirect influence on the location of industries. Today, private enterprises cannot invest on a large scale without complementary investment by some public authority. These public investments need not be planned on a purely competitive basis by local authorities without any recognition of the interdependence of their activities. In many cases, international co-ordination of government investment is badly needed; the examples of transport facilities and electricity are self-evident. Private investors get signals from governments by public investments and other government activities. Before regulating private business directly it may be better first to co-ordinate government activities by international agreements.

Perhaps some of the problems mentioned can theoretically be handled more easily by centrally administered economies without private ownership of capital. But these countries have difficulties in combining international integration with national planning autonomy. In these countries, therefore, sectoral integration is not normally a way to unrestricted economic union.

III. SECTORAL ASPECTS OF SECTORAL INTEGRATION

Those who hesitate to run the risk of surrendering national economic sovereignty entirely to a regional union may try, nevertheless, to capture some advantages by carefully specified sectoral integration arrangements on a regional or worldwide basis. Provided such advantages do exist, they are all the more impressive under conditions of comprehensive integration or general free trade. However, they seem to exist even without these favourable conditions, because they are closely connected with the particular problems of individual economic sectors.

It is evident that many agreements on technical questions belong to this category. Nobody denies, in principle, that much useful work can be done by the international harmonisation of traffic codes and of government orders regulating the technical properties of vehicles and other products to make them less dangerous or more suitable for the environment. International standardisation of medical instruments, pharmaceutical products, electrical equipment and even agricultural products can be reasonable to a certain extent. All of these accords — apart from their technical merits — become more important with increasing interchange across borders. Harmonisation of this sort reduces the scope of administrative protectionism: on the other hand, it can also reduce competition if the regulations are too rigid and do not allow for the improvement of commodities. Too much standardisation can transform open oligopolies with heterogeneous products into closed oligopolies seeking joint profit maximisation. The activities of the EEC authorities clearly demonstrate the ambivalence of this kind of sectoral integration. Some technical regulations for agricultural products obviously were designed to make the protectionist market order more watertight. Moreover, the EEC institutions have continued to strive for additonal competences that would strengthen their authority, irrespective of any practical necessity for passing new regulations. The permanent political crisis of the Community is responsible for this behaviour. But, undoubtedly, many international agreements or regulations on technical matters can be judged primarily by their concrete benefit for the branch of economic activity concerned.

One cannot say as much without qualification for other forms of sectoral integration; yet the direct effects on the individual sectors must be identified. Some of these direct effects can be treated in more general terms, because similar problems arise in different sectors.

Again, the central problem is the international co-ordination of investments in a special sector. The classical approach denies that it is the task of governments to determine directly the size and location of private investment and to co-ordinate its allocation to regions and countries. More competition is expected to lead to optimum solutions or, in any case, to better solutions than those reached by central regulation. According to this view, specialisation and economies of scale are a result of private planning and competition. Private agreements among competitors on co-ordinated investment are considered to be conspiracies and restraints of trade.

The opposite position is taken by all friends of national and international government planning of the economic process. Their arguments are as follows:

Where the optimum size of the plant is large relative to the demand for the product, complete freedom of investment for private enterprise results in suboptimal-size factories and unused capacity, duplication of investments and waste of resources. Therefore, either private international investment cartels — with or without government control — should be allowed, or some government agency should supervise and co-ordinate sectoral investment to prevent misallocations. This precaution is supposed to be all the more necessary for developing countries, which must be extremely careful in using their scarce resources of capital.[9]

At first sight these arguments seem to be convincing, but that they do not lead very far can easily be seen when we ask the following questions;

(1) Is it really true that in cases of very large investments and narrow markets — that is, in cases of oligopoly — private entrepreneurs are not aware of the risks of investment? Do they not try to get all the information

[9] Tinbergen, in *Latin American Economic Integration*, pp. 170ff.; Dell, *A Latin American Common Market?*, p. 138; Wionczek, in *Latin American Economic Integration*, pp. 10ff.; and David E. Ramsett, *Regional Industrial Development in Central America* (New York, Washington and London, 1969), p. 37.

available in order to minimise potential losses, or are they eager to lose money?

(2) Is it really true, as Tinbergen has said,[10] that relatively long construction periods invalidate the accuracy of the market mechanism as a guide for investment decisions? Do entrepreneurs, when investing, take into account only the prevailing prices and never the expected future prices? Do investors under oligopolistic conditions really not know the investments and investment plans of their competitors, especially when the technical units are very lumpy, as in the case of heavy industry, which Tinbergen has in mind?

(3) Are unused capacities really typical for industrial competition under modern conditions? Certainly an oligopolist will retain some idle capacity as a reserve and deterrent against newcomers and the other oligopolists, but is restriction of free investment and of competition really a good device to bring unused capacities of monopolies and oligopolies into operation? Is the number of production units of optimum size in a growing or developing market as fixed as many economists seem to believe?

(4) Private investors may make decisions that are irrational to a certain extent, but can one use the investment-*cycle* argument, as Tinbergen does, to justify an international investment control, which does not solve cyclical problems but decides structural, regional and, in any case, *long-term* allocation of investments in the countries taking part in a project of sectoral integration? Is temporary overinvestment resulting from competition not an incentive for growth?

(5) Why should free decisions on investment cause suboptimal-size factories, if competition and a common market with internal free trade diminish the market imperfections? The common experience is that larger markets give rise to the establishment of larger factories and larger firms without the need for artificial interference, provided that the larger firms are really more competitive. Are the suboptimal automobile plants in South America, which are so often cited, the result of free investment or an outcome of government protection and lack of free trade? Can large firms exploiting economies of scale survive only if competition through the free investment of newcomers and of smaller firms is restricted? Are these economies of scale more important than the '*X*-efficiency'; that is, the gains in productivity resulting from competition in a more dynamic market?[11]

(6) If all of these questions could really be answered in favour of the regulation approach to sectoral integration, do private international cartels or international government agencies know better than do private investors the best size and location of investment in a certain sector of industry? If so, are they willing and able to follow their better insights under prevailing political conditions? What about the accuracy of the several energy forecasts by official agencies during the last twenty years, to cite but one example of

[10] In *Latin American Economic Integration*, p. 173.
[11] Cf. Harvey Leibenstein, 'Allocative Efficiency *vs. X*-efficiency', in *The American Economic Review*, LVI (1966), pp. 392–415.

the doubtful empirical foundations of centralised investment planning?[12]

(7) If it is necessary to co-ordinate the investments of a certain sector through governments and international agencies, with whom should the co-ordination take place? There is a clear answer to this question in only two cases: either the countries included must regulate their trade in the commodities of the integrated sector with third countries in a very rigid way, so that disturbances from outside are excluded, or the whole world must participate.

In any case, centralised international investment planning for certain sectors is an extremely difficult task, and the problems of organising the machinery for negotiating and decision making are not easy to handle. For this reason, a tendency to avoid frequent renegotiations may develop. As a consequence, dynamic alternatives, which might have evolved under the conditions of free investment, are more or less precluded.

Countries without flexible market prices for factors and commodities face an additional problem for sectoral integration: how can one determine the partner with the lowest costs and the most suitable location of production?

With imperfect factor mobility, factor inputs cannot be calculated as if they had identical values. But this is only one of the difficulties to be overcome. Comparative costs cannot be determined for one sector alone, since the general balance of payments has to draw the line between export goods, nontraded goods and import goods.

In favour of international intervention it can be argued that wider information, or publication of investment plans, is useful to prevent over-investment by competing firms. For example, the ECSC has to be notified of all planned investment in the coal-mining and steel industries. The supranational authority of the ECSC has the power to forbid any investment project if the investor plans to finance it with funds from the capital market. The results of this sectoral control of investment are, however, not very impressive.

Finally, one rarely examined problem of sectoral integration by investment control should be mentioned. If some supranational agency decides that investment of a certain sector shall be concentrated in one of the member countries, then funds must be transferred within the community if the savings of the investing country are not sufficient to finance the projects and if funds from outside the community are not available. A common capital market is a precondition not only for general economic integration but also for sectoral integration. In most of the so-called common markets, however, free movement of capital is not permitted and the national capital markets are separated from each other by exchange control, as in the EEC.

For the more special aspects of sectoral integration, the EEC is both an important and interesting example. The main peculiarity of its so-called common agricultural market is a system of lower intervention prices for

[12] Cf. E. F. Schumacher, 'The Struggle for a European Energy Policy', in *Journal of Common Market Studies*, II (1964), pp. 199–211.

important agricultural products, combined with higher target prices, which are relevant in the case of imports from third countries. The internal market prices can move between intervention prices and target prices. In the case of internal surpluses, the intervention agencies of the EEC buy unlimited amounts of products, thereby keeping prices at the intervention level. In the case of internal deficits at the target prices, imports from the world market are possible. These imports cannot be sold at prices lower than the target prices, since variable levies eliminate any difference between a lower supply price from third countries and the threshold price, which is a sort of derived target price for the relevant port of import. Import quotas were abolished, in most cases, and internal free trade was formally established. Many politicians, and even experts, proclaimed that a real common market for agricultural products had been created. But a market, in the strict sense of the word, existed only in so far as market prices moved between intervention prices and target prices. When one of these limits was reached, the mechanism of the market could not work any more, because prices became inflexible and could be changed only by political negotiations conducted in the familiar all-night meetings of the ministers of agriculture. The intervention prices are minimum prices. Minimum prices are not only a device to guarantee income to the farmers, but also an instrument of interregional and international disintegration. When, in one member country, prices reach the intervention point, it is no longer possible for the farmers of other EEC countries to export additional quantities into that country except to its intervention agencies. No reallocation of agricultural production in the EEC can be induced under these circumstances by market prices. The effect of such minimum prices is similar to the effect of import quotas. By the system of minimum and target prices, agriculture is also, in part, excluded from the normal reactions of markets to adjustments of the balance of payments; the details cannot be explained here.[13] At any rate, there never was complete free trade for agricultural products in the EEC, even before the uniformity of prices was destroyed by the monetary compensatory measures that were taken to cope with changes in exchange rates. The very construction principle of the common agricultural market has disintegrating consequences.

Other sectoral schemes of the EEC include the same instrument of minimum and maximum prices. According to Article 61 of the ECSC Treaty, minimum and maximum prices can be introduced for coal and steel, but this regulation has not been applied systematically. The combination of minimum and maximum charges has, however, become effective for commercial road-transport services. This may be a first step towards greater price flexibility for those countries that had applied fixed charges before. The disintegrating effect of the margin-price system continues, nevertheless,

[13] Cf. Hans Willgerodt, 'Der "Gemeinsame Agrarmarkt der EWG". Kritische Betrachtungen zu einer wirtschaftspolitischen Fehlkonstruktion', Walter Eucken Institut, *Vorträge und Aufsätze 49* (Tübingen, 1974).

to exist. In this particular case, the transport branches and individual firms are more vulnerable to the disintegrating effects of the system than are the suppliers from different nations.[14]

Transport rates work like tariffs. Thus, sectoral integration of transport facilities has immediate consequences for the integration of other sectors. Now and then, free-trade associations and customs unions try to protect their transport business against external competition. Such 'navigation acts' mean higher internal transport costs and, for that reason, disintegration of other sectors of such common markets. If an economic union wants to have its own transport facilities as a safeguard against economic and political risks, it is possible to pay subsidies to its own transport business.

In the case of international trade in energy, the problem of risk is conspicuous. In this field, sectoral integration is advisable only if the likelihood of economic or political blackmail can be minimised.

Some basic conclusions are possible. The various sectoral aspects of sectoral integration do not differ as much as it may seem at first sight. Sectoral integrations cannot be judged without considering the interdependence of all sectors of the economy. Some measures that seem to integrate particular sectors have the effect of disintegrating not only these sectors but others as well. Planning of integration for individual sectors can lead to waste of resources, especially when there is no system of flexible prices. Sectoral integration may be a political device concealing nationalism, protectionism and monopolistic combination behind an activity that seems to belong to the field of true international co-operation.

[14] Cf. D. L. Munby, 'Fallacies in the Community's Transport Policy', in *Journal of Common Market Studies*, I (1962), pp. 67–78.

Comments
Zdeněk Orlíček (Czechoslovakia)

I.

When economists speak of sectoral policy or sectoral integration, and of its place in any individual country's general economic policy or in regional integration, they do not always all have the same thing in mind.

The author of the main paper for this working group bases his judgements on his immense personal knowledge of the advantages and disadvantages that result when integration measures are applied in practice. What he says bears eloquent testimony to his profound awareness of the problems of Western economic groups. He speaks as an expert when he analyses the problems of sectoral integration in the context of the conditions of the capitalist economy. Still, his critique does not go deep enough, to the very root of the difficulties. The observed process of integration in the capitalist economy leads him to certain generalisations, to conclusions that do not apply to the conditions of socialist production.

With regard to the question of whether general integration should be approached via partial integration in specified branches, it is well known that in socialist economies the necessary conditions of integration derive from social ownership. Social ownership gives the state a means of controlling basic macro-economic relations nationally and internationally, at any level that it chooses, including the sectoral one. Internationally, any one socialist government has to rely on co-operation with the others. It follows that, even in the conditions of a socialist economy, it is no easy task to co-ordinate all national policies and approaches in order to mould them into a consistent and optimal whole.

II.

The general principles of socialist economic integration are embodied in what is known as the Comprehensive Programme of Socialist Economic Integration. This must be seen in the context of world politics, because it is the political aspects of integration that are dominant at present. The Comprehensive Programme expresses, first and foremost, the long-term overall strategy of economic policy in the CMEA community. Integration by branches forms part of general integration. But socialist economic integration involves more than the sum of the efforts that are brought to bear on integration in specific sectors. Its mechanism is directly geared to the development of co-operation, and is conditioned by the dominant role of the socialist state and by social ownership of the means of production. The initial and permanently active element is mutual consultation among CMEA countries on the fundamental questions of economic policy and of research and development policy, both on a multilateral and on a bilateral basis, due allowance being made for reciprocal interconnections. These consultations aim at harmonising the underlying concepts of economic policy. The agenda of consultations and their actual course in 1973—4 not only confirms the wisdom of the choice of problems, but pinpoints the requirements for their technical solution and for sources of finance to achieve this.

The Comprehensive Programme takes full advantage of the price and value relations aspects of the system of CMEA co-operation, but in so doing places the accent on planning. In effect, it creates a unified system of international planning, even for the long run. There are, of course, problems of both substance and method, and there are inevitably imperfections in so novel a venture. Nevertheless, a beginning has been made in working out the principles of international planning and applying them in practice.

Member countries make every effort to achieve a modern production structure, which, among other things, involves assigning a relatively important place to the sectors of mechanical engineering and chemicals, and within these sectors involves a growing share of branches representing advanced technology. These also are the subject of special attention by the CMEA authorities with reference to socialist economic integration.

Research and development has on the whole proved to be a rather successful area so far. In some branches, programmes for a distribution of production and the specialisation of production have been devised and are working very well. Ball-bearings are a case in point. Successful progress has been made, too, with the development of joint CMEA enterprises, especially in fuels, raw materials, energy and transport, all of them fields of primary concern to member countries.

But any process of integration must proceed by stages, and it is no use wanting to jump ahead and tackle problems not yet ripe for solution. That is why integration is proceeding at varying degrees of intensity, both as regards different branches and different phases of sectoral integration. Many important questions, such as those of price, are susceptible only of step-by-step solution.

One of the major criteria of the efficiency and balanced proportions of the process of integration is a favourable rate of growth of social production and of international trade. Steady progress can thus be made towards one of the most important aims of integration policy — namely, the evening out of the disparities in levels of economic development in CMEA countries.

III.

Even if the sectoral policies of different groups engaged in economic integration have different political and economic aims, and even if these policies are implemented by different means, one can in practice detect certain tendencies common to them all. Take the case of mechanical engineering, where we have a body of empirical knowledge derived from the analysis of world production, of the international division of labour and of international trade. From this, we can draw certain general conclusions about the manner in which integration proceeds.

(1) The sectoral policy of economic communities concentrates to a large extent on engineering industries, which are in the vanguard of technical and technological progress.

(2) In the general effort to introduce activities (sectors, branches, techniques) not yet adequately developed in the community, special attention

is again paid to the engineering industries. Most often, in these cases of new activities, their requirements are covered largely or even wholly by imports from economically and technologically more advanced countries or regions.

(3) The activities that are so introduced into the community represent for it technological and economic progress and enrichment, and thus lessen its dependence on its original factor endowment. With reference to the engineering industries, the choice falls most often on capital goods, including machines, apparatuses and other equipment requiring much research and development work.

(4) The sectoral policy of any economic community is, then, designed first to catch up with the rest of the world, and later to go beyond mere imitation and to develop new technologies.

We all know that the groups that are at present engaged in integration comprise countries at disparate technical and economic levels, and that even the emerging groups themselves differ quite substantially in this respect.

On the world market and on the community's market, every individual producer occupies a double position: one *vis-à-vis* his production partners in the more advanced countries, and the other *vis-à-vis* the firms of relatively less advanced countries. This double position of any firm in the common division of labour has a bearing, too, on its production and exports. In its relations with more advanced partners, the firm, especially at the early stage of co-operation, is a supplier of simpler products or else of high-technology products made with foreign know-how furnished by the more advanced partner; in its relations with less advanced partners, it acts as a pilot enterprise, which transmits know-how to other producers, either local or foreign, and looks for subcontractors.

Just as every producer occupies a double position in the international division of labour, so does every individual country and, indeed, every economic community as a whole.

To take up Johnson's formulation in international trade,[1] products move both downstream, from more to less advanced countries, and upstream, from less to more advanced ones. In the first direction, goods with a high content of invention and innovation predominate; in the second, we mostly find products of imitation and of relatively low value-added.[2]

The countries whose products move downstream obtain certain advantages from the structure of their exports. This is usually expressed, though not altogether accurately, by a surplus in their trade balance. Exports upstream are less easy, for the weaker country's exports must overcome the quality barriers of the more advanced and more demanding market. This is why upstream exports are often associated with a trade balance in deficit.

A trade structure involving downstream exports (more advanced products, with high value-added and a high research content) seems, at first sight, the more advantageous. A structure with upstream exports seems less rational from the point of view of technical progress (products requiring less research,

[1] Harry G. Johnson, 'The Theory of International Trade', in *International Economic Relations, Proceedings of the Third Congress of the International Economic Association*, ed. Paul A. Samuelson (London: Macmillan, 1969), p. 62.
[2] A. I. Kirillov, 'Nekotorie faktory opredelyayouchtiche razvitie mejdunarodnoi torgovli machinami i oborudovaniem', Annex BIKI 8/1970, p. 28.

consumer goods). Nevertheless, even such exports may generate resources for the acquisition of new techniques and, thus, may become an important factor of economic balance, without which there can be no durable progress at all, whether economic or technical. Instead of comparing the economic effects of export structures as such, it may be more to the point sometimes to compare the effects of an export structure in a given territorial set of relationships with those of the import structure in the same setting.

To the extent that the world political situation improves, it creates propitious conditions for the process of integration, for co-operation on a broader scale and even with continuing differences between the countries' social systems and types of economic and social integration, for economic co-operation among all the countries of Europe. The members of the CMEA regard their integration process as an open one.

Comments
Dimitrios Delivanis (Greece)

Willgerodt's conclusions are that

(1) The various sectoral aspects of sectoral integration do not differ as much as it may seem at first sight';

(2) Sectoral integrations cannot be judged without considering the interdependence of all sectors of the economy';

(3) Some measures that seem to integrate particular sectors have the effect of disintegrating not only these sectors but others as well.

I propose, first, to insist on these three points with the help of Willgerodt's arguments, whilst adding my own comments; and, second, to develop the points on which I was not convinced by his paper.

(1) *'The various sectoral aspects of sectoral integration do not differ as much as it may seem at first sight.*

(a) Willgerodt stresses that those who hesitate to run the risk of surrendering national economic sovereignty entirely to a regional union may try to capture some advantages by carefully specified sectoral integration arrangements. I am afraid that the unforeseen consequences of the interdependence within the economy and the constant changes that the latter undergoes may prove very quickly that the arrangements reached do not secure the advantages foreseen, inasmuch as the old principle *pacta sunt servanda* is not always respected by the governments of the world.

(b) Willgerodt mentions that these sorts of arrangements have a greater importance whenever the interchange across borders increases. I submit, however, that when this happens their application will perhaps become very difficult, expensive and time-consuming, thus reducing the importance of the targets the attainment of which had been considered possible.

(c) Willgerodt refers to the international co-ordination of investments and is very objective in presenting the arguments, first, in favour of governmental interference and, second, in favour of settlement by the private businessmen involved. Let me stress how much I am, in this connection, in agreement with Willgerodt, inasmuch as in both cases results are far from being satisfactory for reasons that are well known. The continuous changes, within the economy and of the targets to be realised, have to be considered as the main factors of this unsatisfactory development.

(d) Willgerodt is once more right when he stresses the modest results achieved by the ECSC in directing investments financed through the capital market, and when he reminds us that foreign exchange control on capital movements is in force even now within the EEC, seventeen years after it started operating.

(e) Let me also agree with Willgerodt's sceptical remarks about the developments of the European Common agricultural market.

(2) *Sectoral integrations cannot be judged without considering the interdependence of all sectors of the economy.*

(a) Willgerodt stresses this point at the beginning of the paper, and refers to it twice again whilst mentioning the failure of the common agricultural market in the EEC and the probable danger of the different results of uniform tariff reductions, especially when the tariffs on different industries are not uniform at the outset. Let me add, however, that this has to be considered avoidable if tariff reductions really have to be carried out on a large scale and within a relatively short time. Experience all over the world attests to this.

(b) Willgerodt analyses very accurately how increased integration in one sector can cause a disintegration of other sectors if the sectoral balance of trade runs into deficit, or even if it does not. As a matter of fact, he is right in insisting that the factors of production available have a tendency to be attracted to the most developed sectors, and those are of course those where integration was considered possible and profitable for all involved.

(c) Willgerodt insists on the indirect effects of sectoral integration on sectors not yet integrated, and expects import to increase in non-integrated sectors, I should say owing to the scarcity of production factors as mentioned before.

(3) *Some measures that seem to integrate particular sectors have the effect of disintegrating not only these sectors but others as well.*

(a) I agree with Willgerodt regarding the difficulty of centralised planning in market economies when the government officials negotiating the allotment of industries to the member states are unable or unwilling to accept the locations that would allow the industries to be competitive in the long run. The distribution of industries among the integrating countries will not necessarily be in accordance with the long-run relations of comparative costs and advantages. It is well known that these considerations may be forgotten even where the integration process involves regions of a single country, and, thus, they will certainly not be decisive in international negotiations, even between the most friendly nations. Let us not forget that the degree of this friendship changes often and sometimes rapidly.

(b) The disintegrating consequences of the common agricultural market are simply mentioned but not analysed, most probably because they are considered well known.

I should like to end by referring to some differences I have with Willgerodt.

(a) On his opinion that some elements of the sectoral approach to economic unification can also be found in most plans to dismantle tariffs and quotas I think that this interpretation is too large, as tariff duties may change, may be undermined by monetary devaluation, may be neutralised by price changes and, last not least, may be combined with exchange control or quotas in both ways.

(b) On the idea that small countries may refuse integration if they are afraid that the large powers involved will take advantage of their strength to impose their will. This is, as far as I can judge, somewhat unrealistic. I am sorry to say that large powers may exert pressure on small countries whenever they so desire.

(c) On his belief that the alternative to heavy intervention by international concerted investment control is not *laissez faire* but some sort of market-oriented interventionism. This is rather obscure and I should appreciate hearing more on this. Let me add that Willgerodt has perhaps concentrated too much on the EEC case.

Opening Statement for Group Discussion
Victoria Curzon (Switzerland)

Static trade theory suggests that a sectoral approach to general integration would be unreliable, but that, if dynamic considerations are taken into account, it may under certain circumstances be pursued as an end in itself.

General integration between $n - 1$ countries is already a 'second-best' policy because it does not eliminate all market distortions: goods, services and factors move freely within the integrated area but not between the union and the rest of the world, thus causing interspatial distortions in the allocation of resources. Sectoral integration takes place when goods, services and factors move freely within a sector, but not between it and the rest of the economy. This suggests that intersectoral misallocation of resources is bound to occur. Sectoral integration practised by a group of countries thus gives rise not only to interspatial but also to intersectoral distortions in the allocation of resources.

Another drawback to sectoral integration is that it will be difficult to combine economic efficiency with political acceptability, if the latter implies that each member of the group will insist on an equal or proportionate share of industrial activity. One way of mitigating this problem would be to include as many sectors as there are members, and either plan their location in advance or let the market decide and hope for the best. Either way, the trade-off between political acceptability and economic efficiency is obvious.

The question then arises whether this 'basket' of sectors is to be composed of a series of sectors, integrated within themselves but not with each other, or whether the 'basket' is to be a 'super-sector' within which goods, services and factors move freely. If the former, intersectoral distortions will increase as extra sectors are included in the scheme; if the latter, intersectoral distortions will begin to diminish after a certain point, dwindling to zero as all sectors are gradually encompassed. Only in the latter sense could sectoral integration be viewed as a method of achieving general integration.

It is unlikely, however, that this approach to general economic integration would prove superior to the more widespread method of gradually lifting barriers to the movement of goods, services and factors across the board. Its main attraction for governments may well lie in the possibilities it offers for negotiating an *ex ante* intercountry distribution of integration benefits, on the assumption that the admittedly larger *ex post* benefits of general integration would not be fairly distributed amongst participants.

If general integation is not the desired objective, sectoral integration becomes an end in itself, from which countries may benefit under certain circumstances. If dynamic considerations are taken into account, it is possible that the gains from economies of scale and 'learning by doing', especially among small, previously autarkic countries, may outweigh the static losses from the interspatial and intersectoral misallocations of resources. Sectors offering appreciable scale economies will vary from group to group, depending on the size of the integrating area, the size of the constituent parties and the degree of pre-integration autarky. In Western Europe, for instance, only a few public sectors still offer large and as yet unexploited scale economies, while in many less developed areas other sectors in an intermediate range of products may provide scope for previously unexploited scale economies. The static losses due to the interspatial and intersectoral misallocations of resources should nevertheless be recognised and accounted for.

Report on Group Discussion
Josef Pajestka (Poland)

I.

What can be presented at the plenary sessions is a rather modest attempt at summarising in a few minutes a wide, rich, many-faceted and interesting discussion of the group. I certainly cannot do justice to all the views expressed and issues covered. The more so, since I wanted to take this opportunity to present my own views on certain problems, and these views may not be shared by other participants. One thing can be said about the discussion at the very outset. It helped in hammering out a rather wide and common understanding of the issues discussed. I mean by that the elimination of certain misunderstandings, the finding of a common language and common platform, and the clear definition of the real differences in conceptual approaches.

II.

A very interesting contribution was made by speakers who brought factual analysis and observations concerning specific sectors such as industry, agriculture and infrastructure.

It was a common opinion that infrastructure presents a field that is particularly promising for economic and other co-operation, be it within the integration groupings or within the wider co-operation schemes. It was indicated that the European rapprochement can profit much from co-operation in the various sectors of infrastructure. It was also stressed that co-operation in infrastructure is an important precondition for more intensive economic co-operation in many developing regions of the world.

A most lively discussion developed on the subject of integration in agriculture. Sceptical and critical views were expressed with respect to the progress of agricultural integration within the EEC. In criticising the failure of the concepts underlying agricultural integration, negative consequences of its protectionist assumptions were also stressed. Participants from the socialist countries did not seem to complain about the progress of their international co-operation in agriculture. For the developing countries, agricultural integration was still less in the forefront of their considerations for integration.

The real core of theoretical concepts and integration problems appeared in industrial co-operation, and it was felt that the crucial controversies around the types and strategies of integration are formulated with industrial integration in mind.

If my report on the discussion about integration in specific sectors is limited to just a few, superficial comments (which certainly do not reflect the real value of the discussion), this is because it seems justified, in the limited time available, to concentrate on issues of a more general nature that are of interest to the plenary session.

III.

The group's discussion was helped very much by the opening statement made by Victoria Curzon, who commented on the Willgerodt and Orlíček papers.

Let me indicate first one positive conclusion that we arrived at as a result of the discussion: that sectoral integration can be viewed in two different ways.

First, as an integration strategy in which sectoral integration is a way towards a general integration. For this case the problem consists of appraising whether, how and why the sectoral integration leads towards general integration. This understanding of sectoral integration seems rather widespread among Western economists and it was presented in Willgerodt's paper and Curzon's statement, both of which presented several very interesting arguments for and against the formulated integration strategy.

Second, as a sectoral aspect of any integration scheme, not necessarily presupposing any sequence of integration strategy. This way of looking at sectoral integration appears in the socialist countries and, in certain cases, in integration schemes in the developing world.

There was a lively but useful misunderstanding on that issue. Orlíček's paper presented the second view and was criticised from the standpoint of the first view. I say that the misunderstanding was useful because it led to a clear definition of the two ways of looking at sectoral integration. I felt that there was a widely shared opinion that sharp contradistinction of sectoral *versus* general integration was neither substantiated nor justified. In this respect, a view expressed by Delivanis was quite generally supported.

Throughout the discussion on sectoral integration several arguments were raised supporting its values and, even, its necessity.

(1) It was asserted that, with the growing need for long-run considerations and programming, sectoral co-operation brings about certain benefits that cannot be obtained otherwise. Participants from the socialist countries put particular emphasis on this point, giving many examples.

(2) It was maintained and substantiated that sectoral co-operation allows for better insight and control of the distribution of benefits within the integration scheme. This is particularly important for developing countries. The sectoral approach was also valued for special cases of high social and economic adjustment costs (for instance, in agriculture). It was also indicated, however, that special care should be taken regarding the impact of partial integration ventures on the balance of payments of individual countries.

(3) It was observed that there are certain specific sectors for which sectoral co-operation is especially suitable for technical, economic, and other reasons.

This discussion led to still another conclusion. The majority of participants favoured a wide and rather loose concept of integration of the type presented by Machlup in his Presidential Address, covering market integration, production integration and other measures aimed at adjusting the fabric of individual countries to the requirements of the international division of labour. It was also stressed that integration schemes necessarily require a long-run strategic approach. This point was particularly maintained by economists from the socialist countries.

IV.

In the discussion there were, however, differences of views that cannot be reduced to misunderstandings, since they reflect real differences in conceptual approaches. They are of a general nature and, therefore, I think it justified to bring them into consideration here.

The first view, rather widely held among the Western economists and heard very much during this conference, can be presented in a necessarily simplified formulation as follows: the play of the market forces, with limited interference from state and interstate organisations within large multinational areas is the *integration proper*, and everything else obstructs and disturbs the optimal integration. Hence, sectoral or any other partial integration can be only a second-best option.

The other, opposite view cannot, unfortunately, be presented in a very simple way, since it has to be substantiated. Let me present it first as my own view.

V.

It seems useful first to 'localise' somewhat the integration phenomena. Two comments seem relevant in this respect.

(1) Integration is not an aim in itself, but should rather be viewed as *instrumental* in relation to the objectives striven for by society.

(2) Integration belongs to the field of international, economic and political relations.

These two assertions being accepted, an important problem follows: what is the proper subject of any integration set-up? I submit that the subject is the *nation state* (and the national economy), which is the form in which most societies are organised and which they use to pursue their interests and aspirations. It is undeniable that nation states are principal subjects of international relations and, therefore, also of integration schemes.

Now, let me observe that, while volumes have been written on another subject and agent of economic activities — namely, the *firm* — and on the interactions of firms — that is, the *market* — rather little has been written on the subject of the nation state as an economic agent and on the system of international economic relations.

Let me also observe that, as is certainly well known here, the world is being confronted by dramatic challenges. Only recently, a Special Session of the United Nations called for a new world economic order. What is this about? As formulated by the politicians, it is about a new system of economic, international relations — more just and more equitable.

Let us now take up the problem of what the properties of just and equitable international relations should be. First we must ask how well economics is equipped, in its conceptual framework, to deal with this problem. Extremely poorly, in my opinion. It has not defined the national economy as a subject, a proper agent of economic relations, and has hardly touched the problem of equitable interactions among nation states. This is particularly true of those schools of thought in Western economics that stick to traditional neoclassical theories.

Now, what about the common-market model as the predominant and proper model of integration? I do not discuss its application to the developed capitalist economies, which is a separate problem. I discuss it as a theoretical and general model for international economic relations and, therefore, also for any integration scheme.

If applied in this way, the following argument seems appropriate. All of the market argumentation is based on the assumption of market-*cum*-equity.

We know, however, that the real situation is market-*cum*-disequity; and this is the crux of the matter. Market ideology for international relations may be an ideology for the strong against the poor.

What do the poor and weak have with which to defend themselves against the strong and economically aggressive rich? Not much more than state power. Let us not tell them that this is against theory, against optimum, against welfare. Let us also not tell them that they must get rid of this, the only powerful instrument they have, if they want to benefit from economic co-operation and integration.

While these are general observations, they are very relevant to the problem of sectoral integration. Utilisation of the state for the sake of protecting the interests of the poor and weak is fully justified and not against the theory. The theory should be adapted in order to incorporate the national economy as the proper subject of economic analysis and to open the way for elaboration of the principles of just and equitable international relations. When this is done, one should have no particular trouble in presenting in a theoretical manner the sectoral development integration that is engineered by way of international relations. This, in my opinion, is an urgent need, so much so that it seems desirable that the IEA should give serious consideration to this problem in its future activities.

While not all of this argumentation was accepted by all participants in the working group, one view seemed to be common. The armoury of economic theory must be revised to achieve the solution of the urgent problems of humanity — those of eliminating hunger and poverty, of establishing more equitable systems of international economic relations, and of introducing more rationality globally. This last need involves the theoretical concepts of economic integration.

To conclude with a personal opinion, I believe that, as regards the solution of crucial world problems, the theories of common-market integration, which are very much favoured by traditional Western economic thinking, are misleading. On the other hand, the approaches contained in the socialist principles are appropriate but require better theoretical presentation.

6 Industrial Policy: Location, Technology, Multinational Firms, Competition, and Integration of Product Markets (Main Paper, Working Group C)

Pierre Uri (FRANCE)

Integration does not rest on the assumption that the mere abolition of governmental barriers can create a perfect market. Price equalisation can be blocked so long as there are monopolies with powers of discrimination. Such monopolistic practices can be curbed only by governmental action. It follows that integration is possible only among countries whose governments can agree on common rules and common procedures of decision making. There may be differences of degree, as exemplified by the institutions of the EEC and the CMEA consultations; under looser arrangements, GATT has its own machinery of negotiation and arbitration for traiff reductions, and economic co-operation between East and West is framed by general intergovernmental agreements.

In these circumstances, traditional analytical instruments are of little use. Integration is essentially a dynamic process, by which it is hoped to diminish the obstacles to growth that derive from inefficiency and, to some extent, from the balance of payments. In addition, one should perhaps mention the political aim of reducing inequalities: this is justified by common usage, as a national economy with undue regional disparities is not considered truly integrated. In any event, whether integration comes about through market forces or through planning, it must stand the test of competition, failing which investment would prove to have been misdirected. The question here is how much time to allow, for, clearly, the first new job opportunities and nascent industries cannot be sacrificed at once.

For these reasons industrial policy is something that no country and, for that matter, no regional union can do without, for the very good reason that it takes so long for an investment project to be prepared, be carried out, and, then, produce its effects, that economic activity cannot rationally be governed by the market situation, competition and returns at any given moment. In other words, the *immediate* comparative advantage, as determined by relative prices at prevailing rates of exchange, must give way to *potential* comparative advantage. Not only are the relations of demand and of competition subject to dynamic change, but in addition a nascent industry is in a situation very different from the one it can look forward to once it has taken advantage both of economies of scale and of external economies.

Industrial policy may be explicit or implicit. In centrally planned economies it is, of course, explicit and, indeed, the expression of a fundamental choice. The Soviet Union has given priority to the development of heavy industry so as to hasten the use of modern technology in other industries, even if this has meant retarding their take-off or modernisation. The People's Republic of China, though it does have its own basic industries, went about it the other way round: it concentrated on the creation, or gradual development, of industries that used crude techniques but could get going quickly and could fit into the highly decentralised population pattern of China. In market economies, planning seldom encompasses the whole of industry. To take the example of France, which led the way by launching an economic plan immediately after the end of the Second World War, it will be recalled that this first plan formulated explicit targets for only a few basic sectors – coal and electricity, transport, steel, cement, and farm machinery. The urgent need at the time was the re-creation of resources that were still in short supply; later, as the scope of planning broadened, it became more loosely indicative. The most specific efforts were directed to the development of advanced industries like supersonic aircraft, nuclear reactors, and even rocket launchers and satellites. Sometimes the technical success of these ventures fell short of the hopes placed in them, or their commercial success failed to repay their cost. It is not hard to see why. An industrial policy must be a consistent whole; an appropriate sequence must be observed in creating industries, and a technological spurt is premature without a base of traditional industries sufficiently broad to collect the fall-out. In a sense, an implicit industrial policy like that of Germany, which encouraged investment rather than trying to direct it, generated progress on a more continuous front than did the more explicit policy of France or, to take an analogous example, that of Great Britain.

In advanced and in developing countries alike, industrial policies often have contradictory aims and make use of means that, far from reinforcing each other, often largely cancel one another.

One basic choice is that between allowing and restricting competition, both domestic and foreign. Yet, once the choice has been made, it is hardly ever followed through strictly. There are always branches of industry or individual firms that manage to obtain protection against fast decline. It would be hard to find a country that does not treat its textile or its footwear industry much as it treats its agriculture. Shelter against imports, tax privileges accorded by right or by usage to small enterprises, low-interest credit, official rescue operations when bankruptcy threatens – such measures are applied along with measures having the opposite effect: for instance, the concession of public funds or a generous depreciation allowance to large concerns and spearhead sectors.

The point at issue is not the principle of intervention designed to ease the establishment of one industry or to slow down another's decline. What does matter is whether the aids and protective measures are so applied that they can some day be diminished or dismantled, or whether the situation is likely to get out of hand after so much has been done to buttress uneconomic ventures, which may be a legacy of the past or, on the contrary, premature, so that there is no choice but to go on supporting them on a mounting scale. It is one thing, for instance, to allocate large public funds to research in new sectors where risks are too great to be assumed in full by private enterprise, and quite another thing indefinitely to prolong the life of obsolete forms of production or other kinds of business activity.

Even if the principle of domestic and foreign competition is upheld, there are two very different methods of giving effect to it. One of them does not shirk the harshness of the market. It relies on the optimistic assumption that the elimination of dead branches will lead to the more dynamic growth of other activities, which as a result will have access to an increased supply of manpower and of financial resources. This is what the British Conservative government gambled on. But it is a gamble that can come off only if full employment is maintained and if entrepreneurs are bold enough to invest on a large scale in new branches. These conditions are not easily met. If they are not, all that happens is that there is more unemployment and a rebellion of the workers, so that fresh impetus is added to the inflation that was to be contained by bringing down costs.

The other method is entirely different, but it requires a high degree of continuity and consistency. It looks to the future, but it smoothes the way to it. The idea is that it is not good enough to accept the old free-trade argument that consumers gain by being able to choose imported goods if they are cheaper. For most consumers are also producers, and the more advanced the economy is, the greater and more predominant will be the body of wage and salary earners in the working population. They cannot easily be persuaded that it is to their advantage to pay less for some goods, if a shift to imported supplies puts some of the labour force out of work. Without income there is no choice. And from the point of view of the economy as a whole, low-productivity employment is preferable to no employment at all, since its opportunity cost is nil. Thus, if the argument is to be convincing, it must be addressed to the producers as well. It must be restated in terms of the striking wage differentials between regions, between branches of industry, and even between firms within any one branch. In Western Europe, inter-branch differences in average wages range, at best, from 1 to 2, and in some countries from 1 to 3. Within any one branch, one firm may be paying one-third less than another, and in Japan only half as much.

A meaningful industrial policy, then, must aim at gradual structural change of a pattern that causes social inequalities. It must go to the root of things. Existing wage differentials can be diminished only by a combination of regional policy and the continuous conversion of ill-adapted branches and old-fashioned firms. But the difficulties are formidable, for they are often cumulative. Backward or distressed areas suffer not only from an excess of farm population, but also from the presence of declining industries headed by firms of the wrong structure. The development of social overhead capital or of temporary aids may help industry in disadvantaged regions to get off the ground or to recover, but only on the condition that, at the same time, dynamic firms take on the labour force made redundant by the disappearance of those that have to be closed down. Industrial policy requires the recycling both of manpower and of housing facilities. It is only when it is so conceived, with all of the implications, when it is clearly explained, and when it is accompanied by appropriate income guarantees in case of a change of employment, that industrial policy can count on the co-operation of the workers and their representatives. Only then does it have a chance – other than by scattered pay handouts, which are soon engulfed by inflation – to achieve a reduction of inequalities by gradual changes. In other words, industrial policy so understood is the mainspring of an effective social policy.

Another choice that industrial policy cannot evade, even if it does not always approach it consciously or with clearly defined ideas, is its attitude to domestic competition. Policy in this field effects the size of firms, the relation of large firms to small and medium-sized ones, and, in mixed economies, the dividing line between the public and the private sector. For a long time American industrial policy concerned itself only with the first of these aspects, without bothering about either regional balance or adjustment processes; it is only recently and grudgingly that it has followed the example of other countries in relying on public enterprise for the co-ordinated development of certain river basins, for atomic energy and for space travel. Without much enthusiasm, other advanced countries have recently begun to think about controlling industrial concentration, but in so doing they seem to be afflicted with a sort of schizophrenia leading, in some countries, to opposing efforts on the part of several different public authorities. Some are inclined to encourage mergers with a view to creating firms big enough to hold their own against large foreign concerns; tax facilities are granted to this end, or, sometimes, a public financial institution throws its weight into the balance by buying shares in a prospective merger situation. But in the same countries, and at the same time, other authorities may be trying to prevent the formation of dominant positions. Still others support small and medium-sized firms; not, indeed, in order to help them adjust, but merely to keep them alive, with the support of artificial props. Surely the only way out of such wild confusion is to set specific criteria. The advantages of scale are not the same at the level of production and at the level of marketing, and at the production level they do not always require firms to be growing, provided they are sufficiently specialised.

As regards the delimitation of a public sector, no country – other than those where it covers virtually the whole of the economy as a matter of principle – seems to have any definite theory about what to do with

industry in this respect. Sometimes firms get into the public sector more or
less by accident. In developing countries, full or partial nationalisation has
been applied especially to foreign firms — sometimes by way of reprisal,
but more often in order to regain control of natural resources and to stop
the outflow of funds by profit repatriation. In the industrial countries with
a market economy, an argument can be built for taking into the public
sector those industries the cost structure of which precludes price competition because marginal cost is lower than average costs. Other cases in point
are industries that are heavily dependent on government contracts — the
alternative being strict controls, as, for instance, in the United States — and
industries where research and development expenditure is so enormous and
so risky that it can be defrayed only by a government. Beyond that, there
are mainly two opposing lines of thought. According to one, all the largest
firms should be nationalised, even if they are well managed, while according
to the other they should be taken over only if their management is
incompetent. Another direction is that disposable public funds should
rather be used to set up public enterprises in sectors or regions where private
enterprise has failed to take hold or has left gaps in the industrial structure.
On the nationalisation issue, the British Labour Party is committed to the
first alternative, while the second appears in the joint programme of the
Left in France. The creation of new industries with public funds is a
characteristic feature of Italy's Industrial Reconstruction Institute. But
surely, from the point of view of employment, wage levels and external
balance, it is more effective to make good the gaps in existing structures or
to reorganise them then to take over firms whose productivity is already
high enough to pay decent wages.

Divergences are even more extreme in the matter of the movement of
factors of production, meaning not only labour and capital but also the
establishment of foreign firms at home or of domestic firms abroad. In some
countries growth is achieved with the help of immigrant labour, even if it
creates formidable problems of housing and social integration; in others, it
is thought that the domestic labour force can best be protected by closing
the door to foreign workers. For capital movements, there are no international rules at all. At one end of the scale there are countries that do
not seem to mind how much capital comes in or goes out, and at the other
end there are those that restrict movement in both directions. As regards
direct foreign investment, a country may change its attitude at various times.
Some industrial countries make a distinction between the establishment of
new firms and the takeover of existing ones; such a distinction is more
appropriate in developing countries, for they are often short of outside
capital and, in that case, foreign funds are better applied to the foundation of
new industries, even though, on occasion, there may be definite advantages
in reorganising existing firms. Sectoral discrimination is common in many
countries, even in the United States; but, barring considerations of national
defence, the logic of such discrimination is not always clear.

The net effect of policies that often lack internal consistency and, in any case, are divergent from one country to another is to enhance the bargaining power of multinational firms rather than to reinforce that of each country's government. It may well happen that one country is played off against another. The smaller and weaker a country is, the better is the chance that a foreign firm, whose contribution, as such, is welcome, will be able to obtain protection in the domestic market, tax concessions and subsidies, and perhaps even a guarantee of lasting monopoly by a ban on the establishment of competing firms of either domestic or foreign origin. And governments are likely to outbid each other all the more actively the more they feel that a new industry can provide a supply base for other markets. The point is that the effects on competition differ according to the manner in which trade is organised. Among CMEA countries, there are some that permit foreign firms to have a stake — admittedly, a minority one — in the capital of a joint company. The Soviet Union deals with multinational firms in a number of ways: it may order a factory design from them or even a complete plant, and pay cash; or it may arrange coproduction or compensation agreements leading to a settlement in goods; or it may pay royalties for manufacturing processes or fees for technical assistance. In a system where trade rests on *ad hoc* agreements rather than on a continuous flow of transactions based on relative prices, such disparate attitudes to multinational firms are of no consequence. This is not so in a system of regional integration governed by the market mechanism, where, indeed, divergent attitudes to multinationals produce certain assymetries. This has become only too obvious in the case of the EEC. It has so far proved impossible to work out any sort of common policy towards foreign firms. When one country tried to place restrictions on their entry, it was outflanked from bases elsewhere in the Community, and found itself importing goods made in factories set up outside, without even the benefit of local production and employment. When, on the other hand, some country or other has offered concessions in order to attract foreign firms, the process has tended to become cumulative. Similar asymmetries may well appear in developing countries. Countries reluctant to play host to multinational firms are weakened by those that welcome them most openly and on the most favourable conditions. It is only when a group of countries unite and thus hold out the hope of creating a really large market that a common policy towards multinationals has any chance of being applied successfully. This has been tried by the Andean group. It remains to be seen whether, by making some of its rules retroactive, the group did not go further than it meant to in discouraging the entry of new firms, for these may well fear that other rules they accept may be abrogated in the future. It also remains to be seen whether individual member countries will refrain from making excessive use of waivers.

One must conclude, regretfully, that the closer the markets communicate and the more widely industrial policies diverge, the more arbitrary the location of industries is likely to become, to the detriment of overall welfare.

Let us now see whether this conclusion can be modified in the light of the interrelations of corporate strategy and market integration.

Location choices may be influenced as much by the limitations on integrated markets as by their broadening. A firm may try to jump tariff barriers by installing itself inside the country that has put them up. But the strongest inducement is a large, yet protected, market. This situation is typical of the EEC. Multinational firms of foreign origin have been more successful in occupying this privileged economic space than have even the largest of their European competitors. The reason is simple enough. The newcomers had no particular ties with any one of the member countries, nor any traditional location, and therefore it was easier for them, from the outset, to think in terms of the common market as a whole. Their location decisions responded more flexibly to the regional decentralisation policies of national governments, and, most of all, they were quick to take advantage of such special facilities as any member state offered for development in the national territory or in any one particular region. Multinational firms were helped, of course, by the emergence of an international capital market in Euro-currencies, but, in any event, international investment nowadays no longer requires any actual transfer of funds, as it used to do. The United States applied exchange controls without openly calling that, and thereby drove American firms to raise funds locally, even though the resulting rise in interest rates threatened to cost America as much in short-term capital movements as it had hoped to gain for the balance of payments by reducing long-term transfers.

The next question is what effect the operations of multinational firms have on market integration. In this context it would be a mistake to consider them all in terms of a single, homogeneous model. The one thing that they do have in common is that affiliates of the same group are divided by a difference of principle from independent and competing firms. The latter need not worry about causing losses to others. But a group, to the extent that it really is capable of maximising overall profit, must make sure that what any one affiliate does occasions the least possible losses for others.

Beyond that, distinction has to be made between different types of multinational firms. First of all, there are those that process local resources for sale on the local market. The big food concerns are cases in point. In whatever country they have their factories, they import little and export little. If they do anything for integration, it is in respect not so much of product markets as of manufacturing processes, and even these need not be identical in all cases, but may vary as a function of factor proportions.

Apart from this special category, we may think of the integration effects of multinational firms in terms of two opposing models. The first is that of firms that manufacture components in several countries and assemble them in one of these or even in yet another. This method carries the international division of labour even further than perfect competition would do, for it is one of the assets of multinational firms that they possess a network in which information can circulate and can be exploited even more quickly than in an ideally transparent market. A variant of the integration model is that of a group that simultaneously turns out a differentiated range of end-products in different locations, each of these products being intended for sale on all markets.

By contrast with these models of organisation, there is the case of market-sharing by a group that manufactures comparable products in different locations. This means, in effect, that the group imposes private export restrictions on its subsidiaries or licensees. Such an arrangement may be necessary in certain cases in order to keep down overall costs – as, for instance, when the distribution of goods like motor cars requires an extensive network of after-sale services – but it can have highly distorting effects on the distribution of advantages among the host countries.

Another situation that departs very considerably from market conditions is vertical integration. This goes beyond the division among several countries of different stages of one product, from production of the raw material, through transformation, to actual sale to the end-users. As soon as one affiliate of a group supplies another with components, or with equipment for a manufacturing process, with research results, services or capital, the transfer prices may cease to have any relation at all with those that would correspond to transactions among independent firms. The internal structure of a group may be enough to occasion such distortions, because there is always a temptation to show profits for those affiliates in which the parent company has the highest stake, rather than for those in which it has a smaller or even a minority holding.

Yet, the fact remains that the most serious distortions result from the disparity of industrial policies in different countries, including their consequences for the tax treatment of various forms of capital rewards and for the exchange regulations that govern international remittance.

The haphazard tax concessions that are offered by industrial and by developing countries alike may well cancel each other, at least to some extent, and, in any case, lead to an inequitable distribution of tax burdens within each country. It would be more rational if the country where a multinational firm has its headquarters were to tax its worldwide consolidated profits, subject to deduction of any taxes paid to host countries. Under such a system there would be an inducement for developing countries to raise their tax rates to those current in advanced countries. Tax reliefs might be conceded by the home countries as part of a general programme of development aid, or as compensation for the initial disadvantages of settling in certain regions.

Market-sharing arrangements cannot be impeded by developing countries without the co-operation of industrial ones. The latter could, for instance, bar imports in the case of restrictive practices harmful to any particular developing country. In any event, multinational firms clearly create difficult problems for the control of industrial concentration. Either the home country takes action on its own, which leads to an extraterritorial application of its decisions, or else there would be no control at all, unless the principal countries to which multinational firms belong agree on joint principles and procedures.

The distinctions that have been made with regard to patterns of production help to identify certain typical cases of multinational firms selling, or applying, technologies that may be inappropriate in the country concerned. This happens when firms have the monopoly power to enforce the joint sale of useful processes as well as of some that are not immediately applicable. In the frequent case of vertical integration, the quest for decreasing costs may lead firms to multiply the application of some research result or of some type of machinery without the extra expense of adaptation. In most of the other situations discussed, multinational firms will probably tend to adjust their production methods to relative factor costs; if not, the fault lies not so much with economic calculation as with ingrained human habits.

But there is a more general difficulty that is hard to avoid. The presence of multinational firms may speed up economic growth, but in underdeveloped countries it almost inevitably increases inequalities. These firms offer more modern jobs, and certain social groups have more direct dealings with them or consume their products. Unless the host country spends the tax revenue from these firms, or, perhaps, a levy on their capacity to pay higher wages, in such a way as to spread more widely the benefits of their greater productivity, their presence may become a factor of internal disintegration.

This brief survey of the requirements to be met and of the obstacles to be overcome suggests certain lines that industrial policy should follow if it is to be conducive to integration both within any one country and on the regional or even international scale.

The link between industrial policy and financial and social policy has never been sufficiently stressed, even in industrial countries. The effort to raise the income of the poorest calls for more than gradual structural change in the direction of lifting the performance of different sectors and firms up to the level of the most productive among them. It is also necessary to adapt output to the demand that is thus called forth. Otherwise it may, for example, happen that a rise in the lowest wages pushes up the price of the good bought by the wage earners concerned. Production or imports may not be flexible enough to provide an answer to what must be seen as a primary source of inflation. The aim of planning must surely be to create incentives that speed up the adaptation of real resources to the intended change in the distribution of money incomes.

At the regional level, the dismantling of obstacles to trade among developed countries has worked well enough as regards established industries. But, as regards the more advanced industries yet to be created, co-operation has always come up against each individual country's insistence on obtaining for its producers the equivalent of its own financial contribution. Regional groupings of developing countries are all the less able to rely on the mere removal of obstacles, as there are fewer existing industries, or fewer opportunities for substituting new and more productive jobs for those made redundant by competition. Hence the complementarity agreements. But, even so, the fewer are the projects, the greater is the danger that countries will outbid each other for them, so that their distribution may lead to extra costs for activities in situations that are economically less than optimal.

At the international level, the tragedy of underdevelopment is a measure of the inadequacy of the ideas that have been applied and of the efforts that have been made so far. To be sure, economic theory has been enriched by the recognition of cumulative effects; the volume of investment, for instance, can be larger the higher are existing income levels, and, thus, the gap between countries widens. But when it comes to the overall distribution of aid, it really is hard to discover any sort of consistency. One might have thought that the poor countries would get the more aid per inhabitant the lower their incomes per capita. This has not been the case at all. Or, one might have hoped at least for some other logic, or for some reciprocal relation between financial flows and the rate of growth in recipient countries. Again, there is nothing of the kind.

There is a glaring gap in the analysis of income distribution among countries, just as in the theory of income distribution among individuals. The manifest division between earned income and inherited income is ignored by the models of pure theory and fully recognised only in nonconformist thinking. Similarly, we have to think in terms of the drag of history, and of the lingering effects, first of colonialism and then of *laissez faire* in trade and investment. All of these were bound to lead to unequal trade and to the geographical concentration of development.

Industrial policy has a major function to fulfil today. It is hardly conceivable, of course, to draw up a world plan for the allocation of industry. But it should be possible to hold a general line, with all that it implies. The growth of multinational firms has enhanced the mobility of capital and, also, of management, leaving labour as the sole immobile factor of production. This has simplified comparative advantages, which now rest not so much on factor proportions as on the wage–productivity ratio in each branch. It does not follow that all labour-intensive industries can, or should, be shifted gradually to developing countries. Many modern industries need a great deal of labour, but of a highly skilled kind; and, however high the wage level in advanced countries, unit costs may still be lower there. This is one of the bases for a division of labour. It gives a chance to the industrial policy of advanced countries to work to the joint benefit of their own labour force and of developing countries. To be consistent, acceptable and effective, such a policy must follow a combined, three-pronged approach: developing countries must be supplied with industrial finance; new markets must be opened up for their industrial products; and, at home, full employment must be coupled with generous adjustment aids so as to smooth the way to structural change.

Comments
Ryutaro Komiya (Japan)

I.

In his valuable and very comprehensive survey, Uri remarks that no country or regional union can do without industrial policy. For the purpose of the present discussion, which is largely confined to market economies, industrial policy may be defined as a system of government interventions with industries attempting to change the industrial pattern of resource allocation in order to achieve certain economic and noneconomic aims. In market economies, industrial policy is called for because of the presence, among other factors, of 'market failures'. Any of the causes of market failures (and among these causes are the existence of external economies or diseconomies, significant economies of scale causing the cost curve to decline over a wide range, the absence of the futures market for most commodities under uncertainty, and low interindustry or interregional mobility of labour in the short run) can be a valid reason for governmental interventions and planning, or even for establishing public enterprises in certain areas. Thus, from an economic point of view, it is necessary for the government to engage in an active industrial policy in certain areas because the market mechanism there fails to allocate resources in an efficient way.

Granted, then, that a wide variety of situations in the market economies call for an extensive industrial policy, it is important to recognise the great difficulties in formulating, implementing and administering an appropriate industrial policy. The market mechanism fails under certain circumstances, but the government or bureaucrats in charge of industrial policy not infrequently fail too. Or, we might say, industrial policy often fails to allocate resources in an efficient and/or socially appropriate way.

Coming from a country that has developed a very extensive and elaborate system of industrial policies, I can enumerate difficulties associated with industrial policy in a market economy.

First, policy makers may not be able to predict the future correctly or to evaluate the effects of policy measures properly, and because of this may make wrong decisions. Under the market mechanism, competing firms usually hold different expectations regarding the future, and those firms that predict better than others prosper over the long run. Industrial policy and planning always involve a certain degree of centralisation of prediction and judgement, and this may lead to the danger of putting all the eggs in the wrong basket. Moreover, policy makers who have made a wrong decision are often able to shirk their responsibility, because there is always something they can blame.

Second, since there is always a group of people who benefit, often substantially, from a particular policy, that policy tends to build up vested interests. The interest groups put pressure on the government to pursue a policy that is favourable to them but that may be socially inequitable and/or detrimental to the national interests.

Third, policy makers themselves often have an interest in pursuing a particular industrial policy. Government bureaucrats are subject to Parkinson's law of unlimited expansion and ramification and usually prefer extending government authorities. This is one of the reasons why government interventions in a particular industry tend to be maintained much longer than is justified.

Fourth, extensive government interventions obviously suppress individual initiatives. In the short run, concentration of power in the hands of industrial policy makers may be an expedient for immediate gains, but it may work to impair the energy, creativity and initiatives of the private sector, and could be detrimental to economic and social development over the long run.

It is most important, then, that some scheme should be devised to review and revise the industrial policy at frequent intervals, to disengage the government from excessive intervention, to eliminate policy makers responsible for wrong decisions, and to avoid undue concentration of power.

II.

Uri points out the possibility of conflicts between industrial policy and competition policy. If the extent of intervention under an industrial policy is limited and only moderate, or if indirect policy measures such as tariffs or taxes are used, the conflicts may not become too serious. But, if a more active and extensive policy is adopted and if the government attempts to carry out industry-wide, rigid planning, conflicts are bound to arise. In fact, in Japan the Ministry of International Trade and Industry (in charge of industrial policy) and the Fair Trade Commission (in charge of competition policy) have often been opposed to each other.

The encouragement of mergers and co-operation among firms within an industry, with a view to improving the competitiveness of national firms *vis-à-vis* foreign ones is obviously in contradiction to anti-concentration policy. Government directions or guidelines on production, investment and pricing, whether in an industry dominated by few firms or in an industry in which many small or medium-sized firms operate, are incompatible with maintaining competition among firms. It must therefore be asked, what are possible criteria for minimising conflicts and avoiding confusion?

When a protective industrial policy aims at establishing a new industry within a country, or at renovating an old one, there should be a reasonably fair prospect that the industry will be able to stand on its own within a specific time period. The policy should be based upon evaluation of the long-run, if not immediate, comparative advantage. Protection over a prolonged period without a prospect of its being removed is generally not conducive to national interests. Thus the license, so to speak, of protection and of extensive government regulation of an industry should be issued only for a limited time period, except when the purpose is a noneconomic one.

Although it would be necessary to restrict imports or foreign direct investment and to limit the extent of competition among national firms during the period of the extensive industrial policy, the government should maintain at least some degree of competition between national and foreign firms. If national firms are very heavily protected against competition from abroad or from foreign direct investment, and if domestic prices are out of line with international levels, there would not be much hope that industry would soon be able to stand by itself without protection. During the period of protection, national firms need to earn profits, since they must expand their capacity in order to reach minimum size to enjoy those economies of scale that often are essential in establishing the industry. But the dividend payments and the level of wages and salaries should be regulated, because otherwise the benefits from protection and from restricted competition may be partly dissipated.

III.

Co-ordination of the industrial policies of countries participating in a regional integration scheme should be highly beneficial. In many of the industries in which an extensive industrial policy is called for, economies of scale are a strategic factor in successful industrial development. If an industry in its early stage of development can have an integrated regional market instead of just a national one as its base, it would be easier for it to establish itself. Also, in negotiating with multinational corporations on their prospective investment projects, the member countries can improve their bargaining position by adopting a joint policy and negotiating on a regional level.

As a matter of fact, however, even the EEC, the most advanced regional union in the world, has had little success in co-ordinating its members' national industrial policies or their policies towards direct foreign investment. It is important, then, to ask why the co-ordination of national industrial policies is so difficult.

First, the member countries usually have different views on the future outlook of industrial development and it would not be easy for them to agree on which industries in which countries should be protected and by what policy measures.

Second, the intraregional co-ordination of industrial policy is a non-zero sum, n-person game, and there may be a serious opposition of interests with regard to the distribution of industries under a co-ordinated or integrated industrial policy. An active industrial policy within a regional union usually means greater international division of labour among the members, and the countries may not be able to agree on the pattern of intraregional specialisation, especially where 'strategic' industries are involved. It is possible that some countries gain much while others gain little, or even lose under a certain arrangement. Or, a member country may benefit from adopting a liberal policy towards inward direct investment when all others maintain much less liberal policies. It may be pointed out here that the game—theoretic aspects are also present in the case of the national industrial policy, with some regions within a country gaining and others losing; but on the national level there are various redistributive mechanisms at work redressing the imbalance — for example, through public finance or through mobility of labour and other factors of production. Such redistributive mechanisms are either absent or much weaker in the case of the regional union.

Third, as pointed out above, even within a country there are opposing views on industrial policy, and many difficult problems are left largely unresolved. It would be more difficult to solve these problems on the regional level. As in the case of France and West Germany, even countries that are more or less the same size, have the same per capita income and are at approximately the same stage of industrial development may have considerably different traditions on industrial policy. The relationship between government and industry may vary considerably from one country to another. Certain types of intervention that are acceptable in one country may not be acceptable in other countries.

These considerations suggest that attempts to pursue a co-ordinated, intra-regional industrial policy may encounter much greater difficulties than are involved in a national industrial policy.

Comments
Nuno Fidelino de Figueiredo (Brazil)

Let me focus my comments on some issues that are intimately related to a basic question for Latin American industrial policy: namely, the possible criteria for the location of industries in the context of economic integration.

Our starting point must be the recognition of an existing tendency for 'uneven' location of industries throughout the Latin American region. In very few words, it can be generalised (neglecting, of course, numerous discrepant particular cases, related either to specific industries or particular countries) as follows.

(1) In the discontinuous-process industries — for instance, the mechanical and engineering, textiles, wood, leather and plastic transformation industries — that contributed to the initiation of the industrialisation process in Latin America, and in which a less elaborate technology prevails, there would probably be no pronounced tendencies for locational concentration in a particular country or countries. Concentration would exist, but would favour the existing main urban centres of each country.

(2) In the discontinuous-process industries that are more demanding in terms of technology and market size (mainly those industries involved in the production of capital goods) there would most probably be a tendency for strong and progressive concentration of production in the larger countries and, within these countries, in the most mature existing urban and industrial centres. This is because of the external economies prevalent in this type of industrial activity.

(3) As regards those continuous-process industries that in general are greatly dependent upon some basic natural resource, either as raw material or as a source of energy, we have to distinguish two cases, depending on whether the geographical distribution of the basic resource is more or is less extended throughout the integration region. In the case of a more extended geographical distribution of the resource (and a good example is the iron-ore/steel industry), there would be a tendency for industrial-location patterns of a relatively even nature, following the availability of the basic resource and the minimum economic size of industrial operation. In this case, the costs of transportation would play a very important role, favouring local transformation of raw materials and therefore a wide geographical spread of industry. Alternatively, in the case of a more concentrated distribution of the basic resource, the resulting location pattern of the industry — assuming there is no interference in the interplay of market forces — would necessarily be one of high concentration. Typical examples are offered by the wide range of industries based on oil. The tendencies throughout Latin America towards a 'disequilibrium' pattern of industrial development, following the elimination of tariff and nontariff trade barriers, should be more accentuated in the relatively less developed countries, which suffer from four important disadvantages: the limited size of their domestic markets; the comparative newness of their industrial environment; their less rich and varied endowment of natural resources; and (in some cases) their unfavourable geographical situation in relation to potential regional and extraregional markets for their products.

One conclusion to be drawn from the preceding ideas is the need, from the point of view of the political feasibility of any proposed regional integration scheme, for some degree of 'interference' with free competition, to push the regional location of industries towards a desired goal. What goal should be considered and what kinds of 'interference' would be instrumental for its achievement? In other words, by what ways and means could we accomplish some 'regionalisation' of instruments throughout Latin America? More precisely, what criteria should be adopted to select and orient the (public and private) industrial investments of participating countries?

As a first approach, I think we would all agree in favouring a regional extension of the criterion of private profitability applied in a national context. The investments should be directed towards locations in which the private profitability of capital would be maximised – or, alternatively, in which the unit costs of products would be minimised, this being a social criterion that coincides with the preceding private one in all cases where a situation of free competition is present. In a national context, the locational pattern of industrial activity results from the incidence of factors such as transportation costs of inputs and outputs, cost of communications between the firm and the market, as well as external economies and diseconomies. The incidence of such factors is evaluated and weighed by private and public entrepreneurs, modified by different policies and, in particular, by instruments of economic policy deliberately manipulated to redirect development in certain desired ways.

The regionalisation of the decision process, initially found in a national context, therefore requires not only the elimination of all obstacles to the free movement of goods, but also the free transfer within the region of enterprise and capital (and also of labour, but this is not relevant for the present argument). It also requires that there be a consensus among all participants regarding the promotional goals that modify the cost–benefit balance accepted by the entrepreneurs as a framework for their investment decisions and selection of corresponding investment locations. Out of these three conditions for the regionalisation of industrial-location criteria, the third one – the necessity for all the participating countries to be substantially in agreement about the ways of influencing in any different direction the spontaneous process of location – is, from my point of view, by far the most difficult to fulfil. In relation to this, let us for the sake of brevity consider not the possible regional objectives for supporting the industrial development of the smaller Latin American countries that are reasonably well endowed (here, I believe, less difficult obstacles arise), but the case of the impediments to a regional investment policy that originate in the desire of each and every country for 'industrial balance' (which means different things to different countries). How can we find criteria that are rational and objective and that can be actually and reasonably automatically applied – most probably by regional authorities having some degree of supra-national power of decision – in relation to national goals and objectives differing from one national economy to another? This is especially difficult as it requires comprehension and adoption of the value-system of any given country, together with participation in the complex socio-political system of national decision-making.

Value-systems differ from country to country, reflecting dissimilar situations with regard to levels of development, social structure, national cultural inheritance, and so forth. As a consequence, the pattern of allocation of resources considered socially desirable also differs between countries.

Let us take as examples Argentina and Brazil, which differ substantially from each other as regards GNP per capita, population growth, and the ratio between population and natural resources. It could be expected that the value-system of Argentina would reflect a relative predominance of goals such as internal and external stabilisation of the economy, while Brazil would be more sensitive to goals and national objectives related to the acceleration of capital formation and the rate of growth of the economy as a whole. How do we find a common denominator or, in other words, formulate regional criteria for the allocation of capital resources in Latin America such that both national positions can be satisfied? This example, in my opinion, suggests the extreme difficulty of determining a 'social welfare function' of a regional (Latin American) character, from which to derive criteria for the regional allocation of resources. This happens not only because of the empirical task involved, but also because such a welfare function would be meaningful as an instrument for economic policy only if at least some measure of political integration had been attained. This is clearly demonstrated if one calls attention to the mutual relationship between the allocation of capital resources and the need to compensate any imbalances among the Latin American countries (imbalances produced by the application of the economic criteria based on the free play of market forces), by way of redistributing income among the countries through appropriate fiscal policies. This would amount to applying to the different member countries of a regional group the same kind of balancing (redistributing) policies as most sovereign countries apply through their fiscal and monetary agencies to their own provinces (or to particular areas) when these are on too-divergent economic levels. Is this transposition to the supranational regional level of policies commonly practised within a national economy feasible in the foreseeable future? I think different attitudes towards the problem of regional economic integration in Latin America flow in large measure from different answers to this basic question.

Opening Statement for Group Discussion
Péter Veress (Hungary)

The task of our working group is to investigate the relations between industrial policy and integration.

The study by Uri reflects a thorough knowledge of the subject. It presents the major issues that we have to discuss. The scope of ideas has been further widened by the contribution of Ryutaro Komiya.

Industrial policy may be helped by integration, primarily the implementation of the objectives of various branches. Although in our age the branch objectives of industrial development differ according to the level of economic advancement and the political and social aims of countries or groups of countries, efforts at developing the energy and basic, material-producing branches, at developing the food economy and infrastructure, and, in general, at adapting up-to-date technology are generally similar.

In the medium run, the emergence of several integration groups is a necessity. Should they operate in isolation from each other or set up in unhealthy competition with each other, they may become sources of considerable tension. We ought to examine whether co-operation, or at least the development of a healthy competition, can be insured among the various integration groups.

To the extent that integration makes possible the free movement of capital and, more so, of labour, it may contribute to implementing the regional employment targets of industrial policy, mainly in solving the employment problems of border areas.

Industrial policy may considerably determine what form of integration should develop: vertical integration, where the phases of production are built upon each other, or horizontal integration, which relies on parallel development and production. The endowments and level of development of the member countries may also determine whether vertical or horizontal integration is desirable.

The interrelation of politics and the economy has never been felt so strongly as in our days. The steady process of the development of various kinds of integration may be encouraged or hindered by the political objectives of the individual countries.

It is also well known that the specific systems of economic control and management are not homogeneous, even in countries with identical socioeconomic systems, and the economic mechanisms themselves do not uniformly affect the development of integration either. If the national political will is 'negative', it may render the economic problems more acute; if, however, policy is favourable to the integration process, it may help in bridging tensions due to divergent economic mechanisms.

The improvement of international relations, *détente*, may reduce the political elements — for instance, the armaments race — that distort economic progress and the order of economic values and may have a favourable effect on the rational expansion of the international division of labour both among countries with different socio-economic systems and among those with identical ones. The assertion of an opposing political process diminishes the chances for economic co-operation among countries with different social systems.

In some countries industrial policy is implemented within the framework of a

planned economy, while in others it is implemented within the context of a
market economy.

We, in the socialist countries, believe that a planned economy provides a
better foundation for the implementation of integration. It is, however, well
known that indirect methods — for instance, price and tax policies — also
play an important role in the economic systems of countries with planned
economies. At the same time, efforts at planning can be observed in market
economies. Joining the integration process is necessary for both socio-
economic systems, but there may be differences in setting the specific goals.

In market-economy countries, tensions emerging from the problem of
realisation become the compelling power, while in countries relying on
planned and proportionate development the need to increase the efficiency
of production and to secure harmonious development necessitates more intensive participation in up-to-date forms of international division of labour.
Thus, the question is whether the evolution of integration is prompted by the
desire to accelerate development or by the pressure to remove existing
tensions.

The more comprehensive and the greater the role of the government-operat
industry in an economy, the easier it is to implement the central ideas in the
development of integration. In the socialist countries, the co-ordination of
economic-development objectives and the harmonisation of economy-wide
and individual-branch plans, has resulted in rapid development, and today the
bulk of the socialist countries have advanced industries.

In the process of integration, large corporations of increasingly multinational nature have a determining importance. In market economies, an ever-
closer intertwining of the integration process with the multinationals can be
seen. Views concerning the activities of such multinational corporations differ
strongly. According to some, they may even hinder the implementation of the
goals of industrial policy in certain countries. In our view, the activities of the
multinational firms should be judged according to the following criteria:

- do they promote a healthy structural development of the economies of the
  nations concerned?
- to what extent do they promote a rational, international division of labour?
- do they cause economic and political tensions within individual countries
  or among nations?
- do their oversized dimensions have a paralysing effect on the freedom of
  action of the national governments?
- how do they serve East–West political and economic *rapprochement*?
- what is their effect on the economic and political progress of developing
  countries?

This last criterion is particularly important.

Is it a rule that large corporations, as carriers of integration, are necessarily
of a multinational nature, and is it possible for the co-ordinated activities of
large national firms to substitute for the multinationals? In what cases is it
expedient to create joint ventures or to make efforts at bringing about cartels

In the long run, and in the framework of integration, will small and mediu
sized enterprises restrict themselves to servicing activities, or will they perhaps
join the integration process by performing work for large enterprises by mean

of 'subcontracting'?

For us socialist economists and economic leaders, examination of the activities of multinationals still depends on mainly insufficient information. We have no detailed knowledge and, therefore, cannot formulate a comprehensive opinion about them. There can be no doubt, however, that in the course of the evolution of the economic integration of socialist countries there will emerge enterprises in whose activities several socialist countries will be interested. But joint enterprises founded by socialist countries come about by the will of national governments, serve common interests and, hence, cannot be regarded as equivalents of the multinational firms that operate in the market economies, manage their enterprises according to their own optimum criteria, and may even come into conflict with local social interests. Some joint socialist enterprises have lately been created, but not enough time has elapsed for a fair evaluation of their activities to be possible.

I believe that the questions raised are among the vital topics of our age, and successful discussion in this working group may enrich not only economics, but may also prove helpful to governments in their economic policy decisions and to the appropriate international organisations in arriving at adequate recommendations.

Report on Group Discussion
Harry G. Johnson (UK)

The topic of our group's discussion was the broadly defined one of 'industrial policy: location, technology, multinational firms, competition, and the integration of product markets'. As a result of this rather lengthy menu, our session attracted a great deal of interest, and I consider myself fortunate to have had two co-chairmen, Gatovsky and Cravinho, to share the burden of maintaining an orderly discussion. In fact, such was the pressure of demand from the floor for speaking time, that we used all our allotted time, and to use it fairly were obliged to use the last afternoon for brief presentation of the contributed papers. I mention this since I shall not attempt to summarise that part of the discussion, other than to record that it included a number of contributors who, in greater detail than was possible in the general discussion, made points that were probably of greater enduring interest to the minority who are engaged in concentrated study of the problems in particular areas, countries, or fields of economic interest.

I ought to call attention to one of the central characteristics of the group's discussion — a characteristic that showed itself in a certain identification of approach and topical interest with the country or region to which the particular speaker belonged. One of the subjects included on the agenda, namely the multinational firm, tended to run away with the discussion. There was to some extent an uneasy tug-of-war between concentration on the multinational firm and concentration on the more general concept of industrial policy as such.

The general question of industrial policy involves a division of interest and approach among economists by country-type of origin, in the sense that for the socialist countries 'industrial policy' is basically *planning policy*. For the less developed countries — and to make matters more difficult still, this includes both some smaller socialist countries and some nonsocialist countries, in which planning and competition are mixed in different proportions — 'industrial policy' is *industrialisation* and *development* policy. For the advanced Western countries, 'industrial policy' is an aspiration to outguess the market competition process in deciding what *new technologies* will be socially the most profitable to develop, in order to remain 'advanced'. Much of the discussion on this general strand of economic theory and policy failed to achieve a meeting of minds, because the problem as seen by the advanced-country economists (most of whom were preoccupied by disappointment with the way policy has recently gone in the EEC) is very difficult to understand as a real problem for economists whose minds are used to the much more comprehensive, and in one important sense non-nationalistic, concepts of socialist planning. In addition, there was considerable disagreement among the Western economists who took up the problem of whether conventional concepts of 'competition' *versus* 'planning' properly defined the policy choice. Specifically, when Uri emphasised the point that all advanced countries use a mixture of both competition and planning, at least one contributor pointed to the importance of recognising what he called 'quasi-*non*-governmental institutions' — the use of planning arrangements that are independent of both governments and private enterprise, most noticeably in the field of price control and, more generally, of anti-inflation policy.

If the problem of mutual understanding posed by (country-type or regional) differences in basic conceptions is serious with respect to broad industrial policy, it is even more so with respect to multinational corporations, both because these entities fit quite differently into different systems of formulating, and thinking about national economic and, specifically, industrial policy, and because national experiences and scientific research and thinking about them are at vastly different stages in different countries. There is also a distinct difference, cutting across the broad division between 'socialist' and 'capitalist' economic systems, between small countries and large ones, with the small countries tending to feel especially nervous about the implications of the activities of multinational firms for their national sovereignty and autonomy. There is yet another difference within the small countries, between those that feel comfortable, or at least familiar, with Western corporate enterprise (originally almost exclusively countries of British settlement but now including Japan and various East Asian countries of Chinese cultural affiliation) and those that are dominated by fears of corporate enterprise (in particular this group includes the Latin American countries, whose origin is European, but pre-modern-industrial European).

The result of these wide differences in conception, which are understandable in terms of economic history and international politics, is that economists think that when they talk about the multinational corporation they are all discussing the same animal, when they are not really talking about the same animal at all, or are talking about the same animal at different stages of its life. Thus, the papers and discussion by economists in the non-USSR socialist countries tended to discuss the multinational corporation as if it represented the iniquitous system of capitalism in all of its early-nineteenth-century ugliness. By contrast, the USSR representatives tended to take the view that the multinational firm is a fact of life that a large, industrially advanced country has to deal with, and can deal with, so long as it knows what it is doing. The papers and comments from some of the nonsocialist less developed countries also seemed often to rely more on lively imagination or on cautionary anecdotes and horror stories than on the scientific assessment of quantitative evidence in the light of rational economic analysis of profit maximisation subject to constraints. This was particularly true of the vexed issue of 'transfer pricing', where – as is often true elsewhere in economic policy analysis – it is often assumed, quite wrongly, that the institutional power to fix prices somehow removes the economic constraints that make a particular choice of price optimal, thus leaving an economic vacuum to be filled by the commentator's worst imaginings.

Understandably, therefore, there was considerable behind-the-scenes dissatisfaction (eventually expressed by an Australian speaker) with the failure of most of the commentators to be aware of, and to have learned from the very large volume of scientific research material and theoretical and empirical findings accumulated by economists in such countries as Australia and Canada – and also, one may add, the United Kingdom – where the political problems of investment by the multinational firm have been present for a long time, and where the large amount of serious scientific research on the subject has cumulated into a quite different view of the problem from that that has characterised

European discussions.

In conclusion, I must confess that it is extraordinarily difficult to summarise a discussion so wide-ranging in content, and so lively that it took three co-chairmen to maintain a semblance of control. But the purpose of a working group of this kind is more to stimulate the minds of those present than to produce a coherent set of conclusions for those not present, and I hope that we shall all leave Budapest with new ideas that will gradually coalesce into subsequent writing, lecturing, and research endeavours.

7 Migration and Integration of Labour Markets (Main Paper, Working Group D)

Kosta Mihailović (YUGOSLAVIA)

I. INTRODUCTORY

Within the broad scope suggested by the topic assigned to this working group, I shall focus my attention on migration problems of the EEC.

An analysis of the relationship between economic integration and migration is of course, expected, to deal with both migration within and migration into the Community. However, as regards the last decade, these two kinds of migration are hardly comparable, either in terms of size, or in terms of effects or tendencies. While immigration into the EEC expanded rapidly during this period, intra-Community migration became negligible, despite the overall progress in integration. Between 1962 and 1972 there was a net increase in intra-Community migration of only 138,000 workers. This was roughly equal to a reduction in the number of migrants from the EEC working in Switzerland (137,000). Full employment and the similarity of socio-economic structures provided little incentive for international migration among the EEC countries.

The effects of the free-movement of labour from outside on intra-Community migration thus appeared to be more than modest. Considering its limited scope, it is difficult, if not impossible, to evaluate its impact on national product, productivity and capital formation, as well as on efficiency and factor-price equalisation. In view of these facts, this paper will be directed only to the analysis of immigration from other countries.

II. IMMIGRATION FROM OTHER COUNTRIES

A rapid increase in migration from Southern Europe to the EEC countries was a consequence of the coincidence of several factors. The integration process within the EEC was accompanied by growing protectionism, while expanding production faced serious limitations in foreign trade. The balance-of-payments deficits of South European countries was an obstacle to their own development and a barrier to exports from the EEC countries. On the surface, the insufficient import of goods into the EEC from the Southern European countries has been gradually offset by the import of a labour force, providing from their remittances additional purchasing power in Southern Europe and at the same time scope for further economic expansion in the EEC. The most immediate cause was an increasing demand for labour, under conditions of full employment, in the EEC countries — a demand that was met by an unlimited supply of labour from South European countries. The problem was, however, of a more fundamental nature and cannot be explained by short-range factors only. It also involved structural differences relating to the level of economic development and the accompanying population characteristics.

The growth of migration in the decade 1962–72 was really impressive.[1] The number of migrant workers in the six EEC countries in 1962 was slightly above 1 million, while in 1972 it reached more than 3·5 million (see Table 1). One might assume that the constant growth of immigration into EEC countries during the last fifteen years would not have been possible unless there had been favourable economic effects. However, these effects are difficult to measure with scientific accuracy. Given the unreliability of data on the number of foreign workers, it is hopeless to look for such information as the contribution of foreign workers to the national product or even the amount of wages paid. One of the few quantitative estimates published in the *International Migration Review* concerns Switzerland, but the situation it depicts may to some extent be analogous to the situation prevailing in the EEC countries:

Thus approximative calculations were made in Switzerland between 1964 and 1970. They show that the increase of five per cent per year of the national product is due for half to the increase of foreign labour. During this period, the activities of the migrants is said to have led to an increase of the national income amounting to 2·340 millions of Swiss francs. The wages paid to this labour have been of 800 millions. Who has benefit of the super income?[2]

It is unfortunate that no explanation was given of the method used in reaching these figures. Because of that, the above-mentioned data must be taken with caution, but the contribution of immigrants to the increase in national product and capital formation is not in doubt. Using the tools of neoclassical analysis, Gallais-Hamonno and Bourguignon show that by increasing foreign labour (the stock of capital assumed to be constant) domestic production rises. As a consequence of the fuller use of capital and labour the wage rate declines. Different effects on production and distribution

---

[1] Since the United Kingdom, Denmark and Ireland have only recently entered the EEC, this paper deals with the growth of immigration in the six original countries.

[2] 'The World Conference of Labour and Migration Questions', in *International Migration Review*, VII (Centre for Migration Studies, 1973), pp. 298–9.

TABLE 1

FOREIGN WORKERS IN SOME EUROPEAN COUNTRIES

	1962	*1972*	*Index (1962= 100)*	*Increment 1972– 1962*	*Percentage of EEC immigration 1962 1972*	
Belgium	137,959[a]*	199,611[b]	145	61,652	74·0	64·1
From EEC	102,154	127,962	125	25,808		
France	1,073,820*	1,770,000†	165	696,180	35·1	14·3
From EEC	376,880*	252,249†	67	−124,631		
West Germany	655,463*	2,316,980	353	1,661,517	32·7	24·0
From EEC	345,447	555,992	161	210,545		
Netherlands	32,000*	99,800†	312	67,800	45·6	20·5
From EEC	14,600	20,500[d]	140	5,900		
Luxembourg	22,400*	40,900*	183	18,500	89·3	68·9
From EEC	20,000	28,200	141	8,200		
Italy	1,102*	44,030[a]*	3,995	42,928	60·6	29·6
From EEC	668	13,052	1,953	12,384		
Total immigration (six countries)	1,922,744	4,471,321	233	2,548,577	44·7	22·3
Total immigration from within EEC	859,749	997,955	116	138,206		
Switzerland	644,706*	648,985*	101	4,279	85·4	63·8
From EEC	550,870	413,803	75	−137,067		
Austria	13,100*	186,465*	1,423	173,365	25·2	1·8
From EEC	3,298	3,294	100	−4		
Sweden	121,747*	229,656[c]*	189	107,909	14·8	6 8
From EEC	18,034	15,583	86	−2,451		
Total immigration (nine countries)	2,702,297	5,536,427	205	2,834,130	53·0	25·8
Total immigration from EEC countries	1,431,951	1,430,641	100	−1,310		

Notes:

[a]1961. [b]1971. [c]1973.
[d]This figure includes workers working in the EEC for more than five years.

Sources:

*Heinz Werner, 'Freizügigkeit der Arbeitskräfte und die Wanderungsbewegung in den Ländern der europäischen Gemeinschaft', offprint from *Mitteilungen* (Stuttgart: Kohlbammer, 1973), statistical supplement.
†Commission des Commonautés européennes, *La Libre circulation de la main d'oeuvre et les marches du travail dans la CEE – 1972* (June 1972).

lead to higher profit.[3]

The lack of data does not allow one to estimate precisely the contribution of immigrants to national product and capital formation. But, even if this were possible, the estimate of direct effects would be insufficient. Indirect effects and social gains must also be taken in account. Perhaps the most important of these is the possibility of using a capital-saving model for the purpose of expanding production under conditions of full employment. It is based on an increase in employment in branches with a low elasticity of substitution of labour by capital. Increased production in those branches enables capital to be moved to propulsive branches where the elasticity of substitution is high, and so makes it possible for production to be increased in these other branches as well. This model, called by Böhning 'capital widening',[4] allows, in the short run, for a rapid expansion of production by importing a foreign labour force, which means meeting an increase in demand while reducing risk. The high flexibility of such a model makes short-term combinations with foreign labour feasible.

While the model appears to be consistent, there is nevertheless the question of whether the shifts of capital are geared to those industries that can ensure an optimal technological progress. There seems to be a strong tendency, for one reason or another, to proceed with the traditional labour-intensive industries. Most of these industries cannot face the present and future competition of developing countries unless they import foreign labour. Travis is right in saying that 'the richer countries clearly view migration as an adjunct of customs policy in rescuing labour-intensive and inefficient industries'.[5] But, in so doing, the labour receiving countries raise obstacles to their further technological progress. The utility of labour immigration thus appears meagre, both as a long-range proposition and from the point of view of the national economy as a whole.

Indeed, the role of foreign workers must be assessed within the context of the entire economic structure. Without them, production in many branches would stop, with implications in connected branches and in the entire economy. Some key branches such as mining, construction and car manufacture rely heavily on foreign workers. On the other hand, immigration tends to extend the effective demand on the markets of the receiving countries, thus giving an additional impetus to production, especially in branches that produce goods of low elasticity. Mass production of low quality goods can also progress, owing to a high demand for such goods by

[3] G. Gallais-Hamonno and F. Bourguignon, 'Migration of Manpower versus Migration of Capital — A Cost-Benefit Analysis from the Standpoint of the Developed Countries', CICRED Conference (Buenos Aires, Mar 1974), mimeo.
[4] W. R. Böhning, *The Migration of Workers in the United Kingdom and the European Community* (London: Oxford University Press, 1972).
[5] W. P. Travis, 'The Relationship among the International Movements of Workers, Capital and Goods', Seminar of Demographic Research in Relation to International Migration (Buenos Aires, Mar 1974), mimeo.

migrants. Finally, some very old and depreciated housing is used thanks only to the immigrants' readiness to save on rents.

The financial effects of migration are perplexing, obscure and difficult to understand fully. The major part of the migrants' remittances is used by the governments of the countries of emigration to cover their balance-of-payments deficits, mostly with the countries of immigration. However, a large proportion of immigrant workers do not make any remittances home, but save their earnings locally, thus contributing to the savings of immigration countries. Moreover, it is uncertain whether the migrants get social services, such as health, education and housing, equivalent to their payment of income tax. As far as the human and financial investment in the upbringing of an adult migrant is concerned, there is no doubt that it is an important contribution to the immigration country. There are different opinions as to what extent this investment is compensated, at what level of skill, and with regard to the length of employment abroad.

As far as factor-price equalisation is concerned, immigration has produced no effects within the EEC. Peters shows that relative differences in nominal wages among various countries in the period 1961–70 remained virtually unchanged, but that in absolute terms there was a sharp increase.[6] Even after correction for differences in the cost of living – which, as a rule, is high where wages are high – the differences in nominal wages were not notably reduced. An analysis of EEC statistics for the period 1958–71 gives the same picture, although the growth in absolute differences appears smaller (see Table 2).

According to an earlier EEC study,[7] which gives statistical series on average wages for the period 1955–65, at 1958 prices, Italy recorded the highest relative wage increase of all member countries (index 180), which means that differences between the countries with the highest and lowest wages had narrowed. However, equalisation assumes that the growth rate is in reverse proportion to wage level and that all members of the Community are included. Such a trend could not be demonstrated. West Germany, for instance, was a close second to Italy in the growth index (169) even though it is one of the most advanced countries. But nothing can illustrate the equalisation trend better than the fact that the gross hourly wages in West Germany and France were at equal levels in 1958, while in 1971 they were higher, in West Germany, by 40 per cent.

---

[6] About gross hourly wages for some Community countries, see A. Peters, 'Die wirtschaftlichen und politischen Verhältnisse in der Bundesrepublik als Determinanten für die Wahl des Ziellandes', in *Die Ausländer in der Bundesrepublik Deutschland: Jahresarbeitstagung der Deutschen Gesellschaft für Bevölkerungswissenschaft* (Taunus, Apr 1972).

[7] Commission des Communautés européennes, *Critère à la base de la fixation des salaires et problèmes qui y sont liés pour une politique des salaires et des revenus* (Bruxelles, 1967).

TABLE 2

INDUSTRIAL GROSS HOURLY EARNINGS (US DOLLARS) IN SIX
EEC COUNTRIES 1958–71

	Year	Belgium	West Germany	France	Italy	Luxembourg	Neth lands
Industrial	1957[a]	0·85	0·78	0·76	0·65	1·12	0·67
workers	1971[b]	2·55	2·82	2·00	2·28	2·59	2·60
Index (country with highest wages = 100)	1958	76	70	68	58	100	60
	1971	90	100	71	81	92	92
Absolute	1958	−0·27	−0·34	−0·36	−0·47	–	−0·45
difference	1971	−0·27	–	−0·82	−0·54	−0·23	−0·22

[a] = Estimated figures
[b] = Estimated on the basis of statistics from 1960.

Source:
Expose sur l'évolution de la situation sociale dans la Communauté en 1972
(Bruxelles–Luxembourg, Feb 1973).

III. THE WORKING OF MIGRATION

Any discussion of the economic aspects of migration must keep in mind
that the entrepreneur acts as the initiator of immigration with profit
maximisation as a motive. With economic integration within the EEC, a
chance for additional expansion of production has been created – a
challenge to the entrepreneur's ability in mobilising the factors of production.
Owing to the fact that manpower has gradually become the most scarce
factor, the entrepreneur must mobilise it under the conditions of full
employment at home. The labour force supply was ample in South
European countries, and the entrepreneur took advantage of that by
recruiting migrant workers.

The role of migrant workers in capital formation is twofold; direct and
indirect. On the one hand, immigrants are particularly easy prey for
direct exploitation. Not only do migrant workers take the difficult or
lower-paid jobs, but, in addition, they tend to take those jobs that are
typical of large-scale and semiautomated industries and are monotonous in
the extreme. The strike, in August 1973, of Turkish workers in the Ford
factory in Cologne, when one of their main demands was for the assembly
line to be slowed down, shows the intensity of work required of foreign
workers, who are predominantly young and male, more prone to

conformism in their capacity as 'guests', and preoccupied with earning as much as possible. Moreover, they themselves often impose a work rhythm that is faster than domestic workers would like. The entire system of labour recruitment — including an unlimited supply of foreign labour, regulation of the workers' status, difficulties in obtaining work and residence permits, and the threat of being laid off — not only encourages conformism but also makes it possible to screen immigrants very closely and be further selective of them.

On the other hand, foreign workers exert pressure on the wage levels of the labour market of the host country. The massive numbers of foreign workers make it possible for wages to be relatively lowered, even when immigrants are not in direct competition with domestic workers. The pressure is, of course, much greater when there is direct competition. Immigrant workers who counteract the scarcity of labour make it possible for wages to be maintained at a lower level, while keeping profits at a higher level.

A consequence of the twofold role of immigrant workers in the formation of capital is the dual character of the labour force and the labour market. The phenomenon has always existed, but gained a larger dimension by immigration. In addition to women, who often are paid less than are men in the Community countries, there are significant groups who are discriminated against in the labour market, among whom immigrant workers are very prominent. Thus, instead of, or along with, coloured workers, immigrants, in the majority of cases, fall into the category of disadvantaged groups.

The employment of migrants in unattractive and lower-paid jobs holds true for all parts of the labour market. An analysis of the jobs held by immigrants shows that there is at least one discriminatory factor, if not several such factors, in operation. According to an EEC Commission, some 50 per cent of the workers from non-Community countries in 1971 were employed in construction, metal-processing and textile industries. The jobs in each of these three branches have many features that make them undesirable and discriminatory. And, as Nikolinakos so acutely pointed out, 'discrimination is the ideology of exploitation'.[8]

In addition to its economic implications, the dual character of the labour force also has wide social and political implications. Whereas the entrepreneurs continue to insist on differences within the working class, the trade unions have repeatedly pleaded for integration, homogeneity and solidarity of the working class, irrespective of country of origin.

IV. MIGRATION-INDUCED PROBLEMS

The compliance of the governments of the EEC countries with the employers' approach to migration can be seen in their designation of these workers as

[8] M. Nikolinakos, 'Germany — The Economics of Discrimination', in *Race Today*, III, no. 11 (London, 1971) pp. 372 and 374.

'guest workers'. As a rule, governments make no provision for the families of migrant workers or for additional public spending to expand infrastructure and public services. Workers from sending countries 'go abroad to work' to earn as much money as possible and as fast as possible, in order to achieve some specific private goals. In hopes of forestalling assimilation, governments of the sending countries foster the idea that their workers have gone abroad only temporarily.

The treatment of migration as a temporary phenomenon has served to accentuate all of the short-run primary effects. Viewed in this light, labour migration appears to be the sole possible, if not even optimal, answer for all those concerned. In conditions of full employment, employers see their chance to expand production by using immigrant labour and, thus, maximising profits. The governments of the receiving countries see an opportunity to increase their national product by importing a scarce factor. The workers get a job or a higher wage. Convinced that they have no better alternatives, the governments of the sending countries regard emigration not only as a source of hard currency but also as a way of easing social tensions.

Although the intentions and goals have remained the same, as have the original propensities of those involved, immigration has changed in the course of time. These changes have been caused by the 'maturing' of migration in a 'self-feeding' process, to use Böhning's terminology.[9] As foreign workers began systematically to prolong their stay abroad, the number of married immigrants and of those living together with their families grew. As of 1972, 30 per cent of the foreign workers in West Germany had been living there for more than seven years. Of the total foreign labour force, 74 per cent were married men and 68 per cent were married women. Of the total number of married men, 62 per cent lived with their wives in West Germany, and 92 per cent of the married women lived with their husbands. Perhaps nothing is so indicative as the rise in the number of immigrant children. In West Germany in 1972 there were some 950,000 immigrant children who had been born since 1956.[10]

These problems could no longer remain simply the affair of immigrants. But recognition of the problem implies a change in the economic premises on which the employment of foreign labour is based, and means construction of housing, schools and hospitals for the immigrants and their families. The huge costs of the infrastructure, which may not be postponed any more, have forced the governments of immigrant countries to accept a more active policy of immigration instead of their passive support for the entrepreneurs

[9] Böhning, *The Migration of Workers.*
[10] Source: *Repräsentativ-Untersuchung 72 – Beschäftigung ausländischer Arbeitnehmer* (Nuremberg: Bundesanstalt für Arbeit, Nov 1973). As far as it is known, this survey is the only one of its kind that has been made in the EEC countries. Because of its comprehensiveness, it has been widely used by the author in preparing this paper. It is a fortunate coincidence that the survey was made in West Germany, which is a large and typical country for immigration.

employing the migrant workers. In West Germany, the government has taxed employers DM 1000 for every newly employed foreign worker. This can be regarded as payment for the social costs being caused by entrepreneurs, who had not previously been charged for them. However, this could also be understood as a measure against the employment of new foreign workers. The illegal employment of foreign workers has not been allowed, although it has been tolerated. Nowadays there is rigorous insistance on legal employment according to bilateral agreements. Even before the oil crisis, West Germany decided to stop further increase of immigrants.

All this points out that the effects of immigration have to be reinvestigated in the light of new trends, especially because of the mass nature of the phenomenon. So far, it is not only a question of the huge costs involved in providing the necessary infrastructure, construction of which was initially neglected, but also a question of the high rate of growth of tertiary activities. Because of that the secondary sector has become a subject of long-term import in relation to the foreign labour force. It seems that conflicts between economic gains and social losses are increasing all the time. We should not be too sure that the EEC countries will not follow Switzerland's example in sacrificing some economic gains by introducing a restrictive immigration policy for the sake of maintaining social and cultural standards.

Concerning the emigration countries, the problems are more difficult. Sending countries are torn between a fear of the socio-economic implications of the exodus of their young workers (who, because of pressures on them to assimilate, may stop remitting money home), and the fear that a recession may cause these workers to return. Workers' remittances, as a means to cover a balance-of-payments deficit, are the only clear gain from emigration for the sending countries. However, there comes a question of how long this can be taken into account in the light of prolonged stay, marriage or delayed return home from abroad. The export of labour is a compensation for the insufficient export of commodities, but in the long run such an orientation obviously is dubious. The trouble is that emigration countries have adjusted their finances to income from remittances, which are not then used for creating new jobs. In the meantime, there has been the failure of some other myths, such as the myth of returning home, the myth of acquiring higher qualifications to be beneficially used after coming back home, and the myth that the consumption habits of emigrants will increase the exports of sending countries.

Migration has had many (and some unexpected) social and economic consequences. For example, there is its effect on the age structure of the population; the assimilation problem; the problem of responsibility for the families of the migrants; and the problem of declining agricultural production in areas affected by large-scale emigration. Despite unemployment, it is very difficult to find manpower for mining or similar jobs. As a result, the sending countries of Southern Europe have in the meantime become receiving countries for immigrants from North Africa. In addition, emigrants are faced with a whole complex of difficulties in advanced countries. The feeling of being discriminated against is the inevitable result of poor living conditions, ghettos, social insecurity, lack of support from social and family ties, the red tape of a bureaucracy that seems indifferent because one does not know the language, insufficient integration into society as a result of all this, and so on.

V. TO MOVE THE PEOPLE TO THE JOB OR THE JOB TO THE PEOPLE

The economic and social problems attendant upon migration are obviously formidable both in the EEC and in the South European sending countries. They indicate that migration has exceeded its optimum. Both groups of countries are now making efforts to reduce labour movements to reasonable proportions. Being without real choice, the sending countries have a very difficult task in that respect. The protectionist policy of the EEC against imports of goods from third countries is the cause of a degree of migration that is higher than it would be under the conditions of free commodity exchange. In a situation where labour and commodity exchanges are not accorded the same treatment, it is not possible, from the standpoint of the sending countries, to show whether the scales tip in favour of exporting factors of production or in favour of trade; nor is it possible to determine the justification of the volume of immigration or of investment abroad.

In any case, the possibility that sending countries will take steps to influence the size of emigration is negligible. These countries would have the power to stop emigration but are unlikely to exercise it. Emigration is a substitute for exporting commodities. It is difficult to object to the policy of remedying a balance-of-payments deficit by exporting labour when it seems impossible to develop alternative exports. Sending countries cannot withstand the pressure of this deficit, and fear far-reaching repercussions on their economic development and stability.

Receiving countries have looked upon immigration as a temporary and limited phenomenon and have attempted to justify it with theoretical rationalisations based on assumptions about factor-price equalisation and with implications for the equalisation of incomes, specialisation and the more efficient utilisation of resources. However, it has rapidly become evident that these assumptions rest on a faulty assessment of the nature and duration of migration. Instead of equalisation within the Community, there has been a polarisation of development in West Germany, accompanied by a polarisation of immigration. The consequences of this have been relatively higher wage increases in that country. There is an obvious discrepancy between theory and reality, and this gives rise to much confusion and a large number of open questions.

Any attempt to solve the basic migration questions must first tackle the dilemma of whether to move the people to the job or the job to the people. The starting point here is the fact that industrialised receiving countries make the decision on whether to allow immigration, while firms decide about investing capital abroad. The important question that arises here is, what are the chances that firms will give preference to investing in sending countries rather than to importing manpower?

It should be clear from this paper that migration into the EEC has been at least partly responsible for high rates of profit. This statement does not run counter to the empirical fact that the EEC is the most attractive area for new investment, not only for firms in the member countries, but also for American companies and, most recently, even for the developing countries. A slight share of Community capital has been invested abroad, and of this the United States has taken a good slice. A consideration of the possibilities for replacing immigration with investment in sending countries must begin with existing preferentials, among which profits play a crucial role. Private firms will invest abroad rather than at home if they can earn larger, or at least equal, profits, provided that the social and political risk is minimal and that they can transfer their profits. These provisos are not so easy to fulfil in the countries of investment. Institutional changes are always possible in the long run, and investments are, by nature, long term.

It is realistic to assume that, in many cases, profits could be higher in the emigration countries than in the developed-capital exporting countries. Lower wages because of lower cost of living allow higher profits. To complicate matters, however, large-scale emigration may cause the foreign investor to be faced with a need to pay higher wages, or with the need to make additional investments to substitute capital for labour. In either case, profits drop below the expected level.

There is the further consideration that firms from the advanced countries may not invest in sending countries simply because the latter are providing manpower. The opposite may be argued to equal effect; namely, if investment in sending countries noticeably reduces the supply of manpower, wages will rise and profits will diminish in the receiving countries — unless, of course, there is an unlimited supply of labour. Investment abroad and immigration are often unrelated, being merely two autonomous areas for the action of capital. On the other hand, substitution is not always possible. Substitution of labour by capital may be impeded if a large portion of the immigrant and domestic labour force are noncompeting groups.

In view of all these considerations, it is unlikely that a firm would invest abroad and, thus, forgo the security of institutional conditions, freedom of transferring capital and profits, and the stimulants of the large Community market, just for equal profits. Profits would have to be higher in order to offset these impediments. The allocation of capital into investment abroad and investment at home in order to maximise profits gives to the former a relatively small share. However, even apart from the above-mentioned obstacles, experience to date has shown that capital tends to invest in the developed countries and in large cities. In the present circumstances, capital is reluctant to enter not only developing countries or less developed Southern

Europe, but even the less developed regions of the advanced West European countries. There is no complete answer to why this is so, but, obviously, such behaviour and its consequences on migratory movements must be taken in account.

Viewed from this angle, the probabilities are slight that firms in the immigration countries would make any substantial investment abroad in order to mitigate labour migration. It would seem that self-regulating substitution, in which companies play the key role, could not give an optimal balance between the two alternatives, since it gives immigration a clear advantage. It seems appropriate, therefore, that governments should encourage entrepreneurs to export capital and to cut down immigration. But, there are strong reasons why governments may hesitate to move in this direction. Gallais-Hamonno and Bourguignon hold the opinion that the hesitation of governments may be supported by uncertainties relative to the following issues. Would investment abroad adversely affect the growth rate and, if so, how much effort would be needed to offset it? Are sending countries compelled to restructure industrial production if they invest abroad? How high are the profit taxes levied by the country where the investment is made? Would the receiving countries be prepared to import goods that they are now exporting, at the risk of upsetting their balance of payments?[11]

But, despite all the uncertainties, governments should take action that would induce entrepreneurs to give appropriate consideration to all kinds of externalities relating to migration. Greater government influence could open new possibilities for a comprehensive labour-migration policy to replace the present short-run approach as an historical alternative. A deeper insight into the reality of integration and immigration requires theoretical thinking to concentrate on structural relationships, with due account for social and humanitarian considerations. Such a solution would seem to promise further co-operation between sending and receiving countries.

From the standpoint of structural changes, the international division of labour is the most important. In the past, traditional labour-intensive industry in the advanced countries of Western Europe has served as the driving force in development by altering the predominantly agricultural structure of the economy. However, in this process it has exhausted its forces. In the face of the low wages in those branches — a scarcity of labour and the high social cost of concentration — it is hard to find a good argument, besides protectionism, for prolonging the life of this type of industry. However, labour-intensive branches in sending countries with large pools of unemployed labour could develop generating forces and, by a change in structure, could increase labour productivity, as has happened in the past in the advanced Western Countries.

Clearly, there is now a call for a new, more adequate international division of labour. The EEC countries actually have only capital as an abundant factor

[11] Gallais-Hamonno and Bourguignon, 'Migration of Manpower'.

of production. Their real chance lies in capital-intensive industries. Such a division of labour would, of course, be no basis for long-term specialisation in less developed countries, and factor endowment must be viewed as a historical category. However, such a division would spur a greater commodity exchange and reduce migration to a reasonable level, provided that the import of capital were stepped up at the same time.

Coproduction could take on a very important role if the sending countries were to manufacture those products that require more labour input. Such cases can be found in practice. The international coproduction in the CMEA has been established on principles of specialisation as the cornerstones of integrational processes. This type of co-operation, which diverges from the classical notion of international trade, is better served by planned economies, although it is also practised by firms in EEC countries in their relations with third countries. This possibility is especially attractive for two reasons: on the one hand, the wealth of forms of co-operation provides a high degree of flexibility; and, on the other, the division of labour tends to minimise migratory movements. At present it is difficult to say what the outlook is for such co-operation between the EEC and third countries, even though it has become accepted.

VI. FINAL COMMENTS

The recent experience of the EEC with regard to immigration from third countries reveals two salient points. First, the original assumptions relative to the nature and role of international migration have not proved adequate. Second, theories underlying the migration policies of all partners concerned, with *laissez faire* in their background, can neither explain the reality nor offer optimal solutions. Thus, a fundamental reconsideration of the true character of international migration is needed, to take into account its structural nature and its effects on the economic development of both sending and receiving countries. Such a reconsideration would first of all call for a thorough re-examination of the existing theories, which may find better inspiration in the theory of economic development than in the theory of international trade. It would also call for more sophisticated research and for better statistics, as well as for continuous co-operation among the countries concerned while they formulate and reformulate policies at every stage of development.

Comments
Hilde Wander (Federal Republic Germany)

Mihailovic's paper centres around two basic questions: (1) has liberalisation
of migration within the EEC induced more intensive movements among
member countries; and (2) what were the effects of immigration from third
countries? From statistics and other information, he finds that, despite the
heavy influx of workers from outside the Community, mobility among
member countries has hardly increased, and neither extra- nor intra-
Community migration has been supporting regional economic integration.
The latter fact is reflected, *inter alia*, in the progressive concentration of
labour and capital, in the persistence of wide discrepancies in wage levels,
employment conditions and labour productivity, and in the evolution of dual
labour markets.

In appraising and supplementing Mihailovic's analysis I shall take a
slightly different approach by asking: (1) could one actually expect a material
rise in migration among member countries as a consequence of the removal of
legal barriers, considering the complicated functions of modern labour
migration; and (2) given the multiplicity of flows, the conflicting interests
involved and the different political and institutional settings, what are the
conditions permitting labour migration to promote regional integration? To
answer these questions I shall separate 'Labour exchange among highly
developed economies' from 'migration from less to highly developed
economies'. Such a distinction emphasises the qualitative aspects of migration,
and not only the quantitative ones. It also implies a rejection of neoclassical
theory as a suitable instrument for explaining the economic effects of
migration.

Numbers aside, the multiway exchange of workers of different skills conforms more to the needs of industrial labour markets than does the one way
flows of unskilled labour from less developed regions. Internationally, it represents
an extension of internal labour mobility and implies more productive utilisation of scarce manpower within a wider economic combine; hence, closer regional and functional integration. By contrast, immigration of unskilled labour
is in essence the continuation of internal rural-urban migration, which should
decline with progressive integration. It immediately increases the workforce
of the receiving countries, but not necessarily its efficiency.

Considering the comparatively high share of skilled personnel among migrants from industrialised countries, the slight upturn of intra-Community
migration (excluding Italy) may have contributed more to regional integration
than the statistics suggest. I agree, however, with Mihailović that liberalisation
of migration as such did not provide much incentive. Since motives, objectives
and patterns of migration differ with the migrants' occupation and skills, the
removal of formal barriers was insufficient to stimulate international labour
exchange. While recent improvements in education and training may have
favoured the desire to migrate, prevailing differences in training systems, skill
requirements, employment services and social security schemes in the EEC
tend to bar its realisation. That such and similar factors (for instance, language)
hamper mobility of skills is suggested by the fact that Austrians in the Federal
Republic of Germany, who are less liable to such obstacles, clearly outnumber

the total of migrants from EEC countries other than Italy. Better utilisation of the Community's skill potential would require effective harmonisation of training, guidance, employment and pension systems, along with measures that make the immigrants competitive to the native workforce rather substitutive.

True, regional wage differentials are powerful incentives. Yet, disregarding whether one agrees with Mihailović that on average they were too small to inspire intra-Community migration, one must not forget that the threshold at which such differentials become potent differs for the various groups of workers. More important, expected wage increase is only one among many factors motivating migration. The higher the levels of education, skills and living standards, the more weight is given to prospects for social upgrading, satisfactory working conditions, education opportunities for the children and many other conveniences that may or may not immediately correspond with higher wages. Surely, migrants strive for optimal economic advantage, and it is the most progressive areas that attract the greatest number of them. But such a generalisation implies neither consonant individual behaviour nor conformity with overall economic and social needs. Detailed knowledge is required for explaining the variegated pattern, functions and consequences of modern labour migration.

Slackening migration from underdeveloped regions and the progressive concentration of labour and capital in the urban industrial centres are conspicuous examples of the wide gap between economic and social 'optima'. even under conditions of free factor movement as prevailing in national economies. Many areas are depressed not because of insufficient out-migration, but, rather, because of a continuous loss of skills, which in turn discourages capital investment. Remaining pools of unemployed manpower often consist of workers who are unable to migrate. If such conditions have evolved within the liberal setting of individual countries, how could the removal of legal migration barriers bring about a better redistribution of labour in the EEC? In the case of southern Italy, which is comparatively rich in labour, the recent slowdown in emigration to Community countries corresponds closely to better local employment outlets and declining demographic trends. Moreover, competition with non-Community migrants has become harder. Freedom of movement implies the loss of certain advantages that migrants from third countries are often granted in their working contracts.

There is thus no spontaneity in the relationship between free factor movement and economic integration. Since this already holds true for highly developed competitive markets, it applies even more to differently developed, imperfect economies. In geographical respects, labour and capital are never fully exchangeable, nor does either factor induce development *per se*. Emigration affects all segments of the sending economy, but in a variegated rather than in a fixed manner, depending upon the specific structure of the outflow and the prevailing economic, social and demographic conditions. As for capital, it is the composition that counts, along with its amount. Moreover, migrants and capital investors respond to different incentives. The countries supplying most of the migrants are, generally, not the same ones as attract most capital. On the contrary, the 'self-feeding' mechanism[1] innate in the oneway migration from countries of chronic labour surplus to countries of labour shortage tends to support progressive capital formation in the receiving, rather than in the

[1] See Böhning, *The Migration of Workers, the European Community* pp. 54 ff.

sending, economies.

Nevertheless, this does not suggest that stricter control of migration would be advisable. Apart from direct improvement in the balance of payments brought about by the workers' remittances, emigration — as well as its back-flow — carries important potential advantages for the sending countries in terms of reduced pressure on the labour market, increased per capita income, higher savings and improved work experience. These advantages must be realised by an active economic policy suitable to lead the additional funds and skills into productive channels. Outflow of surplus labour alone is not enough to defeat the chronic shortage of jobs: sufficiently rewarding investment and employment outlets must be opened to utilise the productive potentials of those who remain and of those who return.

With this in mind, I consider it inappropriate to view emigration and the import of foreign capital as alternative strategies for promoting economic development. The gains to be derived from either movement are highly inter-dependent, a fact that rejects the conception of simple choice between 'moving people to the jobs or the jobs to the people', disregarding whether this is understood in a rigorous or in a more flexible sense. 'The golden mean between the two extremes' to which Mihailović refers implies close functional correspondence between the flows of labour and capital and requires adjust-ment of respective structures in the first instance.

With rising capital investment and a higher demand for skills in the sending countries, labour migration will eventually decline in volume, but this does not imply that it will lose importance. On the contrary, it will more and more turn from a oneway into a multiway flow, which is better suited to support regional economic integration. A final solution to the migration problems would therefore depend very much upon the strategies that the sending countries apply to develop their economies. But it is also true that these countries are in a weak position to adjust the flows of labour and capital according to their specific development goals.

From this angle I agree with Mihailović that regional economic integration requires close co-operation among sending and receiving countries, based upon long-term perspectives of growth rather than on short-term labour needs. Such co-operation should not be restricted to the economic sphere, but should be extended to all relevant social and educational fields as well. But I do not see that this would require 'greater government control' over immigration and investment abroad on the part of the receiving countries, if this is meant as direct, unilateral intervention. Rather than controlling the flows immediately government policy should aim at implementing measures and promoting con-ditions that make labour and capital movements better responsive to develop-ment objectives that are mutually accepted and pursued by the sending and receiving countries. Immediate control over migration creates isolated effects in either the one or the other partner country and is not suited to promote regional integration. To minimise migratory movements is no end, *per se*, if the combined interests of all the countries concerned are taken into considera-tion. Such reduction should result, rather, from a change in the occupational and skill structure of labour demand as brought about by spreading develop-ment over a wider geographical area.

Comments
Giorgio Basevi (Italy)

I.

The previous discussant has already presented a brief summary of the two main problems to which Mihailović addresses himself in his contribution, and of the answers he finds. In trying to distil the essence of these problems I shall rather comment on the choice of questions that he makes, look for additional aspects of these problems, and examine the methodology that he uses in giving answers to the chosen questions.

II.

While the two main questions posed by Mihailović were probably the most immediate ones to be asked in a paper on migration and integration of labour markets, it is doubtful whether they go to the heart of the problem. It seems to me that, aside from the objective of political unification, which was at least initially important in integrating the EEC countries, the economic driving forces behind the integration process have mainly been those that are behind capitalist economies in general; namely, the pursuit of profit and, subsidiary to it, of economic growth. From this point of view, asking (1) whether the greater mobility of the labour force resulted in greater intra-Community movements, and (2) what the nature is of the relationships between immigration from EEC countries and immigration from nonmember countries, is, at best, asking proximate questions with respect to the more fundamental one (which, at worst, they may even hide) of whether the greater mobility of the labour force, from both within and outside the EEC, has affected positively the profit and growth rates in EEC countries. This unifying question, it seems to me, may help in answering the subsidiary ones regarding the relationship between product and factor movements, between labour migration and capital movements, and the various degrees of these mobilities within and outside the EEC countries. Indeed, whether one or the other of these movements has taken place may be appreciated and explained with regard to the effect it has had, by itself and relative to the other movements, on the profit and growth rates.

That the questions asked by Mihailović are proximate ones is demonstrated, here and there, in his paper, particularly when he discusses the nature of the relationships between immigration from EEC countries and immigration from nonmember countries. Here he asserts that, by keeping domestic wages down in the sector toward which they moved, extra-EEC immigration allowed for larger profits than would have been possible without this action. Very perceptively, he also points out that, through the use of cheap labour from third countries, the EEC has been able to delay the change in comparative advantage that would indicate the shift of labour-intensive industries to less developed countries. Thus, labour immigration from extra-EEC countries has been a form of protectionism against less developed countries (possibly the same ones from which labour has come). It then would be natural to emphasise that, since this was of no advantage to the domestic workers in the protected sector (whose wages were kept relatively low by immigration), it must have been of advantage to capital employed in these sectors and, possibly, to increasing the overall profit rate.

Again, Mihailović comes near to looking at the problem from this unifying point of view when at the end of the paper he suggests widening the analysis to the question of the choice between moving 'the people to the job or the job to the people'. He does not pursue this line very far, and it is a pity, since, it seems to me, in answering this question the fundamental role played by profit would have come to the surface.

III.

The choice of proximate, if not elusive, questions relative to the fundamental ones explains why Mihailović neither makes full use of the theoretical apparatus to which he refers (mainly the neoclassical theory of international trade) nor looks for possible alternative theoretical frameworks. Suppose we were to look at the matter from the point of view suggested above, What, then, would the theory of international trade tell us? Assume that capital is the abundant fact-or in the EEC, relative to the less developed countries that are involved in labour migration. Trade liberalisation in the EEC has introduced a relative trade discrimination against third countries. Thus, movement of products from them is hampered, while it is favoured from within the EEC. The reduction of trade involved in the first effect tends to reduce the return to capital, while the increase of trade involved in the second would tend to raise the return to capital. In fact, any obstacle to trade (and the common tariff wall is one) tends to lower the return to the relatively abundant factor, which is intensively used in the export sectors. How to reap the advantage of higher returns to capital due to intra-EEC trade creation, while avoiding the disadvantage of lower re-turns due to relative trade reduction with third countries? The natural way out would be to substitute factor movements for product movement. Thus, while product movement is privileged within the EEC, factor movements are privi-leged with respect to the rest of the world, as a substitute for trade, which is relatively discriminated against. Labour immigration from third countries helps in keeping down the wages of the relatively scarce factor (labour) in the EEC, and in raising the returns to the relatively abundant factor.

The question then arises of why, when labour moves in one direction, capital does not go in the opposite direction, or not enough of it does (this is the dilemma of moving the people to the job or the job to the people). Here again the neoclassical theory could be used with some advantage (and has been)[1] to show that the clue is to be found in the effects that the choice has on the return to capital. It can in fact be shown that with labour imports the productivity of capital is increased in the immigration countries and decreased in the emigration ones, and this reduces the incentive of the immigration countries to invest in the sending ones.

The above analysis should be thoroughly formalised, which would require more space and time than is now available to me. My purpose is only to in-dicate how the theoretical framework within which Mihailović moves (mainly, the neoclassical theory) may be able to explain the facts if the right questions

---

[1] For a brief, but clear, summary of the relevant results, see Gallais-Hamonno and Bourguignon, 'Migration of Manpower'.

are asked. Alternatively, the neoclassical framework could be replaced with a neo-Ricardian approach, which helps to emphasise even more clearly the leading role of profit, and throws additional light on the problems involved. The classical Ricardian recipe against the tendency towards falling profits is to lower wage costs. This (apart from unlikely decreases in the domestic natural wage) can be done through technological progress or through imports of cheap-wage goods. Labour immigration from third countries, by lowering the natural wage in the technologically less advanced industries, keeps up the profit rate (and, possibly, the rents that are collected in those particular industries), while technological progress in export industries is the means of offsetting the higher wages that have to be paid to domestic labour working in them. Thus, the development of a dual labour market, to which Mihailović alludes, is a way of keeping up profit rates (and particular rent positions) within the EEC, while at the same time allowing the higher natural wages that are required by domestic EEC workers.

Here again the analysis is only suggestive of the way in which the Ricardian theoretical framework could throw light on the questions underlying Mihailović's paper, when these are looked upon from the point of view of the effects that migration and the connected phenomena have on the distribution of income, particularly on profits.

Opening Statement for Group Discussion
Preben Munthe (Norway)

The subject of this congress is a timely one. During the whole post-war period, and particularly for the last fifteen to twenty years, integration has taken place at a rapid rate in many parts of the world. Thanks to the great technological advances in communication and transport, goods, capital and manpower move with greater ease and lower costs than ever before. Furthermore, because of the political actions taken by many countries these tendencies have been strengthened.

At the same time, it should be remembered that the world is still sharply divided into political—economic zones — the East and the West, the developed and the developing countries, and so on. It is important to keep this in mind. In his opening paper, Mihailović has chosen to deal with labour migration into and within the EEC; that is, an area that is an extreme case of economic integration. An account of labour migration in the world as a whole would, of course, be very different. One would find that migration between East and West is almost nonexistent, that migration within the Soviet Union and the East European countries is a very limited phenomenon, that the characteristics of migration among the developing countries often differ from those of migration in Western Europe, and, finally, that migration from the developing countries in Africa, Asia and Latin America to the developed countries takes place on a limited and selective scale. Therefore, the problems to which Mihailović has drawn our attention are, in a sense, rather special.

What does the phenomenon of economic integration mean to us as economists? Probably the greatest professional challenge is to revise and to extend our traditional economic theory so that it can be more useful for designing economic policies for countries that are strongly affected by developments in other countries within the same economic region. When the economies of several countries are integrated, their economic policies should also, to some extent be integrated. Designing policies for interdependent nations may be particularly important within the fields of monetary and fiscal policies, but, as Mihailović reminds us, labour migration also raises fundamental problems in both the sending and the receiving countries.

Many studies have made it clear that migration is a complicated social phenomenon. Basically, the main causes for moving are differences in employment opportunities and wage levels in the sending and receiving countries, but there are a number of other factors influencing such decisions. A study of the migration among the EEC countries can throw light upon one special aspect: the effect that the abolition of restrictions and the harmonisation of social policy have upon migration. According to Mihailović, the effect has been quite modest. Internal migration has not been stimulated to any large extent, although, as Wander points out, the picture of labour movements within the EEC has many aspects, both quantitatively and qualitatively. Furthermore, a considerable number of the migrants from EEC countries, primarily from Italy, have gone to Switzerland and other non-EEC countries.

When evaluating the migration among the EEC countries, it may be relevant to consider the internal migration within a modern industralised nation. In spite of the high mobility of labour and capital within the United States and the countries in Western Europe, there still exist important wage differentials and significant variations in rates of employment. Also, the experiences of many countries show that, in spite of substantial efforts, both regional problems and problems of low-income occupations have not been eliminated. When this is true within a single country one should perhaps not expect that migration among the EEC countries will make a substantial contribution towards reducing similar differences in the member states.

The effects of labour migration are both economic and social, and both internal and external. Mihailović and Basevi point out that there may be an important discrepancy between the private returns and the social returns from migration. Foreign workers are brought into a country by firms that are unable to recruit local labour, partly because of noncompetitive wage rates. In order to keep the former rate of profit, they have to bring in foreign workers. When so doing, the entrepreneurs do not take into account the social costs to the sending and the receiving countries. If these costs are to influence the firms' decisions, they need to be internalised by means of public regulation, including taxes.

Almost never are public regulations imposed in one country in order to pay for the costs incurred in another country. The situation is similar to the one prevailing when countries pursue their own trade and tariff policies autonomously. However, in the case of the EEC it should not be forgotten that a development fund has been set up and that a regional policy for the whole area is to be conducted. In a way, this may redress the balance between countries gaining and countries losing from migration.

To what extent the nonprivate costs in the labour-receiving countries are reflected in taxes and other regulations is difficult to say. Switzerland, as we were told, has almost stopped all further immigration because of *Uberfremdungsgefahr*. Other countries maintain other types of restrictions. To what extent these measures are effective and efficient is difficult to answer, and I believe that much research remains to be done.

According to the papers, the sending countries are in a weaker position than are the receiving ones when dealing with labour migration. In order to avoid emigration, particularly from regions in which an outflow of younger people would inflict great losses upon the remaining population, a country must either pursue a vigorous regional policy or put restrictions on leaving the country. As we all know, even in countries where public funds for regional developments are ample, there is no easy way to create jobs in backward areas.

One way to stimulate growth is to allow foreign firms to establish subsidiaries. The authorities of the host country or, alternatively, the country from which labour will emigrate, can to a considerable degree affect climate for investment. By guaranteeing to foreign firms a 'fair deal' or even offering subsidies, protection from imports, and so on, investors from abroad can be attracted. An analysis of the alternatives — labour emigration and foreign investments — should be carried out before specific measures for attracting foreign capital are taken. Also, in this field, co-operation between the authorities of the host country and the investing country would be desirable. Therefore, labour-market policies for interdependent countries should include not only measures that influence labour migration, but also foreign investments, and these measures should be designed in co-operation with all of the countries within the region in question. The question of whether people should be moved to the job or the jobs to the people has to do with the mobility of both labour and capital, and is, furthermore, a question of political co-operation across national frontiers.

Report on Group Discussion
Orlando d'Alauro (Italy)

The discussion of the working group on migration and integration of labour markets started from a general point of view but proceeded to a consideration of particular cases.

From the general point of view, the analysis of problems was made with strong reference to the existing ideological political patterns, and attention was focused more on the consequences of migrations than on their causes. In effect, problems of migration have had much more attention than problems of the integration of labour markets.

Some participants stressed the idea that the optimal utilisation of labour is to use manpower forces on their original site, but no one clearly explained how it is possible to do so if one accepts interregional and international systems of the prices of goods.

The classical and neoclassical theories of international trade were mentioned, but there emerged differences of interpretation among the participants. The big question of factor-price equalisation, as explained by Heckscher and Ohlin, and the particular case considered by Samuelson, received practically no consideration. However, the final analysis of Samuelson, presented in 1971, demonstrates that it is important to consider that it is not possible, except in the very particular case of identical production functions, to obtain an equalisation of factor prices — and, especially, to have the same wages — in regions or countries with different endowments of factors. The consequence is that, if one wishes to ameliorate the wages of the less well paid, it is necessary not only to have free exchange of goods, but also to facilitate the movement of factors and, in particular, of labour.

On this argument, however, there were fundamental disagreements. Some of the participants, starting from an individualistic point of view, affirmed that, if it is true that migration has social costs to be really neutralised, it is normally a useful and sometimes necessary instrument in improving the allocation of factors of production without reducing individual freedom and economic efficiency. Others, stressing the importance of the socialist solution of the integration of labour, rejected migration as stimulated by market forces and talked of planned movements of workers to facilitate integration, not for ameliorating the rewards of labour, but only with reference to the necessity of improving the knowledge, training, and technical progress of workers. Migrations, they say, are only marginal for socialist countries, because they have achieved situations of full employment. Workers go abroad only for a short time, and only to improve or to obtain special qualifications.

The contrast between the two points of view is evident; it seems that between them there is no bridge. The difference was clearly seen when an explicit reference was made to the general question of whether 'to move the people to the job or the job to the people'. This question has great importance in market economies, and has some importance also in planned economies if one wishes to achieve rational allocation of all, including human, resources. But this question was discussed only slightly. Some people spoke of the fundamental role played by profit in the solutions given in the market economy and rightly remembered the importance of international capital movements (as 'concomitant' agents rather than substitutes). Others, on the contrary, said that in a planned economy there are governmental controls that establish all the movements, that provide for a division of labour seeking to minimise migratory movements and improve regional investments.

The second part of the discussion was more impressive; it was concerned with special cases of regional integration and labour migration, particularly the case of the EEC.

The thesis developed in the main paper was that economic integration of the EEC has not been supported by strong migratory movements. The abolition of restrictions on movement and the harmonisation of social policy have had only a modest effect on migration within the EEC. And there still exist significant wage differentials and different rates of employment in the EEC countries. Until now, liberalisation has not provoked more emigration and real integration of the labour market of the EEC.

The reason for this — as explained by the main speaker and others — is that the growth of the EEC has utilised an increasing number of immigrant workers from non-Community countries. This immigration has aided the polarisation of development in the EEC and, to a certain degree, has aggravated the regional disequilibrium in the European regions.

The analysis of migration into EEC countries was made with reference to the situation of 'sending' and of 'receiving' countries, with particular reference to Italy as one of the senders. The contribution that the work of immigrants makes to the GNP of the receiving countries was evaluated.

The general idea is that integration in the labour market of the EEC will improve with the new regional policy and with the best utilisation of the Social Fund for compensating the social cost of migration within the area.

With regard to integration of the labour market in the CMEA, the view was expressed that it is strictly connected with the objectives of national full employment, better utilisation of the resources of different countries, and, sometimes, forms of industrial co-operation (such as joint enterprises, and movements of labour for the exchange of experience and special training). It is hoped that there will be an intra-CMEA division of labour that is useful to all countries by means of a planning system that focuses on the growing development and integration of the socialist area.

In substance, all of the participants recognised that the real problems of 'integration by migration' of labour markets are not ignored in planned economies, but are important — and often very important — only in market economies. In these economies, the social and economic effects of migration are paramount. The social costs in sending countries are normally higher than are the social costs arising in the receiving countries — especially costs relating to the forced enlargement of general infrastructures. On the other hand, it was admitted that until now discussion and co-operation between sending and receiving countries has not been easy, for the former are usually in a weaker position. However, the opinion of the participants was that, in the future, closer collaboration between all countries interested in migration — and such collaboration must sometimes include proper measures for foreign investment — will reduce the negative effects of migration and improve the trade and growth of all countries.

8 International Capital Movements and the Integration of Capital Markets (Main Paper, Working Group E)

Peter B. Kenen (USA)

I. INTRODUCTORY

Because we are to look at capital mobility *and* the integration of capital markets, I propose to emphasise dimensions of mobility that find their expression in organised markets — international transfers of instruments like stocks and bonds. I shall not say much about transfers of titles to real property or, at the opposite end of the spectrum, transfers of money in currency markets. In other words, I shall neglect direct investment and, with more serious misgivings, the problems of monetary integration posed by alternative exchange-rate regimes.

The international migration of enterprise — direct investment — has led to large capital transfers in recent years. Happily, it is at last receiving close attention. Economists are looking at the *process* of direct investment, the transfer problem once again, and at the *product* of direct investment, the international rearrangements of output, income, and wealth. We have begun to ask why firms go abroad, how their decisions affect production, employment, capital formation, and economic growth in host and source countries, and how they are apt to influence the composition and direction of international trade.[1] We have also started to investigate the ways in which governments can improve the balance of benefits and costs flowing from direct investment.[2] Unhappily, we have not yet examined intensively the

[1] Theoretical and empirical research on the causes and consequences of direct investment is reviewed by G. C. Hufbauer in 'The Multinational Corporation and Direct Investment', in *International Trade and Finance: Frontiers for Research* ed. P. B. Kenen (Cambridge: Cambridge University Press, forthcoming).

[2] Jones and others have extended the neoclassical analysis of costs and benefits. Hymer offers an 'anticlassical' analysis. Kindleberger appraises the costs and benefits specific to less developed countries. See R. W. Jones, 'International Capital Movements and the Theory of Tariffs and Trade', in *Quarterly Journal of Economics*, Feb 1967; S. Hymer, 'The Efficiency (Contradictions) of Multinational Corporations', in *American Economic Review*, May 1970, and 'The Multinational Corporation and the Problem of Uneven Development', in *Economics and World Order*, ed. J. Bhagwati (New York: Macmillan, 1971); and C. P. Kindleberger, 'Direct Investment in Less-Developed Countries: Historical Wrongs and Present Values', in *International Economics and Development: Essays in Honor of Raul Prebisch*, ed. L. E. DiMarco (New York: Academic Press, 1972).

implications of direct investment for international economic integration — for the unification of markets and of governmental units, to use the distinction stressed by Cooper in his paper for this congress.

But I am not much troubled by my decision to neglect direct investment in this paper. The analysis of direct investment involves two sets of issues, and only one is immediately relevant to the integration of capital markets. Decisions to locate production abroad, the essence of direct investment, are separable analytically from decisions concerning the manner in which a multinational plan is executed. A firm deciding to produce abroad need not even export capital; it can rent a foreign plant rather than buy or build. Furthermore, when a firm does decide to buy or build, it has many ways to finance the project. Instead of using its own funds or borrowing domestically, it can borrow abroad, in the country where it plans to produce or in some third country. Decisions concerning ways to finance a direct investment are no different in character from decisions concerning ways to finance domestic investment.

I have more trouble justifying my decision to neglect transactions in bank balances and the integration of monetary systems. There can be no perfect integration of markets for goods or claims without the perfect integration of national monetary systems. The possibility of changes in exchange rates introduces into international transactions a risk (or cost) that does not encumber domestic transactions.[3] As Mundell and McKinnon have put it, the advantage of money over barter implies that the 'optimum currency area' is the entire world.[4]

There are important reasons for sacrificing this advantage — for using several moneys and altering exchange rates: (1) factor prices are not perfectly flexible; (2) factors are not perfectly mobile; and (3) governments cannot subordinate national aims to those of their neighbours or those of a supra-national monetary agency. Indeed, this last fact succinctly states the case for national autonomy in monetary policy, and autonomy cannot be complete if exchange rates are not flexible.

Fixed or pegged exchange rates interfere with autonomy in two ways. As nations must ultimately balance their external payments — reserves are finite — they have eventually to sacrifice some of their domestic aims. Furthermore, central banks that peg exchange rates cannot hope to control completely the supply of money. When they sell bonds in the domestic securities market they often have to buy foreign currency in the exchange market, especially when national securities markets are closely integrated.

---

[3] It would be wrong, however, to translate this assertion into an attack on flexible exchange rates. The risk of changes in exchange rates cannot be removed by pegging them (or by narrowing the margins within which they can fluctuate). The risk can be removed only by fixing exchange rates forever.

[4] R. A. Mundell, 'A Theory of Optimum Currency Areas', in *American Economic Review*, Sep 1961; and R. I. McKinnon, 'Optimum Currency Areas', in *American Economic Review*, Sep 1963.

Because governments are still determined to conserve monetary sovereignty, there is little chance of a credible commitment to fix exchange rates irrevocably. Central banks, moreover, have sown a harvest of doubt about their ability, let alone their willingness, to honour any such commitment. In consequence, the prospect for close financial integration is, I fear, remote.

II. BARRIERS TO CAPITAL MOBILITY AND INTEGRATION

These reflections on monetary sovereignty introduce two new subjects – the measurement of capital-market integration, and the identification of prerequisites to additional integration.

The last two decades have witnessed large capital movements, not only direct investments and short-term speculative flows, but also long-term borrowing and lending. This growth of borrowing, however, does not necessarily testify to the closer integration of capital markets. The volume of new nonresident issues in markets outside the United States is as yet quite small, and there is little evidence of active trading in 'seasoned' securities; secondary markets for nonresident debt are relatively underdeveloped, even in Western Europe.[5] Furthermore, an increase of flows – of trade in new or seasoned securities – is not the best evidence of integration. To measure the strength of links between markets, one should look at market prices – interest rates in this instance – and the evidence on this point is far from conclusive. There are strong positive correlations between comparable interest rates in major financial centres, especially between national and Eurocurrency rates, and recent econometric work has traced clear structural connections between financial markets.[6] But these correlations and structural connections are not getting stronger.[7]

The widespread use of capital controls and expectations of changes in exchange rates are important reasons for the continuing segregation of capital markets. If all controls were dismantled, however, and exchange rates were thought to be fixed, differences in interest rates would not disappear. There are other barriers to perfect integration – limits on the *willingness* of

[5] L. B. Krause, 'Implications for Private Capital Markets', in *European Monetary Unification and its Meaning for the United States* ed. L. B. Krause and W. S. Salant (Washington, DC: The Brookings Institution, 1973).

[6] The evidence is surveyed in Z. Hodjera, 'International Short-Term Capital Movements: A Survey of Theory and Empirical Analysis', International Monetary Fund, *Staff Papers* (Nov 1973); and R. C. Bryant, 'Empirical Research on Financial Capital Flows', in *International Trade and Finance*. See, also, R. J. Herring, 'International Financial Integration: *Capital Flows and Interest Rate Relationships Among Six Industrial Countries*', unpublished Ph.D. dissertation (Princeton University, 1973); and R. D. Marston, *American Monetary Policy and the Structure of the Eurodollar Market* (International Finance Section, Princeton University, 1974).

[7] See V. Argy and Z. Hodjera, 'Financial Integration and Interest Rate Linkages in the Industrial Countries', International Monetary Fund, *Staff Papers* (Mar 1973).

investors to hold debt instruments issued by nonresidents and limits also on their *ability* to do so.

The most important limitations on *willingness* derive from differences in the costs of acquiring knowledge about domestic and foreign borrowers and from differences in the risks of having imperfect knowledge. Each of these in turn reflects the fact that borrowers and the instruments they issue are not homogeneous. There are many kinds of borrowers and debt instruments, even in a single country, and they differ in many ways. But it is relatively easy to acquire information about large borrowers, the instruments they issue, and conditions in the markets for those instruments. Hence, big governmental units and big corporations — those whose nonfinancial activities cover the largest domains — enjoy the easiest access to lenders. Because they are large, their names are well known. Because they are large borrowers, there are well-developed secondary markets for their obligations, making those obligations more liquid than those of small borrowers.

When one turns from the domestic to the world scene, the heterogeneity of borrowers and of instruments is amplified. Domains of nonfinancial activity are more remote, and lenders are not as familiar with borrowers, even with large ones. Secondary markets are less accessible and, as I said before, are not well developed in many major countries.

Compounding these effects of distance and environment, there are large international differences in legal systems. Three juridical dimensions distinguish domestic from foreign investment; they bear on the costs of acquiring information and of redeeming mistakes. First, there are differences in the immunities and duties that laws confer on artificial persons — governments, corporations, and other borrowers. Second, debt instruments are defined and issued under the specific provisions of laws that regulate accounting practices, the disclosure of financial information, and the rights of claimants in instances of default. Third, the administration of the law is itself an attribute of national sovereignty, and one's rights under law may depend crucially on one's nationality.

I need not enumerate the many circumstances that limit an investor's *ability* to hold foreign assets. Examples will suffice. First, certain financial institutions may be forbidden to hold claims on foreigners or claims denominated in foreign currencies. Second, some institutions are encouraged or required to invest in certain classes of domestic assets, especially in governmental debt. Third, there is the matter of taxation. Tax policies sometimes discriminate against incomes and capital gains arising from foreign investment or, with the same effect, discriminate in favour of certain earnings and gains arising domestically.

III. SOME IMPLICATIONS OF MOBILITY AND INTEGRATION

I turn now to the subject that interests me most — the benefits and costs of capital mobility and of integrating capital markets.

Real gains arise from the more efficient allocation of capital. These may not be as large as we are prone to argue when we teach trade theory, and one devoted advocate of financial integration, Charles Kindleberger, warns against neglecting the numerous costs.[8] These costs relate to 'second-best' situations in which an omniscient government would control capital movements to offset rigidities and imperfections in the national and world economies. But Kindleberger also lists a number of reasons for expecting *net* benefits from integration, especially from unifying capital markets in the developed world. Integration would dilute the monopolistic powers exercised by banks and other institutions in isolated capital markets. It would broaden and deepen securities markets, enhancing the liquidity of 'seasoned' securities and reducing the cost of borrowing. It would match more closely the liquidity preferences of borrowers and lenders by making available a larger assortment of financial instruments.

Additional benefits and costs accrue to the conduct of national policies. I have already mentioned one of the costs – the loss of monetary autonomy under fixed exchange rates. There are, however, two classes of benefits. When capital is highly mobile, monetary policy can be assigned to regulate the balance of payments, freeing other policy instruments for the pursuit of domestic objectives. This is, of course, the simplest statement of the case made by Mundell for pairing instruments and targets.[9] Each instrument, he argues, should be given the task for which it has the largest comparative advantage. His prescription has been qualified many times, and the advent of the 'new' portfolio view of international capital movements has caused some authors to reject it altogether.[10] In my opinion, however, Mundell's prescription has not lost its vitality. The once-for-all changes in portfolios found in the new models arise in the course of once-for-all movements between stationary states. The models *omit* the continuing capital flows that monetary policy is supposed to regulate. In true-to-life economies, saving and investment take place endlessly. Some of the saving finds its way to foreigners; some of the investment is financed by foreigners. Monetary policy can affect these flows; it has a significant comparative advantage in the quest for external balance.

There is, next, a beneficial connection between the integration of capital

[8] C. P. Kindleberger, 'The Pros and Cons of an International Capital Market', in *Zeitschrift für die gesamte Staatswissenschaft*, Oct 1967.

[9] R. A. Mundell, 'The Appropriate Use of Monetary and Fiscal Policy for Internal and External Stability', International Monetary Fund, *Staff Papers* (Mar 1962).

[10] The relevant literature is gathered by M. v.N. Whitman, *Policies for Internal and External Balance* (International Finance Section, Princeton University, 1970). See, also, W. B. Branson and T. D. Willett, 'Policy Toward Short-Term Capital Movements: Some Implications of the Portfolio Approach', in *International Mobility and Movement of Capital*, ed. F. Machlup et al. (New York: National Bureau of Economic Research, 1972); and E. Tower, 'Monetary and Fiscal Policy in a World of Capital Mobility: A Respecification', in *Review of Economic Studies*, July 1972.

markets and monetary unification. A multinational central bank must have access to a multinational financial market in order to conduct open-market operations. If it were compelled to operate in segregated markets, its policies would affect the allocation of economic activity and the distributions of income and wealth. Concern about these side effects could get in the way of its primary aims and limit politically its freedom of action.

The third and final set of benefits and costs arises in respect of the adjustment process — the manner in which a national or regional economy responds to exogenous disturbances affecting its balance of payments. This is the subject that I shall examine formally, in order to investigate suggestions made by Ingram concerning balance-of-payments adjustment under fixed exchange rates, with and without capital mobility.[11]

I shall emphasise a point made by Scitovsky.[12] Because a current-account surplus adds to a country's wealth, it has always to disturb the equilibrium between actual and desired wealth. In consequence, a surplus sets in train changes in expenditure (saving out of income) aimed at establishing a new equilibrium. Furthermore, a change in wealth must alter the demands for all financial assets, not just the demand for money, leading to capital movements or, in the absence of capital mobility, to changes in interest rates. Using these simple notions, I shall refine Ingram's claims for capital mobility and the integration of capital markets. Working with a simple portfolio model, I shall show that mobility does not affect the *size* of the change in income required to restore external balance under fixed exchange rates, but does *slow down* the change in income and reduces the cumulative change in reserves.[13]

IV. A FORMAL MODEL

Consider a small, open economy in which there is no real capital formation. Saving can be offset only by a government deficit or a current-account surplus, and wealth can be accumulated as money, claims on government, or claims on the outside world. The economy produces one commodity, and its price is fixed (at unity) in home currency. Because there is no real capital formation, and saving is carried out only by households, one can neglect the activities of firms, and concentrate on households, banks and

[11] J. C. Ingram, 'A Proposal for Financial Integration of the Atlantic Community', in *Factors Affecting the United States Balance of Payments* (Washington DC: Joint Economic Committee, US Congress, 1962), and *The Case for European Monetary Integration* (International Finance Section, Princeton University, 1973).

[12] T. Scitovsky, *Money and the Balance of Payments* (New Haven: Yale University Press, 1969).

[13] I have dealt with these same themes in my, 'Toward a Supranational Monetary System', in *Issues in Banking and Monetary Analysis* ed. G. Pontecorvo et al. (New York: Holt, Rinehard and Winston, 1967), and 'Implications for International Reserves: Comment', in *European Monetary Unification and its Meaning for the United States*. See, also, M. v.N. Whitman, *International and Interregional Payments Adjustment: A Synthetic View* (International Finance Section, Princeton University, 1967).

government.[14]

As households are the ultimate holders of private wealth, their balance sheet takes this form:

$$W^h = L + (1/r)B^h + W^b, \tag{1}$$

where W^h is household wealth; L is money issued by the commercial banks (there is no currency, and firms hold no cash); B^h is the stock of government bonds (consols) held by households, measured by coupon payments; r is the market interest rate on those bonds; and W^b is the net worth of the comcial banks. (W^b appears in this equation because households own the banks, but it can be altered only by changing the prices of assets held by the banks.)

Because households are the only ones to save, they receive the entire national income. One can therefore write their demand for money as a function of national income, Y, and the interest rate:

$$L = L(r,Y), L_r < 0, L_y > 0. \tag{2}$$

Notice that equations (1) and (2) define the households' demand for bonds; they can acquire bonds only when there is an increase in their wealth or by swapping bonds for money.

Household saving, S, will be made to occur whenever there is any difference between desired wealth, W^s, and actual wealth, W^h:

$$S = \lambda(W^s - W^h), \quad 0 < \lambda < 1, \tag{3}$$

where

$$W^s = W(r,Y^n), \quad W_r > 0, W_y > 0 \tag{4}$$

and

$$Y^n = Y - T. \tag{5}$$

Here, T is the net transfer (lump-sum tax *less* subsidy) from households to government.

Finally, impose an important restriction on the demands for wealth and money. Let $W_y > L_y$, so that an increase in household wealth due to an increase in income will increase the demand for bonds.

Turning to the balance sheet of the commercial banks:

$$W^b = L^c + (1/r)B^b - L, \tag{6}$$

where L^c are the banks' reserves (the liabilities of the central bank), and B^b is the stock of government bonds held by commercial banks. Assume, moreover, that the banks hold only those reserves needed to satisfy the fractional requirement imposed by the central bank:

$$L^c = qL, \quad 0 < q < 1. \tag{7}$$

---

[14] Under additional assumptions set out in P. B. Kenen, 'Capital Mobility and Financial Integration', (mimeo, 1974), one can also neglect certain interest payments that would otherwise complicate the government budget, the balance of payments, and the definition of household income.

By implication, any change in the banks' investible assets will be reflected in their holdings of bonds.

The central bank holds bonds and foreign-exchange reserves:

$$W^c = \pi R + (1/r)B^c - L^c, \tag{8}$$

where π is the price of foreign currency in terms of home currency; R is the stock of foreign-exchange reserves (in foreign currency); and B^c is the stock of government bonds held by the central bank. (Changes in the asset prices, π and r, are fully reflected in W^c, the central bank's net worth, and have no other effect on the model.)

The total stock of government bonds, B, must equal the holdings of the several other sectors:

$$B = B^h + B^b + B^c + B^f, \tag{9}$$

where B^f is the stock held by foreigners. Furthermore:

$$(1/r)\,\dot{B} = G - T, \tag{10}$$

where G is government expenditure, and $\dot{B}$ is the rate of change in the stock of bonds. (Dotted terms denote continuous rates of change; terms like dB denote comparative-static changes.)

Similarly, the balance of payments determines the rate of change in reserves:

$$\pi\dot{R} = (X - \pi M) + (1/r)\,\dot{B}^f, \tag{11}$$

where X and M are merchandise exports and imports, respectively, and $\dot{B}^f$ is the rate of change in foreign holdings of government bonds. The trade balance depends on the exchange rate and income:[15]

$$(X - \pi M) = M(\pi,Y), M_\pi > 0, M_y > 0. \tag{12}$$

Finally, national income is defined by

$$Y = (Y^n - S) + G + (X - \pi M) \tag{13}$$

in the familiar Keynesian manner.

My model employs two institutional constraints and a strong behavioral restriction:

(a) Define perfect capital mobility by making B^f endogenous and fixing r; foreigners are willing to buy an unlimited quantity of domestic debt at a constant interest rate. Absent mobility, set B^f at zero and make r endogenous.

[15]The assertion that $M_\pi > 0$ is another way of saying that the Marshall–Lerner–Robinson condition is satisfied. This familiar elasticities condition is the only route by which the exchange rate affects the model. Households hold no foreign assets, and the demand for money makes no allowance for spending on imports. Thus, the model disallows the asset and money-stock effects stressed in recent work by Dornbusch (see Rüdiger Dornbusch, 'Currency Depreciation, Hoarding, and Relative Prices', in *Journal of Political Economy*, July–Aug 1973).

(b) Define pegged exchange rates by fixing π and making R endogenous. Define freely flexible exchange rates by making π endogenous and fixing R.

(c) Suppose that the government always maintains a balanced budget by varying its tax collections against its expenditures, so that $\dot{B}$ is always zero.[16]

Assumption (c) makes the level of taxes endogenous, leaving us with only three policy instruments: changes in total government debt, changes in central-bank holdings of debt, and balanced-budget changes in expenditure. It also helps to simplify the model, which can be rewritten in four statements:

$$W^h = \pi R + (1/r)(B - B^f) - W^c \tag{14}$$

$$qL(r,Y) = \pi R + (1/r)B^c - W^c \tag{15}$$

$$\lambda[W(r,Y-G) - W^h] = M(\pi,Y) \tag{16}$$

$$\pi \dot{R} = M(\pi,Y) + (1/r)\dot{B}^f \tag{17}$$

The first defines households' wealth; the second says that the demand for bank reserves must equal the supply; the third says that saving must equal the trade balance; and the fourth defines the change in foreign-exchange reserves.

V. THE COMPARATIVE STATICS OF FINANCIAL POLICIES

In a stationary state, all stocks are constant. By implication, $\dot{B}^f = \dot{R} = 0$, the trade balance is zero, and there is no saving. Invoking these conditions, differentiate totally equations (14) to (17) and set $\pi = 1$. After additional simplifications:[17]

$$
\begin{bmatrix}
1 & -1 & 0 & W_y & \theta_r \\
0 & -1 & 0 & qL_y & qrL_r \\
0 & 0 & 1 & -M_y & 0
\end{bmatrix}
\begin{bmatrix}
(1/r)dB^f \\
dR \\
(M_\pi)d\pi \\
dY \\
(dr/r)
\end{bmatrix}
=
\begin{bmatrix}
(1/r)dB + (W_y)dG \\
(1/r)dB^c \\
-dX^a
\end{bmatrix}
\tag{18}
$$

[16] This assumption is borrowed from D. K. Foley and M. Sidrauski, *Monetary and Fiscal Policy in a Growing Economy* (New York: Macmillan, 1971). It is not insistent with another made below, that there is a permanent increase in the total debt, dB. An increase in debt can be accomplished by a *temporary* increase of expenditure or decrease of taxes.

[17] See Kenen, 'Capital Mobility and Financial Integration'.

where

$$\theta_r = (1/r)(B - B^c) + rW_r > 0$$

The matrix in (18) reduces to three columns when one chooses between fixed and flexible exchange rates, then between perfect and no capital mobility. The disturbances listed in (18) can be interpreted as follows:

dB: a once-for-all increase in government debt accomplished by a temporary increase in expenditure or a decrease in taxes;

dB^c: a once-for-all open-market purchase of government debt by the central bank;

dG: a permanent increase in government spending, balanced by a permanent increase in taxes;

dX^a: a permanent increase in the foreign demand for exports.

Table 1 presents the comparative-static effects of the first two policies. (The effects of dG resemble those of dB.) Consider first the effects under fixed exchange rates with perfect capital mobility. As newly issued debt will be bought by foreigners at a constant interest rate, there is a one-to-one relationship between dB and dB^f, and an increase in debt can have no effect on domestic income. There cannot even be a change in reserves. To issue additional debt, the government must run a budgetary deficit, and this will

TABLE 1

COMPARATIVE-STATIC EFFECTS OF FINANCIAL POLICIES

Variable	*Perfect mobility*		*No mobility*	
	$(1/r)dB$	$(1/r)dB^c$	$(1/r)dB$	$(1/r)dB^c$
FIXED EXCHANGE RATES				
dY	0	0	0	0
dR	0	-1	$(qrL_r/Q) < 0$	$-(\theta_r/Q) < 0$
$(1/r)dB^f$	1	-1	$-$	$-$
(dr/r)	$-$	$-$	$(1/Q) > 0$	$-(1/Q) < 0$
FLEXIBLE EXCHANGE RATES[a]				
dY	0	$(1/qL_y) > 0$	$-(rL_r/L_yQ_\pi) > 0$	$(\theta_r/qL_yQ_\pi) > 0$
$(1/r)dB^f$	1	$-(W_y/qL_y) < 0$	$-$	$-$
(dr/r)	$-$	$-$	$(1/Q_\pi) > 0$	$-(W_y/qL_yQ_\pi) < 0$

$Q = \theta_r - qrL_r > 0$

$Q_\pi = \theta_r - (W_y/L_y)rL_r > 0$

[a]The change in the exchange rate, $d\pi$, is always equal to $(M_y/M_\pi)dY$,

be reflected by the trade balance. Hence, borrowing will change the current and capital accounts by equal, but opposite, amounts, leaving reserves intact. An open-market sale by the central bank has the same effect on the capital account, but such a sale swaps bonds for money, not for goods, and has no effect on the current account. In consequence, an open-market sale causes an equal, but opposite, change in reserves. The table, then, replicates a familiar theorem: under fixed exchange rates, perfect capital mobility deprives the central bank of any control over the stock of money.

When capital is immobile, the results are different, but even in this instance, there can be no permanent change in income. In the absence of any alteration in the exchange rate or in the foreign demand for exports, the long-run equilibrium level of income is fixed by the requirement that trade be balanced. New results obtain only in respect of the interest rate and reserves. Government borrowing and open-market sales have the same effects on the interest rate and on the demand for money. The effects on reserves, however, differ between the two policies *and* from what they were with capital mobility: borrowing reduces the stock of reserves; an open-market sale raises it. The reasons for this difference can be stated in two ways – by invoking the requirements of monetary equilibrium or by describing the forces affecting trade. Because each policy reduces the demand for money, it also has to accomplish a reduction of supply. An open-market sale reduces it too much, and the economy has to import money (by running a trade surplus). Borrowing does not reduce it at all, and the economy has to export money. The *processes* set up by the two policies guarantee these results. By raising the interest rate, each policy induces saving by households, leading to transitional reductions in income and imports. This is all that happens with an open-market sale; it adds to reserves. But government borrowing is the direct cause of a transitional trade deficit, and this deficit is larger than the reduction of imports induced by saving; it expels reserves.

Under flexible exchange rates, three of the policy outcomes feature permanent changes in income because they lead to permanent changes in exchange rates. (There can be no such change in the fourth instance, government borrowing with capital mobility, as the current and capital accounts move in opposite directions, precluding excess demand or supply in the foreign-exchange market.) Consider, first, an open-market sale when capital is mobile. Because it produces a capital inflow without changing the trade balance, it causes the exchange rate to appreciate, depressing domestic activity. This familiar explanation, however, is not sufficient to account for my results. The capital inflow is temporary, yet the changes in income and the exchange rate are permanent. Furthermore, the same things happen when capital is not moblie. Again, we must invoke the requirements for equilibrium in the money market. When exchange rates are flexible, the central bank does not intervene in the foreign-exchange market. Hence, an open-market sale reduces the supply of money, and there must then be a reduction in the demand for money. This calls for a decrease in national income, an increase in the interest rate, or a combination of the two. With capital mobility, the interest rate cannot change; the reduction in demand must be accomplished by reducing income. In the absence of mobility, the reduction in demand is partially accomplished by an increase in the interest rate, and the decline in income is smaller. In both instances, however, the demand for imports declines, and the price of foreign currency has to fall.

Turning finally to government borrowing when capital is not mobile, there is a permanent increase in income and a permanent depreciation of the home currency (to offset the larger demand for imports). The increase of the interest rate caused by borrowing reduces the demand for money, but there is no change in the supply. There must be an increase of income to take up the excess supply.

It is difficult to compare these results with those that others have obtained concerning the effectiveness of various policies. Many models deal in flows, not in stationary states. Furthermore, the fiscal policy studied here — an increase in the stock of debt — is not the one that others have examined. And even when the outcomes resemble those obtained elsewhere, the reasons are not the same. My conclusions, then, are cast in slightly different form from those found in other papers on this subject.[18]

(1) Arrangements in the foreign-exchange market are more important than arrangements in the capital market for the effectiveness of monetary policy. It will have no permanent domestic impact when the central bank must intervene in support of fixed exchange rates. Arrangements in the capital market are important mainly for the size and the speed with which the policy's influence is felt or dissipated.

(2) The two sets of arrangements interact elaborately in their influence on the effectiveness of fiscal policy. When capital is perfectly mobile, fiscal policy has no permanent domestic effect; new bonds are sold directly to foreigners, leaving reserves (exchange rates) intact. When capital is not mobile, fiscal policy has effects similar, but opposite in sign, to those of monetary policy. Under fixed exchange rates, borrowing reduces reserves. Under flexible rates, it causes a permanent depreciation and stimulates domestic activity.

VI. THE COMPARATIVE STATICS AND DYNAMICS OF AN EXOGENOUS INCREASE IN EXPORTS

I come finally to the question that my model was designed to answer: how do arrangements in capital markets influence the size and speed of the adjustment to an exogenous change in the demand for exports? Answers are given by Table 2, which shows the comparative-static and quasi-dynamic

---

[18] See, however, R. I. McKinnon and W. E. Oates, *The Implications of International Economic Integration for Monetary, Fiscal and Exchange Rate Policy* (International Finance Section, Princeton University, 1966).

TABLE 2

COMPARATIVE-STATIC AND DYNAMIC EFFECTS OF AN AUTONOMOUS
INCREASE IN EXPORTS (dX^a) UNDER FIXED EXCHANGE RATES

Variable	Comparative-static effect	Dynamic effect
	PERFECT MOBILITY	
dY and $\dot{Y}$	$(1/M_y)dX^a > 0$	$\lambda[(X-M)/(S_y+M_y)] > 0$
dR and $\dot{R}$	$(qL_y/M_y)dX^a > 0$	$qL_y \cdot \lambda[(X-M)/(S_y+M_y)] > 0$
	NO MOBILITY	
dY and $\dot{Y}$	$(1/M_y)dX^a > 0$	$(Q/Q_n)\lambda[(X-M)/(S_y+M_y)] > 0$
dR and $\dot{R}$	$(Q_\pi/Q)(qL_y/M_y)dX^a > 0$	$(X-M) > 0$

effects of a permanent exogenous increase in exports. For definitions of Q and Q_π, see Table 1, above. Here

$$Q_n = q\lambda\theta_r \left[L_y/(S_y+M_y)\right] - qrL_r > 0.$$

The comparative-static effects derive directly from equations (18). The dynamic effects are obtained by taking the time derivatives of equations (14) and (15), setting $\dot{B} = \dot{B}^c = \dot{G} = \dot{\pi} = 0$ and $\pi = 1$, and combining the results with equations (16) and (17). Writing the results compactly:

$$
\begin{bmatrix}
1 & -1 & 0 & 0 \\
0 & -1 & qL_y & qrL_r \\
0 & 0 & -(S_y+M_y) & -\lambda\theta_r
\end{bmatrix}
\begin{bmatrix}
(1/r)\,\dot{B}^f \\
\dot{R} \\
\dot{Y} \\
(\dot{r}/r)
\end{bmatrix}
=
\begin{bmatrix}
-1 \\
0 \\
-\lambda
\end{bmatrix}
(X-M), \qquad (19)
$$

where $S_y = \lambda W_y$, the marginal propensity to save.

The comparative-static effects are unambiguous. Capital mobility does not influence the size of the permanent increase in income. It affects only the change in reserves by way of its effects on the demands for bonds and money. When capital is mobile, the increase of demand for bonds that is caused by the increase in income is satisfied by buying bonds from foreigners. When it is not mobile, the increase in demand for bonds cannot be satisfied, and the interest rate must fall. Household shift from bonds to money, eliminating the excess demand for bonds but increaseing the excess demand for money. The economy must import additional money, enlarging the cumulative increase of reserves.

The dynamic arguments round out this analysis. They show that the *rates of change* of income and reserves depend importantly on the presence or absence of capital mobility. This assertion can be proved by subtracting from each outcome *with* mobility the corresponding outcome *without* mobility.

Starting with the rates of change in income,

$$\dot{Y}_m - \dot{Y}_n = -\theta_r[\lambda(W_y - qL_y) + M_y][\lambda(X - M)/(S_y + M_y)Q_n] < 0. \qquad (20)$$

The *rate of change* of income is smaller with mobility at every point in time during the adjustment to an exogenous change in exports. Income rises more slowly in response to an increase of exports and falls more slowly in response to a decrease of exports. (Equation (20) does not say so directly. It compares $\dot{Y}_m$ and $\dot{Y}_n$ at times when the trade balance would be the same. The inference, however, is straightforward.)

Turning to the rate of change in reserves,

$$\dot{R}_m - \dot{R}_n = -[\lambda(W_y - qL_y) + M_y][(X - M)/(S_y + M_y)] < 0. \qquad (21)$$

The argument of this equation is the same as the expression for $(1/r)\dot{B}^f$, the capital flow, in Table 2. This is because $\dot{R}_m$ and $\dot{R}_n$ are evaluated at points in time when the trade balance would be the same with and without capital mobility; the difference between the rates of change in reserves can testify only to capital movements. But this result, while simple, is not trivial. It reinforces Ingram's case for capital mobility. Mobility reduces the rate at which reserves decline when a country suffers a reduction in exports.

Combining this result with the one obtained above, capital mobility can be said to serve two related functions. First, it slows down the endogenous decline in income caused by an exogenous reduction of exports. Second, it mutes the need to hasten that decline by applying deflationary policy that will conserve reserves.

Comments
Robert A. Mundell (Canada)

For fifteen years the problem of short-term capital has been studied intensively in the International Monetary Fund (IMF), by academics, bankers and research organisations, and at conferences, and there has been a significant increase in our knowledge of its determinants. The theory of the subject, however, has not progressed as rapidly as necessary to establish significant generalisations. Perhaps this is because of the turmoil of exchange markets in recent years and the tendency of the subject matter to outrun our grasp of the changes in the monetary environment. The proximate causes of capital flows change with the international monetary system; and not only the regression coefficients of capital-flow equations but also the structural formulation of the systems in which they are embodied need to be altered.

The major causes of short-term capital flows have altered with the exchange system. Under the gold-exchange standard and adjustable-peg system, capital shifted from deficit to surplus currencies, leading to the huge 'overhang' of dollar balances held by central banks and by commercial banks in the Euro-dollar markets, often encouraged by swaps and repurchase agreements. Exchange-rate uncertainty combined with rigid but not fixed exchange rates led to enormous interest-rate differentials in the crisis period needed to offset potential capital losses from adjustments in the peg. After the shift to floating rates, differential rates of inflation took over as a major determinant of interest differentials. Capital moves to equalise rates of return, and the law of one price holds in the capital—money market as in every other. After the increase in the oil price, exchange-rate changes induced by shifts in investments of oil surpluses created grave distortions of purchasing-power parity relationships and artificial cycles of exchange rates, interest rates and prices. We have still not resolved the problem of finding the equilibrium pattern of exchange rates.

The major problem of research in this field is that attention to the study of the trees may have hindered our understanding of the economic forest, which is itself left unstudied and, by policy, unattended. In the past few years the world economy has been blasted by immense shocks. We are now in the midst of an inflationary recession the origins of which can be traced to the break-down of the international monetary system. Short-term money flows and international financial markets have been chaotic, confidence in the stability of the Eurodollar market has broken down, and depression seems just around the corner.

The gold-exchange standard broke down in August 1971 and with it the dollar discipline accepted by the countries whose exchange rates were pegged to the dollar, and the gold discipline accepted, in principle at least, by the primary reserve centre. The Bretton Woods system was replaced by the 'Smithsonian system' after the Azores agreement to devalue the dollar. The distinguishing feature of the Smithsonian system (which did not last much more than a year) was a system of rigid exchange rates without convertibility. It retained the intervention system based on key currencies, but ignored the need for global regulation of international reserves. There was no ceiling on the reserve media nor any mechanism to prevent the inflationary finance of deficits. Even gold values in international reserves became inflation-elastic to the ex-

tent that the price of gold rises with inflation and gold reserves can be used as
collateral at market-related prices for extensions of international credit (as
recently agreed between Germany and Italy). The increases in the official price
of gold merely whetted the expectations of speculators and a public that is increasingly concerned with the anxieties of preserving capital in an inflationary
world.

The Smithsonian system broke down shortly after the second devaluation
of the dollar. It merged into the system of floating exchange rates, which had
been championed by the United States Treasury since 1971. The major defect
of this system, for the United States as well as for the rest of the world, is that
it failed to erect a barrier to excessive reserve creation.

The new system thus makes a substantial change in the global money-supply
function. Violent price increases under the gold standard and even the gold-
exchange standard were inhibited by the liquidity constraint of a declining
real value of gold. This effect is broken under the present system as the money
supply becomes accommodating either through a still rising money multiplier
that increases potential Eurodollars or greater monetary expansion in the
United States. International reserves and Eurodollar deposits have more than
doubled since 1971, as the monetary system has accommodated the increased
need for reserves. But cause and effect interact; both the bullionists and the
banking-school advocates have their day. Reserve-money creation raises prices
and price increases increase reserve money through the inflationary finance
of deficits. The price of many basic metals and other materials tripled, and
the price of gold and oil quadrupled. The economist does not have to look
for political causes of these changes in prices when the economic rationale
stares him in the face. The price of oil would not have quadrupled under the
gold standard or a disciplined international monetary system; big deficits
would have prompted sharp adjustment, lowered the flow of funds and
weakened the cohesion of OPEC (the Organisation of Petroleum Exporting
Countries).

Turning now to the major problem of global policy, we have two major
problems − inflation and unemployment. To stop inflation we need to control international liquidity and excessive domestic monetary expansion. The
IMF needs to develop the estimates for the *world money supply* that were
made in the Fund in the early 1970s. It is only when the global totals of
money, including the 'stateless' money of the Eurodollar deposits, are taken
into consideration that the full inflationary role of the current 'system' can
be appreciated. There is little point to controlling M_1 or M_2 in the United
States without also regulating their counterparts in the dollar markets overseas. The total of Eurodollar deposits has been the fastest growing single component of world money and there is little point in controlling 'Stateside'
money without also controlling 'Euromoney', which uses Stateside money as
a reserve base.

The great inventory boom of 1972−4 peaked in early 1974 and commodity
prices have been coming down. This is partly a consequence of the sudden increase in oil prices as non-oil inventories are liquidated to finance higher oil
bills, and as the accelerator effects of speculation in commodities are reversed.
But its impact on the consumer-price indexes is felt only with a lag. In combination with the high price of oil and an incipient wage explosion, we risk

much higher unemployment. The cost of living will continue to rise as wages rise to catch up with past losses of workers' real income. Full employment will not be compatible with falling material prices, rising money wages and higher oil costs. Unemployment is already excessive in the OECD countries. Moreover, the increase in oil prices implicit within the OPEC revolution amounts to tens of billions of dollars. If a steep world depression is to be avoided, the implicit tax will have to be offset by tax reductions of a huge magnitude in importing countries. The major responsibilities here lie with those countries — the United States, the Federal Republic of Germany, and Japan — where there is unemployment and whose external positions are able to accept the international implications of tax reduction. These countries must take the lead in initiating reductions in tax rates. As the situation worsens, the magnitude of stimulus needed rises. But the thrust of the stimulus should come from fiscal ease, not monetary inflation. Short-term capital imports will help to finance the tax cuts.

The appropriate policy mix for inflationary recessions requires a split of our monetary and fiscal instruments, using expansionary fiscal policy to cope with excessive unemployment, and monetary restraint to curb excessive inflation. Tight money and fiscal ease lower both inflation and unemployment, and tend to improve the capital account of the balance of payment more than they hurt the balance of trade. The two financial instruments have differential effects on inflation and unemployment. The differences arise because of the homogeneous character of wage, price and money changes, differences between national and international impacts, aggregate supply *versus* aggregate demand changes and even expectational effects. And just as monetary and fiscal policies are totally different instruments, so the rate of inflation and the level of unemployment are differential targets. Tax policy has a comparative advantage in altering the equilibrium level of unemployment and the rate of monetary expansion on the rate of inflation.

I see ahead a substantial reduction in our standard of living if we do not take steps to restore a stable international monetary system and put our macroeconomic policies back on the track. When this is done the instabilities due to volatile short-term capital movements will be converted to adjustment-easing lending that reduces the stress of sudden change. The best hope in my judgement lies in a movement toward fixed exchange rates with convertibility of most currencies into a major key currency along optimum-currency-area lines, and convertibility of the major key currency into an asset like gold or a currency based on the special drawing right or agreed alternative.

Comments
Alexander K. Swoboda (Switzerland)

I.

In discussing the topic assigned to this working group, Kenen has served us
well in avoiding the Charybdis of platitudinous generalities without running
into the Scylla of tedious discussion of the details of barriers to capital movements. For, on a general level, what more is there to say than that, in a perfect
world, unimpeded movements of capital would lead to more efficient resource
allocation, and that, in an imperfect world, the usual problems with second-
best analysis prevent us from making any broad generalisations?

After raising a few questions about the nature, prerequisites, and recent
evolution of capital-market integration, Kenen focuses on the latter's implications for the conduct of national policies. Loss of monetary autonomy is seen
as the main cost of financial integration and capital mobility. Benefits include
increased effectiveness of monetary policy for balance-of-payments purposes,
the creation of a single market within which to carry out open-market operations in the context of monetary union, and improved adjustment to autonomous trade-balance disturbances under fixed exchange rates. The formal mode
that constitutes the main part of Kenen's paper elaborates on this last point,
among other issues, and concludes that capital mobility does not affect the
extent to which income has to change in order to restore payments balance,
but it does reduce the required rate of change of income and the cumulative
change in reserves.

Space limitations imposed on discussants' comments prevent me from doing
full justice to the many insights contained in Kenen's paper. I shall confine myself to a few general remarks, and to a discussion of Kenen's model and its conclusions.

II.

Capital markets are integrated if the price of the future in terms of the present
for like borrowers and lenders, and as embodied in identical instruments, is
equalised over the integrated area; that is, if the law of one price holds. The
absence of obstacles to trade in claims, together with competition and equal
and free access to information, ensure that capital movements (arbitrage in
claims) will equalise returns on comparable assets. But all assets are not identical; one of the reasons why such a wide variety of assets is traded, both
nationally and internationally, is, of course, the need to reconcile the preferences and expectations of lenders and borrowers and of various subcategories
within these two broad groups.

It should therefore not surprise us to find divergences among interest rates,
both nationally and internationally. Judging the degree of capital-market integration through reference to interest-rate comparisons is fraught with difficulties and a number of questions can be raised in this context.

First, under what circumstances can national interest rates on otherwise
identical assets differ — that is, capital markets be *dis*integrated? Obviously,
some obstacles to arbitrage must exist: in the very short run, these may take

the form of transactions and information costs; in the longer run, regulatory (for instance, differential taxes that discriminate between residents and non-residents) or discriminatory monopolistic practices must be invoked.

Second, under fixed actual and expected exchange rates, money rates of interest should be equalised in integrated capital markets. Under flexible rates, or when actual and expected exchange rates diverge, it is the notoriously difficult-to-measure *expected* yields on assets that are identical in every respect but currency denomination that should be equalised.

Third, some assets may not be traded internationally simply because they are tailored to national preferences or regulations. The fact (if it is a fact) that, as Kenen notes, 'when one turns from the domestic to the world scene, the heterogeneity of borrowers and instruments is amplified' is not convincing evidence of less integration internationally than nationally. The crucial question is whether interest rates tend to differ more within one nation than among several. To my knowledge, this question has not been investigated empirically; one promising technique that, with suitable modifications, could be applied here is the one developed by Hans Genberg to examine whether inflation rates differ significantly under fixed exchange rates from country to country.[1]

The distinction between traded and nontraded assets could also fruitfully be incorporated in models designed to study the loss of monetary autonomy due to the integration of capital markets. This has been done by Branson, by Dornbusch, and by Kenen in a more extended version of his study.[2] In such models *and in the short run*, it is possible to affect local interest rates, through monetary policy, even though some assets are 'perfectly mobile', by carrying out open-market operations in nontraded assets — or by creating 'nontraded assets' through controls. The effectiveness of such policies, however, depends crucially on the degree of substitutability between traded and nontraded assets. Furthermore, once one allows for the effect of changed interest rates on income, prices and, hence, the balance of trade — the intermediate or 'adjustment' run — the initial effect of the monetary policy will weaken and tend to disappear in the longer run.

This implies that whatever gain in monetary autonomy is achieved through controls or by acting on the relative supplies of traded and nontraded assets will be a short-run one only — the higher the 'capital mobility', the shorter the run.[3] Moreover, the gain in monetary autonomy from lack of financial in-

[1] See H. Genberg, 'A Note on Inflation Rates under Fixed Exchange Rates' (unpublished manuscript, May 1974). Genberg finds that, on average over his sample period, inflation rates among major OECD countries differ no more from each other than do measured inflation rates among United States cities. I suspect a similar finding would arise from applying a modified version of this test to interest rates.

[2] See, for instance, William Branson, 'Macroeconomic Equilibrium with Portfolio Balance in Open Economies', *Seminar Paper no. 22* (Institute for International Economic Studies, University of Stockholm, May 1972); Rüdiger Dornbusch, 'Capital Mobility and Portfolio Balance' (mimeo, June 1974); and P. B. Kenen, 'A Portfolio Model of Adjustment with Four Financial Assets', *Princeton University Working Papers in International Economics*, G-75-01.

[3] This point is emphasised in two articles of mine. See A. K. Swoboda, 'Equilibrium, Quasi-Equilibrium and Macroeconomic Policy under Fixed Exchange Rates', in *Quarterly Journal of Economics, LXXXI*, Feb 1972, and 'Monetary Policy under Fixed Exchange Rates Effectiveness, the Speed of Adjustment and Proper Use', in *Economica*, May 1973.

tegration may not exist at all, even in the short run, if goods markets are integrated. Under fixed exchange rates, goods arbitrage insures that money prices of traded goods move in harmony, and monetary policy can have an effect on income or prices only if it can affect the terms of trade, which is quite unlikely except in the very short run, or if the country where the policy is undertaken is large enough to affect world prices, incomes or interest rates.

To sum up, the loss of monetary autonomy arising from capital market integration is minimal (it is limited to short-run effects if any), and one cannot but agree with Kenen that exchange-rate, rather than capital-market, arrangements, are the important factor in this respect. The freedom that flexible exchange rates allow is control over the general price level, but recent experience in many countries indicates that it may be a freedom not worth having.

III.

Kenen's formal model is designed to analyse the extent to which capital mobility frustrates monetary independence and facilitates or hinders adjustment to exogenous trade disturbances. I shall limit my comments to the fixed-exchange rate case.

Kenen's comparative-statics results are, with but a few exceptions, well established in the literature.[4] The model, however, differs from traditional ones In particular, and these are worthwhile features, capital movements result from stock adjustments and saving reflects adjustments between actual and desired wealth. This makes possible a clear distinction between the steady state and an explicitly described adjustment path. Other features of the model may be less attractive. In particular, prices are assumed to be fixed and, concomitantly, output is strictly demand-determined; also, wealth is defined so as to assume no discounting of future tax liabilities associated with the servicing of the public debt.

The complexity of Kenen's model (especially with respect to disaggregation of balance sheets) makes it difficult to see what specific assumptions and equations produce his specific conclusions. Careful examination of the model however, reveals that its results derive from only a few key assumptions and equations and can readily be understood.

To illustrate, consider the effect of an open-market purchase of securities ($+dB_c$) under fixed exchange rates. Kenen concludes that the *equilibrium* level of income is not affected, whatever, the degree of capital mobility, but that, with perfectly mobile capital, the equilibrium interest rate remains constant, whereas it falls when capital is immobile.

These results are mainly determined by four equations in Kenen's model: equation (1), the definition of household wealth; equation (2), the demand for money; equation (3), the saving function; and equation (13), the goods-market equilibrium condition, which states that national income is determined by aggregate demand 'in the familiar Keynesian manner'. This last equation, taken in conjunction with the saving equation, is sufficient, to produce the

[4] See Mundell's early work, as illustrated in R. A. Mundell, *International Economics* (New York: Macmillan, 1968). Cf. also the two articles cited in note 3 above.

conclusion that an open-market operation does not affect the equilibrium level of income under fixed exchange rates, whatever the degree of capital mobility. For, by definition, investment is zero and so is saving in equilibrium; taxes are assumed to be equal to government expenditure. Equation (13) then is: $Y = Y + (X - M)$. The term in parentheses must be equal to zero – that is, the value of imports must be equal to the exogenously given level of exports. As income (with a fixed exchange rate) is the only determinant of imports, the equilibrium level of income is entirely determined once the exogenous level of exports is given.[5] (The equilibrium value of equation (13) is depicted as the line TT in the figures below). This conclusion of Kenen's is perfectly consistent with the one reached within the standard Mundellian model – though in the latter it occurs because there is only one level of the money stock compatible, *ceteris paribus*, with payments equilibrium, even though saving need not be equal to zero and capital may flow even in equilibrium.[6]

Whether the interest rate is affected by an open-market operation depends, in Kenen's model, on the effect of that operation on household wealth. Remember that for saving to be zero, as it must be in equilibrium, desired and actual wealth must be equal. A fall in the interest rate reduces desired wealth, so that only a lower level of actual wealth is compatible with equilibrium at lower interest rates. Assuming for simplicity (unlike Kenen, but this makes no essential difference here) that households own the central bank, household wealth is equal to the sum of the value of foreign-exchange reserves and of bonds held by residents, that is, in Kenen's notation

$$W^h = R + (1/r)(B^h + B^c + B^b) = R + (1/r)(B - B^f), \qquad (1)$$

neglecting W^e, which, in any event, is assumed to be constant.

Consider an open-market purchase of securities under perfect capital *mobility*. A fall in the interest rate is prevented as foreigners sell the bonds to the central bank, which loses an equivalent amount of reserves. Household wealth does not change, since the reduction in R is matched by that in $(1/r)B^f$ (or, equivalently, the increase in $(1/r)B^c$) at unchanged $(1/r)(B^h + B^b)$. When capital is *immobile*, however, $B^f = 0$ and an open-market purchase of securities – which leaves the total of bonds outstanding, B, constant by definition – can increase B^c only at the expense of B^h and B^b. At the initial interest rate, wealth has not changed yet, but portfolio balance – Kenen's equation (2) – has been disturbed, since the stock of money has increased. The rate of interest tends to fall, but at a given level of income this implies that desired wealth falls and, hence, dissaving and a corresponding trade deficit take place; some of the money that has been created is now destroyed as foreign-exchange reserves decrease. However, the initial rate of interest cannot be restored, since, with unchanged B and r and diminished R, actual wealth has fallen below its initial level and below desired wealth for saving to occur. In other words, since the open-market purchase induces a loss of reserves that reduces actual wealth, the interest rate has to fall in order to restore equality between desired and actual wealth.

A simple graphical illustration may help clarify Kenen's result. The initial

---

[5] Incidentally, for consistency with the treatment of saving, imports should be made a function of expenditure and not of income in Kenen's model.

[6] See Swoboda, in *Economica*, May 1973.

equilibrium of the economy is described in Figure 1. TT is the locus of combinations of income and interest rate that, for given exports, equilibrates the balance of trade. It thus depicts, for $G = T$ and $S = 0$, Kenen's equation (13), the demand-determined level of output. SS represents the various combinations of interest rate and level of income for which desired wealth is equal to a *given* level of actual household wealth, say W_0^h. These two schedules are sufficient to determine the equilibrium rate of interest, r_0, and the level of income, Y_0. For convenience, we can also draw in the money-market equilibrium schedule LL — Kenen's equation (2). LL will pass through A since the money stock is an endogenous variable under fixed exchange rates and in the absence of neutralisation operations.

Suppose, now, an open-market purchase of securities takes place. If capital is *mobile,* household wealth is unchanged, and income, the rate of interest and the money stock are not affected. As the domestic assets of the consolidated

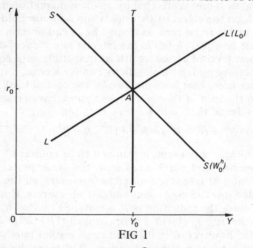

FIG 1

banking system have increased by $(1/r)B^c$, its foreign-exchange reserves decrease by the same amount. The case of *immobile* capital is illustrated in Figure 2. The decrease in household wealth attendant on the loss of reserves shifts the SS schedule to $S'S'$; for every level of income the rate of interest must be lower than before in order to bring desired wealth in equality with the lower level of actual wealth, W_1^h. In the final equilibrium at B, the rate of interest must be lower than before. As, again, the money supply is endogenous, it increases to L_1 so that LL shifts to $L'L'$. This illustrates Kenen's conclusion that the loss of reserves is smaller when capital is immobile.

It is interesting to inquire why these differences between the case of capital mobility and that of immobility do not appear in other models.[7] The main reason is simply a difference in the definition of net wealth. If one assumes that future tax liabilities are discounted by the public, an open-market operation fails to have a wealth effect in the final equilibrium. Any change in holdings of government bonds is compensated for by opposite changes in 'holdings'

[7] The 'standard' result is that the interest rate will not be affected, except during the transition to equilibrium. See Swoboda, in *Quarterly Journal of Economics, LXXXI.*

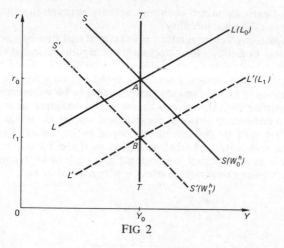

FIG 2

of future tax liabilities. This is, of course, the main issue in the controversy surrounding Lloyd A. Metzler's conclusion in his justly famous 'Wealth, Saving and the Rate of Interest' (*Journal of Political Economy, LIX*, Apr 1951). This is not to deny that a real balance effect arises in the transition to equilibrium. In the final equilibrium, however, real balances are restored to their initial level through an equiproportionate change in the price level in the closed economy, and through a return of the nominal supply of money to its initial level in the small open economy.

Finally, let me comment only very briefly on Kenen's conclusions concerning the effect of an exogenous change in exports. That the impact on income in the final equilibrium is independent of the degree of capital mobility is perfectly obvious from equation (13), or from realising that the shift in *TT* in our figures is the same irrespective of whether capital is mobile or not. This result contradicts the one obtained from 'Keynesian' models in which *flows* of capital are responsive to interest rates, in the type of model that Ingram had in mind. These would predict that the income change is greater when capital is immobile than when it is mobile. The reason is that, with capital mobile, part of the burden of overall payments adjustment is borne by the capital account relieving pressure for trade-account (and, hence, income) adjustment. To the extent that flows of capital are characteristic of the adjustment period, this provides indirect support for Kenen's second conclusion, that income adjustment may be slower with than it would be without capital mobility.

IV.

In conclusion, I should like to add a few questions to Kenen's menu for discussion. For the sake of brevity, I shall list them without discussion.

(1) To what extent, and in what sense, is capital-market integration affected by whether fixed or flexible exchange rates rule?

(2) Does the degree of capital-market integration have anything to do with the *choice* between fixed and flexible rates? In particular, how is the purported

insulation of national macro-economic activity through flexible rates affected by the degree of capital mobility?

(3) If capital-market integration is beneficial and first-best, except for the Kemp—Jones—Connolly—Ross optimum tax argument, and if the loss of national sovereignty due to integration is minimal under fixed exchange rates and inexistent under flexible ones, what is the rationale for the proliferation of controls on capital movements that we seem to be witnessing?

(4) In keeping with the general theme of this congress, how much validity is there to a distinction between regional and worldwide integration? In particular, how relevant are the criteria developed in the theory of customs unions, for instance, to the issue of whether a piecemeal approach to capital-market integration — as exemplified in a regional approach or in free mobility confined to particular categories of assets — is beneficial or not?

Opening Statement for Group Discussion
Raymond Bertrand (France)

I. INTRODUCTORY

The integration of capital markets, whatever that means, appears in a quite different light according to the degree of political and economic union that the countries concerned want to achieve. Either we consider nation states that are, and want to remain, separate — in which case the questions relate to the optimal degree of freedom of capital movements between them; or we assume that a group of nation states wants to form an economic union — that is, achieve full integration. In this case, the questions relate to the role, timing and conditions of the integration of financial systems as part of the process of economic union.

Broadly speaking, the first case corresponds to the type of problems met by industrialised countries in the OECD, where rules and procedures for co-operation concerning international capital movements have existed for nearly fifteen years. The second case is illustrated by the efforts of the EEC to move towards integrated capital markets.

II. CAPITAL MOBILITY BETWEEN SEPARATE NATION STATES

Let us leave out tightly centralised and collectivist economies, where each capital transaction is supposed to satisfy tests of social utility. Among market economies, like those of the OECD countries, government practice and international co-operation have evolved similar attitudes toward international capital movements. Private capital transactions are basically considered as socially positive, unless shown otherwise. Governmental interference with capital transactions is widely differentiated, depending upon the nature of the operations. Banking operations and short-term capital transactions (both outward and inward) are often subject to strict regulations, because they interfere more directly with the conduct of monetary policy and with the management of external reserves. Portfolio transactions are sometimes regulated where capital flight is feared, or when domestic market disturbances require it. As a rule, direct investment is left alone, except for foreign entry in some industries. Commercial credits are, as a rule, completely free.

On the whole, this approach makes economic sense, since it provides a broad range of second-best solutions for adjustment policies, on the one hand, and for resource allocation, on the other. Capital controls are preferable to trade controls for the adjustment of temporary and cyclical disequilibria; they do not cure the causes, but help to gain time in order to work out solutions. Direct investment, on the other hand, is the main vector of international resource allocation, is less prone to speculative or short-term influences, and needs a climate of stability.

From the point of view of short-term adjustment, much depends, of course, on the exchange-rate regime. With clean floating rates, two major reasons for using capital controls would be removed, since monetary policies would be autonomous and external reserves irrelevant. With fixed rates, or with very dirty float, we are back in the real world. Peter Kenen has attempted to demonstrate that capital controls then accelerate the changes in internal demand necessary to restore equilibrium, and call for larger changes in reserves. That may be the case, under very restrictive assumptions, although I confess to being somewhat doubtful about the effectiveness of causal links between capital movements and internal demand via interest rates and the level of investment.

In any case, international balance (and adjustment of domestic demand to it) is perfectly compatible with sustainable net capital outflows or inflows. What is lacking, both in the international attempts to co-ordinate balance-of-payments structures and in theory, is a set of criteria that would permit us to judge the social utility of alternative patterns of international net flows of real and financial resources. For years we have seen Italy as a capital exporter, Canada and Norway as large capital importers, and Japan shifting from a net importer to a net exporter position. The OECD as a whole used to be a net capital exporter to the rest of the world; after the oil crisis it is a net importer to the tune of $40 billion a year. Clearly, net external savings are not a function of total wealth or of income per capita. I wonder if they should be.

III. INTEGRATION OF CAPITAL MARKETS WITHIN AN ECONOMIC UNION

In the perspective of full economic union, integration of capital markets does not simply mean full capital mobility among the parts of the union. It also implies the replacement of separate regulatory frameworks by one central machinery for the regulation of credit, interest rates, financial institutions and securities business.

Assume that an economic union of certain nation states is the objective. Assume that, in its final stage, it involves a common currency, pooled external reserves, and complete freedom of payments and financial transactions within its territory. The question, then, is how to reach the ultimate stage, and, in particular, where and when capital-market integration should fit into the whole process.

I should argue that financial integration (defined as full capital mobility plus central regulatory machinery) should come at the end, and, in any event, not before currency and monetary unification. In this context, the loss of autonomy of national financial policy is not a 'cost' of capital-market integration, since the whole exercise postulates the substitution of a larger decision unit for the previously autonomous ones.

Both financial and monetary integration are not continuous processes; they include, at some stage, qualitative institutional thresholds where key policy responsibilities are transferred from existing nation states to a supranational organ of the union. As long as existing national organs feel responsible for their exchange rates, monetary reserves, interest rates and money and credit expansion, they cannot avoid having to react in times of high stress by some sort of control over transfers and financial transactions with the other states, including those with which they intend to form a union, notwithstanding all commitments to the contrary. The motivations to intervene have to be eliminated first, and alternative adjustment mechanisms must be ready. Failure to recognise this basic fact explains what little success the EEC has so far achieved in financial integration. In this perspective, detailed and thorough harmonisation of regulations of various types of financial institutions, or commitments completely to liberalise partial sectors of operations, do not touch the heart of the matter.

Progress along these lines is not cumulative, and is always in danger of retrograding, in the same manner as progress toward permanently fixed exchange rates within a group of currencies. Instead of stating that integrated capital markets help to conduct a unified monetary policy, I should say that a unified central bank and a central authority able to redistribute public funds and credit among the regions of the union are the preconditions for a unified capital market. Whether such perspectives are good or bad is entirely a matter of subjective political choice. But, clearly, full integration will remain a political rarity, and does not provide a model for the world.

IV. INTEGRATION THROUGH THE INTERNATIONAL MARKETS

Meanwhile, many of the technical benefits expected from the integration of capital markets have been obtained through the Euromarkets for short and long money (increased competition between banks and issuing houses — capacity to raise very large amounts — transparency of interest rates and conditions — depth and flexibility). These markets have grown quickly during the last decade because they were outside of national regulatory frameworks, and they helped resolve the not-infrequent conflicts between national policies. Remember the periods when American, British or Swedish companies were (as in some cases they still are) prohibited from taking money across the exchanges for investment abroad, and, simultaneously, were prevented from borrowing or issuing bonds in the country where they wanted to invest.

True, these markets have developed quite a few problems of their own, but remedies were found. In any case, the Euromarkets will have a major role to play in the redistribution of oil money.

V. CONCLUSION

Capital mobility is not an end in itself, but a means of achieving several functions of the international economy. Capital movements can be destabilising or run contrary to domestic objectives, and this justifies some degree of control, preferably under international surveillance. Such controls should be modulated according to the potential international benefits and national costs of various types of capital transaction. In short, full capital mobility is out of the question among nation states.

Technically, the international market already provides many advantages to be expected from such integration. Policy compromises can thus be worked out between national goals and the common need for international allocation of resources.

Economic union, by removing national constraints, makes full capital mobility possible, provided that sufficient regulatory powers are vested in the monetary and financial organs of the union.

It is impossible for all countries simultaneously to be net capital exporters or net capital importers. The pattern of transfer of real and financial resources in any given period results from market forces and from national policy stances on demand, exchange rates, interest rates, and so on. It is open to question whether full capital mobility alone would optimise this structural pattern, assuming that operational criteria of optimality were available. But it is even more doubtful whether an optimal pattern could result from intergovernmental agreements.

Report on Group Discussion
Herbert Giersch (Federal Republic Germany)

In four sessions, Working Group E dealt with international capital movements
and the integration of capital markets. The paper by Kenen, the comments by
Mundell and Swoboda, and the opening statement by Bertrand were followed
by a discussion on the basis of a detailed agenda.

While the broader aspects of Kenen's paper concerning the barriers to, and
the costs and benefits of, capital mobility formed the background of much of
the group's work during the succeeding sessions, his specific model for determining the implications of capital mobility for individual countries under
fixed and flexible exchange rates was dealt with by only a limited number of
specialists. Swoboda's geometric interpretation revealed the essence and the
limitations of the model. Bertrand's opening statement complemented the
theoretical analysis with a number of observations on the policy aspects of
capital-market integration.

The first part of the ensuing discussion was devoted to some general aspects
of capital-market integration. The question was put of whether greater flexibility of exchange rates may have a disintegrating effect on international capital
markets. This fear was considered unjustified, however, since the only realistic
alternatives — capital controls or abrupt parity changes at irregular intervals —
would certainly be more disintegrating. Moreover, the market has already in-
vented an appropriate instrument for coping with present-day exchange rate
risks: loans denominated in terms of a basket of currencies.

There was a debate about whether, and in what sense, national economics
can insulate themselves from outside disturbances by means of flexible exchange rates if capital markets are closely integrated. It was argued that, even
under perfect mobility, countries would be free to choose their rate of inflation, allowing an upward float to insulate themselves from world inflation.
But it was emphasised that different time lags with respect to factor and commodity prices make it very difficult for a country to return to relative price-
level stability in a short period of time.

The question of whether there can be a case for capital controls aroused a
number of comments. It was pointed out that controls are more harmful for
long-term capital movements and direct investment than for liquidity transfers.
On the other hand, there may be political objections to foreigners buying up
domestic property. Nevertheless, on economic grounds, capital controls were
considered justifiable only under very specific conditions, for instance, as a
second-best solution if there are irremovable impediments to trade and to
labour migration.

The idea that there may be a case for regional capital-market integration
comparable to that for a customs union did not find support if it implied
erecting a common system of controls *vis-à-vis* third countries. There was,
however, agreement on the desirability of measures for regional capital-
market integration aimed at reducing market imperfections, international
differences in taxation, and other institutional factors.

The second part of the discussion dealt with regional capital-market integration and with capital movements in Western Europe. The suggestion contained in the opening statement, that West European capital-market integra-

tion must be preceded by monetary integration was confronted with the American experience that capital-market integration had strengthened centralising forces in the Federal Reserve system.

There was a long debate about whether it is desirable and possible to increase capital flows from the highly developed central areas of Western Europe to the peripheral areas in the north and south of the EEC. While the desirability of a regional policy bringing about the regional dispersion of private investment was not questioned by European economists, doubts were expressed regarding its probable effectiveness. It was emphasised that any regional policy would be effective only if it were conceived of as a long-term strategy and were not abandoned when it produced no result in the short term. Regarding the view that regional policy should aim essentially at redistributing income for consumption, it was argued that regional policy could not be regarded as a zero-sum game, since it promised a better utilisation of idle resources at the periphery and reduced congestion in the agglomeration centres of the central areas. As to the instruments, the opinion prevailed that incentives would be superior to controls. Exception to these views was taken by a participant from the GDR, who objected that to use incentives would be to give in to the profit motive, which he considered to be at the root of regional imbalances.

Colleagues from the USSR drew the group's attention to the size of American direct investment in Western Europe and its concentration in particular industries. They argued that, in the future, American investment in Western Europe would slow down as a result of recent exchange-rate changes, the narrowing of the technological gap, and the consequent changes in the relative rates of profit. They also predicted that American direct investment would be spread more evenly among industries and regions, thus intensifying competition. In evaluating direct investment and the financial operations of multinational firms, our Soviet colleagues claimed that American-based multinational corporations had predominantly disintegrative effects on the economy of Western Europe, whereas the formation of European multinational firms would support the forces of West European integration.

The mutual financing of large enterprises within the CMEA, and the role of the international investment bank, were the subject of the third part of the group's discussion. A number of communications on this proved to be very informative for Western economists, although it was felt that the integration of economic terminologists is in need of improvement. The group learned that there are three types of international corporate financing: joint construction agreements, joint enterprises ('joint-stock companies without stocks'), and coproduction agreements. Where borrowing is involved, repayment tends to be in kind. The implicit real rate of interest is estimated to amount to 3 or 4 per cent. Participants from CMEA countries expressed the hope that the resources of the international investment bank would be enlarged to allow it to play an increasing role in CMEA integration.

The fourth topic on the agenda was the issue of capital transfers in the framework of East—West co-operation. The group heard that individual CMEA countries were borrowing in international markets on the same terms as were other borrowers, while loans from Western governments were obtained at interest rates of 6—7 per cent, often combined with long-term trade contracts.

There followed a report on the direct participation of Western private firms in enterprises in Yugoslavia, and specific answers were given to questions raised by the audience. Three points appear to be worth mentioning. First, the recipient country is interested not only in the capital transfer, but also, and perhaps even more, in the transfer of technology. Second, experiments with joint ventures in Yugoslavia have been very successful. Third, it was regretted that the extent of Western participation in joint activities was as low as 2 per cent of total investment in Yugoslavia.

The fifth part of the discussion concerned the stake of the developing countries in the functioning of the international capital market. This question was seen to be of paramount importance, since development aid from governments and from intergovernmental institutions is unlikely to increase to the extent necessary to cover the needs of those developing countries that are facing a deterioration in their terms of trade as a result of increases in the price of oil and impending food shortages. In these circumstances, direct investment is bound to play an increasingly important role, notwithstanding its drawbacks, which were particularly stressed by economists from the USSR and the GDR. Several speakers emphasised the point that developing countries that want to attract foreign investment should avoid exchange controls and other forms of currency overvaluation. It was reported that empirical studies have shown overvaluation to be important in explaining why some countries have experienced a decline in their share of total international investment.

Much thought was given to the problem of how the additional revenue that the oil-producing countries will earn in future could be channelled into investment in the less developed world. Suggestions were made for creating both new institutions and new instruments. As regards institutional aspects, a representative of the World Bank group described the efforts that the World Bank, the International Development Association and the International Finance Corporation are making in channelling funds from the rich to the poor developing countries. It was acknowledged that there may be a need for corresponding international institutions that could facilitate the raising of funds to finance the balance-of-payments deficits of those industrialised countries that are already heavily indebted to private international lenders. As far as new instruments are concerned, several speakers came out in favour of issuing index-linked bonds denominated in an international unit of account. This would enable the oil producers, who cannot readily absorb real resources, to be offered an asset that would protect them against the risks of unanticipated devaluation and inflation. The advocates of this proposal suggested that the index-linking of bonds would raise the supply of oil and facilitate the recycling of finance. It was admitted that such protection should not be withheld from domestic savers either.

These suggestions led to the last topic on the agenda — a general discussion of the present problems of the international capital market. In the diagnosis, attention was focused on the shortening of the debt structure due to the acceleration of inflation in all Western countries. Parallels were drawn with the period before 1929. Some participants feared that disinflationary policies would go too far and would lead to a crisis, unless countries with surpluses adopt appropriate policies. Among possible measures mentioned were exchange-rate adjustments and the use of fiscal measures and index clauses as a means of minimising the negative effects on the output of restrictive monetary policies.

9 Monetary and Fiscal Integration (Main Paper, Working Group F)

Alexandre Lamfalssy (BELGIUM)

I. INTRODUCTORY

This paper deals with the expedience and the possibility of creating a currency area, as well as the economic steps by which it may be achieved.

This is a subject that has been widely debated in terms of economic analysis, thanks above all to the pioneer work of Robert Mundell, the 'father' of the concept of an optimum currency area. I do not propose to say anything new on this matter, nor even to present a summary of the theoretical debate.[1] Rather, I shall examine the specific case of monetary integration as conceived and pursued within the EEC; I shall explain why the attempt has failed and show the implications of this failure for other aspects of economic union; and I shall discuss why it is worth trying again and how best to do so.

The terms 'monetary union' and 'currency area' will be used here interchangeably. In either case, what is meant is a geographical area made up of several countries, each with its own currency, but an area within which exchange rates are fixed once and for all, and capital movements and payments are entirely free.

II. THE FAILURE OF THE EEC'S ATTEMPTS AT MONETARY INTEGRATION

The success of any attempt at monetary integration must be measured by facts, not by official statements. And the facts are plain: between 1969[2] and spring 1974, both parities (or central rates) and the market rates of exchange of EEC currencies against each other have altered more frequently than

[1] For an overall review of theoretical work concerning an optimum currency area, see Pascal Salin, 'La Zone monétaire optimale', in *L'Unification monétaire européene* (Paris: Calmann-Lévy, 1974). This volume also contains other contributions on the same subject, as well as a full bibliography. See also *The Economics of Common Currencies*, ed. H. G. Johnson and A. K. Swoboda (London: Allen and Unwin, 1973), which is a symposium of papers (submitted to a conference held in Madrid in March 1970) on optimum currency areas.

[2] It was on 12 February 1969 that the Commission submitted to the Council the first concrete scheme for monetary integration, known as the Barre plan.

during the first ten years of the Common Market. The German mark, the guilder and, to a lesser extent, the Beglian franc have appreciably risen in value against the lira and the French franc, which remained tied more closely to the dollar than to the German mark.

Nor can much comfort be drawn from the manner in which these fluctuations actually happened. The European agreement on the joint float of European currencies *vis-à-vis* the dollar was modest enought in its aims; it did not preclude parity changes, but merely involved joint limits to the exchange-rate movements around certain central rates, which themselves remained open to change. Personally, I have always thought that such an agreement was somewhat spurious, in that it gave all market parities an illusion of stability. The purpose, of course, was to achieve real stability, but this cannot be expected from an arrangement setting a limit to *continuous* exchange-rate movements while leaving the way open for *discontinuous,* and possibly large, parity changes. If I have left myself without forward cover and incur an exchange loss because the Deutschmark central rate is revalued against the Belgian franc, it is small consolation to me that this revaluation has in fact not infringed the rules of the Community 'snake'.

Yet there is something to say for the snake. First and foremost, central banks have had to intervene in the market for other EEC currencies, and these direct interventions have had the effect of a real, if slight, diminution of the role of the dollar in international affairs. Another good point is the frequency of these novel operational contacts among the central banks of the countries adhering to the agreement.

By the spring of 1974, even these meagre consolations had melted away. Three of the four leading currencies in the EEC – the pound sterling, the French franc and the lira – are floating freely, and, in effect, the snake applies solely to the Deutschmark area, comprising the Belgian–Luxembourg franc, the Dutch guilder, the Danish krone and its Swedish and Norwegian counterparts. The joint float really has precious little to do with the EEC as such. The Belgian franc still has its two-tier market, now dating back more than twenty years. As of 16 April 1974, the result, in practice, is that the 'official' Belgian franc is touching bottom with respect to the German mark, while on the capital market it has dropped right through the bottom (which, formally, does not exist at all) to the extent of about 2 per cent. Note that there is nothing in this situation to infringe the working rules of the European joint float.

As regards the freedom of payments and capital movements, the Community policy has no tangible result to show at all. To be sure, external convertibility, as established in 1958, still survives, but the geographical area to which it applies in no way coincides with that of the EEC. This, perhaps, does not matter very much. On the other hand, what does matter is the total absence of any sort of *common* policy with respect to the numerous restrictions imposed on capital movements in the current battle against speculative, or 'hot', money. European central banks have assembled an impressive arsenal for this purpose, but I have been unable to find one single weapon anywhere that makes a distinction between capital originating in other EEC countries and capital from elsewhere. The technical reasons for this are plain: without some sort of common external tariff, there is no way of making out a 'certificate of origin'.

The inescapable conclusion is that monetary integration within the EEC has made no progress at all. With reference to the hopes and intentions expressed in 1968 and 1969 on the basis of the gratifying progress of the Community in other fields in the past ten years, we have gone backward, rather than forward, in monetary matters. The 'gradualist' approach, which was meant as a combination of — or perhaps just a compromise between — the 'monetary' view and the 'economic' view, has led to an attempt to foster integration by gradual and parallel steps as regards both currencies (narrowing the margins of fluctuation, concerted policies on official exchange rates) and economic policy (co-ordination of budgetary and monetary policies, short-term reactions to business conditions). Why has this approach failed? Was it because of its own inadequacies? Or is the geographical area of the EEC one that, for a number of reasons, simply defies being transformed into a currency area? Or did unforeseen events outside the Community make it impossible to achieve monetary union?

III. THE ILLUSIONS OF THE GOLDEN AGE AND THE DISTURBING INFLUENCES OF INTERNATIONAL ORIGIN

The Common Market started in 1958 under exceptionally favourable circumstances, the effects of which lasted, by and large, until 1967–8. In those ten years or so, member countries of the EEC experienced faster and more steady economic growth than did most of the world's other industrial countries, except Japan. Inflation was contained within tolerable limits. Apart from a brief scare about the lira, no country suffered any large or persisting deficit in its balance of payments. And, except for a minor revaluation of the German mark in 1963 (a venial sin), intra-Community parities underwent no change. Thanks to these circumstances, the proposed customs union was achieved ahead of schedule.

I have had occasion to explain elsewhere,[3] without the benefit of hindsight, what reasons led me at that time to ascribe these results to a happy constellation of circumstances rather than to the internal dynamics of the EEC. To some degree or other, all member countries enjoyed export-led growth, which had been made possible by a number of factors (abundant supply of labour, relatively small military expenditure, high propensity of households to save, and so on), of which the most important was the systematic undervaluation of European currencies. It was this that made room for persisting current-account

[3] *The United Kingdom and the Six: An Essay in Economic Growth in Western Europe* (London: Macmillan, 1963); 'Europe's Progress: Due to Common Market?', in *Lloyds Bank Review*, Oct 1961; 'Contributions à une théorie de la croissance en économie ouverte', in *Recherches économiques de Louvain*, Dec 1963.

surpluses in the balance of payments, by which alone this type of growth can be sustained.

We now know that this situation was inevitably unstable. It could have lasted only if the European current-account surplus had been offset by capital exports, preferably to developing countries. If, at the same time, the current surpluses of the United States had similarly been offset by capital exports to developing countries, then we might have found ourselves in an idyllic world where the direction of the transfer of real resources was politically acceptable and where, at the same time, there would have been reasonable stability in the world distribution of exchange reserves.

Since 1968 things have been going badly. The United States' current-account surplus was replaced by a deficit; American capital exports grew, but the bulk of them went to Europe. Thus, Europe found itself at the receiving end of long-term capital as well as of hot money, both flows being attracted by the undervaluation of European currencies, principally the German mark. Even before then, gold and foreign-exchange reserves had begun to pile up in European hands, and this accumulation could continue so long as the deterioration in the net American position gave rise to no major concern about the dollar; once serious misgivings about it began to be felt, around 1969–70, the flight from the dollar set in and speculative capital took refuge in the currencies of those European countries that had so long and so persistently enjoyed balance-of-payments surpluses. But these movements were *selective*; not all European countries 'benefited' from them to the same extent. Hence, inevitably, the resulting pressures were of different strengths, so much so that exchange rates had to be adjusted and the stability of intra-Community rates came to an end.

Europe's governments and monetary authorities can claim some excuses for having stood by, powerless, as European dreams of monetary integration went up in thin air. Even with international circumstances at their most propitious, as they were until 1968–9, currency union would have come up against more difficulties than would customs union; it involved politically more sensitive matters and, since the removal of tariff protection had already deprived national policy makers of one of their major weapons, the *domestic* problems arising within any one member country (Italy in 1963–4, France in 1968–9) would in any event have made things hard for the protagonists of monetary integration. By ill fortune, the authorities had at the same time to cope with the collapse of the international monetary system and with the innumerable technical and political problems due to international disturbances. Confidence in the dollar crumbled, the role of gold changed and its price on the free market rose four-fold; the United States set the world's leading currencies afloat; international liquidity, which until then had been regarded as so insufficient that special drawing rights had been created, suddenly became overabundant and, more-over, because of the gold imbroglio, impossible to measure. In other words, virtually all the working hypotheses upon which governments had reasoned for more than twenty years simply ceased to apply.

IV. THE DETERIORATION IN THE TERMS OF TRADE OF INDUSTRIAL COUNTRIES

To the effects of the dollar devaluation were added, more recently, those of the spectacular rise of raw-material prices, those of oil above all. This price explosion implies a deterioration in the terms of trade of industrial countries, especially in Europe. This in turn is bound to have two consequences: first, these countries' balances on current account must deteriorate; and, second, the transfer of real resources to countries producing raw materials will demand sacrifices in the form of a slow-down in the rate of increase in consumption and/or investment — hence, slower economic growth.

The effects will not be the same for all member countries of the EEC. Some will suffer more than others. Here we have a second, quite new, reason for the instability of exchange rates *within* the EEC. Plainly, it was for these reasons that the French government, anxious to gain a competitive advantage for French exporters, took the franc out of the snake and allowed it to depreciate.

V. LARGE-SCALE CAPITAL MOVEMENTS

The two 'external' factors of disturbance — the crisis of the international monetary system and the rise in raw material prices — would not have had such devastating effects on European monetary integration if the international economic setting had not been dominated by large-scale capital movements.

A number of facts, reforms and spontaneous developments have all worked in the same direction of stimulating capital flows. The introduction of general external convertibility in 1958 gave nonresidents the right of free exchange transactions in all currencies except that of the country of domicile of the bank at which they keep their deposits;[4] this created an appropriate institutional framework and, at the same time, considerably curtailed the power of control of the central banks.[5] The way was thus open for the spectacular

[4] A nonresident with a deposit of, say, guilders at a London Bank was always — even at the height of the recurrent sterling crises — free to transform his money into German marks. But he was not always free to switch from some foreign currency into sterling and *vice versa,* and British residents had even less freedom.

[5] The idea behind external convertibility was that it did not impede any country's monetary policy, since it did not affect the balance of payments (say, of the United Kingdom, in our example). It is true that a transaction such as that mentioned in the previous note has no effect, either direct or indirect, on the sterling rate; but it certainly does have an effect on the exchange rate of the guilder and the mark, and, at least temporarily, escapes Dutch and German central-bank control. The German central bank, of course, retains the power of prohibiting the buyer of marks from using them to acquire German domestic financial assets; but, in the meantime, the owner of Deutschmark balances will have the full benefit of any revaluation of the mark, having done his bit to make this inevitable. External convertibility thus gives every individual central bank the illusion that it can isolate its own currency from capital movements. But this isolation can be achieved only by curtailing another country's freedom to isolate its currency, and therefore is, collectively speaking, an illusion.

growth of the Eurodollar market. Now, it is a fact not open to doubt that the Eurocurrency market, as a whole, provides the perfect transfer mechanism for capital movements, whether genuine or speculative. So does the Eurobond market, but on a smaller scale. Finally, the multinational branch network of a dozen or so big banks provides the means of quick and efficient transfer of funds. Of course, the most perfect mechanism would have remained inoperative if businessmen had not chosen to use it. This condition too was fulfilled, when the increasing interpenetration of Western economies led to the exponential growth of foreign trade. The leads and lags, caused sometimes by differential rates of interest and sometimes by expectations of changes in market rates of exchange or parities, are in effect capital movements via the privileged, and often officially favoured, channel of foreign trade. Their potential size grows with the growth of foreign trade.

The increasing number of multinational firms has made the connection between foreign trade and capital transfers even closer. The reason lies in two characteristics of multinational firms not shared by even the most powerful importers and exporters of any single country: their branches in different countries systematically trade with each other, and their cash management, in most cases, is centralised. Any decisions that the central finance management takes in the light of its overall view of the international interest-rate structure, or of exchange risks, thus make an immediate impact on the whole branch network. They influence the choice of the currency of the sources of finance and of the market on which to raise them, as well as the timing of payments; in short, they accelerate the leads and lags in lower gear. These decisions may, of course, also lead to 'true' capital movements.

VI. IS THE EEC AN OPTIMUM CURRENCY AREA?

The question arises of whether the failure of attempts at monetary integration in the EEC must be attributed solely to international disturbances. There is more than one indication to the contrary. The fact is that certain *internal* conditions for the creation of an optimum currency area have not been met, and still are not at hand.

This applies, in the first place, to intra-Community mobility of factors of production and, hence, to the formation of factor prices compatible with the existence of a currency area.

Labour statistics show that, barring only the migration of Italian workers to other EEC countries, mainly Germany, the bulk of migratory movements originated in Mediterranean countries that were not members of the EEC, and were not intra-Community flows. Moreover, Switzerland attracted proportionately more Italians than did Germany, and among Germany's 'guest workers' a much higher proportion came from Mediterranean countries other than Italy, especially in terms of the respective size of labour-exporting countries. In terms of the mobility of labour in the EEC (or should we say in the optimum area of Germany?), Yugoslavia and Turkey accounted for a bigger share than

Italy did. Nor do the time series of statistics reveal any increase in intra-EEC movements of labour – either in absolute figures or relatively with respect to other labour flows – to correspond to the progress of trade integration in the Community.

So much for the statistical figures, which are, assuredly, far from perfect. But beyond that we note the total absence of any sort of machinery for wage bargaining at the Community level. To be sure, it appears that contacts do exist both among employers' federations and among trade unions, but, to the best of my knowledge, no attempt has been made so far in either case to define common attitudes in wage negotiations. A case in point is that wage indexing in relation to the cost of living is a practice very unequally distributed among member countries; in Belgium, it covers all wages, in Germany none. At a time of rapid inflation this is bound to lead to wage disparities.

The factor of production 'enterprise' has no greater mobility in the EEC than has labour. Although there are no full statistics on this matter, all partial surveys available suggest that American firms have played a preponderant part in direct investment in the Community, or, at any rate, have played a far bigger part than have EEC firms. This can be explained by many perfectly sound reasons, such as comparative costs, the establishment of the common external tariff, and the size of American corporations. But the question remains: are we justified in speaking of the *differential inflow* of American direct investment into Europe as *intra-EEC mobility* of firms? In a certain sense, yes – for it has contributed to an equalisation of factor costs. But is this a sufficient definition of mobility?

A second, oft-mentioned condition for the creation of an optimal currency area is that its member countries should have a fairly similar 'inflation propensity'. Such a similarity, incidentally, would not be entirely dissociated from the criterion of 'wage formation' mentioned above, but it is clearly influenced by other factors, of which the most important are the rate of increase in labour productivity and the strength of the aversion to inflation felt by the economy's policy makers. In this there are very wide divergences among European countries, and these divergences matter all the more as inflation gathers pace throughout the world.

Several explanations suggest themselves. In Italy during the last few years, and in France in 1968–9, there have been wage rises clearly originating in the country's own political and social developments – witness the fact that these wage rises had no, or only a minimal, effect on neighbouring countries. In Britain, the blame rests not so much with rising wages, as with the extremely slow pace of productivity gains. If the United Kingdom continues on its productivity trend of the last fifteen years, and money wages increase at a rate at least matching that of the other EEC countries, then the value of the pound must inevitably decline gradually against other EEC currencies.

Finally, the battle against inflation plainly occupies different places in the scale of priorities in economic policy of different countries. It tops the list in the Federal Republic of Germany, whose anti-inflation policies are always the promptest, the strictest and the most lasting in Europe.

There are therefore good reasons to doubt whether there is anything optimal about the EEC as a currency area. Yet there are counter-arguments that, in my view, are weighty enough to win the day in the debate.

First, there is the matter of foreign-trade integration among member countries of the EEC. It is a fact that intra-Community trade has grown fast, for whatever reasons; it is a fact, too, that full unification of the international trade of the EEC countries would greatly reduce their degree of openness – which is another way of saying that intra-Community trade is larger in volume and tends to grow faster than does each individual member country's trade with nonmembers. This statistical observation does not, of course, warrant any *certain* conclusions about optimality, but it does create very strong presumptions.[6]

Second, we must ask ourselves whether the customs union has any chances of survival without monetary union. My instinct is to say no. It could perhaps be shown, with reference to the elementary principles of the theory of comparative advantages, that, once customs duties are abolished, the division of labour among members of the customs union can increase, regardless of the level of intra-union exchange rates. But it can certainly *not* be proved that exchange-rate *variations* would have no disturbing influence at all on the working of a customs union. Devaluation or revaluation of any one country's currency is bound to be regarded by the others as an indirect means of reviving tariff protection and, thus, of altering the trade flows. Moreover, at a given structure of external trade, such a measure will always specifically affect the position of some industry or another, and will thereby introduce some disturbance into trade relations. If, in addition, it became clear that any one country tried systematically, by repeated devaluations, to keep its currency undervalued (France is always suspect in this respect), the other countries would be bound, eventually, to demand retaliation and, in the extreme case, even the introduction of specific protection.

Third, allowance must be made for the social cost of uncertainty as the result of intra-Community exchange-rate fluctuations.[7] As long as effective exchange-rate fluctuations were limited to an occasional, and isolated, change in parity, it might, at a pinch, have been possible to neglect this cost. It cannot be neglected at a time of frequent and sizable variations in official or market exchange rates.[8]

[6] Certainty would require proof that the degree of openness so measured does, in fact, correspond to a certain proportion of substitutable/nonsubstitutable commodities (cf. R. I. McKinnon, 'Optimum Currency Area', in *American Economic Review,* Sep 1963), as well as to a certain marginal propensity to import (cf. M. Whitman, *International and Interregional Payments Adjustment: A Synthetic View,* Studies in International Finance, Princeton, 1967).

[7] R. A. Mundell, 'The Cost of Exchange Crises and the Problem of Sterling', in his *International Economics* (New York: Macmillan, 1968).

[8] One cost, which is seldom mentioned in theoretical writings but is patent to any banker, is the transformation of industrialists into currency speculators. Exchange cover

The fourth argument in favour of transforming the EEC into a currency area derives from the international monetary crisis. What would happen if the EEC were *not* to become a currency area? The Western world is not made up of a large number of countries of comparable size. If it were, I should perhaps have no major misgivings in the case of a possible collapse of what remains of the European Community. In such a world, it would not be absurd for all currencies to float, nor would it be absurd, as an alternative, to return to a somewhat revised Bretton Woods system, in which gold, upvalued, would resume its place and in which special drawing rights would allow balanced liquidity creation, with the IMF supervising such parity changes as become indispensable in case of basic disequilibrium. However, the Western world comprises the giant American economy, which, for obvious reasons, would play a dominant role *vis-à-vis* an 'atomised' Europe. It is no use expecting any reform of the international monetary system; once confidence in the dollar is restored — and we are well on the way to that — the Western world will simply adopt the dollar standard. This could go on working almost indefinitely, provided that the relatively stable current-account surplus in the American balance of payments is not greatly exceeded by capital exports. This situation would correspond to the Kindleberger—Salant model, with the United States playing the part both of the world's banker and of its centre of industrial entrepreneurship. In other words, without a European currency area, the individual European countries would inevitably be drawn into the dollar area.

By contrast, the transformation of the EEC into a currency area would create the indispensable conditions for an international reform by which the Western world would become at least bipolar and, perhaps, with Japan gaining more autonomy, even tripolar. From the point of view of political balance in the world at large, I am inclined to regard this solution as distinctly preferable and of great benefit not only to Europe but also to the developing countries and even to the United States. Of course, I am bound to admit that this statement involves a generous measure of political value judgement.[9]

VII. PROSPECTS

Where then, do we go from here? On what lines can we make a new approach to monetary integration in Europe, at a time when the failures of the past are glaringly obvious and also easy enought to explain?

Here, in outline, are a few propositions on which I stand ready to say more in the discussion:

(1) The world economy is in a state of profound disturbance, more so even

is often expensive and there is a great temptation to reap exchange profits; it is small wonder, therefore, that management skills are increasingly being applied to this purpose. This is the kind of temptation that has long afflicted manufacturers using raw materials subject to strong price fluctuations.

[9] I fully subscribe to the content of R. Mundell's profession of faith, and to the terms in which he states it, in his paper 'A Plan for a European Currency', in *The Economics of Common Currencies*.

than in the years 1969 to 1973. The rise in oil prices entails a fundamental re-structuring of external balances; the rise in other raw-material prices is reshaping the whole body of relations between industrial countries and those that produce raw materials; the impact of these two facts on the industrial countries will be differentiated, but no one knows how; and, finally, the quickening pace of international inflation may well lead to increased dispersion of national inflation rates around the average and thereby cause even more disturbance to exchange equilibrium.

(2) The political will to fix, once and for all, the mutual exchange rates of European currencies appears to be weaker than before.

(3) In these circumstances, I regard the open and free floating of European currencies against each other as the lesser evil compared with the efforts to keep the diminished snake alive, because (a) if the snake survives, it will tend to create a Deutschmark zone, which would have serious political drawbacks; and (b) if the snake perishes, in spite of all efforts to keep it alive, then the idea of a concerted policy of central banks, which even now is open to a good many doubts, will be discredited for ever. Currencies should be allowed to float freely for as long as it remains impossible to foresee the end of present disturbances. When oil prices have settled on a more stable equilibrium level, when the runaway rise in raw-material prices has stopped, when we can see whether inflation in industrial countries shows signs of subsiding or assumes the proportions of hyperinflation, *then* it will be time to think again about a concerted exchange-rate policy.

(4) Meanwhile, we have to admit that national authorities must be free to adopt whatever level of exchange rate suits the aims of their economic policy, and that their freedom to do so must not be subject to any constraint. But, as a counterpart of such complete freedom, they should gradually yield some of their sovereignty in other fields, with the intent of creating the *structural* conditions for the establishment of a currency area. These reforms should not stop short at the simple slogan of 'co-ordination of monetary and fiscal policies'; they should go deeper and prepare the way for a process of optimal adjustment of interregional balances of payments.

(5) The action programme for these reforms should aim:

(a) to promote effective freedom of movement for labour inside the EEC;
(b) to encourage wage bargaining at the European level;
(c) to facilitate direct investment across EEC frontiers, not only by abolishing exchange control, but also by removing other obstacles;
(d) to make possible the gradual interpenetration of financial circuits inside the EEC;
(e) to put into effect a policy of regional aid and to endow the aid fund with means that would be massive enough to act as a factor of income redistribution; and
(f) to make a start on introducing a joint European fiscal system, which, in case of regional imbalances, can act as a redistributive factor.

(6) If such far-reaching reforms are to be carried out, it is impossible at the same time to go ahead with efforts designed to freeze intra-Community exchange rates. In the present international climate, no European government would be prepared to forego its freedom of action with regard to exchange rates. Rather than force governments to go slow on integration in fields such as those listed above, it seems to me preferable to avoid placing any restrictions on this freedom.

Comments
Carlos Massad (Chile)

I should like to examine some of the consequences that may arise if an international monetary system is developed on the basis of a 'bipolar' or 'tripolar' universe, with exchange rates fixed within the poles and floating between them — which seems to be Lamfalussy's view of the Western world.

Unlimited official intervention would be required to keep intrapolar rates fixed. The necessary financing for such intervention could be provided by some form of mutual credit arrangements among central banks, as it has been in the past. On the other hand, floating interpolar rates would usually move in an equilibrating direction for each pole as a whole,[1] even though not necessarily for every individual component of each pole. If interpolar floating were to be completely free, official interpolar intervention would, by definition, be excluded. Private intervention, however, would play the role of smoothing out exchange-rate changes. If such a role were desired for the private sector, it would have to be able to accumulate the currencies in which to intervene.

As indicated above, official interpolar intervention is precluded if rates are to float freely between poles. However, each pole will have a cluster of developing-country currencies pegged to it through official intervention, and the effective exchange-rate changes of these currencies will depend both on the composition of the international transactions of each country and on the movement of the rate for their own pole *vis-à-vis* the rate for other poles. While it is to be hoped that such movements would serve an equilibrating function between poles, they may not — and, in general, will not — be equilibrating for currencies within the cluster, thus complicating the adjustment process for them.[2] It would usually be difficult, or costly, for the less developed countries to float their currencies, since their money and foreign-exchange markets will be undeveloped, their importers and exporters less sophisticated, and access to relevant information more difficult for them than for the major countries. Hence, for them to float or to change their exchange rate frequently would imply a transfer of real resources because of the demand for coverage abroad.

Furthermore, in some cases the exchange rate with a particular intervention currency becomes a political banner, with all the consequences of rigidification. Or, economic circumstances may be such as to render adjustment of the external sector through income changes less costly than it would be through exchange-rate changes.[3] A variety of reasons, then, indicate that the less developed countries — or most of them — will maintain fixed rates with the main currency of their poles through unlimited official intervention.[4] The floating of the main currencies would impose additional adjustment needs up-

---

[1] Or for the most important component of the pole, meaning the component with the largest participation in the total external transactions of the pole.

[2] Pegging to a 'basket' of currencies does not solve this problem, at least in a market economy. The relevant indicator for each importer and exporter is the specific rate affecting him, and not the 'basket' rate.

[3] Depending on the relative importance of the external sector, marginal propensity to import, composition of imports and exports, and so on.

[4] Pegging usually does not imply a free choice of either the policy or the currency.

on them, while considerations of uncertainty would lead their central banks and other foreign-currency holders to diversify their holdings.

This analysis implies certain effects on the demand for reserves. From the point of view of the monetary authorities of the poles, free interpolar floating will generally mean a reduction in their demand for reserves with which to face fluctuations created by their economic circumstances *vis-à-vis* other poles, while unlimited intervention to keep fixed rates within the pole would create no substantial net additional need for reserves. The desired composition of reserves would change, so that monetary authorities would favour a larger accumulation of currencies of other countries in the pole, or of drawing rights on other central banks of the pole. Furthermore, the private sectors would generate an increased demand for the currencies of other poles, and so assume a new, or at least expanded, intervention role.

The relative impact of the decrease in demand for reserves by the official sector and of the increase in demand for foreign currencies by the private sector on the total demand for international liquidity is an empirical question that it is perhaps too early to answer, particularly under conditions of managed rather than free, floating. However, it is possible to draw at least a tentative conclusion regarding the transfers of resources involved in the accumulation of reserves. Increased holdings, both private and official, of each other's currencies would largely cancel out, so that currency accumulations would minimise any intrapolar resource transfers. Hence, additional needs for future reserves or for international liquidity could be satisfied with little or no real resource transfer by the poles, a more favourable situation than one in which a single major currency is accumulated by all other countries.

Unfortunately, this outcome would not apply to less developed countries. First, their demand for reserves would increase because of the additional adjustment needs created by the floating of the currency or currencies of their poles. Second, their own currencies would not be accumulated by any other countries and, hence, there would be no offsetting, or netting out, effect. They would have to accumulate additional reserves and would have to pay for them, in the present or in the future, with real resources. Here is the link in reverse!

This analysis implies some particular direction of movement in the international monetary system. The private sector can play a greater part in intervention only if it accumulates additional currencies, and the intervention needs of the monetary authorities within the pole also point in the same direction. Any reduction in the demand for reserves and international liquidity within the pole would then take the form of a reduction in demand for assets other than currency holdings, and particularly for special drawing rights. The role of special drawing rights in the system would thus be diminished; any increases in liquidity would be provided through mutual credit agreements or similar arrangements, which, as in the past, would exclude most less developed countries. The developing countries would generate an increased demand for reserves, including special drawing rights, but their influence on world affairs would be too small for the increased demand to be of much consequence for the system.

I believe that the above conclusions would, in general, also hold if the currencies of the poles were subject to managed floating. The official demand for reserves would probably tend to be smaller under managed floating than under fixed rates, and smaller still under freely floating rates, while the increase in demand by the private sector arising from a change from fixed to floating rates, would, in general, be smaller under managed floating than under a freely floating system.[5] I incline to the conclusion that the difference between the effects of the two systems on the demand for reserves and international liquidity and on their composition may be more noticeable in quantity than in quality, and that in both cases the demand for special drawing rights in the most influential countries would be reduced. The expressed desire to install these rights in the centre of the system may thus be frustrated, at least for some time.

But all is not lost. Under managed floating there is still the pervasive $n - 1$ problem. As is well known, the freedom to move an exchange rate in a particular direction through intervention is limited by the movements of other rates. If there are to be n poles and n independent exchange rates, some outside element has to be introduced into the picture. Each pole would wish to be able to intervene to keep its exchange rate at any desired level with respect to the new element and, if it is to do so efficiently, the new element must be generally accepted and usable.

Hence, even though a multipolar world points in a different direction, the limitations of such a system may soon lead to additional support for something like special drawing rights. However, this seems to be a case where the short-term does not lead to the desired long-term results, or – at any rate – only through a series of crises. (Does this mean that monetary reform cannot proceed by stages?)

The free floating of all currencies without polar arrangements would produce results not much different from those set out above. If the outcome were to help promote a politically desirable objective, like the building-up of a monetary union in the EEC, it would at least be some consolation. However, I am not convinced by the 'lesser evil' type of argument used by Lamfalussy; and I am even less convinced that the reforms he suggests as necessary to prepare the ground for additional steps towards ensuring the optimum adjustment of interregional or intrapolar balances of payments are more possible, less costly or more relevant with a free float than otherwise. EEC-wide wage negotiations would be extremely difficult, or irrelevant, if the free float were to fulfil reasonably well its job of insulating one economy from disturbances originating elsewhere, and of avoiding or minimising the external effects of domestic policies.

In those circumstances, inflation rates would tend to diverge rather than converge, and there is no reason to expect that the presence or absence of floating would affect the performance of domestic productivity. Because of the added uncertainty of floating, direct international investments among EEC countries may be discouraged rather than encouraged, and there would be no reason to think that there would be a regional aid policy. Furthermore, floating rates and highly mobile short-term capital may make for larger fluctuations of exchange rates around their long-run trends,[6] while the upward price effects of exchange-rate movements may be self-perpetuating.

The effective mobility of labour would not be enhanced by the presence of

[5] In so far as the official sector intervenes to smooth out exchange-rate movements.

[6] See, for example, Mundell's discussion of this problem in his *International Economics*, Chapter 11.

uncertainties regarding exchange rates. In any case, if goods are mobile enough and imports and exports fairly diversified, the relative immobility of labour does not necessarily prevent price equalisation,[7] so that labour mobility may not be of major significance. On the other hand, unless it can be shown that wage differentials have increased within the EEC, the fact that labour is apparently less mobile inside the EEC than outside is no evidence of a currency area. In fact, the reduced mobility of labour may be the by-product of an increasing intra-EEC mobility of goods and of other factors of production. We are left with a gradual interpenetration of financial paths within the EEC and with the preliminary outline of a European fiscal system. These two areas of reform, important as they are, may not be decisive by themselves.

I should not dare to suggest an alternative strategy for the EEC, not knowing enough about the prevailing economic and political circumstances. But I suppose that I could reasonably ask once again whether it is too late for a drastic acceleration of the rate at which integration is proceeding.

[7] The analysis of this point is in H. G. Johnson, 'Factor Endowments, International Trade and Factor Prices', in *The Manchester School of Economics and Social Studies,* *XXV,* no. 3 (Sep 1957). See also H. G. Johnson, 'The Possibility of Factor-Price Equalisation when Commodities Outnumber Factors', in *Economica, XXXIV,* no. 135 (Aug 1967).

Comments
John H. Williamson (UK)

Lamfalussy's paper is representative of present thought in accepting as fact the failure of the attempt to create a European monetary union (EMU) by 1980. The principal question that he discusses is why the initiative launched by the European Community failed. He suggests three possible reasons:

(1) that external events – the breakdown of the Bretton Woods system, the rise in commodity prices, the increase in capital mobility – have created an international environment that has undermined the possibility of progress toward monetary integration;
(2) that the EEC is not an optimum currency area; and
(3) that the strategy adopted to promote monetary integration – a gradualist approach with heavy emphasis on an early reduction in intra-European exchange-rate flexibility – was misguided.

By contrast with Lamfalussy, I find the first of these reasons the least, rather than the most, compelling. In part, this is, because of scepticism about the thesis that undervaluation is systematically favourable to economic growth. One can agree that there are important insights in the theories of export-led growth that Lamfalussy has been instrumental in propagating, notably (a) the stimulus to investment that results from the assurance that payments constraints will not compel the authorities to deflate output, and from the ability profitably to supply markets that are sufficiently large to permit the realisation of economies of scale; (b) the greater efficiency of investment that is designed to serve a market of adequate size; and perhaps (c) the greater ease of shifting resources from net exports to investment, rather than from consumption to investment.[1] But none of these factors suggests that a continuing transfer of real resources to the rest of the world is, in itself, a cause of growth.[2] There is therefore no more reason for expecting that an end of those transfers, as a result of currency realignments, will hinder growth, than there is evidence that it has done so. More generally, it scarcely seems conceivable that a well-designed strategy for achieving an unambiguously desirable goal would have been thwarted by events that must surely have increased the benefits of securing that goal. Finally, as Lamfalussy concedes, the international monetary crisis presented opportunities for accelerating the process of monetary integration. The fact that these opportunities were not exploited points towards one of the alternative explanations.

[1] If a cyclical expansion is export-led, accommodation of the accelerator-induced rise in investment does not require a compression of consumption, and, therefore, a redistribution of income away from labour, as tends to be the case with a consumption-led boom. (This line of reasoning was suggested by the analysis carried out by T. F. Dernburg in 'The Macroeconomic Implications of Wage Retaliation against Higher Taxation', *IMF Staff Papers*, (Nov 1974).
[2] See M. Whitman, 'International and Interregional Payments Adjustment: A Synthetic View', in *Essays in International Finance no. 19* (International Finance Section, Princeton University, 1967).

Perhaps, then, the EEC does not have the characteristics of an optimum currency area? In considering this hypothesis, Lamfalussy discusses the extent to which the EEC satisfies the various criteria for optimum currency areas that have received prominence in the literature: factor mobility, consistent propensities to inflate, and openness of the constitutent economies to each other. Despite his conclusion that the first two of these criteria provide little support for viewing the EEC as an optimum currency area, he argues that there are other considerations that, collectively, are powerful enough to justify support for EMU. I applaud Lamfalussy's unadvertised abandonment of the conventional search for a single criterion to identify the desirable extent of the currency domain, and his adoption of a more prosaic cost-benefit approach that recognises the relevance of a multiplicity of factors and seeks to weigh one against another. But I question his assessment of the benefits, which seems to me to exaggerate those that he considers, and to neglect one factor of major potential importance.

The first benefit considered by Lamfalussy stems from the growth of intra-EEC trade, which has increased the openness of the European economies *vis-à-vis* one another and, therefore − according to McKinnon's classic argument − has increased the benefits of currency union. The direction of this effect is clear enough, even though the appropriate measure of openness is ambiguous; but it is far from clear what degree of interpenetration would 'justify a definite conclusion' that a unified currency area was optimal. In view of the fact that trade interpenetration among the European states remains markedly lower than that among individual states in the United States,[3] I question the conclusion that 'the presumption is very strong'.

Lamfalussy's second claim is that the customs union is likely to break down without monetary integration. However, the reasoning used to justify the conclusion seems to overlook certain crucial distinctions. Specifically, exchange-rate changes that neutralise differential cost trends seem more likely to ease than to intensify protectionist pressures; those that are merely 'noise' will add to the uncertainties of foreign trade and may thereby reduce the benefits of the customs union, but there is no reason to suppose they will lead to pressure to destroy the customs union; it is only those that result from the pursuit of 'competitive' policies by the member states that seem likely to threaten the consequences envisaged by Lamfalussy. Since, as already indicated, I do not share Lamfalussy's faith in the growth-promoting qualities of payments surpluses, I believe that the scope for competitive policies is restricted to cyclical stabilisation.

The third benefit Lamfalussy cites is the removal of the social cost of the uncertainty stemming from exchange-rate fluctuations. I do not doubt the existence of this benefit, but I hesitate to give it great weight on the basis of anecdotal evidence alone.

The final benefit mentioned by Lamfalussy is the enhanced power of a monetarily unified Europe to withstand absorption by the dollar standard. It is easy to agree that European influence in international monetary affairs would be enhanced by a capacity for joint action, and that circumstances could arise in which the EEC may wish to create arrangements of its own.

[3] See N. Kaldor, 'The Dynamic Effects of the Common Market', appendix I, in *Destiny or Delusion*, ed. D. Evans (London: Gollancz, 1971), pp. 81−2.

It is much less obvious that such arrangements need include complete currency unification.

I therefore give less weight to the benefits enumerated by Lamfalussy than he does. On the other hand, I also feel that he has neglected a most important topic that probably adds to the case for monetary union, at least for those with an egalitarian welfare function. This involves the interaction between fiscal integration (a subject within the terms of reference of this working group, despite its neglect by Lamfalussy) and monetary union. In the first instance, one may expect monetary union to accentuate regional problems, on account of demonstration effects tending to raise wages in regions where productivity is relatively low.[4] Because unemployment is more visible than poverty is, and because a regional policy to remedy unemployment has a minimal cost to the community as a whole,[5] one can expect the intensification of regional problems to stimulate political pressures for fiscal integration. If regional unemployment were restored to its previous level as a result of fiscal transfers, the new situation would differ from the initial one solely in the distribution of income, which would be more equal.[6]

While the case for regarding the EEC as an optimum currency area is not, in my view, sufficiently overwhelming to justify any precipitate moves towards EMU, I am prepared to join Lamfalussy in disputing the view that the failure of EMU can be explained by his second reason. Since I have already challenged his first explanation, I am left with his third possibility – that the strategy that was adopted was misguided. I am content to be left with this explanation. In a monetarist world where the locking of exchange rates could be enforced by following the gold-standard rules of the game at minimal cost in terms of output deflation, price inflation and social disruption, a strategy based on the early reduction of intra-European exchange-rate flexibility would have stood a chance of success. In the Europe of the 1970s, it was bound to fail, even if it had been accompanied by a commitment to the gold-standard monetary policy, which economic theory demonstrates to be essential to the maintenance of fixed exchange rates. It was bound to fail because the cost of adhering to that commitment, in the absence of such preconditions as factor mobility and consistent propensities to inflate, would have been prohibitive.

The alternative strategy, as sketched by Lamfalussy towards the end of his paper, goes to the other extreme. If one waits for the restoration of price stability before launching any new monetary initiatives, one risks a long wait. (Moreover, national authorities cannot all have 'complete freedom' regarding their exchange rates, if only because of the $n - 1$ problem.) I

---

[4] The analysis is developed in my paper 'The Implications of European Monetary Integration for the Peripheral Areas', in *Regional Policy and Economic Sovereignty* ed. J. Vaizey (forthcoming).

[5] See B. Moore and J. Rhodes, 'The Effectiveness of Measures to Promote Growth in the Peripheral Regions of the United Kingdom', ibid.

[6] In principle, fiscal integration may be able to secure these benefits even without monetary union. To that extent, the argument depends on the hypothesis that monetary union is, in fact, likely to spur fiscal integration, which seems to me highly plausible but not beyond challenge. See W. M. Corden, '*Monetary Integration*', *Essays in International Finance no. 93* (International Finance Section, Princeton University, 1972), p. 38.

see no convincing reason for not complementing his proposed structural reforms with a new monetary initiative,[7] provided only that it does not seek an unrealistically early locking of exchange rates or the restoration of an adjustable peg that is unworkable in an era of capital mobility.

[7] Some ideas on the form that such an initiative might take were developed in G. Magnifico and J. Williamson, *European Monetary Integration* (London: Federal Trust, 1972).

Opening Statement for Group Discussion
Marina von Neumann Whitman (USA)

The major point on which Lamfalussy and the discussants of his paper appear to agree is that the Werner Commission was wrong.[1] Or, to put it a bit less baldly, the conclusion that one is forced to draw is that a monetary integration plan designed for one sort of world has proved inappropriate and incapable of survival in a quite different one.

Lamfalussy himself would apparently go further and stand Werner on his head. That is, he would for the time being, entirely abandon efforts at monetary integration and focus on other aspects of policy integration, including the fiscal aspects. Massad and Williamson seem to think that this is going too far, and I agree, as will be made clear in one of the points below. In any case, this is only one of a number of questions central to the problem of how — and, indeed, whether — to put the European Humpty Dumpty together again. Let me list a few that I regard as particularly compelling.

(1) As is appropriate in a conference conceived and organized by Fritz Machlup, I begin with a plea for a more precise definition of monetary integration. The three authors in our present session appear to regard it simply as unalterably fixed exchange rates. Many others, however, would argue that monetary integration requires a common monetary policy, perhaps even a unified central bank as well. Corden has gone so far as to term a system of unalterably fixed rates unaccompanied by these other characteristics as 'pseudo exchange-rate union', because of what he regards as its inevitably unstable and self-destructive character.[2]

(2) Monetary integration, as approached by the EEC, involves rather precise rules and obligations. The process was conceived and undertaken within the framework of the Bretton Woods system, which also had the characteristics of a relatively formal 'monetary constitution'. But, for a variety of reasons, I doubt very much that the world is going to have a new monetary constitution in the near future. Rather, we are likely to operate with a much more informal, *ad hoc* system for some time to come. Can the EEC partners set up 'rules for integration' in a world without rules? Or, if they cannot, will they also find ways to approach integration in a more informal, *ad hoc* fashion than they did before?

(3) Most of the literature on optimum currency areas has implicitly assumed that a currency area is coterminous with a policy area in all its aspects. But, as Cooper has so convincingly described in his paper for this congress, different functional areas may — and sometimes do — have different domains. Is this a serious problem in the European case? Is the optimum domain of a customs union, for example, different from that of a currency area, or that of a currency area different from that of a fiscal area? If so, can it be practical to institute such different domains, or must one simply choose the best compromise as the domain for a total policy area?

[1] Pierre Werner (chairman), *Report to the [EC] Council and the Commission on the Realization by Stages of Economic and Monetary Union in the Community* (Brussels, Oct 1970).

[2] W. M. Corden, *Monetary Integration.* Essays in International Finance No 93 (Princeton: International Finance Section, April 1972).

That is, in what circumstances and under what conditions does it make sense to have different, and perhaps overlapping, jurisdictions for different functions?

(4) Apropos of the previous point, there is the following conundrum: why have the EEC countries done so well in trade integration and so poorly in other aspects of economic integration? I refer here not only to the failure of monetary integration, but also to the apparent lack of progress toward integration of capital markets. Kindleberger's comment[3] of more than a decade ago — that, while European trade integration was progressing directly, its financial integration appeared to be taking place indirectly, via the United States — appears to remain largely true today. We need to know why this is so, and what it implies for monetary and fiscal integration in Europe.

(5) Some interesting work has been published lately by Niehans,[4] who suggests that, contrary to widespread belief, the gold-exchange standard system is not inherently unstable *except* in the context of secular inflation. The same thing may well be true of a system of fixed rates implied by monetary integration. If prices were completely stable, one would have only to ensure that the initial exchange-rate relationships were equilibrium ones in order to make monetary integration work. But with inflation, unless the rates of price increases are identical in every participating country, exchange rates are bound to get out of line. And, the higher the average rate of inflation, the higher the variance is likely to be, and the faster any fixed pattern of exchange rates will diverge from equilibrium. Among regions of a single country, very high mobility of both goods and factors of production tends to keep regional rates of inflation from diverging very much. That is, structural similarities imply similar Phillips curves for different regions, while the relatively high degree of homogeneity within a given country means, presumably, that regional indifference maps are also similar. Taken together, these assumptions imply that the optimum trade-off points with respect to inflation and unemployment do not diverge much among regions of a single country. Therefore, the welfare cost of maintaining a common inflation rate, as required by monetary integration, is probably reasonably low. It is also compensated by other interregional (that is, national) policies, particularly fiscal transfers. But among nations, where both Phillips curves and indifference maps are likely to differ substantially, one can show that the welfare cost of maintaining the common inflation rate required by a currency area is proportional to the magnitude of the divergences among optimum national rates of inflation.[5]

(6) The above suggests that monetary integration must be accompanied by

[3] C. P. Kindleberger, 'European Economic Integration and the Development of a Single Financial Center for Long-Term Capital', in *Weltwirtschaftliches Archiv*, XC, no. 2 (July 1963), pp. 189–209.

[4] Jurg Niehans, 'The Flexibility of the Gold-Exchange Standard and its Limits', *The Economics of Common Currencies,* ed. Harry G. Johnson and Alexander K. Swoboda, (Cambridge, Mass., 1973), and 'Reserve Composition as a Source of Independence for National Monetary Policies, in *National Monetary Policies and the International Finance System,* ed. Robert Z. Aliber (Chicago, 1974).

[5] M. v. N. Whitman, 'Space Prosperity and People Prosperity: The Delineation of Optimum Policy Areas', in *Spatial, Regional and Population Economics*, ed. Mark Perlman et al. (New York, 1972).

measures (a) to reduce structural differences and, thus, lessen the degree of divergence among optimum inflation rates in the component countries of the area, and (b) to compensate the remaining welfare losses resulting from adherence to a common inflation rate. A clear implication of this view is that monetary and economic integration must proceed in parallel fashion, one cannot get too far ahead of the other. Very possibly, in other words, optimum currency areas are not born but made. Here I not only agree with Massad and Williamson, but am puzzled by Lamfalussy's final point. He appears to regard monetary and economic integration as competitive or substitute goods rather than, as is the usual view and as I have argued strongly here, complementary ones. I hope we shall learn more of his views on this question.

(7) Finally, to what extent do the integration efforts of the socialist countries contain analogies to this controversy about how the various functional aspects of integration fit together (and, particularly, to the controversy over the 'monetary' *versus* the 'economic' approach to integration)? I should very much like to hear the views of economists from Eastern Europe regarding the relevance of this whole question to their own problems and concerns.

Report on Group Discussion
Raymond Barre (France)

I. INTRODUCTORY

Working Group F was concerned with the monetary and fiscal aspects of integration. These are controversial matters and have been much debated in recent years. The group had the benefit of a paper by Lamfalussy and of introductory comments by Williamson, Massad and von Neumann Whitman, which provided a basis for searching and interesting discussions.

While fiscal aspects were not neglected, it was the monetary aspects of integration that attracted most interest, especially with reference to economic and monetary union within the EEC.

In this brief summary I cannot mention every speaker and do justice to all of the contributions to the debate. Instead, I shall try to summarise the discussions under two main headings, in the hope of giving as objective as possible an account of the different points of view expressed.

II. CONCEPTS OF MONETARY INTEGRATION

East and West hold different concepts of monetary integration, and the dissussions provided an opportunity to define these more sharply.

In socialist countries, where the economy is planned and where foreign trade is balanced on a bilateral basis, the point that is regarded as essential is to integrate such 'real' processes as production, foreign trade, investment and research. Their integration is planned and synchronised, and incorporates monetary and financial integration. Monetary relations are the result of real processes. Hence, the problem of the convertibility of currencies does not arise in the CMEA countries in the same terms as it does in capitalist market economies.

At present, monetary integration in the East works through a multi-lateral clearing system based on transferable Soviet roubles. Economists from socialist countries are aware of a number of difficulties that stem both from inter-country disparities in levels of production and of productivity, and from differences in national price systems and the conditions of fixing exchange rates.

It was suggested that, while the multilateral clearing may be adequate for trade among CMEA countries, a somewhat higher degree of convertibility would have the advantage of encouraging certain investments of common interest and may also be helpful in relations among the people of Eastern countries.

But convertibility, in the socialist view, has social aspects that could work to the detriment of workers in the less developed countries. If, therefore, convertibility were to be introduced, due allowance would have to be made for its possible social implications in the CMEA countries.

As regards the monetary relations of CMEA countries with the rest of the world, where different economic systems are the rule, Eastern economists said that they would like to see a new international monetary system that takes account of the economic transformations of recent years. This system should be open to, and serve, the interests of all countries, regardless of economic and social regime and level of development. The system should be linked to gold, but Eastern economists made it clear that they were not advocating a return to the gold standard of the past, but rather the use of gold as *numéraire* in the international monetary system, seeing that they do not regard special drawing rights as being sufficiently universal and neutral to fulfil this function.

In the West European countries that are pursuing monetary integration, all currencies are freely convertible in the market against each other and also against nonmember currencies. This free convertibility is an essential factor in the expansion of foreign trade and financial transactions, and it is thanks to it that trade integration has made so much progress in the EEC since 1958.

What, however, does monetary integration really mean in this regional group? Some argue that monetary integration should lead to the formation of an area comprising several countries whose currencies are linked by fixed and unalterable exchange rates, with complete freedom of capital movements and payments. Others want to go further and add a common monetary policy conducted by common monetary institutions, headed by a common central bank.

It was pointed out that, when the six (as it was then) member governments of the EEC adopted their programme of economic and monetary union (EMU) in March 1971, they in no way dissociated the two approaches. The final aims of EMU were:

(1) freedom of movement for people, goods, and capital;
(2) fixed and unalterable exchange rates;
(3) common medium-term and short-term economic policies and also common structural policies, especially in regional and social matters;
(4) harmonisation of direct and indirect taxation; and
(5) common institutions, backed by a common system of central banks.

This third approach fits in with the working group's view that monetary union cannot be made to work without a set of instruments and measures by which to reduce structural inequalities among member countries and to offset such welfare losses as may result from the acceptance of a common rate of inflation.

III. MONETARY INTEGRATION IN THE EEC

The discussion covered four main topics: appraisal of results so far, feasibility of economic and monetary union in the EEC, the reasons for recent difficulties, and prospects for the future.

(a) In appraising the results achieved so far, some say flatly that it must be accepted as a fact that the EEC's attempt to create a monetary union by 1980 has failed. This failure is manifest in the unilateral floating of the pound, the lira and the French franc, in the absence of any joint policy regarding speculative money movements, and in the postponement of the first tax harmonization measures proposed for Stage One. Attention was drawn to the glaring contrast between the Community's success with its customs union and its failure with monetary integration.

But others argued that it is wrong to talk as though monetary union were intended to come about all at once, that the process of monetary integration did not really start until April 1972, and, therefore, that its results so far must not be compared with those of the customs union, which had the benefit of ten years of propitious economic conditions and a powerful international trade liberalisation movement. These speakers recalled that since 1969 the EEC has, after all, developed consultation procedures, has intensified collaboration among the central banks of member countries, has set up machinery for mutual assistance, and has founded the European Monetary Co-operation Fund. They also stressed that the currency 'snake' is still working, in spite of the recent floating of the French franc, and, indeed, that it remains the nucleus of a currency system specific to a number of countries, some of which do, and some of which do not, belong to the EEC. In these circumstances, the issue cannot be prejudged at this stage; it cannot be taken for granted that the Community's attempt at monetary integration has been a failure, just because it has encountered difficulties largely due to international factors; nor, on the other hand, can eventual success be taken for granted.

(2) Subsequently, the working group was led to discuss the question of whether economic and monetary union of the EEC countries is at all feasible.

In the first place, is the EEC an optimum currency area? Some had their doubts, because of deficient intra-Community factor mobility and also because of the varying inflation propensity in different member countries. Others made a case for monetary union in the light of such factors as the growing trade interdependence of the EEC countries, the need to safeguard the customs union, the danger that repeated adjustments of exchange rates may vitiate the conditions of competition and provoke reprisals, and, finally, the risk that isolated European countries may be absorbed by the dollar standard.

However, the weight of these factors was contested. In particular, it was suggested that trade interpenetration among EEC members still remains markedly lower than that among individual states in the United States, and that, in any case, the EEC can enhance its influence on international affairs by means other than complete currency unification.

There was broad agreement on the general difficulties that, exceptional circumstances apart, stand in the way of EMU. These difficulties have to do with member countries' divergent views on what rate of inflation is tolerable; with structural disparities, especially of a regional nature; with the need for broadly based financial solidarity as a condition of intra-country transfers of resources; and with the fact that EMU implies progressive shifts of sovereignty from member states to Community institutions.

Economic and monetary integration is, without doubt, first and foremost a political process and, as such, defies prediction.

Finally, it was pointed out that the enlargement of the EEC had complicated all of these troublesome problems and had made them even harder to solve. Indeed, it was asked whether the enlarged Community is capable of intensified integration, or whether it is bound to drift towards becoming a mere free-trade area. This was regarded as the fundamental question, and was seen as having created more uncertainty about the future of European economic and monetary union than had all of the EEC's monetary difficulties in recent years.

(3) The reasons for these recent difficulties were discussed at some length. There was general agreement that many of them were due to international factors. But the main responsibility for them was attributed to the choice of the monetary strategy of limiting intra-Community exchange-rate fluctuations. This was regarded as premature. Is it possible, in a world where most currencies are afloat, for certain European countries to adopt a system of reduced exchange-rate flexibility? Is it possible, in a world without rules, to lay down rules of monetary integration and to stick to them?

It was suggested that the countries of Europe could have taken advantage of the international monetary crisis in order to speed up the process of monetary integration. But governments were afraid of the risks of such acceleration, and preferred a gradual approach. It was pointed out too that, while the EEC had narrowed the margins of exchange-rate fluctuations, it had never precluded parity changes.

By limiting the margins of exchange-rate fluctuations, it was hoped to foster intra-European trade and to encourage member countries bound by a common monetary constraint to co-ordinate their economic policies more closely. The internal troubles of the 'currency snake' were explained by the failure of the countries participating in the joint float to draw the consequences of their chosen monetary strategy: there was no closer co-ordination of economic policies, no harmonisation of interest-rate policies, no massive increase in reciprocal credits, no concerted central-bank intervention *vis-à-vis* the dollar.

(4) Finally, the working group discussed the future of monetary integration in the EEC. There were some who recommended that Community currencies should be left to float freely until the present international disturbances abate; only then will the time be ripe for a concerted exchange-rate policy. Others saw continuing merit in keeping intra-Community exchange rates as stable as possible, especially with a view to their priority aim, the battle against inflation.

There was general agreement that the European countries should do what they can to create, progressively, the structural conditions necessary for monetary union. The Working Group heard a proposal for a new monetary initiative in the form of a European currency unit to circulate alongside national currencies and be used in certain trade and financial transactions. This, it was suggested, may attract to Europe some of the huge financial resources that are now accumulating in the hands of petroleum producers.

IV. CONCLUDING COMMENTS

In concluding this report, in which I have tried my best not to pass over in silence such differences of opinion as were expressed, I am pleased to record full unanimity on one point: the hope that monetary integration, in the East as in the West, will come about in a spirit not of political rivalry, but of co-operation among large organised regional groups.

All members of the working group felt that their frank discussions had helped them to a better understanding of current attempts at integration, of the difficulties that these have encountered, and of their potential long-term benefits.

10 The Socio-Political and Institutional Aspects of Integration (Main Paper, Working Group G)

József Bognár (HUNGARY)

There are two things that are important to understand about the socio-political and institutional aspects of economic integration.

(1) The complicated interdependence that is created between politics and economics during the transformation of the economic system. Politics play an extremely important role in issues of integration, since the contracting parties making the decisions and weighing the achievements are the national states themselves.

(2) The relationships between the modernised economic system and the existing political, social, and institutional system, including their dynamically changing interests.

The kind of influence that the economic integration of groups of countries can have depends mainly on three conditions. The first of these is *the socio-economic system of the integrating countries.* Usually integration takes place among politically homogeneous countries, and there can be radical differences in the fundamental reasons for integrating. Developed capitalist countries obviously integrate in order to strengthen the capitalist social system by exploiting the achievements of the scientific—technological revolution and thus giving further impetus to their economic growth. On the other hand, socialist countries expect the strengthening of the economy to consolidate and promote the socialist social system.

The second condition is *the type of integration grouping.* It might be said that whether a grouping is primarily based on market forces or is a production-developing integration governed by central plans is determined by the socio-economic system of the countries involved, since the developed capitalist countries have mainly integrated markets, while the socialist countries have integrated mainly to develop production. This statement, however, is not quite exact, because market (that is, commodity and money) conditions are integral parts of production-promoting integrations, while controls such as economic programmes, state interference, planning, and economic-political decisions play an important role in West European integration. It is also evident that the type of integration exerts an influence of its own.

The third condition is *the economic policy pursued by the member states that have integrated.* The notion of economic policy is used here in its broadest sense to include the totality of conditions and problems inherited from the past (level of advancement, capital surplus or deficit, excess or shortage of labour, regional differences, and so on), as well as the measures taken or planned by the member governments to improve the current situation.

I shall not touch upon the economic integration of developing countries in this paper, for two related reasons. First, these associations should be regarded as regional economic co-operation and not as integration. The domestic economies of these countries have not yet developed to the point where the increasing share of classical foreign trade can be replaced by co-operation or by the division of development tasks. Trade within this regional grouping comprises no more than 5 to 12 per cent of total foreign trade. Within the Central American regional grouping, trade between the member countries represents about 20 per cent, of the total, but the population of the participating countries is less than 12 million. Second, the socio-political changes taking place in individual developing countries are usually not related to economic ties to other countries in the region but to the creation of the domestic socio-political structure necessary for economic growth.

The European Economic Community is looked upon mainly as a market grouping of industrially advanced countries belonging to the capitalist system. All the member countries except Italy are rich in capital and have no labour reserves. While in most of them the per capita national income is high (middling in Italy), the regional differences are great and are even growing in some countries.[1]

Political factors had a decisive say in the creation of the Community. All political systems and governments have had to cope with the scientific—technological revolution as a component of policy, but the acceptance of economic necessities, the objective economic conditions and postulates, can be coupled with different political systems depending on the situation and the intentions of the government. It is obvious that common interests constitute the most decisive impulse in any integration efforts, but a nation state's interests, which are in the last resort class interests, are more than the totality of all economic interests.

What were the major political motives behind the political decision to create the Community?

(1) The creation of economic conditions under which capitalism could function smoothly, without major crises and excessive cyclical fluctuations, while maintaining full employment. The absence of dynamism, major cyclical fluctuations and unemployment are indicative of the inefficiency of the ruling class, especially where there are antagonistic class relations.

(2) The creation of economic conditions attesting to the superior vitality

[1] Commission des Communautés Européennes, *L'Evolution regionale dans la Communauté, Bilan analytique* (Luxembourg, 1971).

of the capitalist economy as against the socialist economy. Fearful of failing to achieve these conditions by their own driving forces, the developed capitalist countries tried to prevent the economic growth of the socialist economies, or at least to slow it down, by embargo or other measures of discrimination. In other words, in this period West European economic integration was looked upon by many 'as an instrument of building up the anticommunist front'.[2] Those were the days when the cold war was concentrated in Europe and when NATO was created, on the initiative of the United States.

(3) The termination of the centuries-old Franco-German hostility and desperate rivalry. This goal has been achieved in the changed constellation of world politics and the world economy, although other conflicts have cropped up in the new situation, as was to be expected.

(4) The intention to match as far as possible the economic and technico-scientific potential of the United States.

(5) The development of new arrangements to replace the disintegrated colonial system.

The creation of the EEC convincingly substantiates the historical experience that large enterprises or industries can associate on the basis of purely economic interests and create units of a qualitatively higher order. But the linking of the structures and processes of national economies — mainly with a view to constituting a large economic unit out of member countries — can be achieved only through political decisions. When political decisions do open the way toward integration, common economic interests become active and exert a powerful influence upon socio-political and institutional factors.

Nevertheless, the economic achievements and socio-political changes are assessed on the basis of the differing value systems of the various segments of an antagonistic society and affect them in different ways. Integration brings certain advantages and disadvantages. How they are divided among the participating members or among different social classes or strata constitutes a critical problem.

The idea of the signatories to the Treaty of Rome was to turn a customs union into an economic union in the 1970s. Economic union presupposes the elimination of differences in tax and income policies, a co-ordinated development of the industrial structure, *rapprochement* of currency and credit policies, and, eventually, the introduction of a common currency. In this connection the question has been raised of whether it is possible in a modern state to separate economic and political functions. Is it possible to leave political and other noneconomic functions in the hands of a nation and deprive it of the instruments necessary for performing these functions?

These problems were discussed with dramatic force and eloquence by

[2] Gunnar Myrdal, 'The Efforts toward Integration in Rich and Poor Countries', Lecture in Mexico City, Oct 1966.

the late Imre Vajda, a Hungarian economist who died all too soon.[3] I shall briefly cite his conclusions, with which I totally agree.

(1) Economic union is not a stepping stone on the road to political union but a possible and desirable consequence of political unions.

(2) Political union means the creation of a new state, with all the imponderable consequences this involves. Further research is needed to clarify what transitional forms may come into being in the process.

(3) Although political institutions are determined by the forces and relationships of production, economic interests – judging by our experience thus far – are by themselves not enough to create a union.

According to Vajda, 'the economic foundation of a nation state rests on the high share of national income that is redistributed'.[4] In view of this, let me add the following to the points already mentioned.

(4) The power relationships of integrating countries undergo substantial changes, which may be due to uneven distribution of the advantages deriving from the integration or to differing development dynamics in the integrating countries. Paradoxically, these two different causes trigger an identical reaction – a determination to strengthen the national economy.

(5) In the case of a selective (nontotal) integration, some sectors of industrial production (not to mention agriculture and services) may achieve optimum dimensions within the national frameworks that are provided by the member countries of the West European integration. This point is that in the leading industries efficiency in investments and costs of production improve as much as, or more than, growth of output, whereas in many other production branches advantages of scale are negligible or of a negative value.

(6) The structure of a nation's economy influences its political-power position both inside and outside the integration. This fact prompts the middle powers (which were the big powers before the Second World War) to 'protect' their economies as power centres and to make them competitive. It prompts the small countries to consolidate their economies to achieve material advantages through rationality and, in this sense, to make them competitive. These two different endeavours lead to identical results – the strengthening of the national economy – although this process takes different forms (modernisation of structure and greater mobility and elasticity).

(7) Many conflicts can be observed between the political and economic drives of the individual nations. In such cases, the politically stronger countries try to gain economic advantages by political force. If one country attempts to influence the distribution of economic advantages by noneconomic means, this induces the partner or partners to mobilise their noneconomic (mainly political-power) forces. In this manner, competition between nations is transferred from the sphere of economic rationality to

[3] Imre Vajda, 'Integracio, gazdasági unio és nemzeti állam' ('Integration, Economic Union, and Nation State'), in *Közgazdasági Szemle*, no. 4 (1966), inaugural address at the Academy. [4] Ibid., p. 402.

the sphere of power politics, strengthening 'traditional' conflicts inherited from the past.

Consequently, in summing up the changes that the West European integration has brought about in the political relationships of the members, as well as in the relationship between the integrating countries and the outside world, the following conclusions can be drawn.

(1) The processes tending to attenuate conflicts between the West European economies, and the consequences of the scientific and technological revolution, have strengthened during the past twenty years. In spite of its many conflicts, regional integration is the outcome of this process and should thus be considered progress compared with the disintegration that took place between the two world wars. Of course, under antagonistic social conditions, disintegrating tendencies exist even within an integration grouping, both in the socio-political and in the economic sphere.

(2) Integration has helped substantially to overcome the 'traditional conflicts' that have led to three great wars — including two world wars — in the past hundred years. It is perhaps not necessary to emphasise that, although some traditional conflicts have been resolved, new conflicts have emerged.

(3) Experience shows that conflicts arise also with the entrance of new member states to the integration grouping. At first, tensions among the members are mitigated to a certain extent, but later they increase, aggravating the political, social, and institutional problems that crop up. These conflicts may be exacerbated by the fact that the old members regard the conditions of admission as an occasional compromise with the rules of the game (that is, the 'price of admission'), while the new members look upon the compromise as a position from which to carry on their struggle for further benefits. The newcomers have to use considerable persuasive force if domestic opinion is very much divided on the issue of their joining the integration grouping (this happened with the admission of the United Kingdom to the EEC).

(4) Experience also shows that a nation's economic and noneconomic interests include driving forces that are indispensable in the present stage of development. This is why plans for an economic union seem to be unrealistic.

(5) The West European economic grouping was started at the time of the cold war, with intensive American support 'as an instrument of building up the anticommunist front.'[5] With the lessening of international tensions, this goal lost much of its militancy but not its 'Western exclusiveness' or its closed character through regional protectionism. These factors obviously make it difficult for the Community to build up fruitful and mutually advantageous relations with the socialist countries and the developing world. A regional integration in our day can be looked upon as up-to-date and positive only if, by its openness, it promotes a new international division of labour and the

[5] Gunnar Myrdal, *op. cit.*

creation of a new world economic system.

(6) The joint organisations of an integrated grouping are not institutions above governments, since the governments establish them in order to perform specific high-level technical tasks associated with the improvement of the forms and methods of co-operation. Every institution, however, tends to develop according to its own laws, and in running its course may confront the interests and power structures that originally created it. The joint apparatus starts to regard itself as 'the would-be bureaucracy of the economic union', the cohesion of which rests on loyalty to the integration interests. This is why the EEC has more than once had to face the opposition of the governments of its members. This happened, for instance, in the discussion of the joint market for agricultural products, of the problems of the coal, iron and steel concerns of West Germany, and in connection with the legal status of European corporations. The apparatus is characterised by a technocratic attitude that not only disregards the past, which is an important constituent of the present political situation, but also fails to realise that economic and technological rationality is one of the components of future political relations. Even some of the economic differences of the present are the result of the political relationships of the past.

Integration has actually changed or is changing substantially the socio-political problems of certain countries. In analysing these, it is necessary to realise that complex social processes are usually the combined and accumulated effect of many factors, and that integration as a response to economic necessities is only a part of new premises and a new way of thinking.

Without any intention of classification, I divide into three groups the socio-political effects of integration. Underlying this division are the intentions of the bodies making decisions in relation to existing socio-political processes. I assign to the first group the short-term direct effects that can be eliminated by improving 'techniques' within the integration system. Included here, for instance, would be the adoption by the EEC of a common agricultural policy, under which it was necessary to transfer the subsidy systems of the individual countries into an integrated system (that is, raise them to the level of the Community). This resulted in problems fo farm structure, as shown by the Mansholt plan of 1968. In connection with this plan, it soon became evident that the establishment of 'optimum farm dimensions' brought the economic goals into serious conflict with political interests. The consequences of the conflict were dealt with by the 1972 directives of the Council of Ministers (the pension premium, programmes of special training and retraining, the location of industries in agricultural areas, and so on).

Another example is provided by the case of the European Social Fund, which was set up with a view to preventing the social tensions that arise when the industrial structure is modernised and the importance of some economic sectors downgraded. The Fund is meant to mitigate the problems associated with retraining, resettlement, and income reduction, although its activities have not yet evolved on large scale.

I assign to the second group the specific combination of direct and indirect effects that have produced essential changes in the structure (that is, in the weight of the components of the structure) of the West European capitalist system. I wish to emphasise two of these changes

(1) The enormous increase in the economic functions and activities of the government (the monopoly capitalist government, of course). The capitalist governments of today try to boost production, to redistribute a large share of national income, to finance large investments and a significant proportion of scientific research, to avoid or moderate crises, to establish currency equilibrium, to stimulate structural changes, and to put a brake on inflation.

The increase in the economic functions of government requires the employment of a growing number of experienced and energetic economic managers. In a number of countries, it has become the practice for the exponents of monopoly capital to take over the management of economic affairs on the government level.

(2) The big monopolistic companies have gained in strength over the small and middle-sized companies. The big companies are often said to be the vanguards of integration, whereas small and middle-sized companies resist integration, or at least try to do so. There is no doubt that here, too, the need for economic rationality comes into conflict with socio-political interests. The representatives of these smaller companies have acted as the safe bases of the existing system and the changing governments. This is why serious efforts are made to 'convince' these companies, which are to be adapted into the economy, that the new structure will still be acceptable to them. They are promised a substantial increase in income or offered the illusion of independence. An assessment of the significance, intensity and depth of these changes will convince us that integration is not only an economic issue but a political-power question.

Into the third category I assign indirect effects that, while they are diametrically opposed to the intentions of the power centres making politico-economic decisions, are the necessary consequences of the processes they trigger.

(1) The struggles of the working class, of left-wing parties, and of trades-unions against monopoly capitalism have gained strength and support from the masses. This struggle is now fought not only to improve the economic position of the working class but also to achieve an equitable distribution of incomes; the right to participate in factory management; and other political ends. It is becoming clear to growing numbers that it is not sufficient to fight *against* something: it is also important to fight *for* something. The appearance of the democratic alternative in different forms is the direct consequence of the realisation of this fact. In certain countries the democratic alternative, having transgressed the bases and frameworks of the old political parties, or having even disrupted them, has actually come to the threshold of winning a majority in elections.

(2) The dissolution of the traditional political structure of the bourgeois

democratic states has begun and is accelerating. This dissolution can be
traced to the conflict between economic forces and interests undergoing
rapid change, on the one hand, and the political structure, on the other. It
manifests itself in growing instability. One example is the weakening of the
elements in politics and economics that formed the governing majority
in the past. More and more countries are headed by governments based on a
minority or a very small majority that is under growing pressure from the
masses and the constant threat of being outvoted in Parliament. More and
more often efforts are made to establish a 'strong state' under the pretext
of restoring stability. Economically advanced modern societies need a
strong state power,[6] they say. The structure of the modern state is built on
ever-bigger organisations, including mammoth companies, electronic brains,
long-term programmes, integration systems, and research machinery, all of
which need strong central government.

The alternative is formulated in the statement, 'either big enterprises or
the state', but these two are obviously so intertwined that this choice has
only rhetorical value. The demand for strong government today is clearly
directed primarily against the representatives of opposing class interests,
against the exponents and partisans of the 'democratic alternative'.

If we weigh the time lag between economic processes and their indirect
socio-political consequences, it becomes evident that the socio-political
phenomena analysed above are the products of a period when economic
growth was relatively rapid, there was full employment, foreign-exchange
rates were stable, and the rate of domestic inflation did not exceed 2–3 per
cent annually. At times of slower economic growth, accelerated inflation
(even 'stagflation'), and a lower employment rate, the conflicts become
sharper. The assumption that economic prosperity, with rewards that are
distributed very unevenly, will satisfy all and sundry has proved to be an
illusion, and in economic crises dissatisfaction becomes even greater.

Turning now to the social and political problems connected with
socialist integration, I should like to stress again that there is no practical
value in abstract integration models based on a system of norms (the 'ideal
integration') that disregards the socio-political system, the stage of economic
development, and the economic and political situation. There is no such
thing as abstract or general integration. There are only concrete integrations,
with very specific characteristics. Integrations take place among nations,
and the functions are therefore inseparable from the distribution of tasks
among these nations, and the plan according to which international co-
operation is regulated. Integrations formed by the two fundamental social
systems differ from each other also with regard to the way in which the
role of the member nations is conceived. (We shall come back to this
question later.) In socialist integrations, there are problems that are solved
by the member countries, and perhaps not even by economic means;

[6] Ferdinando Scianna, 'Interview with Maurice Duverger', in *L'Europea*, II .

whereas, in Western Europe, attempts are made to solve these issues within the Community. Two examples of this are: (1) the establishment of the optimum farm size in agriculture; and (2) the relation between free migration of labour within the integrated area and full employment in each country.

The development of optimum farm size in the EEC was started in 1968 under the Mansholt plan. I do not want to talk about the relevant implications. In the socialist countries the optimum farm size was established by organising co-operative farms, mostly by political methods. An integration obviously need not be concerned with problems that can be solved in the individual countries. If we consider the dimensions of an integration independently of the size of the member-nation economies, we may come to the conclusion that the EEC covers a vaster area than does the CMEA, because the former is concerned with issues that are disregarded by the later.

The free movement of the factors of production, including the labour force, is an essential achievement of West European integration in the EEC. The introduction of rules permitting this is rational when there is an 'over-supply' of labour in some member countries and a manpower shortage in others. But is the free migration of labour necessary when there is full employment in the member countries? Full employment naturally does not mean that labour supply always coincides with demand in all regions. Furthermore, in certain trades young labour can acquire greater skill in industrially advanced countries. At times when investment reductions are made to maintain economic equilibrium, manpower may be temporarily released and certain companies may have excess capacity. This is why in the socialist region there is some migration of labour under organised (institutional) conditions. If, however, there is full employment in the member countries, flow of labour between countries plays a limited role and cannot acquire the significance, for instance, of the appearance of surplus Italian labour in West European countries.

Socialist integration is an economic grouping of countries belonging to the socialist community with a view to accelerating the economic growth of the members of the system and to optimising their structure in relation to one another. The framework in which the forces and factors of production develop today is still the domestic economy, although there are a growing number of problems that can most rationally be solved on the international level. The road to closer *rapprochement* and to complete internationalisation is through the socialist development of the member countries and their economies. The question is: what is meant by national interest and how is it related to integration interests in this system of thinking? National interest, which is determined in the last analysis by economic conditions, is more than the totality of economic interests, since different nations develop under different external and internal conditions. The totality of these conditions, which include the political, security and cultural spheres as well as economic interests, can be regarded as national interests. The material basis on which this relies is separate national property and the corresponding distribution system. The international interests, which are the main concern of an integration, form a whole, with national interests as its component parts. It follows logically that an integration has no interests separate from national interests, and that is why no supranational organisations have ever been set up within the CMEA. Yet, neither can the national interest emerge in a pure form within the integrated interest, since the interests of economically co-operating nations do not, and cannot, completely coincide. If the material basis of the national interest is separate national property, then the economic ties linking the socialist nations will mainly assume the form of commodity and money relations. In such circumstances, the only principle that can underlie the establishment of an equilibrium of national interests is the exchange of equal values. Socialist integration is a regulated, planned process that materialises in the form of exchange. Therefore, commodity, money credit and foreign-currency conditions may act as incentives in this system and thus as efficient instruments in the development of the operation of the entire integration.

In stressing the importance of national interest, it is necessary to point out that the national interests of socialist states cannot be determined without taking into account the internal and external conditions of socialist development and the historic mission of the working class and the socialist community. Soviet economists have done pioneer work in investigating the relationship between the member countries' economies and an integration that is certainly one of the key issues of progress in socialist development.[7]

Political factors also played a decisive part in the creation of the CMEA. Most of these factors were in the sphere of common interests, which have a lion's share in all integrations, although here again 'interests' means much more than the totality of economic interests. Among other political factors were coercive effects such as blockades or embargoes imposed by capitalist countries. These had to be counteracted in the course of development.

I should like to emphasise two of the common interests promoting political decisions.

(1) After the Second World War, an essential change took place in the global position of socialism: whereas there had previously been socialism in one country, there was now socialism in several countries. The new historical and political situation compelled the socialist states to develop relationships in compliance with socialist principles and with a view to promoting progress in all socialist countries. This endeavour was naturally concerned not only with the economy but also with security, foreign policy, and culture.

(2) One of the epoch-making purposes of socialist economic co-operation is to secure better conditions and a framework for worldwide competition with capitalism. The coercive element of the economic blockade or embargo imposed by the leading capitalist countries could be offset only by mutual

[7] Among Soviet economists, I should like to mention with special emphasis O. Bogomolov, M. V. Senin, M. Maksimova, and Y. Belyaev. Their works and studies have been instrumental in shaping my views.

assistance and close co-operation. The socialist countries joined forces, both politically and economically in a part of Europe that had not been affected by the great social and economic upheavals of the industrial revolution. Thus, in the economic sense this area remained a marginal one, a periphery, while in the political sense it became the arena for various nations, nationalities, cultures and religions to fight one another. The hostilities and passions were, of course, fostered by the old ruling classes and by the great powers fighting one another for hegemony, and not without success. This painful truth is not altered by the fact that the conception of co-operation can also be traced further back along the progressive line of the history of Eastern Europe.

In this area, inflamed by national hostilities and by conflicts between nationalities, the creation of political and economic co-operation obviously demanded much circumspections and persuasion from the young socialist systems. The socialist countries had to achieve a new social structure by totally transforming the economic one. Such a transformation required a dynamic policy of industrialisation in countries that had not yet achieved the middle stage of development. In implementing the great task of structural transformation – one that has been in the forefront of progressive national endeavours for several decades – a decisive part was played by the Soviet Union, when – under embargo conditions – it ensured raw-material supplies and opened its vast market for the products of the new industries. It is common knowledge that large economic units have undoubted advantages in building up economic contacts. The crucial question is whether the large economic unit we have in mind uses the advantages deriving spontaneously from power relationships and available even in the case of formal equality of exchange, or whether it is deterred from doing so by other, socio-political and ideological forces. In the co-operation between the Soviet Union and the member states of the CMEA, socio-political, ideological factors have proved so strong that economic-power relationships have never asserted themselves unilaterally.

This fact seems to indicate that the political factors underlying integration (economic co-operation) have played a very important part both during the normal functioning of the community, and at times of cyclical and structural change.

Not only must fundamental interests coincide in an integration, but in addition a balance must be attained between the opposing interests that necessarily arise when new decisions or bilateral agreements are made. The co-ordination of economic interests is much more difficult than, say, the co-ordination of foreign politics or of strategic interests, since economic interests (the economic interests of enterprises, and the economic situation and security of the workers) are very deeply and directly rooted in the society. When interests conflict, equilibrium must be achieved within the integration grouping or in bilateral relations, since the road toward general (integrated) interests is through the observance of specific national interests.

Nonantagonistic opposing interests may arise in a number of problem areas. One of these is the adjustment of national structures to the integration structure. It may happen, mainly in the first phase of industrialisation, and later, at several crucial points in development, that individual countries insist on interpreting the national industrial structure in a manner that was correct in the past but is currently outdated. The contrary, of course, may also occur. At critical points of development, the system of distribution of tasks between integrated and national economies undergoes a change under the impact of the scientific—technological revolution and of different economic factors. In such cases, two systems of requirements come into conflict: one is economic rationality as expressed in integration, the implementation of which is expected to accelerate the development of the community; the other is the principle of equality and sovereignty of nations, stipulating that substantial issues can be solved only by unanimous agreement of the participating countries.

These issues have always been handled with utmost tolerance in the decision sphere of socialist integration, permitting the members that comply with the new concept to proceed in that direction and allowing the members that insist on the earlier concept to refrain from joining the programme in question. If this were not so, one would either have to renounce the development that is objectively possible or certain countries would feel that integration was an obstacle to the further development of their national industries. Now, if the economic programmes projected in the new plan are carried out successfully, and if industries producing expensively, with low output or without safe markets, create economic, social and political problems in some countries, then, after a certain time has elapsed, the point will have been reached for everybody to accept the new principles of specialisation and of distribution.

Similar conflicting interests arise on the question of equalisation. There is general agreement that socialism has to eliminate the economic, cultural and other discrepancies that still exist among the member countries as a heritage of the past; yet it must develop dynamically in order to attain a favourable position in competition with capitalism. Equalisation is achieved both through the growth of each country's economy and as a result of multilateral co-operation, including mutual assistance among the socialist countries. The process of equalisation obviously requires and presupposes the friendly assistance of the more advanced socialist countries as well as the maximum mobilisation and rational utilisation of the resources of the less advanced economies. The dimensions and the structure of this assistance are, however, inseparable from the dynamics of the industrially more advanced countries, which, in turn, influence the worldwide competition with capitalism. It is therefore necessary to co-ordinate the two requirements rationally, since the development of the entire community cannot be stopped by the narrowest bottleneck either in an economy or in international co-operation.

By the nature of things, conflicting interests arise in various problems of foreign trade, such as in the structure of exports and imports. The conflicting interests are generally based on objective foundations. In many instances, however, the conflict is only apparent, being due to the fact that national prices, values and incentives fail to reflect real economic interests. In such cases, apparent economic interests seem to be real, and real economic interests are unclear.

During the expansion of economic ties, common as well as conflicting interests may arise in the micro-economy and in various branches. It often happens that enterprises and branches discover new opportunities for co-operation that may require investments in two or more countries. In such cases, the relevant enterprises and branches make co-ordinated efforts to obtain investment development credits from the decision-making authorities. From the point of view of the nations involved, such partial interests appear as development alternatives in the course of drafting their five-year plans.

In analysing the domestic effects of integration, a few words must be said about the correlation between institutional structures and the managerial system, about conflicts between technical and economic considerations, and about the positive effects of integration on the modernising of production structures.

In order to control and promote co-operation on the governmental level, governmental bodies are created with parallel structures. This facilitates regular consultation among member states, the exchange of information on past experience, and the planned co-ordination of the various development concepts.

The communist parties of member countries play an especially important part in stimulating the development of socialist integration, in formulating new concepts and programmes, and in shaping public opinion on integration In our view, it is particularly beneficial that the initiatives are not in the hands of a technocratic mechanism that, while it may be on a high level, is by its very nature likely to become divorced from the masses and to underestimate the weight of public opinion. Besides being permanently associated with economic and international tasks, the communist parties maintain structural and many-sided contacts with all strata of the society and are thus capable of weighing carefully in advance the socio-political effects of the measures, steps and changes connected with integration.

Integration also has an important influence upon the co-ordination of management systems. There may be a high degree of decentralisation of decisions in domestic economic questions, depending on the intentions of the governments. In matters affecting relations within the community, the decision level of the other countries (their degree of centralisation or de-centralisation) must be taken into account. In international relations, we can proceed only from obligations undertaken on an equal footing: if one government guarantees the selling and buying of certain commodities, then the government of the other party must make the same guarantee, irrespective of the way in which the domestic economy is administered. If there are significant discrepancies in this respect between management systems, they must be bridged in the spirit of mutual equity.

Certain conflicts between technical and economic considerations may occur even within domestic economies. Technical optimum is well known to differ from economic optimum. In international co-operation, the dispute may arise not among the spokesmen of the national economies, but perhaps between the representatives of the technical optimum and those of the economic optimum. This difference should be borne in mind.

Finally, let me point to a factor that affects the thinking of different strata of the population — namely, that integration has a very substantial reorganising and rearranging effect on large enterprises. In the first phase of industrialisation, certain enterprises were established that did not operate profitably. Today this circumstance is no longer associated chiefly with technical standards or with labour, but rather with an assortment of products. It is therefore often rational to give up trying to manufacture the end-products in every branch in every country. This is how the principle of vertical integration was adopted, within which the damand of outer markets becomes decisive. In this manner, subsidised factories often become economical and more productive through integration. This process, which gained particular impetus after the adoption of the Comprehensive Programme, has compelled these enterprises to enter into more negotiations, to achieve more careful co-ordination, and to acquire more knowledge of markets. The vertical division of labour within the Comprehensive Programme has for many years stabilised the position of the participating enterprises and demonstrated to the workers in the factories and branches that a rationally established integration makes possible the solution of the most complicated problems.

In the decades to come, integration is going to have very important and complicated tasks to perform in shaping the world economic system. Inherent in important and complicated tasks are many conflicts. Conflicts are also inherent in the relationship between integrated groupings, which may represent radically different socio-economic systems. Finally, the economic actions of integrated communities take place in a world economic environment pregnant with conflicts yet becoming more and more interdependent. Although the actions of the communities are coherent, certain moves are directed more 'inward' and others more 'outwards'. The 'inward' moves, however, determine and limit the zones of outward actions, while the 'outward' moves have an impact on the zone of inward actions. When optimising — economically and politically — the relationship and the division of tasks between the community and member nations, it is of the utmost importance to act with great circumspection along the 'zones of internal actions'. A national economy is an organic economic framework of history and tradition, of property and distribution conditions determined by its system of interests, a framework within which its economic potential can, at a given time, be best mobilised. This situation, especially in selective and nontotal integrations, continues for a long time, even though international property and distribution conditions and economic methods are constantly gaining ground.

Integrations serve the future not only by improving their own economic systems but by developing and promoting a new international division of labour. In compliance with the requirements of this new international division of labour, they must promote the development of trade and the distribution of tasks among different integrated blocs and lay new foundations for the system of an efficient division of labour with developing countries.

The first task means the development of co-operation and the distribution of duties among countries belonging to different social systems, as the safest economic guarantee of lasting peace and security. The second task presupposes the development of measures, methods, and systems of incentives in which – in addition to exchange really based on equal values – a growing role is played by various preferences, by the redistribution of part of the income, by the marketing of different raw materials, and by the participation of technologically advanced countries in the economic development of the countries that produce these raw materials. This is the only way in which it will be possible to transfer institutionally to the developing world as much energy as will be needed (along with the energies of those countries appropriately mobilised and efficiently utilised) to bridge the current alarming gap between developed and developing countries and to lay down the foundations of a new international division of labour.

If, in understanding and solving these tremendous tasks, the integrated communities display sufficient wisdom and determination, they may share in the transition from the old system of international division of labour to the new one.

Comments
Robert Marjolin (France)

I. INTRODUCTORY

I have read Bognar's report with great interest; though not always in complete agreement with some of his views on West European integration, I should like to say how well written I consider his paper to be and how penetrating its analytical thought.

For my part, I shall confine myself to a number of comments (based largely on personal experience) on some of the socio-political causes and conditions that in the 1950s brought the European Communities into being, and in the 1960s led to the establishment of the Common Market more or less in the form in which it had been originally envisaged. I shall conclude with a few words on the institutional and socio-political aspects of future developments, particularly in relation to the conversion of the customs union into an economic and monetary union, the principle of which was agreed upon in 1969 but which is still in the project stage.

II. THE BIRTH OF THE EUROPEAN COMMUNITIES

Any integration in Western Europe would have been physically impossible if the countries wishing to form a customs union had had different economic systems. In fact, they all had a capitalist-type market economy. More important still, was perhaps, the fact that society was of the pluralistic type featuring many centres of decision. In all cases, competition played a vital part, often in prices but primarily in product quality, product innovation, after-sales service, and so on.

However, it would be wrong to think that the economic systems of these countries were exactly the same. In every case governments had a considerable share in total economic activity, though it varied from country to country. There were differences in the extent of nationalisation, in government action with regard to the redistribution of wealth, and in the measures taken to stabilise the economy. In terms of the degree of government intervention in economic affairs, the member countries could be split into two camps. On the one hand, there were the Federal Republic of Germany and Benelux, with market economies on the American pattern, and, on the other, France and Italy, where bureaucratic influences played a much more important part. Even in the private sector, the principle of free competition was subject to varying degrees of limitation from country to country.

In addition, economic integration would have been impracticable if the political systems of the nations endeavouring to join together had differed very sharply. All, in fact, were parliamentary democracies, although, a few years after the foundation of the Communities, France became a semi-presidential democracy. A multi-party system and trade-union independence in relation to political power were two essential, lasting characteristics of the member countries. Any country with a different political system was almost automatically excluded, even though it might be regarded as qualifying geographically for admission into a West European union.

Apart from these general conditions, there was the fact that the Six had reached a comparable level of economic development in spite of considerable variations in per capita income and regional development.

Moving now from conditions to causes, we can easily list a number of factors that had considerable importance during the 1950s, though subsequently their significance lessened or even vanished.

The wish to prevent any future military conflict between France and the Federal Republic of Germany was in the minds of the founders of the European Coal and Steel Community. Today, such a conflict is unthinkable. The disintegration of colonial empires also played an important part, since it demonstrated to member countries that their future was no longer overseas, but in Europe.

There is no denying the fact that the political tension existing at that time between, on the one hand, the United States and Western Europe, and, on the other, the USSR and the other East European countries helped to strengthen the move towards unity in Western Europe. Even so, I should like to stress that at no time was there any intention to prevent or to impede development in the socialist economies. The trade restrictions introduced in the 1950s and 1960s had other origins and stemmed from other considerations.

In contrast to these background causes, there were two other factors that had decisive influence. First, there was the fact that the nations of Western Europe aspired to a standard of living comparable to that of others more favoured by history and, in particular, of those on the other side of the Atlantic. Second, there was the underlying feeling that if Western Europe failed to unite it would cease to play any part in world affairs and would finally lose control of its own destiny.

III. THE SETTING-UP OF THE EUROPEAN COMMUNITIES

Whereas originally the three Communities were practically on an equal footing, the Economic Community quickly came to be the most important of the three and to offer the greatest potential for future development. The integration of Western Europe provided to be essentially a matter of trade.

The result of this has been a considerable development in trade in goods and services among the original six member countries. For most of the countries, well over half their foreign trade is accounted for by dealings within the Community. This *de facto* integration constitutes the strongest bond in the unity of Western Europe.

Certain clauses had been introduced into the Treaty of Rome in order to prevent the most powerful industrial countries (primarily the Federal Republic of Germany) from crushing the weakest or, at least, impeding their development. These clauses have not had to be invoked or, if so, only exceptionally and for different purposes. France and Italy, which in 1957 and 1958 were, in the view of certain gloomy prophets, were headed for economic disaster, are the two countries that have derived most benefit from the movement towards integration.

To the extent that it has accelerated general economic growth in its member countries, the EEC has also helped, if not to solve, at least to make less intractable two important economic problems with socio-political aspects:

agriculture and regional development. However, we should not be blind to the fact that, at least as far as the second of these two problems is concerned, we are still a long way from a final solution, or even from a situation that could be regarded as tolerable.

With regard to the institutional aspects, majority rule has proved, at least in relation to major issues, to be either an illusion or a possibility for the remote future. All decisions touching the interests of one or more member countries on points of vital interest to them, and even many others as well, are taken unanimously. It would be wrong, therefore, to regard the European Communities as technocratic structures. More important still, experience has shown that the unanimity requirement was not an insurmountable obstacle when it came to taking important decisions in the common interest.

The enlargement of the EEC in recent years has presented the Six and some of their neighbours with a very difficult problem, especially as regards the accession of the United Kingdom. Temporarily settled in 1971, the question has now been reopened under conditions with which we are all familiar.

The United Kingdom's reluctance to throw in its lot irreversibly with that of the Six is understandable, principally by reason of its traditional role in world affairs, the attachment of the British population to institutions that none of the events over the past few centuries has succeeded in shaking, and the special place of trades unions in the country's political history.

I shall not be so bold as to attempt to forecast how this problem may be solved. It could be that a reduction, or at least a levelling off, of its financial contributions, together with minor reforms in relation to the common agricultural policy, would make it possible for the United Kingdom to confirm its membership. Another way out would be for the United Kingdom to opt for associate status. It would remain a member of the customs union for industrial products, but would be relieved of all its other obligations.

Relations between the EEC and the United States, though still highly satisfactory, have altered in recent years. From the very start, the integration of Western Europe has always been supported by the Americans, both for political and for sentimental reasons. Throughout the 1950s and 1960s, Washington encouraged West Europeans to search, together with America, for a more satisfactory balance than would be possible between an American super-power and a fragmented Europe.

In Europe there was much concern to make up the lag in technology and management as quickly as possible. This problem has proved to be far less acute and far less serious than many considered it in the 1960s. Western Europe has made very rapid progress and the gap has nearly been closed.

This, and the now stronger economic position of Western Europe explain why the United States, particularly since 1969–70, has been showing a livelier concern for its immediate economic interests. Relations have remained very friendly but have become more businesslike. This is a natural trend reflecting the change that has taken place in the balance of economic power between the countries on either side of the Atlantic.

IV. THE MOVEMENT TOWARDS ECONOMIC AND MONETARY UNION

From the very start the EEC was designed as an economic and monetary union but it was only when the customs union was complete — both industrially and agriculturally – that the question of its development into an economic and monetary union really came to the fore.

The Six (and now the Nine) have been looking for the road to take for over five years. So far, the hoped-for results have not been achieved. There are many reasons for this lack of any spectacular breakthrough. Some are accidental, including the difficulties through which the dollar has been passing in recent years. The persistent weakness of the United States currency, which fell to its lowest value about a year ago, prompted differing reactions from countries in Western Europe and threatened the stability of monetary relationships within Europe.

Since 1973, high rates of inflation in all countries have aggravated this problem. Perhaps the worst feature of the situation, from the viewpoint with which we are concerned, is that inflation rates vary greatly from country to country; though under 10 per cent per annum in the Federal Republic of Germany and the Netherlands, they are as high as 15 per cent or more in France, Italy and the United Kingdom.

Finally, the decision of the oil-producing countries, at the end of 1973, to raise prices has already had a considerable impact – and one that will become even more serious as time goes by – on balances of payments on current account of countries in Western Europe; they are now deep in the red in most cases. There is still no way of knowing how, and by which devious routes, the capital flows will arrive, particularly from the Arab countries, to finance these deficits.

It must be admitted that setting up an economic and monetary union would in any case have been difficult under such conditions. However, there are grounds for hoping that these problems may become less acute. What is more, the determination to join forces in facing these problems and finding their solutions seems to be taking shape in the EEC countries.

The principal difficulty is political. Sovereign states can join a customs union without any serious inroads on their sovereignty. All they do is give up the right to use certain instruments of economic policy, such as the raising of customs tariffs or the imposition of quantitative restrictions. But, in the main, each country remains master of its own economic policy. For example, it can devalue or revalue its currency with a minimum of consultation if it considers such action to be necessary.

Things would be different in an economic and monetary union. The Community institutions would inevitably have a far more important function than at present, and national governments would find their room for manoeuvre considerably restricted. Movement towards economic and monetary union is, in practice, inseparable from the movement towards political union.

The future of this great design will be decided in the next few years. But even if the agreed objectives are not achieved by the target dates, the cohesiveness of Western Europe in matters of economic policy will certainly gain ground and the development of trade and economic relations in general will strengthen it every day.

Comments
Roman Moldovan (Romania)

I.

I shall try to address some problems that, in my opinion, define certain aspects of the socio-political and institutional framework for international economic collaboration. More precisely, these aspects pertain to a set of principles and rules that can be instrumental in promoting this collaboration for the mutual benefit of all interested parties.

In approaching the theme of our debate — social, political and institutional aspects of integration — we start from the concept that the intensification of international economic co-operation, which is a characteristic feature of the contemporary world, can be observed at world, regional and subregional levels. The essential units of the contemporary world economy are the national economies. As independent entities, they facilitate and promote international economic relations. Understandably, each country first promotes collaboration with other countries in the same geographical area, as neighbouring countries certainly are better placed than others are to blend harmoniously their economic and political relations. These interdependencies are not specific to a given geographical area; they have a universal character, deriving from the universal character of the international division of labour. The intensification of these interdependencies has led economic thought towards the conceptualisation of certain new dimensions of economic life.

Economic *rapprochement* and the establishment of long-lasting relations between countries constitute an observable economic process. However, the interpretations of this process in economic theory are often contradictory. Sometimes they tend to confer on this component of international economic co-operation attributes and distinctive features that seek to particularise it and even to differentiate it qualitatively from the phenomenon of economic co-operation itself.

II.

In order for the evolution of international economic relations (the sequence of facts and actions that confer on it a progressive content) to meet the requirements of social development and human needs, it is necessary to state firmly the following principles: the right of each people to decide its aspirations for itself; the right of all countries to complete sovereignty and national independence; the right of all countries, whatever their size, economic level or social system, to freedom and unhindered participation in international life and in the efforts to solve the major problems confronting the international community; the principle of noninterference in the internal affairs of other nations; the right of each people to be the master of its national riches and resources; the right of all countries to have access to raw materials, to modern technologie under mutually advantageous agreements, and to the resources necessary for their economic and social development; the requirement that under no circumstances should raw materials, sources of energy, and international economic relations generally, be used as a means of pressure or interference in the internal affairs of other countries. This indivisible set of principles, which life itself imposes as an inevitable necessity in international economic relations, represents the fundamental theoretical, political and methodological premises for finding and promoting various forms of concrete economic collaboration.

III.

The essence of socio-political and institutional aspects of the intensification of international collaboration at both world and regional scale cannot be investigated in their contents without relating these aspects to the requirement of wiping out underdevelopment and of reducing differences between the levels of economic development of nations, in order to create for all people the opportunity to enjoy the benefits of modern civilisation. The political, social and institutional effects of the integrational phenomena are conditioned by the necessity to establish new economic, commercial and monetary relations on which a new international economic order could be based. This new order should take into account the special needs and stimulate the economic and social progress of developing countries; it should open the markets of developed countries for the industrial goods of developing countries; and it should ensure the transfer of technology from industrial to less developed countries. Intensification of interdependencies is impossible without mutually advantageous collaboration and co-operation. All peoples are interested in the establishment of a new world economic order based on equity, the essence of which should be defined by all countries, whatever their size. Intensification of interdependence in the world economy incvitably makes every nation interested in building up a new economic order, because crisis phenomena and instability in one part of the world unavoidably affect the situation in other parts.

The development of national economies opens new possibilities and, implicitly, new necessities in the realm of the intensification of international economic collaboration and co-operation, both bilateral and multilateral.

IV.

The reality of international economic life demonstrates that the participation of nations in the international division of labour, and the degree of their participation in the world economic activity, is decisively determined by the level of development of their national economy, by its diversification and by its ability to adapt the achievements of the contemporary revolution in science and technology. Life itself demonstrates that a well-developed and diversified economy, far from meaning autarky, is, on the contrary, better suited for an efficient participation in the international division of labour.

The experience of socialist development in various countries attests to the advantages derived from participation in the international division of labour. Intensification of collaboration and co-operation in various forms, including subregional arrangements, is conditioned by the development of the tendency toward the internationalisation of productive forces. The manifestations of this trend give shape to a comprehensive system within which regional and subregional patterns of co-operation must be considered as open subsystems, as component parts. According to this concept, in order to be in concordance,

with the essential realities of the contemporary world, groups set up to facilitate co-operation (regional, subregional or worldwide) should be open groups,
positively contributing to the development of their member countries and
promoting international economic relations in the world as a whole.

In the world economic circuit — a basic element of the structure of interdependencies — important changes are taking place the role and scope of which
make them determining factors in the evolution of the international division of
labour. Two processes, evolving dialectically, are conspicuous in the development of international economic relations: one of specialisation and the other
of collaboration, co-operation and integration. At the same time there is to be
observed an accentuation of the process of shifting from exchanges between
industry and agriculture to exchanges between one industry and another; from
exchanges of raw materials and semi-products for finished goods to exchanges
of goods of a similar kind from this point of view; from exchanges of relatively
simple goods to exchanges of ever more technically elaborate products having
an even higher content of complex labour. There occurs a gradual diminution
of the gaps between the national values and international values of internationally traded goods and services.

These changes taking place in the international division of labour represent
new steps in the evolution of its pattern. For the time being they are restricted
to economic exchanges among the countries with developed and diversified
economies. However, most of the world's countries — the developing countries
— are still in the various stages of intersectoral specialisation and, hence, are
limited to exporting a relatively small range of goods. This limitation has an
adverse influence on the pattern of their foreign trade.

Besides evolution of traditional forms of collaboration like the commercial
exchange of goods and services, the changes occurring in the world economic
circuit are most visible in the emergence of new forms of co-operation in production, technology, management, financing and sales. Such forms acquire an
ever-growing specific weight. These new forms are more compatible with the
phenomenon of intensified international specialisation and are more likely to
use the potential and to meet the requirements of modern (or modernising)
national economies.

V.

To an ever-growing extent, the forms of multilateral relations are blended with
the forms of bilateral relations. The latter acquire a relatively larger importance
as a result of co-operation in production that implies long-standing relations,
mutual knowledge and continuous bilateral contacts and contracts. Taking into
account the ever-growing role of international economic collaboration as a
factor influencing the economic growth and social progress of nations, the
countries strive to organise and institutionalise their mutual economic relations
in order to maximise the benefits accruing to the parties.

The international economic organisations contribute greatly to the task of
stimulating and promoting exchanges of material and spiritual assets between
nations. At the same time, I think that we agree that the assertion of their constructive role in international economic life is directly related to the degree to
which they promote collaboration, remove hindrances and barriers of any kind

between countries, stand for voluntary collaboration, have an open character, and encourage nondiscriminatory practices by all and with respect to all interested countries.

VI.

Of special importance in the investigation of socio-political and institutional aspects of integration — particularly in connection with the role of international organisations and institutions — is the problem of the levels of economic development of participating countries. Equalisation of these levels and elimination of discrepancies between them must be based on agreement and supported by the activity of international organisations.

Regional and sectoral agreements must be promoted by institutions that are broadly open towards the world economy as well. An implication of the recognition that, in every instance, states and economies are autonomous entities within the world economic system is the necessity of avoiding those forms of integration that have a transnational or even a superstate character. These two forms are liable to result in the opposite of integration; as a matter of fact, they hinder the intensification of collaboration and co-operation on a world scale and the desirable evolution in the pattern of international division of labour.

VII.

Attaching due importance to the place of the international economic organisations in supporting countries in their efforts at obtaining mutually beneficial economic co-operation, I ask your permission to refer to my country, Romania, which participates in a great number of international economic, financial, monetary, technical and scientific organisations, on world, regional and sectoral levels. Romania manifests its confidence in the capacity of these organisations for establishing an adequate framework in which countries and governments, the authorised representatives of the peoples, may achieve mutual understanding and freely accept co-operation, with the aim of finding solutions to questions of mutual interest. In this respect, we may mention Romania's participation in the intergovernmental organisations of the United Nations system, the GATT, and others, as well as her participation in the activities of nongovernmental agencies.

Consistent with her foreign policy, Romania has continuously developed economic relations on many levels with the socialist countries, being one of the founders and an active member of the CMEA, and participating actively in the elaboration and realisation of the Comprehensive Programme adopted in 1971.

VIII.

The intensification of co-operation between socialist countries that are members of the CMEA, and the broadening economic integration of these countries are being carried out by various methods designed to ensure the realisation of the provisions of the Comprehensive Programme. This programme defines the contents of economic integration of the CMEA member countries, a process conceived as the intensification of the international division of labour, which is required to equalise the levels of development of the national economies of the member countries, to modernise their structures and to establish condition for stable connections among the main branches of their economy, science and technology. The CMEA has an open character and does not promote the formation of a closed bloc. On the contrary, it is required to favour both the intensification of mutually advantageous economic collaboration and each member country's participation in the world division of labour.

IX.

In our capacity as economists, we are inclined in this Congress to overemphasi the economic aspects of international relations. However, we must note that under present-day conditions economic collaboration is not only a necessity for the economic progress of each country; it is also an essential condition for international *détente,* for peace and security among peoples.

Life has demonstrated, and continues to demonstrate, that the promotion of free economic relations, on the basis of the new principles being asserted today in international life, is eventually conducive to the creation and consolidation of an atmosphere of peace and understanding among peoples, to a world of peace and collaboration in all the fields of international life.

Opening Statement for Group Discussion
Roger Dehem (Canada)

The questions that we are going to debate are important and delicate ones. They relate to historical developments, factual situations, ideological frameworks and national aspirations. We shall discuss facts and ideas that for some are sound and for others unacceptable.

One of the aims of this congress has been the search for a common denominator in our ways of thinking. This common denominator could be reason, in its eighteenth-century meaning.

To make things clear, it is important to draw distinctions. The subject-matter is so complex and confused that it is useful to separate its many elements, and to discuss them individually.

First, there is *the interpretation of historical realities*. Bognár has suggested an interpretation of East European and West European integration along Marxist lines; that is, by stressing class antagonisms. Marjolin has told us of his disagreement with this approach, at least so far as concerns Western Europe.

A second main topic of discussion could be *the evaluation of the efficiency of existing institutional arrangements in the East and in the West*. This is a complex issue, because efficiency can be evaluated only in relation to the objectives that are supposed to be pursued. These aims could be

(1) the abundance of material goods,
(2) the preservation of individual freedom,
(3) the preservation of an official and exclusive ideology, and
(4) the strengthening of military power.

Only the first of these objectives could be considered purely economic, the others being conventionally regarded as political. It would be interesting to try to make explicit the nature of the aims of existing institutions. We could have a most useful debate.

After discussing the origin of the present-day situation, which tragically divides us into two camps, and, after having made explicit the finality of the institutions under which we live, we might discuss *the desirable and probable development of these institutions*.

If economics were the only concern, we might refer to Cooper's contribution on the optimum integration areas. This problem is an important one only for the EEC, where the economic objectives are paramount. But pure economic rationality belongs, unfortunately, only to the realm of Utopia. Socio-political realities have been moulded by national traditions, and by organised, vested interests in the economic and political fields. These extra-economic factors are precisely those that, in the West, are hiding behind the screen of national sovereignty. They are currently hindering the progress of the EEC towards an economic and monetary union.

Given the national political realities, one may wonder whether an economic and monetary union would be a reasonable objective. Would it not be more proper to look for a 'second-best' solution that would be consistent with existing national constraints? This is what I personally should favour.

I should thus be close to Moldovan's position. He is rightly concerned about how national prerogatives may be safeguarded in the context of an integration system that is inappropriate to national aspirations.

In this respect, we should remember that integrating institutions have not been born out of pure reason with unanimously recognised and freely expresse common objectives. We may have to deal with an asymmetrical institutional system that is imposed upon the weaker members. In the EEC, the system has been freely negotiated between nation states, which are fully and primarily aware of their national interests, but which have tried to increase their nationa advantage through a multinational integration system.

It has become more and more obvious that, after a period of euphoria corresponding to its first ten years of existence, the EEC has recently come up against the problem of distributing the gains of integration. Until about 1968, each member state felt itself to be a gainer from the Community arrang ments. The cake to be distributed was getting larger, as was each slice of it. But relations among member countries have become more antagonistic as som members have attempted to bend the institutions and common policies towards their own ends.

Besides these three main issues that I should like to see debated (the interpretation of historical realities; the efficiency of existing institutional arrangements; and the desirable and probable development of these institutions), there are a number of secondary issues that I think merit discussion. Three of these are outlined below.

(1) *The role of freedom in economic integration.* Machlup reminded us of Adam Smith's principle that 'the division of labour is limited by the extent of the market'. The forefather of modern political economy did not speak of integration, but he meant it. He wanted to explain that the liberation of man from artificial constraints brings about an abundance of goods through a *spontaneous* division of labour.

In evaluating economic and social achievements since the Treaty of Rome, it is important to understand that economic growth is to be ascribed essentially to the private initiatives that have become profitable thanks to the liberalisation and the extension of markets.

In discussing integration institutions, we should beware of superficial evalu tions. Economic progress in the nineteenth century was not the result of an accumulation of stratified bureaucracies, but was the consequence of the dismantling of the mercantilist apparatus that had preceded it.

(2) *The effects of integration on the distribution of incomes.* This is a statistical question. Perhaps Marjolin will be able to bring some light on the subject, in order to dispel ideological preconceptions.

(3) *The effects on integration on the national identity of member countries* The importance that is attached to this issue varies considerably from one country to another. It is very much an issue in Canada. In Western Europe, on the other hand, it is hardly an issue at all, except perhaps in the United Kingdom. This would be an extra-economic question that could be discussed if time permits.

Report on Group Discussion
Shigeto Tsuru (Japan)

The range of topics opened up by the main paper of this working group was not only extremely broad, but also so interdisciplinary that it has not been easy to traverse the entire field with any degree of satisfaction. In addition, it may be frankly admitted, with an inescapable feeling of regret, that, with only a few exceptions, economists from Western countries did not choose to appear in the working group's arena of discussion. The result was that, despite the relevance of the topic to both East and West, the extent of fruitful dialogue that the group was able to achieve was severely limited. What follows is a faithful account of the discussions that took place. If it fails to reveal a *dialectic* process, this is mainly due to the fact that, while there definitely was a *thesis*, there was practically no *antithesis* and thus, necessarily, no *synthesis*.

The starting point of the discussion held in Working Group G was the idea that it is not possible to appraise the significance of economic integration in economic terms alone. The processes of regional economic integration that are developing in the world today are not purely economic phenomena. They entail profound social, political and institutional aspects, which should be thoroughly studied.

In the course of the discussion, speakers referred to the contents of the main paper submitted by Bognár, as well as to the two discussion papers presented by Marjolin and Moldovan. They also raised some new problems, expressing sometimes controversial points of view.

In general, the discussion centred around four foci: (1) the background or causes of economic integration; (2) the social aims of economic integration; (3) the institutional forms of integration; and (4) the socio-political and institutional consequences of such integration.

As regards the first of these — the sources of origin or causes of economic integration — many speakers supported the view that integration processes appear under the impact of certain objective factors. The most important of these is the rapid development of productive forces in the national economies of many countries, influenced by extraordinarily rapid technical progress. The growing size of enterprises, the internationalisation of production, as well as progress in the field of transportation and communications, all create both the conditions and the need for closer international co-operation and integration. Some speakers thought that political forces played a secondary role in the development of economic integration, coming into action with a certain delay and supporting only a phenomenon created by the objective factors mentioned above. Other views attributed a more active role to political factors, as will be mentioned later in connection with *de facto* integration. It was, however, generally agreed that, if in the past there have been some examples of enforced integration, economic integration today is possible only by the common agreement of the interested countries.

The second problem concerned the social aims of economic integration. Many speakers stressed that, in the case of the socialist countries belonging to the CMEA, raising the standard of living of the working class is a primary and direct aim of economic integration, while the other important aim is the equalisation of the general level of economic and social development of the member countries. Some speakers mentioned that the founders of the EEC in Western Europe also had in mind raising the general welfare of the society by means of economic integration.

There was a general opinion that the institutional forms of economic integration depend very much on the characteristic features of the socio-economic and political systems of the countries concerned. This is especially clear in the case of the two main regional integration organisations, the EEC and the CMEA. Opinions were even presented that, in view of the great differences involved, we should talk separately about capitalist and socialist integration. However, some speakers maintained that there are certain institutional problems common to both types of integration and that they should be carefully studied.

The dependence of institutional arrangements on the socio-political system is visible when one takes into account the different methods of multilateral co-operation within the CMEA and the EEC. It was asserted that the stress, in the socialist countries, on the co-ordination of national economic plans and on the arrangement of specific ties between member countries in the sphere of industrial production has led to the establishment of appropriate institutional forms that do not exist in the EEC, an organisation composed of market-economy countries.

It was pointed out that, in the absence of a formal institutional framework, there may be cases of *de facto* integration as a result of the influence exerted by the economy of a dominant power on the economies of other countries. Such a *de facto* integration could emerge as the outcome of a political situation caused by the Second World War and may continue for a long time.

In connection with the socio-political and institutional consequences of integration, the problem of national sovereignty and economic integration was raised by many speakers. It was generally observed that economic integration may be compatible with the sovereignty of the member state of the integrated organisation. Certain limitations to the full freedom of action of particular states, agreed upon by the member states, do not constitute an infringement of their sovereignty, because they are self-imposed limitations. In this connection, decision making in the organisation was discussed. Some speakers thought that unanimity is needed in this process, as is the case in the CMEA. They criticised the principle of majority voting, as it is sometimes applied in the EEC. Others maintained that even with majority voting the individual interests of member countries can be properly secured.

Another topic of discussion connected with the problem of national sovereignty was the role attributed to the common organs in the EEC and the CMEA, respectively. The superiority of the solutions adopted by the CMEA in this respect was stressed by a number of speakers; but there was no one present to dispute this claim.

The problem of national sovereignty was also approached in the context of the relations between the great powers and the smaller countries. The impact of the United States, which is not an EEC member, on the countries belonging to the EEC was critically commented upon, and the need for Western Europe to develop political independence of the United States was stressed. As far as the relations between the USSR and other member countries of the CMEA are concerned, it was asserted that they are based on the principle of national sovereignty and equality, and that it is very important that their common ideology creates a political climate conducive to the strenthening of mutual economic ties in the best interest of all member countries of the CMEA.

Some speakers drew attention to the fact that integration leads to an expansion of the functions of the state in the economic sphere. This is so not only in the capitalist countries but also in the socialist ones. In the latter, some new functions appear in connection with the international co-ordination of economic plans and economic policy, as well as with new relations among the economic ministries, scientific institutes, and production units of the CMEA member countries.

Another very important problem discussed was the long-term social consequences of economic integration. Some speakers expressed the opinion that, because of the new institutional setting created by the economic integration of the CMEA countries, the working classes in these countries find new forms of mutual co-operation, and as a result their consciousness of the international solidarity of the workers is strengthened. New social forces seem to be appearing and are starting to influence the economic and political situation in the EEC countries. But there was no common agreement on the scope and character of the social consequences of economic integration within the EEC. Many speakers referred to a growth of class contradictions in the West European countries. In this connection, the opposite interests of farmers in different countries were mentioned, as was the new situation of the British working class. The opposite interests of the working classes in the labour-exporting and labour-importing countries were also stressed. On the other hand, the view was presented that economic integration does not influence class relations in Western society. It was held that the farmers in the EEC countries are satisfied and that the workers are interested in the broadening of markets. Some speakers attributed the growing role of large monopolistic corporations in the West European countries to the progress of economic integration. In this connection, the role of multinational corporations was mentioned. The creation of the EEC has facilitated their operations and growth. It was indicated, however, that the development of multinational corporations expresses the very logic of private capital, the integration processes notwithstanding.

With regard to the social consequences of economic integration, the need was acknowledged for a multidisciplinary approach, especially for co-operation between economists and sociologists. This could contribute to a better understanding of the problems involved. It was also said that efforts should be made towards assuring a uniform understanding of concepts applied by Western and Eastern economists when investigating and analysing the processes of economic integration.

The last major problem discussed in the working group was finding ways and means of fostering closer co-operation between the two regional integrations in Europe, the EEC and the CMEA. It was the unanimous opinion of the participants that such co-operation would be advantageous to both sides and that there is now an urgent need to find appropriate forms for this co-operation. Some speakers believed that closer co-operation between the CMEA and the EEC may facilitate an increase in economic assistance to the developing countries and contribute to the preservation of world peace.

In concluding my report I should like to say that the general atmosphere of the discussion in the Working Group G was a friendly and constructive one. Notwithstanding some differences of opinion, all participants showed a willingness to understand and appreciate the position and views of their colleagues. Such an attitude is conducive to the achievement of progress in the understanding, among economists of differing ideologies and methodologies, of important economic processes taking place in the modern world.

11 Integration of Less Developed Areas and of Areas on Different Levels of Development (Main Paper, Working Group H)

Eduardo Lizano (COSTA RICA)

I.

Among the main features of international economic relations in the years following the Second World War are the attempts that have been made to establish programmes of economic integration among less developed countries. These schemes have been implemented throughout the Third World, and particularly in Latin America and Africa.

Nevertheless, the outcome of these programmes has been disappointing and the results meagre. In certain cases, members have decided to abandon the programme; Chad, in the Central African Customs and Economic Union, and Honduras, in the Central American Common Market (CACM), are examples. In other cases, the 'normal' way in which programmes work is through a series of crises. This is true in the East African Community and, at present, in the CACM. Some other schemes — for instance, those of the Latin American Free Trade Association and the Regional Co-operation for Development — stagnate for years. Lastly, in other cases — the Association of South-East Asian Countries, and the many proposals for co-operation among the Arab countries — it has proved impossible, after years of work, actually to get programmes started.

All these factors — the instability of membership, the recurrent crises, the lack of progress, and the great difficulties in launching the programmes — create doubts about the very possibility of integrating less developed countries, and about the utility of integration as a means of accelerating economic growth in these countries.

The purpose of this paper is twofold: first, to analyse the relationship between integration and development, and, more specifically, to discuss why less developed countries participate in integration programmes; and, second, to examine the main problems that have arisen in schemes of economic integration involving less developed countries.

[1] The author wishes to thank L. N. Willmore, whose comments and criticism proved most helpful in the preparation of this paper.

II.

Programmes of economic integration have several effects, both on member countries and on nonparticipants. The main sources of these effects are the characteristics of the schemes with regard to mobility of goods and factors and the common external tariff. The greater the freedom of movement for goods and factors and the higher the external tariff, the more pronounced will be the consequences of integration. Some of the effects have been classified as static and others as dynamic, the former relating mainly to the reallocation of factors of production, to problems of consumption and to the terms of trade. The dynamic effects are related largely to the way in which integration alters the possibilities for economic growth in participating countries.[2]

It is generally agreed that integration does not have the same meaning for less developed countries as for advanced countries, for the attention of the latter is focused on the static effects of integration, whereas in the case of less developed countries the dynamic effects are the significant issue. The developing countries have, at least conceptually, two alternatives for the fostering of their economic growth. The first is the autarkic path, which can be dismissed quickly, given the high costs it imposes. The second one, a so-called 'outward-looking' path of development, in which exports are concentrated in a few traditional products, does not offer good prospects either. The main reasons are well known: with few exceptions, the export products of less developed countries are very unstable, the economic growth of countries following this path of development depends heavily on the economic situation in the industrial countries, and, finally, the industrial centres have established so many obstacles to trade and migration that it is very difficult for developing countries to obtain the benefits of their comparative advantages. In the light of this situation, most of the developing countries have been seeking alternative strategies for economic development. It is from this standpoint that integrating becomes important, because these countries regard entry into an integration scheme as an alternative, midway between the autarkic and the 'outward-looking' paths of development. Integration takes something from both of them: from autarky, the protection of the integration area from outside competition through the common external tariff; from the 'outward-looking' path of development, the opening of the national markets of each of the member countries to regional competition. So, the integration programmes involving less developed countries should be seen much more as an alternative path of economic development than as a way of allowing a better allocation of a given stock of factors of production.[3] That is the main reason why, in dealing with integration schemes involving developing countries, less attention should be

[2] J. A. Jaber, 'The Relevance of Traditional Integration Theory to Less Developed Countries', in *Journal of Common Market Studies,* Mar 1971, pp. 254–67.

[3] Sidney Dell, *Trade Blocks and Common Markets* (Constable, 1963); and Béla Balassa, 'El Desarrollo economico y la integración', in *CEMLA*, 1965.

given to a discussion of the trade-creation and trade-diversion effects,[4] which since Viner's seminal contributions to the subject, have been the traditional way of judging economic integration of developed countries. With less developed countries, it is much more important to examine the opportunities that integration opens for the growth and diversification of their economies, through the possibility of establishing new productive activities, especially industrial activities. In fact, in the vast majority of less developed countries, industrialisation has become such a prominent aim that several authors consider it a public good.[5]

In short, for less developed countries, the real alternative is not between free trade and integration, but between the national protectionism of each country and integration – in other words, regional protectionism.[6] Integration thus becomes a means by which developing countries can strive for goals that each country could not reach on its own without an unbearably high cost. More specifically, integration permits developing countries, first, to promote industrialisation at a lower cost than does autarky, and, second, to increase the bargaining power of member countries in relation to third countries. This point of view has been questioned in several quarters. Recently Kraus[7] has indicated that, although integration is superior to national protectionism, it does not mean that integration is the best way to promote industrialisation. Export subsidies actually could be used for the same purpose by less developed countries, and at a lower cost than regional protectionism. It follows that 'so long as governments have the option of granting and adjusting direct production subsidies, customs union will not be the most efficient protective mechanism in the public goods case'.[8]

Several comments can be advanced against Kraus's argument.

(1) The possibility of using export subsidies in order to foster industrial growth presupposes that it is possible for the less developed countries to export manufactured goods. But this is not the case, given the manifold obstacles that the developed countries, as well as the developing countries, have estab-

---

[4] This does not mean that these two effects are not present in integration schemes involving developing countries. There is trade diversion inasmuch as goods that previously were imported from third countries are now imported from partner countries; there is trade creation inasmuch as goods that were produced in the countries are now imported from other member countries.

[5] See the following well-known articles: Charles A. Cooper and B. F. Massell, 'Toward a General Theory of Customs Unions for Developing Countries', in *Journal of Political Economy*, Oct 1965, pp. 461–76; and H. Johnson, 'An Economic Theory of Protectionism, Tariff Bargaining, and The Formation of Customs Unions', in *Journal of Political Economy*, June 1965, pp. 256–83.

[6] R. F. Mikesell, 'The Theory of Common Markets as applied to Regional Arrangements among Developing Countries', in *International Trade Theory in a Developing World* ed. R. F. Harrod and D. C. Hague (New York: Macmillan, 1963), pp. 205–29.

[7] M. B. Kraus, 'Recent Developments in Customs Union Theory: An Interpretative Survey', in *Journal of Economic Literature,* June 1972, pp. 413–36.

[8] Ibid., p. 428.

lished in order to control their imports.[9]

(2) Export subsidies could produce more distortions than does the protectionism of the regional external tariff. That would be the case if the individual countries were to enter into an export-subsidy competition, each trying to attract new industries by granting more subsidies than the other countries. This sort of race will not take place in the case of the common external tariff, because it is, by definition, equal for all the members[10] and it will be enough to set tariff rates that provide mutually acceptable protection from foreign competition.

(3) Export subsidies are more prone to generate retaliation from the other countries than is integration. This is especially true when, because of the subsidies, other countries begin to import goods (for instance, textiles) that are 'sensitive' even in developed countries.

(4) Export subsidies are not an adequate policy measure for reaching other aims of economic integration. Specifically, they do not allow the less developed countries to improve their bargaining position.

(5) Finally, the administrative and political difficulties of export subsidies should not be overlooked.

Thus, it does not seem that export subsidies are a good substitute or an accepable alternative for integration of developing countries. For them, integration remains a valid way of reaching the two goals of industrialisation and an improved bargaining position.

III.

As was mentioned at the beginning of this paper, the results so far obtained from integration programmes involving less developed countries have not been satisfactory. The actual outcome lags far behind the initial expectations. The obstacles have been numerous and complex and quite difficult to overcome.

In this section, attention is paid to some of the more important of these problems.

DISPARITIES AMONG MEMBER COUNTRIES

The initial disparities among member countries, and the way in which integration may accentuate these differences, has become one of the most significant problems for the further progress of integration schemes.

[9] In relation to export subsidies, Cooper and Massell (in *Journal of Political Economy*, Oct 1965, p. 474) argue that 'an industrial sector based on production for export may be exceedingly difficult to establish and maintain. Not only are the industrial markets of advanced economies difficult to enter economically, but obtaining the necessary political co-operation would be very unlikely'.

[10] In the case of a free-trade area in which there is no common external tariff, the countries could fall into the same temptation. This is one of the reasons why there seldom are cases of free-trade areas among developing countries.

The first point that should be cleared is the one related to the concept of disparities. Many factors differentiate countries. These can be economic, cultural or geographical. However, there are two particularly important factors: the opportunities a country has of promoting economic growth; and the capacity of a country to take advantage of these opportunities. All of these factors, taken together, are responsible for the fact that countries have different opportunities for growth and different capacities for taking advantage of these opportunities. Consequently, some countries progress more than others.

Integration can make initial disparities worse. It is clear that integration gives rise to 'backwash' and 'spread' effects, but the former seem to be stronger than the latter in the case of integration schemes involving developing countries.[11] Economic units, especially industrial enterprises, are not located evenly throughout the integration area; on the contrary, there is a strong tendency towards concentration and the formation of development poles. The main factors that influence this polarisation trend are various. First, the initial disparities themselves make it more difficult for the most backward countries to have the political and technical skills required to prevent the mechanisms of the integration programmes from worsening the disparities. Second, the concrete nature of the integration scheme may complicate matters if, for instance, integration is conceived of as just the establishing of free trade and the free movement of factors. In this case, the polarisation effect would be stronger.[12] Third, if the 'periphery' is rich in natural resources, complementary factors of production are likely to move from the 'centre' to the 'periphery'. Obversely, if the 'periphery' lacks natural resources, factors will flow from there to the 'centre'.[13]

The initial disparities and their possible widening during the integration process represent a serious problem for the progress of integration. As has been stated previously, the poorest countries do not have the necessary skills to negotiate agreements for the protection of their own interest. The diversity of aims within an integration scheme is in direct relation to the different levels of development that the member countries have attained, and the more diverse

[11] R. D. Hansen states that 'backwash effects play a far greater role in unions of underdeveloped countries; the more marked the initial disparities in such union, the more the backwash effects tend to predominate' ('Regional Integration, Reflections on a Decade of Theoretical Efforts', in *World Politics,* June 1965, p. 256).

[12] '[I]ntegration cannot take place merely on the basis of the most efficient allocation of resources because that would result in the rich getting richer and confirm the dependence of certain countries on the pattern of monoculture' (E. B. Haas and P. C. Schmitter, 'Economics of Differential Patterns of Political Integration: Projections about Unity in Latin America', in *International Organization,* autumn 1964, pp. 405–37).

[13] In the long run the polarisation problem loses relevance as the growth poles change over time. The cumulative process is not an endless one; history shows how many important financial, commercial and production poles have declined and even disappeared. See P. T. Bauer, 'International Economic Development', in *Economic Journal,* Mar 1959, pp. 105–23. Nevertheless, the problem pertaining to the integration programmes among less developed countries is of an immediate nature.

the aims of the countries the more difficult it is to reach a workable agreement. When disparities are evident, very often the countries expect too much from integration, believing that it alone can solve the problem of disparities; and because of this they may postpone internal measures that are indispensable for economic development. Lastly, the larger the disparities, the greater the pressure on the more developed countries, even if they are poor, to make concessions in favour of the more backward countries of the group. The final consequence is that large disparities among the member countries weaken the integration scheme, disruptive crises occur quite often, and the whole programme is therefore questioned.

DISTRIBUTION OF BENEFITS AND COSTS

The issue of the distribution of benefits and costs of integration among the member countries remains one of the most complex and difficult problems of integration. In all the integration schemes there have been some countries that have considered that the costs that they have to bear are excessive in relation to the benefits that they obtain. This fact gives rise to permanent tensions and conflicts and to so-called distributive crises.

Economic integration creates opportunities and problems at the same time. It leads to new benefits and new costs and the member countries have to find ways and means to distribute them. The benefits and costs that accrue to a country depend on its own economic conditions as well as on the specific measures that the integration programme contemplates. The conditions comprise the amount and the degree of utilisation of the factors of production, the economic policy that a country follows in relation to matters such as monetary affairs, exchange rates, wage policy, foreign investment, and the type of social organisation that the country has. The disparities that arise from the specific measures of integration related mainly to the free trade of goods (changes in trade flows, price levels, the allocation of factors of production, and fiscal revenues), mobility of factors (supply and demand of factors), financial arrangements, and possible agreements regarding the geographical distribution of industries. These conditions and disparities determine the way in which the member countries take advantage of the new opportunities that integration offers, and, to a large extent, the way in which the benefits and costs of integration are distributed among them.

Nevertheless, the difficulties do not stop there. The concept of benefits and costs of integration is, in itself, a very elusive one. A benefit for one country may be a cost for another (for example, the migration of labour under conditions of labour shortages or in a situation of unemployment). Not all of the countries participating in an integration programme have the same objectives, and each one will judge subjectively the benefits it receives. The costs that

[14] R. Erbes, *L'Intégration économique internationale,* Paris: Presses Universitaires de France, 1966), p. 131.

each country is prepared to accept depend upon the alternatives available to it.

These conceptual problems make it difficult to have a clear idea of the distribution of benefits and costs of integration and their true meaning. Leaving aside some methodological points, that is the main reason why the several attempts that have been made to measure the benefits and costs of integration and their distribution have been of little use.[15] It also helps us to understand why, though all integration schemes have recognised the necessity of securing an 'equitable' distribution of net benefits (benefits less costs), very little progress has been achieved.

This is why solutions to this complex problem should not be sought primarily for the purpose of improving the measurements of the total benefits and costs of integration, but rather for helping countries to negotiate integration treaties that take account of the interests of all parties involved. The crucial need is not so much to measure the benefits and costs of integration and their distribution, as to rally the countries' participation – that is, to adopt a set of measures that make each of the countries feel that it is obtaining net benefits. The fact that none of the integration programmes has yet been able to find the right solution to this problem means that more thought should be given to it.

IMPORT SUBSTITUTION

The 'outward-looking' path of development has been considered inappropriate for promoting economic development because the evolution of developing countries would depend heavily on the economic situation and the policy measures taken by the advanced countries. It was supposed that integration would help to change this pattern of growth, by facilitating the domestic production of previously imported goods. But the experience accumulated so far in most integration programmes is that the result of import substitution industrialisation (ISI) has not been satisfactory.

Within the integration programmes ISI has brought the following new problems.

(1) It has made the economies less flexible because of the changes that have taken place in the structure of imports.

(2) It often represents an obstacle to the development of export-oriented activities, simply because it increases the costs and prices of many of the inputs required by activities that are both industrial and agricultural. The competitive position of a country diminishes and it is more difficult to diversify the production structure of the economy. The country will thus remain dependent on the production of those few traditional export products for which it has

[15] For a systematic survey of this problem, see E. Lizano, 'La Distribución de beneficios y costos en la integración entre países en desarrollo', document prepared for the United Nations Conference Trade and Development (United Nations, 1973), TD/B/394.

such high comparative advantages that they will not be in danger, even with the increase of costs caused by ISI.

(3) It has stimulated foreign investment in the form of 'tariff factories', especially when the external common tariff is highly protectionist. Although foreign investment helps to increase production and change the structure of the economy, the country becomes more dependent upon the advanced countries. More and more investment and production decisions are made abroad, based on the interest and strategy of international companies, rather than on the interests of the host country. Many foreign companies settle in the integration area to avoid the protective tariff, but have little or no interest in exporting to third countries, and that makes it more difficult for developing countries to increase their exports. Lastly, foreign companies send sizable amounts of exchange abroad; and, under certain circumstances, that represents a heavy burden on the balance of payments.

(4) ISI has aggravated at least two social problems. ISI generally comes together with customs duties exemptions for the import of capital goods. This makes the use of capital-intensive techniques more attractive and reduces employment opportunities. The situation is even worse if one takes into consideration the fact that the integration process, by widening the market, makes it easier to replace the traditional artisans by industrial production; in the latter the labour inputs per unit of production are less than in the former. All of this happens in countries that already have serious employment problems.

A second problem arises in that ISI has a negative effect on the distribution of income. This arises from the increase in the price of goods due to integration and the fact that the owners of the new industries are seldom the former owners of the handicraft industries to whose replacement that integration contributes.

The conclusion, ISI promotes the creation of certain (mainly industrial) activities that generally speaking are unable to compete on the international markets; hinders the development of export-oriented activities; increases the dependency of the economy; and worsens some social problems. Even so, a certain degree of protectionism and of ISI is necessary in order to get industrialisation started. However, most integration programmes have been unable to carry out a low-cost policy of import substitution.

SOVEREIGNTY

One of the important lessons that integration programmes have already given is that there is hardly any possibility of progress without some degree of co-ordination of the economic and social policies of member countries. Countries will not be able to continue managing their instruments of economic policy as they did before integration. Tariff policy is probably the first instrument of economic policy that has to be regionalised, but others must follow shortly afterwards. To lose control over instruments of economic policy is to lose sovereignty.

The requirement for policy co-ordination raises difficult problems for less developed countries, especially if they have become independent in recent years. Integration would mean losing something of what they have just obtained after waiting for many years.[16] On the other hand, many developing countries are still in the first stages of building a pluralistic society, and, under these circumstances, governments want to have as much control as possible over economic policy. Very often, the struggle for power in a developing country is intense changes of government are frequent and commitments are not maintained.[17] The consequence is that most developing countries are not prepared to remain participants in integration schemes that would require the surrender of important instruments of economic policy or substantial limitations on their use.

POLITICAL SUPPORT

Finally, it is necessary to mention a socio-political issue. Economic integration as a political process requires the support of social groups with sufficient powers; otherwise integration cannot progress. The consolidation of integration depends, to a large extent, on the support the programme obtains from social groups that consider integration to be convenient for their interests and ideas. One characteristic of integration schemes in less developed countries has been the lack of permanent political support.

It is true that certain groups have given their support to integration movements in the earlier stages of their development. This is the case, for example, with industrialists, who are the ones who benefit the most from integration, given the new investment opportunities that the programme creates. Many intellectuals have seen in integration the possibility of diminishing the ties of dependency, and bureaucrats believe that integration may help them to solve some internal economic and social problems. Nevertheless, after some time, the initial support to a large extent disappears. Industrialists soon realise that they have to compete with foreign companies that are usually stronger than they are; the import substitution process tends to become exhausted; and the disputes among the industrial groups of the member countries can be quite severe. The intellectuals are frustrated because integration does not reduce dependency but only changes the nature of the phenomenon. The bureaucrats soon learn that they lose control over the use of important instruments of economic policy and that they have to face new problems for which they are not prepared. The regional bureaucrats, on the other hand, quickly find how 'overpoliticisation' hinders the possibility of transforming plans into reality. So the initial enthusiasm diminishes or even disappears. At best, integration without political support stagnates.[18]

[16] H. Bourguinat, *Les Marchés communs des pays en voie de developpement* (Librairie Droz, 1968), p. 142.

[17] J. S. Nye, 'Patterns and Catalysts in Regional Integration', in *International Organisation*, Autumn 1965, pp. 870–84.

[18] In addition, those social groups whose position (economic and political) is in danger because of integration will not only not support it, but also take every opportunity to try to bring the programme to an end.

IV.

Four main conclusions can be obtained from the experience accumulated
through the various integration programmes involving less developed countries.

(1) Economic integration offers less developed countries an alternative way
to accelerate economic growth, but it is necessary to avoid expecting too much
from it. Integration cannot be a substitute for the internal efforts and measures
that each country has to take. In Castillo's words, 'economic integration is not
a way to evade reforms by exporting the problems to the rest of the region'.[19]

(2) The progress of integration programmes depends on political support
from the important social groups that the movement is able to gather.

(3) From the point of view of international economic relations, integration
should not be considered, at least under present conditions, as a step towards
some sort of new universal economic order.[20] Integration of less developed
countries should be conceived of as an effort to overcome some of the main
obstacles that these countries must surmount in order to promote their own
development.

(4) Hicks has rightly pointed out that 'though the poorer nations are
anxious to become more wealthy, they do not wish to lose their national
identity in so doing'.[21] Consequently, given the disparities and the tendency
for them to increase, and given also the complex problems related to the distribution of the benefits and costs of integration, the integration schemes
should, from the start, pay attention to the distributive aspects. When dealing
with integration of less developed countries, it is not possible to postpone
till later the solution of distribution problems, because if this is done the
programme in question will not progress very far.[22]

[19] Carlos M. Castillo, *Growth and Integration in Central America* (Praeger, 1965),
p. 113.
[20] A. Marchal, *L'Integration Territoriale,* (Paris: Presses Universitaires de France,
1965), p. 13.
[21] J. R. Hicks, *Essays in World Economics,* (London: Clarendon Press, 1959), p. 167.
[22] A. Etzioni, 'European Unification: A Strategy for Change', in *World Politics,*
Oct 1963, pp. 32–50.

Comments
Geoffrey R. Denton (UK)

Lizano's paper discusses different levels of development in the context of integration programmes involving less developed countries. But many of the points he makes apply also to the problems raised by different levels of development among advanced countries. I have chosen to examine these problems with reference to the United Kingdom within the EEC. Lizano comments that integration efforts in less developed countries have suffered from instability of membership, recurrent crises, and lack of progress; this may in many quarters be regarded as a fair description of the problems of the EEC in the 1970s. Certainly his complaint about bureaucratisation and overpoliticisation creating frustration would be shared by many British officials and businessmen faced with adjustment to EEC membership, while the awareness of the negative aspects of membership for the United Kingdom has certainly offset any tendency to think that integration is a way of evading reforms by exporting national problems to the rest of the region. While it will be broadly agreed that differences in levels of development are, in general, wider, and must be more serious for integration efforts among less developed countries, they are certainly not negligible among developed countries.

It is well said that, whereas the traditional static gains have been used to justify integration of advanced countries, dynamic effects are the essence of the case for integration of less developed countries. But dynamic effects are certainly important in relation to integration beyond the customs union — for example, the development of a common industrial policy in the EEC. They are also significant in cases where the net static advantages of membership are small for any one country in an integrating group. Uncertain, but supposedly larger, dynamic gains were decisive in the discussion, in the early 1970s, of the economic costs and benefits of the United Kingdom's membership of the EEC.[1]

The role of integration in providing a degree of protection for economic development even in the advanced countries, through a common external tariff or in other ways, also should not be minimised. Although internal reallocation of existing resources may have been the most significant aspect of tariff removal in the EEC, since resulting trade diversion was relatively small, the EEC has provided a decisive measure of protection in the common agricultural policy. As a consequence of integration, other increases in effective protection have been avoided only on account of the difficulty in agreeing on, and implementing, common policies in areas such as public procurement. While less developed countries may see integration as a means of initiating industrialisation, more advanced countries certainly see it as a means of protecting existing industrial development as well as of fostering it further.

The crux of the problem of areas at different levels of development is reached in the discussion of whether integration widens or narrows disparities. Lizano suggests that 'backwash' effects are stronger than 'spread' effects for

[1] J. H. Williamson, 'Trade and Economic Growth' in *The Economics of Europe*, ed. J. Pinder (London: Charles Knight for the Federal Trust, 1971).

the less developed countries; but so may they be for integration among advanced countries. While in the latter case the initial disparities may be less than for less developed countries, political, social, institutional and behavioural handicaps can cause divergence rather than convergence in the economic fortunes of advanced countries, while integration programmes may certainly tend to intensify the disparities and inhibit corrective action by governments through reducing the range of policy instruments open to them. Certainly, in the discussion of the so-called 'renegotiation' of the terms of the United Kingdom's accession to the EEC, we see an example of the phenomenon, usually assigned to integrations involving less developed countries, in which the structure of one member economy, interacting with the structure of the integration programme, seems designed to make the integration experience of that country unfortunate. The United Kingdom has low investment, low growth, low productivity, poor industrial relations, a high rate of inflation and much social and industrial discontent relative to the other members of the EEC, excepting possibly Italy. These structural problems alone would make for difficulty in facing the challenge of integration. In addition, however, the United Kingdom has a higher proportion of trade with third countries, larger net imports of food, and a chronic balance-of-payments deficit, all of which put it at a financial dis-advantage in a Community that finances its budget, for historical reasons predating United Kingdom entry, from a common external tariff, levies on agricultural imports, and, soon, from part of the proceeds of a common value-added tax.

As Lizano remarks, the larger the economic disparities, the greater the pressure for redistribution of the gains among the members, and the more probable that integration will break down in a wave of political bickering about the structure and terms. He assumes that it is the richer countries that are called on to help the poorer, but the case of the United Kingdom in the EEC raises the interesting example of the poorer new entrant being called on to subsidise the richer founder members, because they have already devised a structure of integration that is unfortunate from the new entrant's point of view. The 'renegotiation' undertaken by the British government in 1974 should be regarded as an attempt to redress this balance, especially in the light of further circumstantial changes detrimental to Britain since the original terms were negotiated.

The political strains, and the likelihood of the integration breaking down, are probably even greater in this case than in the more normal case of richer countries subsidising poorer ones. For a very high degree of sympathy with the problems of a poorly placed member is needed if countries are to agree not only to revise financial arrangements that previously brought them advantages, but also to repoen the issue of the structures of integration that have been created out of hard-fought compromises over many years of negotiation.

It is sometimes suggested that structural changes in the integration programme are not needed to meet this and similar cases, that some redistri-butive budgetary formula can be added very simply, or, alternatively, that the problem can be met by advancing the integration into areas of policy that will bring a net benefit to the disadvantaged country.

In the UK–EEC context this has been taken to mean early progress with the European Regional Fund, a larger Social Fund providing redundancy payments, and, possibly, an industrial policy. Unfortunately, each of these items is politically extremely contentious, precisely because each of them, to bring net benefits to one country, must impose net costs on other members. Thus, distributional equity is not likely to be rapidly achieved, and will probably be possible only at the expense of very large, and even excessive, new common policies, since, with each member fighting for its share, only large and expensive programmes can generate net transfers substantial enough to balance out the earlier inequitable programmes. Moreover, unforeseen economic developments affecting members unequally would continually jeopardise the equity of structures so laboriously evolved.

All of this points to the necessity to structure integration so as to build in a flexible and appropriate *automatic* response to the changing circumstances of existing, and potential new, members. Budgets should be related to some sensible measure such as relative GNP, rather than linked, for historical accidental reasons, to the size of imports from third countries, or the proportion of food grown at home. The structure of the EEC must be capable of coping, without the need for constant 'renegotiation', with fluctuations in the integration fortunes of any member as a result of changing world food prices, energy prices, resources patterns, or exchange rates.

Of course, the decision of each country on whether to join or stay is finally taken not only on the basis of the apparent equity of the distribution of gains among the members, but also by comparing its situation within and outside the integration (Lizano's 'commercial' *versus* 'political' distribution of gains). As Pinder[2] has shown, British entry of the EEC probably involved a number of irreversible changes in its trading situation *vis-à-vis* the rest of the world that would make the alternatives to membership appear even less attractive, should the United Kingdom pull out, than they appeared before entry.

The discussion of import substitution in less developed countries does not seem to have much relevance to integration *per se*, though it is an important concern of those interested in development. The major relevance of integration is that, by widening the market, it is supposed to facilitate the introduction of industrial production. Lizano mentions this in the pejorative context of the creation of unemployment among the traditional artisans whose labour is replaced. But industrialisation that is fostered by trade creation that follows internal tariff removal (as opposed to that induced by external tariffs, export subsidies, or other protective devices) would have many advantages as an import-substituting policy.

Questions of sovereignty appear as relevant for advanced as for developing countries. It is not easy to judge whether a recently acquired freedom from colonial or pseudocolonial tutelage constitutes a greater inhibition on regional integration than does a centuries-old tradition of national independence. In both cases, any perceived loss of sovereignty within the integration must be offset by the increase of sovereignty in other directions: *vis-à-vis* third

[2] J. Pinder, 'The Costs of Pulling Out', in *New Europe*, Jan 1974.

countries, multinational firms, and the like. The difficulty here is that the loss of sovereignty in integration, being the result of specific political decisions, is transparent, while the loss of sovereignty in other ways tends to result from the often unobserved operation of autonomous economic forces. The strongest antidote to the fears of loss of sovereignty in the EEC must be the depiction of the helplessness of individual national governments in the face of monetary disturbances, energy crises, and similar problems.

Finally, however, there remains the choice between regional and worldwide integration, a choice presented in the title of this congress. For countries whose economic and political prospects are readily identified as lying within a particular region, the decisions implicit in the foregoing discussion are likely to generate sufficient momentum to support a process of increasing integration, though, even in such cases, the stimulus of external threat or pressure probably is needed — if historical precedents are valid — to overcome vested interests and inertia. In the past two decades or so, much autonomous commercial integration has already taken place across the boundaries of the major politically integrated or integrating regions of the world, whether these are advanced or less developed regions.

The less developed countries have an alternative to costly and difficult industrialisation behind the external barriers of an integration programme. This lies in the possibility of continuing and enhancing integration with the advanced economies through normal flows of trade in raw materials and manufactures, of capital and technology, and of labour. An advanced area such as Western Europe has a similar alternative to pursuing its economic development via the protection and discrimination of an internal integration. Whether this alternative is chosen must depend on the creation of acceptable structures (that is, structures meeting criteria of equity, flexibility and automaticity similar to those discussed above for integrating areas) for world trade and for other international economic transactions.

It has long been observed that, while governments in the EEC talk about common industrial policies, such policies are already being chosen both by private firms and by public authorities in interdependence with American-based multinationals and other third-country interests. This form of integration would be politically and socially more acceptable if suitable reassurances could be obtained about its continuance under conditions acceptable on all sides. To be economically and politically acceptable, integration needs a structure of rules, a code of conduct, to ensure that the gains are equitably distributed, 'commercially' and 'politically', among the members, that they continue to be equitably distributed in the light of unforeseen changes in the relative economic circumstances of different countries, and that allowing interdependence to increase does not incur excessive risks of economic disruption through the defection or excessively selfish policies of another 'member'. These principles of political economy apply to all kinds of integration: official or private, advanced country or less developed country, regional or worldwide.

Comments
Mahbub ul Haq (Pakistan)

Lizano offers a comprehensive and useful review of the literature on economic integration among less developed countries. My reservations are threefold.

First, I have the impression that he conceives of the objectives of economic integration rather narrowly, as the achievement of higher growth rate and/or greater economic efficiency in the framework of regional integration. He mentions strengthening of 'the bargaining position of member countries vis-à-vis third countries', but does not return to this aspect. I find this strange in a world dominated by discussions of what made possible OPEC's action on oil, and of whether similar integration of national policies is possible for other commodities. If we follow the excellent categorisation of types of economic integration given by Balassa in his paper, it is obvious that the scope for 'policy integration' has increased recently. In a broader sense, I tend to view economic integration among less developed countries as part of the effort to improve their economic position vis-à-vis the developed countries. The chances for this seem to have improved recently, partly because the old power structures are crumbling and at least some OPEC countries are in a position to have enough financial surpluses to underwrite, if they so wish, the bargaining power of other raw-material-producing countries in negotiating a better deal.

Second, even within the narrow framework of regional integration, I should have thought that there was greater scope today for economic integration among some oil-exporting and oil-importing countries — particularly those oil exporting countries (like the Persian Gulf states) that lack absorptive capacity, and those oil-importing countries (like Egypt) that have more ample opportunities for investment. Some studies have projected the potential accumulation of financial surpluses in the hands of a few small OPEC countries (Saudi Arabia, Libya, Kuwait and the United Arab Emirates, which, despite the large area they cover, have a total population of only 12 million) at between $500 billion and $1000 billion in 1985, in view of the limited domestic absorptive capacity of these economies. Surely there is both motivation and finance available here to seek greater regional integration within the Arab world. As such, I find Lizano's rather muted and pessimistic tone at odds with the rather exciting times that we live in.

Third, I believe that there are ways of co-ordinating the legitimate interests of the developing countries while overcoming some of the problems mentioned by Lizano. For the Third World, one of the lessons of the recent events is that there are a number of things they can do by their own actions, without having to beg the international community for small favours. For instance, if the developing countries are really serious about promoting their manufactured exports to the developed countries, as well as increasing trade within the developing regions, they can set up a general preferential system through a simple, bold stroke: the developing countries can agree among themselves to devalue by a large and uniform margin, say 50 per cent, the exchange rates for their manufactured exports and imports traded with the developed nations.

Unless developed countries resort to competitive devaluations, such action would immediately establish a collective competitive edge for the manufactured exports of the developing countries in the markets of the developed world. It would also establish on a regional basis the conditions of import substitution that Lizano mentions, since imports from the developed world would become universally more expensive for all developing countries, encouraging them to buy from one another. As a result, trade among the developing countries would be likely to increase, both in a regional context, because of the geographical proximity of some countries, and overall. I believe that an impersonal and general price action of this kind stands a much greater chance of success than does the attempt to negotiate a series of preferential agreements or economic integration involving only a few countries. At least, it is worth studying in today's climate how the collective economic interests of the developing countries can be promoted by making some innovative departures from the traditional theory and practice of regional economic integration.

Comments
Gunal Kansu (Turkey)

I. INTRODUCTORY

Ample evidence exists on the extent of gains that can be expected from specialisation in industrial production within the framework of economic integration. Studies carried out for the five countries of ASEAN (the Association of South-East Asian Countries), for example, indicate that, for the thirteen industries investigated, fixed investment cost can be lowered by as much as 40 per cent, and unit cost of production by about 30 per cent in regional plants, which have a capacity four times greater than do individual national plants.[1] Engineering data on some selected industries elsewhere in the world reveal similar results.[2]

However, despite such substantial savings, industrial integration has not progressed as rapidly as expected and outcomes have been disappointing. Not a single industry, for example, has been established in ASEAN; the experience of the Regional Co-operation for Development with 'joint enterprises' has come to an almost total halt; and the East African Community has suffered serious setbacks in recent years. Naturally, a host of factors, both economic and noneconomic, have played a role; but, among them, the possibility of the concentration of economic activity and, hence, the polarisation of gains from integration in relatively more advanced and industrialised countries has definitely been a major factor.

In fact, as Lizano rightly argues, 'integration can make initial disparities worse', particularly if integration is conceived of as just the establishing of free trade and the free movement of factors. As a result, a number of methods have been devised in order at least to contain the process of polarisation of benefits that is often associated with economic integration among countries at different levels of development. These methods can be grouped in two broad categories:

(1) methods through which the actual *ex-post*, or anticipated, imbalances in the distribution of benefits of integration are compensated by a transfer mechanism, such as regional development funds or transfer taxes; and

(2) methods through which location decisions with regard to the siting of industry are influenced, or directly regulated, by a system of industrial planning before imbalances take place.

Of these two, the second appears to be more effective. For, although the transfer of financial resources from a more to a less industrialised country is a form of compensation for the losses incurred by the latter, it is mainly

---

[1] *Economic Cooperation for ASEAN*, Report of a United Nations Team (London: Metcalfe Cooper and Hepburn Limited, 1972).

[2] See, for example, 'A Simple Partial Equilibrium Model for Measuring the Costs/Benefits of Regional Co-ordination in Certain Kinds of Industries', unpublished study by UNESOB, ESCOB/PP/72/9.

the long-run technological and cumulative growth effects of the industrialisation process itself that are more important, and that cannot, therefore, be wholly compensated by some form of income transfer.

II. PLANNED ALLOCATION OF INTEGRATION INDUSTRIES

The planning of integration implies the allocation of individual industries, or groups of industries, to member countries. In most integration groupings, however, where the scope for co-operative action and the policy options at the disposal of decision makers are limited, it will not be possible to implement a comprehensive joint industrialisation programme in which the whole range of industrial activity is 'assigned' to individual countries. In most cases, it will usually be more practical to concentrate on those more critical industries that exhibit strong economies of scale and require large capital outlays by actually 'allocating' them to member states through intergovernmental agreements.

The primary purpose in the allocation of industries within an integration grouping is to find a compromise solution between what may be called the 'efficient' and 'equitable' distribution of a given number of industries in order to decentralise the process of industrialisation. What is meant by the 'efficient' solution is a given distribution of industries within the grouping in which each industry is assigned to its least-cost country; that is, to the country where the unit cost of production, inclusive of transport cost, is minimum. The equitable solution, on the other hand, can be defined as the distribution that conforms with an agreed equity criterion.

As an equity criterion, several indexes can be suggested, bearing in mind, however, that equity is, in the main, a subjective concept for which no precise mathematical formulation can be found. One such criterion, for example, may be found by taking each country's relative share in the total income of the integration grouping. Or, alternatively, the share of industries to be allocated to a country may be determined on the basis of the size of that country's market in relation to the total group market for the products of the industries to be distributed.

Once the criterion of each country's share is formulated, the next stage in the allocation of industries is to concentrate on the benefits to be generated by a package of industries in order to determine each country's 'share of industries'. For the sake of simplicity, the following may be mentioned as the main benefits accruing from the establishment of a number of industries: (a) total value-added; (b) the level of intra-grouping exports to be generated; and (c) expected level of employment.

Assuming that these benefits can be approximated in quantifiable terms, then the equitable distribution of a given package of industries that will also decentralise the process of industrialisation would be the one in which the total benefits derived from them are distributed in proportion to the relative share of each country's market in the total value of sales of all products to be manufactured by the particular bloc of industries.

However, different industries exhibit different characteristics with respect to costs, income, employment and trade; and the countries involved are faced with different scarcities. As a result, in the determination of each country's equitable share of industries, a number of complex issues arise to which there appears to be no easy solution. Because of the multiplicity of benefits, weights must be assigned to them in order to approximate the 'total benefits', but the importance of each of these benefits will differ for each country. An economic grouping generally does not constitute one single economic entity. The factors of production are not normally allowed to move freely within the grouping. This implies the existence of separate markets for factors of production, even if the national markets have been integrated by liberalising the whole trade. Under these circumstances, there will not be one single set of prices and, as a result, the value of total benefits will be 'indeterminate' for the integration grouping as a whole.

This problem is likely to be even more pronounced for countries at different levels of development, because of substantial differences in relative factor proportions (associated, by definition, with the levels of development). As a result of these difficulties, it may be more practical not to attempt to combine various benefits in a single index for the whole group.

A United Nations team of experts that examined ASEAN followed a similar approach to industrial integration. Prefeasibility studies were carried out on some industries. In these studies three alternative solutions were compared in some detail, namely (a) national solution, (b) ASEAN solution, and (c) no development. In addition, a number of 'illustrative package deals' were put before the governments.

Each project was ranked according to its best location within the group. In the first illustration, the industries that were location-sensitive were assigned to their best locations. The footloose industries were then allocated, so as to balance out, to the greatest possible extent, the distribution of benefits. In subsequent approximations a better balance, or a more equitable distribution, was sought by rotating some of the less location-sensitive industries among the member countries.

It is clear that the process described may help contain the process of industrial polarisation as a result of integration by allowing the establishment of some key industries in every country on the basis of its market share. It will not, however, be sufficient to reduce the disparities that exist. If the sense of political cohesion among the member states is strong enough for the adoption of more ambitious objectives to reduce income disparities, or to accelerate the process of industrialisation in the poorer countries, a number of instruments may be suggested. As far as the approach described in this paper is concerned, the equity criterion suggested above for the allocation of industries can, for example, be modified so as to permit the allocation of more industries to the less industrialised members than the size of their domestic markets would warrant. Other instruments that could be used include nonreciprocal tariff cuts, and extension of credits through a regional bank.

Comments
Dharam P. Ghai (Kenya)

In his paper, Lizano has touched on the great upsurge of attempts at integration in the post-war period and the difficulties they have run into, particularly in the developing world. This situation is hardly surprising. Integration among any group of countries is an inherently difficult process. There are usually no immediate, spectacular gains to offset the inevitable and complex short-run problems. As Lizano has stressed in his paper, effective economic integration involves the loss of sovereignty in the use of a wide range of instruments bearing on social and economic policy. The co-ordination of fiscal, monetary and other policies can be a cumbersome, costly and, often, irritating process. Since the short-term gains are seldom adequate to compensate for these disadvantages, it is apparent that the success of integration schemes in their early phases must depend on other, overriding considerations. And, indeed, this appears to have been the case with most of the successful schemes in the post-war period.

The driving force behind the European attempts at integration, as represented by the EEC and EFTA, was the political imperative to seek a role for Western Europe, independent of both the United States and the Soviet Union. The birth of the CMEA owed much to the cold-war tensions of the early post-war years. Likewise, in the Arab world, in Africa and in Latin America, the initial fervour for integration was provided by the drive for regional and continental unity, the need to consolidate newly-won independence and to enhance bargaining power. Economic considerations were, of course, always present, but it is doubtful that they played a leading role in the establishment of these schemes.

Lizano has touched on most of the economic and political obstacles that have hampered the working of integration schemes among developing countries. There is, however, an important source of difficulties that is not reflected in his discussion. Reference is made here to the issues that arise when countries with different economic systems come together in an integration scheme. Many of the regional groupings among developing countries incorporate members with significantly different economic systems. This is the case, for example, with the East African Community, the Permanent Consultative Committee of the Maghreb, and the Arab Common Market; and was the case with the Andean group until the overthrow of the Allende regime. The coexistence of ideologically diverse states within a single trading bloc raises issues relating to the role of foreign private investment, relationships with third parties, and a number of other aspects of social and economic policies. But the most important implications arise in the field of trade, and it is to this that the rest of my discussion is devoted.

In a centrally planned economy, the volume, composition and, often, the source of imports and the amount and destination of exports are determined in accordance with the priorities of the annual plan. Thus, conventional integration schemes with an emphasis on trade liberalisation through the abolition of tariff barriers may not be relevant in a situation of this sort. Similar issues are posed by the existence of state trading enterprises. These are to be found both in developing countries whose economies are guided by markets, and in those whose economies are centrally planned; but their relative importance and functions may vary a good deal between the two types of economies. In a centrally planned economy, they are seen as an essential attribute of a socialist economy, whereas, in a market developing country, they may be brought into being to serve a variety of *ad hoc* purposes. The existence of state trading enterprises makes it possible to circumvent the provision of nondiscriminatory treatment of all products originating in the member states of the integration scheme. There are several ways, of varying degrees of subtlety, through which state trading enterprises may, in their purchases, be able to discriminate in favour of domestic suppliers and against those from other member states.

Discrimination of the above sort may also arise in the market economies, even in the absence of state trading enterprises. The existence of monopolistic or oligopolistic trading firms, particularly where they are linked to manufacturers in countries outside the trading bloc; the well-known prejudices in favour of imported products from the industrialised countries; more developed financial and marketing links with developed countries than with the member states of a trading bloc – all are possible sources of bias in importation policies that militate against the expansion of intraregional trade.

The above examples point to the sort of difficulties in the field of trade that have arisen in a number of integration schemes involving developing countries with different economic systems. It is clear that any attempt to solve them, either through the adoption of a wholly market-economy method of integration or of a centrally planned variety is likely to end in failure. An eclectic approach, drawing upon the techniques of both types of integration arrangements and adapting them to the specific situation of a particular trading bloc, is likely to be more fruitful. Some of the approaches that may prove useful are indicated below.

In situations where trade is hampered by a scarcity of foreign exchange and/or by the practice of foreign-trade planning on the part of some members, it may still be possible to expand intraregional trade in stages by agreed amounts or proportions. This can be done by setting aside certain amounts of foreign exchange, which can be increased progressively over time, for the exclusive purpose of promoting intraregional trade. The advantages of such techniques are that they permit intraregional trade to expand relatively smoothly, they shield it from the vicissitudes of balance-of-payments problems, and they are compatible with the system of foreign-trade planning that is practised by economies of the centrally planned type. Similar techniques have been used in the Arab Common Market, in the CMEA and in the GATT for the reintegration in world trade of the European socialist countries.

In the conditions characterising most developing countries, one of the best ways of promoting trade is through the joint planning of regional industries. This can be made compatible both with market economies and with centrally planned economies. It can also ensure an equitable distribution of benefits flowing from the industrialisation brought about by economic integration. If it is carried out in a balanced manner, it could take care of the specific difficulties associated with foreign-exchange scarcity and the planning of foreign trade. Although most integration schemes involving developing countries have, in the past, found it difficult to reach an agreement on the allocation of regional industries, the experience of the Andean group has so far been relatively successful.

The difficulties that are associated with state trading enterprises could be resolved in a number of ways. In the first place, the state trading enterprises in a country could be reorganised to allow them to compete with each other. If they are allowed autonomy in their operations and are required to compete with each other in their purchases and sales, their behaviour may approximate that of private traders. The adoption of this system is perfectly compatible with public ownership of the means of production and exchange, as is shown by the operation of state trading enterprises in such socialist countries as Yugoslavia and Hungary.

If this solution is for some reason not possible or acceptable, it may still be possible to move towards an approximation of this system by devising a set of rules for the operation of the importing and distributing monopolies. The purpose of these rules would be to ensure that imports originating from the member states are in all respects treated identically to domestic products. It would be necessary to have rules to ensure that state trading enterprises import promptly to satisfy domestic demand and that their decisions to import take into account the duties that are payable on imports from outside the region. A system of this type has been devised and implemented in the East African Community.

Opening Statement for Group Discussion
Helen Hughes (Australia)

An evaluation of the stream of economic benefits and costs arising from various types and levels of integration should be the central concern of the study of the economics of integration. Of course, such a cost — benefit calculus can have meaning only in relation to alternatives that range from highly autarkic national economic policies to a movement toward worldwide trade liberalisation. Changes in trade are only part of the total stream of benefits and costs. It seems, from the opening discussions of this congress, that, for the EEC and for the CMEA countries, the overall economic impact of integration is a moot point. Relatively wealthy countries can afford to be cavalier about cost—benefit calculations, and to regard economic effects as secondary to political objectives. Developing, or even lagging industrialised countries cannot. It is, therefore, not surprising that Lizano's paper and Denton's, Kanasu's and Ghai's comments implicitly and explicitly focus on cost — benefit issues, while ul Haq's paper explores alternatives to integration.

Given the growing evidence of the difficulties of integration, the traditional basis of pro-integration arguments requires re-examination. For developing countries, the core of the argument has traditionally been concerned with the benefits of economies of scale in manufacturing. It was assumed that the terms of trade for primary exports would decline and that industrialisation was *the* 'engine of growth' of development that would increase output, productivity and employment. It was also thought that it would be impossible to export manufactured products from developing countries. For 'small' countries, integration was therefore regarded as a necessary concomitant of industrialisation.

All of these assumptions have turned out to be wrong. There has not been a long-term decline in the terms of trade for primary products. Countries that are productive, diversified, primary-product exporters have done very well indeed. Some 'small' countries that have not joined integration groupings have led in the industrial-growth stakes. Exports of manufactures from developing countries have grown at an average of some 15 per cent during the 1960s and early 1970s. It is true that there are market-access difficulties (among developing, as well as into developed, countries), but the growth of manufactured exports in developing countries is still accelerating. There are now some forty developing countries with significant exports of manufactured products, but, with the exception of El Salvador, common-market members are notable by their absence. Undue protection for industrialisation not only hinders the export of primary products, but also makes the export of manufactures difficult unless steps are taken to offset the import-substitution bias.

Another group of issues that require consideration are those that have largely been ignored in the integration literature. First, there are important questions of political economy. Most developing countries emerged from colonial or neocolonial periods with little capacity for planning and administration. The management and administration of integrated regional programmes is difficult. It requires prolonged negotiations and takes up a disproportionate share of very scarce skilled staff.

Perhaps the greatest cost of integration is the strengthening of the tendency towards economic autarky. For small countries, integration seems to promise an opportunity to invest in capital-intensive and technologically complex industries, even when the total integrated market is still very small and internal transportation costs are high. Once inward-oriented industrialisation is established, it tends to persist. In theory, it is possible for a common market to protect domestic industries and subsidise exports; in practice, fiscal conflicts make it very difficult, if not impossible.

Ghai has pointed out the difficulties that arise among countries with different national objectives in an integration grouping, and Denton has stressed the difficulties that a 'lagging' country faces by limiting its policy options on entering a common market. Successive levels of integration require the giving up of more and more instruments of fiscal, monetary and other policy control in favour of harmonisation. Poor and lagging countries give up such instruments at considerable cost.

It is well known that integration leads to difficulties with regard to the distribution of gains among the members of an integrated grouping. These difficulties are greater for countries at low and different levels of development than for relatively homogeneous industrialised countries, and limited fiscal resources make it much more difficult to deal with them. In the past, little attention has been paid to income distribution effects within countries. In practice, because of the association of integration with inward-oriented capital-intensive industrialisation, integration has led to a worsening of income disparities between urban and rural areas, and within urban areas there has been a tendency toward the creation of an élite 'modern' sector group at the expense of employment and mass consumption. In fact, among the developing countries, integration has largely been integration of the élite groups in the capital cities, with a consequent neglect of intranational regional development.[1]

Practical considerations have frequently been ignored in integration proposals. As Kanasu has stressed, there is no doubt that scale is important in many industries, but the gains of complementarity that arise from advanced regional integration planning are difficult to gauge in advance. In developed countries, where industries already exist, the measurement of actual gains and, thus, the 'horse trading' that takes place over the location of industry is much easier. In any case, in developed-country integration planning, the emphasis is not on the sharing of single-plant industries — which consequently, are monopolies, with all their attendant costs — but on the gains from increased competition. There are gains from competition in developing-country common markets, but the planners' emphasis is usually on the complementary, rather than on the competitive aspects of industrial growth.

The role of multinational corporations *vis-à-vis* integrated markets raises interesting issues. For countries desiring capital-intensive and technologically complex industrialisation, and focusing particularly on sophisticated consumer goods, multinational corporations offer important technical and other

[1] A. Kuklinski, 'Integration and Regional Policies in Developing Countries', contributed paper to the working group.

advantages. In the past, unfortunately, many developing countries have tended to give such multinational corporations excessive protection and other incentives and, as a result, the multinationals have reaped high monopoly profits. Integration is sometimes seen as an instrument for reducing competition among countries for investments by the multinational corporations, and, hence, as a way of reducing excess incentives and monopoly profits. There is a great deal of scope for co-operation by developing countries in reducing incentives. However, the proposition that integration is necessary for this needs careful examination. The multinational corporations are foremost supporters of integration among developing countries because integration tends to create larger markets for the type of sophisticated consumer products in which they have the greatest comparative advantage. They are usually confident of being able to negotiate favourable conditions with integration groupings. It is important to note that an industrialisation strategy directed toward increasing employment and satisfying mass needs, is much less attractive to multinational corporations than is the more traditional, sophisticated consumer-goods type of industrialisation. Many basic industries require less input from, and are less attractive to, the large multinationals than is the case for differentiated consumer goods. The social orientation of a country's industrialisation policy is the main determinant of its dependence on multinationals.

The effect of integration of developed countries on developing countries cannot be ignored. There is some evidence that trade liberalisation is determined by the least liberal member. The CMEA countries, particularly, but also the EEC countries, provide to developing countries much less access to their markets than do independent developed countries. Access has also been growing more slowly in the last decade. Moreover, the EEC's current negotiations with individual developing countries and developing-country groupings are somewhat reminiscent of nineteenth-century 'divide and conquer' approaches to trade with colonial and neocolonial countries.

For developing countries, the benefits of integration clearly have to exceed the costs if it is to be worthwhile. Some countries see important political advantages in integration. The Regional Co-operation for Development and the Association of South-East Asian Countries (ASEAN), which are often regarded as integration failures, are, in fact, rather successful international political organisations. ASEAN is also playing a role in exploring possibilities of economic collaboration of various types. On the economic side, however, the view that the record of a more complex type of integration experience among developing countries has been poor is gaining strength. Several members of integration groupings think that the costs have exceeded the benefits. Empirical research in a cost–benefit framework is required to clarify past experience and indicate fruitful approaches for the future. It would be tragic if the economic costs of relatively complex levels of integration were to be ignored. In the meantime, alternative approaches of economic co-operation can be explored. Ul Haq has pointed to the possibilities of partnership between resource-rich and labour-rich countries. At present, developing-country trade restrictions against other developing countries are much greater than developed-country restrictions against developing countries. Yet trade is growing among developing countries and it offers major prospects. Selective trade liberalisation, including package deals for raw materials and components among groups of countries, are promising lines of approach. The harmonisation of policies toward foreign investment does not require a high level of integration. It is, perhaps, salutary to remember that international transportation and communication networks can operate very efficiently with minimal integration.

Report on Group Discussion
Indraprasad G. Patel (India)

The justification for some form of integration among a number of relatively small and predominantly nonindustrial countries is well known to economic theorists. As a policy, integration has also been endorsed by leaders of public opinion in many developing countries. And, yet, the fact remains that the many schemes that have been floated in recent years for regional or sub-regional integration of less developed countries, particularly in Africa and Latin America, have not been characterised by resounding success; and, in Asia and the Middle East, regional integration has so far not even been seriously attempted. Part of the explanation for this failure to implement what economic theory, commonsense and statesmanship alike so clearly dictate is undoubtedly to be found in a lack of political will or of social and political cohesion. As economists, however, it is more appropriate for us to ask whether the failure so far of the integration movement among developing countries can be ascribed, at least in part, to faulty economic reasoning or to misplaced emphasis or to failure to take care of some legitimate economic concerns.

Perhaps the fundamental and primary mistake made in so many attempts to promote integration among developing countries has been to follow a wrong model or analogy — namely, that offered by industrially advanced countries, which are more concerned with the rationalisation of existing industries than with the co-ordinated development of new ones. For that reason, trade policy as the primary instrument of integration may not be appropriate to the conditions of developing countries, which may well need, basically, a co-ordination of investment planning with only such concomitant aspects of trade liberalisation as are essential for underpinning the planning of investment.

Secondly, there has perhaps been a tendency to assume that what is feasible, and indeed necessary, in the long run is in fact equally so in the short run. Merely by creating demand we do not create an internal source of supply, either soon or at reasonable cost.

There is perhaps a third economic fallacy that explains the relative lack of success in developing-country integration: the tendency to think too much in terms of economies of scale in relation to industrialisation — as distinct from agriculture, development of common resources such as rivers, or of facilities such as transport, power generation, scientific research, training and financial institutions. The rationale for integration — that is, for a pooling of demand and resources — applies to all these spheres as much as to industriali-sation; and a healthy and rapid development of other sectors and the efficient utilisation of resources that transcend purely national boundaries are necessary anyway if a healthy and rapid process of industrialisation is to be sustained. The neglect of opportunities for export to the rest of the world would also add to the cost of policies of integration.

In short, integration is only a tool — and only one of many tools — of development. It has to be applied in a measured, selective, or step-by-step manner, with investment planning, rather than trade policy, as its primary thrust, and without undue concentration on industrialisation to the neglect of other areas where economies of scale and common action equally apply.

Having said that much, one should hasten to add that if there is any rationale in economic integration, it must imply a certain discrimination or exclusiveness through trade policy *and* a certain bias in favour of inward-looking development. Unless we recognise this, we run into the opposite danger of throwing the baby out with the bath water. If the pace of progress in developing countries is to be a measured one, it still must be forced or deliberately accelerated; and trade policy that is liberal within, and not quite so liberal in relation to the rest of the world, is a necessary ingredient of such an accelerated process of growth. Similarly, while export-led growth is possible for some time, the question is whether such a process can be carried far, and whether, sooner or later, every country does not need to develop a rather diversified economic and industrial structure, without which even export-led growth cannot be sustained. If this is so, the only question is whether the cost of such diversification or structural transformation should not be minimised by attempting it on a regional or subregional basis rather than on a national basis.

Again, apart from strictly economic considerations, there are larger political and cultural factors that dictate integration among groups of poorer nations. Thus, in addition to economic growth, economic independence from powerful industrial nations is also an objective for countries only just emerging or struggling to emerge from colonial or neocolonial rule. Again, if international inequalities of income and wealth, and even affluence *per se*, are beyond a certain point morally repugnant, we are entitled to ask: is it not better that the economic growth of the poorer countries should not be predicated upon growing demand from, and, therefore, growing prosperity among, the more affluent countries, which are already exhausting and polluting our common human heritage to an intolerable extent?

In short, sooner or later, co-operation and co-ordination among developing countries on a regional or subregional basis must begin to assume more explicitly the attributes of integration proper — with an emphasis on trade policy and a broad-based industrial structure. If so, we should try to find answers to some of the problems that arise in any process of integration. Perhaps the most important problem to tackle is the assurance that the process of integration does not perpetuate or accentuate the backwardness of some countries or regions, but instead promotes the more harmonious and equitable growth of all regions. On a similar plane, the benefits of integration should be shared by all sectors of society and not just by a small sector connected with the development of new industries. Industrialisation confined to the production of hitherto imported luxuries or concentrated in one or two urban centres will not command the acceptance of the community at large and therefore surely will jeopardise the continuance of any such scheme of integration. It has been felt, however, that inequalities, whether interregional or between classes, are a reflection of the overall social and political structure of each society, rather than essentially the products of the process of integration; and only those countries that have internally accepted the values of equality are likely to endorse them effectively *vis-à-vis* other partners in a scheme of integration.

The broader question of the calculation of the costs and benefits of integration so that one can ensure that they are equitably distributed is a rather difficult problem even conceptually, as the traditional framework of static neoclassical theory, particularly international trade theory, is not appropriate for the purpose. On the other hand, if one were to calculate long-term effects, it could be only on the basis of programming models involving so many assumptions that no policy maker would be likely to accept the conclusions derived from them – unless, of course, he were already inclined to do so. Similarly, on one practical aspect of integration – how to allocate industries among participating countries rationally – it is hardly possible to throw any definitive light except to note the inappropriate-ness of using either national or international prices for the purpose. Problems of calculating costs and benefits, or of choosing techniques, or of making investment decisions, arise not only in relation to integration, but also in relation to national development. The present working group can hardly claim to have found acceptable solutions to these fundamental problems, which have divided so many brilliant members of our profession into warring factions. The only comment with which everyone in the group seemed to agree was that each participating nation must benefit to some extent from integration and that this benefit should be such as can be seen and appreciated by policy makers, trades unions and ordinary people, and not just by bureaucrats or model builders.

Nowadays no discussion on any subject is complete without some reference to multinational corporations and to the oil-producing countries. On multinational corporations, it was agreed that care should be taken to ensure that they are not the main beneficiaries of integration and that countries participating in any integration movement should invariably develop a common policy towards them. Regarding the oil-producing countries, it was felt that their newfound wealth could be usefully employed to promote regional integration or co-operation, primarily in the Arab world but also in a wider context.

The question was also raised of whether the oil producing countries could not help the developing countries generally by strengthening their bargaining power. Surprisingly, integration as a means of strengthening the bargaining power of the developing countries was not emphasised during the discussion.

There was also not much discussion on the impact that integration involving one group of developing countries may have on other developing countries. On possible co-operation or integration among developing countries as a whole, an interesting suggestion was made, but not discussed: that the developing countries should devalue their exchange rates by a uniform margin for their manufactured exports and imports traded with the developed nations.

It was emphasised that the experience of socialist countries in integration had important lessons for developing countries, particularly with regard to the reduction of regional disparities. The socialist countries are endeavouring to assist the integration efforts of developing countries by helping them to establish key industries. They are also systematically developing their trade relations with the Third World, and this process could be assisted to the extent that integration among less developed countries promotes planned development among them.

Concern was expressed about the restrictions that the industrially advanced Western countries still apply against imports, particularly manufactured imports, from developing countries, and about discriminatory trading arrangements with different groups among the poorer nations.

Finally, if the ultimate objective of each conference is to prepare the ground for the next one, I should like to pass on a suggestion made in our discussions: that the International Economic Association should organise a special meeting of economists from the Third World so thaty they could discuss their common problems without being inhibited by considerations of courtesy or discretion.

12 Integration by Market Forces and through Planning (Main Paper, Working Group I)

Oleg T. Bogomolov (USSR)

I. INTRODUCTORY

The development of integration processes in international economic (and not only economic) life is a characteristic feature of the modern world. The concentration and internationalisation of production and the new requirements of economic, scientific and technical progress add up to the objective basis for the emergence of integrating communities that differ from each other in socio-economic terms. These communities are an important factor in the world economy, notably in Europe. At the same time, a regional instead of a universal basis for integration may contain within itself definite contradictions, which come to the surface when an integrating community resorts to some form of collective protectionism.

The benefits of international regional economic integration (the subject of this analysis) and its influence on the efficiency of social production explain why there is growing interest in it in various parts of the world. However, the view of the advantages of integration and the purposes and methods of the policy that are designed to make use of these are very different in the two major integration communities – the CMEA and the EEC – and this is a reflection of their different political and economic systems.

Now and again, the CMEA's plan-integration methods are held to be ineffective as compared with the market-integration methods of Western Europe. This kind of contrast greatly oversimplifies and distorts the actual state of affairs.

For one thing, it would be wrong to regard integration through planning as being incompatible with the market and socialist commodity and money relations. Economic planning under socialism implies a development of commodity and money relations both within individual socialist countries and between them. These relations are a necessary element of the planned economy within the national and the international framework.

On the other hand, there is no consensus at all among the theorists and practitioners of West European integration about its being an automatic international system based exclusively on market relations. Let us recall the November 1962 polemics between Ludwig Erhard and Walter Hallstein about the meaning and benefit of economic programming in the EEC. Today, Western economists no longer debate the need for programming or dirigisme, but the limits, scale and methods of state intervention in integration processes.

In the opinion of a group of West German authors,

It takes something more than free trade to ensure even free trade over a long term. Today, politico-economic intervention by the state is so frequent and diverse that the lifting of trade barriers alone cannot help to attain even the limited aim of free trade. The aim of establishing a homogeneous economic space all the more demands common politico-economic responsibility and joint decisions in various spheres.[1]

The Italian economist Ugo Papi has written about the co-ordination and harmonisation of the major economic directives[2] as a condition for integration.

Let us leave aside the question of the reality of such proposals under an international economic system based on the principles of private enterprise. We in the socialist countries believe that truly balanced economic development and economic co-operation are attainable only under socialist social property and relations of equitable co-operation and mutual assistance, and not under competition and operation of the principle of force. However, the statements quoted above are important in that they show that the purely market concept of West European integration has been shaken.

All of this impels one (in line with one of the tasks of the present congress) to compare the two existing types of integration in the light not only of the differences between the planning and the market mechanisms of the CMEA and the EEC, but also of their antithetical social foundations, purposes and results.

II. PURPOSES

In the Preamble to the Treaty of Rome the founders of the EEC declared their resolution 'by common action to ensure the economic and social progress of their countries by eliminating the barriers which divide Europe'. In effect, the intention, in the first stage, was to ensure the free movement of goods, persons, services and capital among the member countries, to even out the conditions for competition, and to establish a common market to function like an internal market. In the second stage, ranging over the 1970s, the aim has been set to move on from the customs union to an economic and

[1] *Neun für Europa. Die EWG als Motor europäischer Integration* (Eugen Diedrichs Verlag, 1973), p. 32.
[2] *Dizionario di Economia* (Turin, 1967).

monetary union, implying the elimination of differences in national fiscal systems, the harmonisation of tax and income policies, the co-ordination of structural changes in industry, the promotion of development in lagging regions, alignment of monetary and credit policies, and, ultimately, the introduction of a common currency.

The idea is to eliminate a number of economic restrictions, in the first place giving greater freedom of action to big business, and to stimulate the concentration of capital and production. In addition the establishment of a common trade and economic policy and of a preferential trade regime within the framework of the Community is designed to strengthen the competitive positions of members *vis-à-vis* American and Japanese companies and to build up a common front in relations with the socialist states.

Only very recently have EEC leaders made statements about integration purposes like the need to adapt, supplement and rationalise industrial structures, to accelerate technical progress, to do away with regional differences in industrial levels, and to ensure social progress for the population; but, in effect, these purposes have not been backed up by any concerted mechanism for implementation.

Socialist integration within the CMEA framework sets itself the aim of achieving rapid economic, scientific and technical progress in all of the member countries, and raising the material and cultural standards of their peoples through deep-going structural changes in the economy in accordance with the objective requirements of scientific and technical progress. It is aimed to rationalise the use of their aggregate economic potential, to promote the concentration and specialisation of production, to intensify scientific and technical co-operation and to even out disparities among the economic development levels of the different countries.[3]

Thus, in contrast to West European integration, the primary aim of which is to establish a common market, the integration of the CMEA countries has from the outset been oriented toward joint efforts in tackling, above all, production and technological problems, shaping a modern, highly efficient economic·structure in the member countries, accelerating scientific and technical progress, and rationalising the international division of labour.

In implementing their integration, the CMEA countries have opted for the objective-and-programme approach, which implies the joint formulation of major socio-economic goals and the elaboration of a complex of measures to achieve these. Among the aims of their integration are the strengthening of the socialist community's position in the world economy, improvement of the competitiveness, on world markets, of the goods produced within the CMEA framework, and, consequently, the further invigoration of the worldwide trade and economic ties of the CMEA countries.

---

[3] *CMEA, Comprehensive Programme for Further Extension and Improvement of Co-operation and the Development of Socialist Economic Integration by the CMEA Member Countries* (Moscow, 1971), p. 9.

III. MECHANISM

Decision-making procedures in the CMEA and its agencies, on the one hand, and in the EEC Commission and Council of Ministers, on the other, differ from each other in a number of important ways. The CMEA countries' integration rules out, as a matter of principle, any supranational prerogatives for the Council itself, whereas integration within the EEC framework provides, in principle, for development precisely in this direction. For the time being and by virtue of necessity, decisions taken in the Council of Ministers must be unanimous, but it is intended to introduce majority voting as soon as possible.[4]

The principal method in the CMEA's activity is the co-ordination and synchronisation of the interests and purposes of the member countries through the co-ordination of national economic plans, the formulation of common principles and the solution of the problems that arise. The CMEA adopts only those recommendations to which all countries whose interests are affected by the co-operation project under discussion consent. It has no powers to impose any decision against the will of an interested country. Obligations in international law arise for the participants only when the relevant intergovernmental agreements are concluded on the basis of these recommendations.

Many Western analysts are known to regard the endless co-ordination efforts in the EEC Commission, and the eventual achievement of a consensus on the basis of the least common denominator, precisely as implying repudiation of the principle of decision making by a qualified majority. However, West European integration theorists have expressed other, and perhaps even weightier, considerations. Thus, R. Dahrendorf wrote,

> While this may sound paradoxical, the inter-state formula is more binding on each of the governments than the supranational function. . . . In practice, for instance, majority decisions on farm prices, to say nothing of economic union, may mean, for the time being, only that those remaining in the minority will go their own way.[5]

A comparison of these two antithetical judgments sheds a stronger light on the advantages and the profoundly democratic character of the CMEA's approach.

Still, some Western economists have continued to regard the CMEA's lack of supranational prerogatives, and its lack of centralised decision making on behalf of the individual governments, as essentially the main obstacle in the

---

[4] The transfer of a part of the national governments' competence to the EEC has so far been most pronounced in the sphere of agricultural policy. 'Thus, the Community now already constitutes a well-established politico-economic level which rises over and above the national states' (*Neun für Europa*, p. 26).

[5] *Die Zeit*, 9 July 1971.

way of socialist economic integration. Naturally, no convincing evidence is set forth to show how this could complicate matters. What is more, the very same economists insist that the success of socialist integration is being hampered by the centralisation of economic decision making in the CMEA countries. The inconsistency and incompatibility of these two conclusions is immediately obvious and makes one question their validity.

There is a growing realisation in the EEC that its initially chosen way of mutually opening up markets and competition as the main element of the integration mechanism is inadequate. New tasks call for joint economic planning and programming. A group of competent West German specialists insist that 'on the European level decisions must be taken on the co-ordination of programmes, long-term planning of investments, including decisions on rationalising production structures.[6] But it is just there that the EEC has shown itself to be helpless, while the CMEA has demonstrated its obvious superiority.

The EEC has yet to set up an efficient mechanism for co-ordinating sectoral structural policy, and this may in part explain the difficulties faced by the coal, steel, shipbuilding, textile or chemical-pulp industries of all the countries in the Community. Despite the fact that co-ordination of transport policy was envisaged in the Treaty of Rome, no substantial results have been achieved in this area.

Integration by uncontrolled market forces produces structural disproportions and even leads to the decline of whole regions and branches of the national economy that fail to survive in the competition. François Perroux says that, under imperfect and monopoly competition, it is not the less efficient but the less powerful enterprises that are inevitably eliminated, because the economic and financial groups involved receive, over and above their classical profits, additional profits that arise from monopoly or oligopoly.[7]

While West European integration has lifted some official limitations in the way of mutual trade, thereby accelerating its growth, it has failed to produce the homogeneous economic conditions (as regards price levels, credit conditions, taxation, the level of wages and social benefits, and so on) that, in accordance with neoclassical theory, were to have brought about an optimal allocation of resources across the sectors on the scale of the Community as a whole.

The method of partial alignment of market conditions has proved to be impotent in the face of problems bearing on the main lines of modern industrial progress. One consequence of the lack of an efficient mechanism for scientific and technical integration in the EEC was the duplication of efforts that led to two costly colour-television systems being developed (the German PAL and the French SECAM). Some economists say that, with

[6] *Neun für Europa*, p. 139.
[7] *Économie appliquée*, XXI, no. 2 (1968), p. 394.

reservations, one may well speak of a common market in textiles, automobiles or biscuits, but there can be no question of one when it comes to aeronautics, atomic energy, space, or information.[8] Euratom, the common research programme, has not yielded the desired results, and nor have the efforts to formulate a common energy policy. The consequences of this failure are being most keenly felt today.

Such problems are tackled differently within the CMEA framework. Here, joint planning activity provides the basis for successful efforts in accelerating scientific and technical progress in each member country, enlarging the scale of production of many types of products, developing a common infrastructure, and transforming and mutually adapting the production structures of the individual countries with a view to giving greater depth to international specialisation and co-operation in production. Joint planning activity includes mutual consultations on basic aspects of economic policy, joint forecasting of development in the key industries, and co-ordination of five-year national economic plans and research and development plans. Recently, the CMEA countries have started to practise joint planning (formulation of concrete programmes for co-operation) in some lines of production so as further to concentrate and specialise production. Joint planning covers research and development projects, investments to enlarge production, the loading and specialisation of industrial facilities, and deliveries of the products involved.

Joint planning has an overriding role to play in directing integration processes in the CMEA countries, because their economies are organised on socialist lines, with the state plan as the chief regulator of economic life. The practical potentialities and efficiency of this arrangement will be seen, for instance, from the development — from the ground up — of powerful lines of production with a high degree of specialisation and co-operation within the CMEA framework: ships and railway carriages in the GDR and Poland, coaches and buses in Hungary, battery-driven trucks in Bulgaria, and electric locomotives and power and rolling equipment in Czechoslovakia. There is also the modern petrochemical industry built up in these countries on the basis of guaranteed oil and gas deliveries from the USSR, and the joint construction of international oil and gas pipeline networks (through the Druzhba oil pipeline alone, these countries are supplied with 50 million tons of oil a year).

Of course, the CMEA countries' mechanism for planning joint activity is not entirely free of shortcomings and needs to be improved. Thus, steps are being taken to make the co-ordination of five-year plans more effective and efficient, especially when these bear on investments. Kohlmey, a prominent GDR scientist, believes that

> there is need to include value factors, like prices and credits, in the co-ordination of medium- and long-term plans to a greater extent than has

[8] *Communauté européene*, no. 133 (1969), p. 10.

been done up to now. There is also the problem of how to take account, in co-ordinating plans and concluding trade agreements, of investments in joint economic projects and the effect they yield, investment credits and projects for international specialisation of production. . . . There is need to tackle the problem of striking a balance between bilateral and multilateral plan co-ordination.[9]

The CMEA countries intend to project and co-ordinate their economic development with each other over the long term — meaning, at present, from now until 1990. This will help them to tackle especially large-scale and advantageous integration projects, to solve jointly the raw-material and energy problem, and to go over to deeper and more intensive forms of international specialisation and co-operation in production.

One of the CMEA's virtues is its mechanism for close scientific and technical co-operation among the member countries and for the integration of their scientific and technical potentials. This is promoted by the exchange of technical documentation, generally free of charge (it has been estimated that, had this been sold at world-market prices, it would have cost the member countries at least $20 billion over the CMEA period), joint implementation of key scientific and technical research projects (almost 900 national organisations are involved in joint work on roughly 1100 research subjects), and the establishment of international research centres and design offices. This mechanism has, for example, facilitated the design and production, on the lines of international specialisation and co-operation, of a common CMEA third-generation computer system known as 'Ryad'.

While admitting that the CMEA is in a position to tackle on a macrolevel the major problems in international economic integration, many Western specialists contrast this with the EEC's achievements in integration on the microlevel — that is, on the company level. This matter calls for special consideration, because of the obviously great importance of direct co-operation ties and direct technological co-operation among the enterprises of different countries. But it is just as obvious that there is no ground at all automatically to identify the growth of co-operation ties with the advance of integration.

Co-operation on the level of enterprises can be deepened either through the conclusion of co-operation agreements or through mergers, shareholdings, or the establishment of mixed companies or subsidiaries. In the West, there is considerably greater risk attached to co-operation links among independent industrial companies than there is to intracompany links, and as a result the former have not been developing as intensively as the latter. The authors of *Neun für Europa* say that 'the establishment of subsidiaries apart, co-

---

[9] Gunther Kohlmey. *Vergesellschaftung und Integration im Sozialismus* (Berlin: Akademia Verlag, 1973), p. 154.

operation across national borders is clearly rare'.[10] Besides, data on the international intercompany agreements on co-operation that have been concluded by the EEC countries indicate that the number of intra-Community agreements is roughly the same as the number of agreements between EEC countries and third countries.[11]

The transnational corporations stemming from the EEC countries can be regarded as an instrument of European integration only with great reservations. They are now a powerful economic factor virtually outside the control of the Community, and frequently operate contrary to the interests of West European integration and outside its framework. Some industries that are crucial from the standpoint of technical progress are dominated by transnational corporations run from the United States.

Contrary to the view held by many Western economists, that state regulation of external economic ties in the CMEA countries tends to blunt initiative in developing international co-operation of production on the level of enterprises and industrial associations, the facts indicate that the process is a very intensive one, with measures being taken to enhance it further. On the level of industrial associations and ministries, the CMEA countries have concluded seventeen multilateral agreements on specialisation and co-operation in production, covering over 1700 modern engineering products. There are over 1000 bilateral agreements of this type involving industrial organisations of the CMEA countries, which have set up nearly thirty sectoral economic and scientific-and-production organisations whose main purpose is to deepen specialisation and co-operation in production and to rationalise the loading of industrial and transport facilities.

The international concentration of production now in progress within the CMEA framework cannot be directly compared with what is going on in the EEC, because of the different scale and forms. Thus, the Organisation for Co-operation in the Bearing Industry co-ordinates development for the purpose of specialising virtually the whole of the bearing industry in the CMEA countries. The large-scale international economic organisations — Interatomenergo, Interelektro and Intertekstilmach — now being set up will tackle similar problems in producing electrotechnical equipment and equipment for atomic and electric power stations and for the textile industry. It is also intended to arrange joint ventures with ownership by shares. For instance, the GDR and Poland are together setting up a large-scale textile mill. An important feature of all of these international economic organisations of the CMEA countries is that none of them is dominated by any of the participating countries but that all are joint undertakings in the true sense of the word.

There are many difficulties in the way of developing co-operation links

---

[10] *Neun für Europa*, p. 116.
[11] *CEPES/RKW. Grenzüberschreitende Unternehmenskooperation in der EWG* (Stuttgart, 1968), p. 205.

among the CMEA countries on the sectoral level and, according to the well-known Soviet economist Yuri Shiryaev, these arise from the differences in the organisational structure of industry in those countries, the degree of concentration of their production and the level of export specialisation of their enterprises. If these relations are to be further deepened, there is a need 'to bridge the existing gap between the foreign-trade and the technical-production activity on the sectoral level'.[12]

By contrast with West European integration, market relations in the CMEA countries' integration have a subordinate — even if important — status with respect to the planning instruments of integration. The fundamentally important feature of these relations is the absence of competition, of the free play of prices, and of any speculative or one-sided gains and losses for the individual participants.

Let us bear in mind that the market mechanism of West European integration has not functioned smoothly and has not always ensured the achievement of the desired goals. Its weakness has already been exposed in that, with the advance of tariff 'disarmament' and the freer movement of capital, there has been a build-up of administrative, tax and other barriers. This mechanism is being undermined by mounting inflation, for the establishment of the EEC has facilitated the importation not only of goods but also of inflation. The world monetary crisis has exposed the imperfections of the EEC's monetary integration mechanism and has cast doubt on the fundamental principles of the Community. Helmut Schmidt, when Finance Minister of the Federal Republic of Germany, declared that 'the struggle over tariffs constituting an average of 8 per cent of the value of imported goods is ridiculous when compared with changes in par values of 30, 40 or 50 per cent, which in a matter of years have done very much more to alter the countries' chances with respect to exports and imports'.[13]

Monetary upheavals have posed a threat to the common trade regime and the system of agricultural protectionism within the EEC framework. The massive movement of tens of billions of Eurodollars has kept economic life in the EEC in a feverish state. There is also the strong impact of the rising price of oil and of some types of imported raw materials.

Without abandoning their fundamental line of developing their commodity and money relations in a balanced manner, the CMEA countries seek to enhance the role of these relations in deepening the integration process. With that end in view, they have been working to improve prices in their trade with each other, and to specify the exchange rates of the national currencies, and have taken steps to extend the functions of the transferable rouble, their collective currency.

Price levels in intra-CMEA trade differ from current world levels. This is due to the fact that CMEA prices remain stable throughout the period of the

---

[12] Yuri S. Shiryaev, *The Economic Mechanism of Socialist Integration* (Moscow: Ekonomika Publishers, 1973), p. 156.
[13] *General-Anzeiger*, 22 Aug 1973.

five-year trade agreements (and now and again for even longer periods). These prices are fixed on the basis of average world prices for the four or five years preceding the conclusion of the trade agreement. This helps to purge world prices of any speculative elements and short-term considerations.

The CMEA countries realise how important it is that prices in their trade with each other should exert an active influence on the development of specialisation and co-operation in production within the CMEA framework and also boost deliveries, to these countries' markets, of goods for which demand is not being fully met.

The settlements system of the CMEA countries is based on the principle of multilateral clearing, the currency here being the transferable rouble with a fixed gold content. The CMEA countries have set themselves the aim of gradually making their collective currency convertible. One of the pre-requisites for the convertibility of the transfer rouble is an extension of economic ties between the CMEA countries and other states on a mutually advantageous basis. In addition, broader participation by the CMEA countries in international credit operations, including operations through their International Investment Bank, should help to solve the convertibility problem.

IV. SOME RESULTS

A general conclusion concerning the virtues and shortcomings of the two integration mechanisms considered above will, it appears, largely depend on the degree of internationalisation of economic life achieved within the CMEA and the EEC, on the social results of the process in both parts of Europe, and on its influence on the normalisation and improvement of the world economy as a whole.

The starting levels must necessarily be considered in any assessment of actual progress in the sphere of integration involving the national economic systems. The CMEA countries did not have any deep-seated historical tradition of close economic links. Up till the Second World War only an insignificant share of their foreign trade (from 1 per cent to a maximum of 15 per cent) consisted of trade with each other. For the EEC Nine, the pre-war figure was roughly 30 per cent. In the early post-war years, the development levels and the economic structures of the CMEA countries were likewise not very favourable for their economic co-operation.

If, despite all these unfavourable circumstances, the Soviet Union and the East European countries have rapidly moved closer to each other economically, the explanation will of course be found not only in the economy but also in the socio-political sphere, in the community of their vital interests. In a sense, the West's cold-war policy, trade discrimination and credit blockade have acted as a catalyst for integration processes within the CMEA framework.

By 1950, the CMEA countries were conducting 60 per cent of their overall foreign trade with each other, and this level has been maintained since then; by comparison, the nine EEC countries conduct 50 per cent of their overall foreign trade with each other. In 1950, trade among the CMEA countries was valued at a very modest 4·5 billion roubles, while in 1973 it was 47·5 billion, with the volume multiplying nearly ninefold. The CMEA countries' trade with third countries increased roughly in the same proportions.

The bulk of the CMEA countries' raw-material, fuel and energy requirements is met within the framework of their community. Although the CMEA members have never sought to set up a closed economic grouping, the high level of their self-sufficiency in energy, fuel and raw-material supplies constitutes an important advantage over the EEC in this age of ours, which abounds in all manner of surprises.

Among the important achievements of the integration of the CMEA countries are the link-up of the national electric-power grids; the establishment and the steady expansion of the system of transnational oil and gas pipelines, constituting the basis of the future common fuel economy of the CMEA countries; and the establishment of a common railway-car pool, which by early 1973 consisted of 230,000 cars (in terms of four-wheeled units).

The new stage of co-operation in the CMEA countries in the 1970s is marked by an even greater pooling of their financial, production and labour resources on an international basis. The International Investment Bank, set up in 1971 with an authorised capital of over 1 billion roubles to finance projects for intensified integration, is only one expression of this process. Another is their agreement to finance jointly the construction of a large, 500,000-tonne chemical-pulp plant in Siberia. The details of similar large-scale projects are now being worked out.

The CMEA countries' economic integration has been a factor behind the rapid growth of their industrial potential. In 1960, for instance, the CMEA countries were generating less electric power than the EEC Nine (404 billion as compared with 426 billion kilowatt hours), and were producing less steel (86 million tonnes as compared with 98 million tonnes). By 1973, the situation had been reversed: the CMEA countries were generating 1217 billion kilowatt hours of electric power, as against 1033 billion kilowatt hours in the EEC countries; and were producing 178 million tonnes of steel (EEC, 150 million tonnes).

The establishment of the EEC has led to more intensive trade among the member countries (from 1958 to 1971 it increased sevenfold, as against a threefold increase in trade with third countries). The EEC countries have achieved some pooling of funds on the Community level: they have a common budget (about 4 billion units of account in 1973), mainly to finance the agricultural fund, and also a number of other common funds. They have several common programmes and sectoral projects.

In the social sphere, the consequences of integration processes in the

CMEA countries, on the one hand, and the EEC countries, on the other, are highly diverse and largely antithetical. Within the EEC, the intense concentration of capital and the growing power of the monopolies, going hand in hand with ever-greater interference in economic life by the national states, have sharpened many social contradictions impinging on the interests of the working people, the small consumers, and large groups of taxpayers, and have led to the ruin of many small and medium enterprises. Indeed, far from containing inflation, integration has, in effect, whipped it up. The CMEA countries are not faced with such a situation.

Competition and the growing mobility of the factors of production within the EEC framework have not reduced but rather have intensified the uneven distribution of resources among the regions. This problem was first considered in practical terms only recently, and the Nine have started to discuss ways to set up a common fund for regional development.

From the outset, the CMEA has concentrated on the problem of evening out disparities in the economic development levels of the individual socialist countries. That steady progress is being made will be seen from the much faster economic growth of countries like Romania and Bulgaria, as compared with the other CMEA countries. Today, national income per capita in the CMEA's European countries is within 20–25 per cent of the average, providing evidence of relatively homogeneous economic conditions in the region.

The two integrating communities also have a different role to play in the modern system of worldwide economic relations. The establishment of an economic bloc in Western Europe has had a painful effect on the interests of many countries and areas throughout the world, resulting in what is usually known as 'diversion of trade' and what Machlup, I believe, has called 'distortion of trade'.

For all practical purposes, the CMEA is not fenced off from third countries by any discriminatory barriers. In recent years, the CMEA countries' trade with third countries has grown faster than has their trade with each other.

The system of co-operation within the CMEA framework tends to create considerably fewer problems in organising extensive European co-operation than does the EEC, with its tariff barriers and discrimination against third countries.

While admitting that the EEC discriminates against third countries, some American specialists insist that the state monopoly and planning of foreign trade in the CMEA countries is also discriminatory. That is something that we in the CMEA cannot accept. The state monopoly and the state plan are the basis of the CMEA countries' economic ties both with each other and with third countries, whereas the EEC applies different trade regimes inside and outside the Community – a procedure that, in affect, amounts to discrimination in the direct and immediate sense of the word. Moreover, the socialist countries have never made their co-operation with the Western countries contingent on the latter's abolition of private enterprise. It is just as unreasonable to make this co-operation contingent on the abolition of state planning of external economic ties and the introduction of a spontaneously functioning market economy. The distinctions between the two socio-economic systems have nothing to do with the questions of discrimination, nonextension of the most-favoured-nation principle, and other artificial barriers in the way of broad international co-operation.

State regulation of the external economic relations of the CMEA countries, along with these countries' large-scale integration projects, open up additional opportunities for co-operation with the West. These opportunities will be available whenever the West is ready to take advantage of them and to establish co-operative relations with the CMEA countries on a new, equitable and long-term basis. This implies, above all, a readiness to conclude long-term economic agreements; to develop industrial co-operation; to finance the construction of industrial plants, the products of which could be used to repay credits; to extend scientific and technical co-operation; and to organise the joint development of new machine designs and new technologies.

European reality is represented by the two types of integration, which can coexist, compete and establish businesslike relations with each other. If they are to do so, all discrimination must be done away with, most-favoured-nation treatment must be reciprocally accorded, and the development of mutual ties on a bilateral and multilateral basis must be stimulated.

Comments
Gottfried Haberler and John P. Hardt (USA)

It is a pleasure to comment on Bogomolov's stimulating paper, because, even when there is disagreement in substance, there is a community in linguistics — the language of modern economics. Unfortunately, we can deal with only some of the many points that were raised.

I. REGIONAL INTEGRATION, PROTECTIONISM AND DISCRIMINATION

Regional integration is the subject of Bogomolov's paper. We shall follow him and concentrate on the CMEA and the EEC as representing integration by planning and through the market, but we should keep in mind that, in addition to the regional integration taking place in the EEC, the Western World has been experiencing a process of wide-spread integration. This process is based almost entirely on market forces, for, practically speaking, there exists no planning on a worldwide scale. Worldwide integration stems from two sources: first, the reduction of tariffs and other trade barriers negotiated through the GATT and the IMF; and, second, the reduction in cost of air and sea transport. The success of this process of worldwide Western integration through the market is measured by the fact that since the last war Western trade has grown enormously and — despite numerous currency crises — without interruption.

Bogomolov is critical of the view that the planning method of integration in the CMEA is ineffective as compared with the market method used by the EEC. For one thing, centrally planned economies, too, can make use of market prices in their planning. It is true that socialist countries have found it necessary to make more and more use of decentralised pricing. But we agree with Bogomolov when he says that, in contrast to the case with the EEC, market relations in the CMEA countries' integration have a subordinate status.

However, the EEC is not based 'exclusively on market relations'. The Western economies are 'mixed economies'. The public sector is everywhere much greater than it was fifty or a hundred years ago. It follows that a mere customs union today does not have the same power to integrate as it had in the nineteenth century. But it is also true that, in the West, the great bulk of international trade is conducted by private business — not only by *big* business but also by *small* firms. Elimination of trade barriers does not bring about *full* integration, but it is a big step in the direction of integration.

We agree with Bogomolov that *regional* integration poses special problems and dangers. Economic efficiency and growth may be impeded by 'collective protectionism' and discrimination against outsiders, irrespective of whether market forces or central planning methods are used. Tariffs and other barriers to the free flow of goods and services in and out of the EEC are discriminatory and not conducive to the most effective division of labour. But protectionism and discrimination appear, although in different forms, in a regional association of planned economies such as the CMEA. In contrast to the case with the EEC, protection may be assured by the supply plans of CMEA countries without resort to tariffs, quotas, or other controls used in market economies. The test of the extent of this protection can be provided by assessments of the CMEA products and processes that are noncompetitive in price and quality in Western markets.

Economic policy in the EEC has been hampered by the lack of centralised decision making for the community as a whole. For example, the accession of new members and important trade concessions to outsiders are still subject to the veto of any member country. This handicap is, however, greatly mitigated by the fact that the great bulk of economic transactions are handled by the market and do not require decisions by the national or Community authorities.

It stands to reason that the lack of supranational prerogative is a much greater handicap for the CMEA than for the EEC, because in the CMEA there is no free market. Every major economic decision is a government decision. In passing, we should like to point out that there is no contradiction between (a) emphasising the defect, just mentioned, in the structure of the CMEA, and (b) the proposition that an individualistic decentralised market economy is likely to be much more efficient and productive than a centrally planned economy. For, once the market has been replaced by central planning, economic rationality and efficiency require that the central authority be able to act decisively, without the handicap of a unanimity rule (the crippling effects of which are evident from the difficulties experienced by the Polish parliament in the days when every member of it had a right of veto).

Of course, centrally planned and market economies are not likely to converge in their institutional arrangements. Indeed, convergence is not necessary to engage in trade, although recent flexibility permitting direct access of Western firms to end-users in CMEA countries has been most helpful. However, as long as centrally planned economies establish their import plans with preference for domestic over foreign suppliers, they are discriminating. The preference for higher-priced or lower-quality domestic over foreign products implies some form of discrimination. Centrally controlled import plans in the CMEA countries may be likened to import quotas elsewhere.

Discrimination may apply to either imports or exports. The Soviet Union's sales of petroleum within the CMEA are a conspicuous case of export discrimination. Crude oil is sold to CMEA countries at a price that is currently less than one-quarter of the world-market price that Western countries have to pay for Russian oil. The USSR bought oil from Iraq for $6 a barrel and resold it to Germany for $18. Natural gas is bought from Afghanistan and Iran at $6·5 and $10·3 respectively, per 1000 cubic metres, while Russian gas is sold to Austria (for hard currency) at $13·8 and to Poland and Czechoslovakia (for inconvertible currencies) at $18·3 and $19·5 per 1000 cubic metres. (See *The Economist*, 3 Aug 1974, p. 67.)

Most Western economists criticise Western tariffs and other restrictions on the free flow of goods and services. We find that the agricultural policies of the EEC are excessively protectionist and discriminatory. But we cannot agree with Bogomolov when he calls the EEC a 'closed economic bloc'. The EEC tariff has been almost halved in multilateral negotiations under the GATT. Therefore, the problem of discrimination against outsiders is no longer as serious as it was, except in the field of agriculture. The EEC agricultural policy not only damages outsiders, but is also a burden on the EEC consumers. On the other hand, some outsiders (for example, the USSR) have profited from sales at cut-rate prices of EEC surplus stocks of butter and other commodities.

Balassa has shown that the enormous expansion of intra-EEC trade was predominantly *not* at the expense of outsiders; in other words, it constitutes, for the most part, 'trade creation and *not* trade diversion' (see Chapter 1 above).

Bogomolov says that, in contrast with the EEC, 'for all practical purposes, the CMEA is not fenced off from third countries by any discriminatory barriers' We cannot accept this proposition. Any regional integration necessarily implies some discrimination against the outsiders. How much there is in the case of centrally planned economies, where foreign trade is monopolised by the state, is, for the reasons mentioned earlier, extremely difficult to say.

Bogomolov mentions the fact that 'in recent years, the CMEA countries' trade with third countries has grown faster than their trade with each other' as an indication of the CMEA's openness (absence of discrimination) *vis-à-vis* outsiders. We believe that the more rapid growth of trade with third countries partly reflects something different — namely, the absence of genuinely multi-lateral trade and of convertibility of currencies inside the CMEA area. Balassa has shown that intra-CMEA trade is still cramped by strict bilateralism. The growing trade of CMEA countries with third countries is due to the growing need for high-technology products not available in the CMEA, and thus constitutes an escape from the cramped trading conditions inside the CMEA. By trading with the West, CMEA countries take advantage of the market convertibility of Western currencies, which allows them to enjoy — to some extent — the benefits of multilateral trade. They can thus buy their imports where the prices and other conditions are most favourable, and not (as in intra-CMEA trade) where they happen to have an outlet for their exports.

We agree in principle with Bogomolov that the United States and the EEC should grant most-favoured-nation treatment to CMEA countries — that is, should charge the same duties on imports from the CMEA as on imports from elsewhere. But it must be recognised that in practice this is made difficult by the fact that it is hard to get reciprocity from socialist countries for most-favoured-nation treatment, because tariff concessions from centrally planned economies do not mean anything.

II. MONETARY INTEGRATION AND THE MOVEMENT OF PERSONS

In the EEC the free movement of goods (customs union) has been accomplished but monetary integration in the sense of permanently fixed exchange rates, let alone in the sense of the creation of a common currency, has not yet been achieved.

However, the importance of this failure should not be exaggerated. It must not be forgotten that in the market the EEC currencies are, by and large, freely convertible into each other as well as into American dollars and other Western currencies. The important thing for trade, integration and economic welfare in general is *market* convertibility and not convertibility into gold. Market convertibility means (a) that anybody who wants to import from abroad can buy the foreign currency that he needs in the market, either at fixed rates or, if the relevant currencies are floating, at the current market rate, and (b) that the exporter can convert the currency that he acquires into the currency of his own country or into some other currency. Market convertibility has greatly contributed to the huge growth of trade between the EEC countries and other Western countries, a growth that has not been interrupted by any of the much-publicised currency crises.

Here, we may mention inflation. Although the sharp rise in prices in all Western countries since 1973 is a very serious development, we cannot agree with Bogomolov when he attributes inflation in Europe to the integration in the EEC. Inflation has been equally strong or stronger in many non-EEC countries, and the CMEA countries have by no means remained free from inflation.

What is the state of monetary integration in the CMEA? We understand that the objective is to move towards a 'transferable rouble' as a common medium of exchange. But we are told that CMEA countries with currency surpluses are *not* free to convert them into other currencies, or into goods and services of their choice. Balassa points out that intra-CMEA trade is still conducted, by and large, on the basis of bilateralism. This is the very opposite of convertibility and monetary integration. It is an extremely serious impediment for trade and for a rational division of labour, which partly explains why in the CMEA, unlike in the EEC, external trade has grown faster than has internal trade.

Another form of integration in the West is that represented by the large migration of labour within the EEC and from third countries to EEC countries; this has been highly beneficial for all concerned. In the EEC countries the immigrants have been invaluable in taking over certain jobs that the more highly skilled and more expensive native labour force is reluctant to accept. The immigrants have earned much higher wages than at home and have acquired useful skills, and their home countries greatly profit from the large sums sent home by the foreign workers.

Western economists and governments are fully aware of the social and political frictions and problems created by large numbers of foreign workers. It is therefore not to be expected that the influx of foreign workers will continue at the high rate of recent years. But, as far as it goes, the migration of labour is clearly a form of integration that goes well beyond the boundaries of the EEC.

We are told that there are potential labour surpluses in the CMEA countries and shortages in others. It would be interesting to have an evaluation of this problem. How much migration of labour has there been in the CMEA? Is more of it expected? Is it possible that foreign workers from non-CMEA countries will be used in CMEA countries?

Still another form of Western integration is that represented by the enormous tourist trade among EEC countries and across EEC boundaries. There is no discrimination here between EEC countries and others. Everybody is free to travel as he pleases, for pleasure or for business, without special permission and often without a visa. These forms of integration must not be forgotten when comparing the effectiveness of the market method and of central planning.

III. STRUCTURAL INTEGRATION THROUGH LONG-TERM JOINT PLANNING

Bogomolov gives examples of long-term joint-planning of industrial structures and of large-scale investments involving CMEA countries. In this area, he says, 'the EEC has shown itself helpless, while the CMEA has demonstrated its obvious superiority'. Unfortunately, it is not possible, on the basis of Bogomolov's few examples, to form a judgement on how much the CMEA has achieved along these lines. It seems that comprehensive figures are not available.

For the West it is even more difficult to evaluate the scope of joint planning, because most of it is done by private firms, even medium-sized and small ones, about which statistics are not available. Bogomolov quotes a German source as saying that, 'the establishment of subsidiaries apart,[1] co-operation across national borders is clearly rare'. Referring to another Western source, Bogomolov says that 'the data on international intercompany agreements on co-operation that have been concluded by the EEC countries indicate that the number of intra-Community agreements is roughly the same as the number of agreements between EEC countries and third countries'. This information does not indicate the importance of such agreements. It confirms, however, that the EEC is not a 'closed bloc'.

Many American firms have established subsidiaries in Europe and have co-operative arrangements with European firms, a tendency that has been intensified by the formation of the EEC. This development helps to boost output and to accelerate growth in the EEC through the importation of American technological know-how and management methods. (In recent years, many European firms have started to operate in the United States.)

Bogomolov mentions as a conspicuous failure of EEC programming the inability to agree on a common colour-television system. This, surely, is a wasteful duplication. But it was not a failure of the market. Private enterprises would have had no difficulties in establishing a single system. It was a failure of government planning. We may further observe that CMEA countries adopted the inferior French system, presumably for political reasons.

Bogomolov stresses that 'The CMEA countries' integration rules out, as a matter of principle, any supranational prerogatives for the Council itself'. In other words, the CMEA operates on the basis of unanimity and not of majority rule. The EEC, on the other hand, intends to introduce majority rule in the future.

For centrally planned economies, the absence of supranational power (unanimity) surely is a serious handicap in the process of integration. True, frequent references are made to specialisation and joint planning of new industries. Presumably, if one of two CMEA countries has a clear comparative advantage in new industries, a unanimous decision about the location of such industries according to the comparative cost situation can be reached. But very often the situation is not so clear. It would be interesting to learn how decisions are actually made in such cases, in the absence of majority rule. How is the comparative advantage evaluated in the absence of scarcity prices?

In the EEC, for the time being, the absence of majority rule is much less of a handicap, because the largest part of trade and the corresponding investment decisions are made by private business, including small enterprises. International division of labour is not dictated by government decisions, but is largely deter-

[1] It is not clear why subsidiaries should be disregarded in an evaluation of the importance of transnational industrial operations. We argue that the creation of subsidiaries is an especially desirable form of transnational industrial operation because it fosters competition. Other forms, such as international intercompany agreements, are likely to lead to undesirable monopolistic practices.

mined by market forces according to the principles of comparative advantage.

Balassa points out that efficient international division of labour in the CMEA is handicapped 'by the centralisation of economic decision-making'. It stands to reason that government monopolies, which have to reach unanimous agreement, must confine themselves to a limited number of large projects. In the West, by contrast, there are thousands of large, medium, and small firms that are constantly on the lookout for opportunities to import and export consumer goods, machines and other capital equipment, to invest abroad and to set up joint ventures, thereby extending the international division of labour, maximising output and accelerating growth.

With regard to co-operation between Western and socialist countries, Bogomolov says that it is 'unreasonable to make this co-operation contingent on abolition of state planning of external economic ties and the introduction of a market economy [on the part of the socialist countries]'. There seems to be a misunderstanding here. For the West to pose such conditions would, of course, be out of the question, and we cannot imagine that any Western economist has made such a suggestion. In our opinion, the United States and other Western countries should unconditionally grant most-favoured-nation treatment to imports from the East. In other words, imports from socialist countries into the United States and into the EEC should be subject to no higher import duties and other charges (and no more restrictive regulations) than imports from other nonmember countries. It should however, be understood, that a customs union, such as the EEC or the CMEA, is not obliged to allow duty-free imports from nonmembers. Concessions that members of a customs union make to each other are *not* subject to most-favoured-nation rights of any third country.

All that socialist countries can reasonably demand is that the EEC should not impose higher duties on imports from socialist countries than on imports from other nonmember countries. It is in the nature of any customs union that it discriminates against outsiders. But the discrimination should be the same for *all* outsiders.

It may be true, as Bogomolov says, that integration through the market could occasionally lead to 'structural disproportions' and to the decline of certain regions. This risk is the price that the West has to pay for rapid progress. Western economists and policy makers are fully aware of these dangers. The EEC has set up a large regional fund to help regions that may be hurt by integration. Actually, no important case has arisen so far of a region whose depression can be attributed to the integration effort.

In the past, 'structural disproportions' have sometimes led to general depressions and to the decline of certain regions, relative to other regions, occasionally even in absolute terms. But there has not been a single case of a severe depression in any EEC country or in the United States in the post war period, although there have been mild recessions. True, the recent period of rapid inflation poses the danger of a recession. But it would lead too far to go into these problems. Neither the inflation nor the danger of a recession resulting from policies of abrupt disinflation has anything to do with regional integration.

There exist, of course, *relatively* depressed, or actually poor, regions in the EEC (Southern Italy and Scotland are examples), but regional differences have become smaller during the EEC period. When the EEC was set up and trade barriers were dismantled, there was some apprehension that some industries would get into trouble when they became exposed to competition with more highly developed German industries, and that this would result in temporary dislocations and unemployment. Actually, the economies of the six (now nine) countries have adjusted smoothly and rapidly, so that it has been possible to eliminate tariffs ahead of schedule. Modern capitalist-industrial countries have once again displayed an amazing capacity to adjust quickly to changing conditions.

Comments
Witold Trzeciakowski and Jerzy Mycielski (Poland)

I. INTRODUCTORY

Integration cannot be looked upon as an automatic international system, based mainly on market relations. Socialist integration sets itself the aim of achieving rapid economic progress through fundamental structural changes in the economy, rationalisation of the use of the economic potential of all integrating countries, promotion of concentration and specialisation of production, and efforts to even out the level of development of all participating countries.

This complex process must be consciously managed and hence it belongs to the domain of 'social engineering': joint socio-economic goals are formulated and corresponding measures are elaborated to achieve them. Final social goals should determine the basic principles of integration and should dictate the choice of economic tools and mechanisms, not *vice versa*. Efficiency cannot be treated as the only and ultimate goal of development. There are also social and political considerations of fundamental importance that must exist exert a decisive influence upon the character of integrative processes. The consequences of this approach for socialist integration are summarised in the stimulating paper by Bogomolov.

Parallel to the nonefficiency considerations there exist externalities, indivisibilities, uncertainties, and economies of scale, specifically in long-term integration processes. These explain the importance of joint, direct planning measures, including the co-ordination of five-year and one-year plans; joint investment projects (multilaterally agreed integration ventures); and rationalisation for production structures. However, with the constantly increasing diversification of production and trade, there is a growing demand also for indirect tools of planning. As, in Bogomolov's words 'The CMEA countries' integration rules out, as a matter of principle, any supranational prerogatives for the Council itself', integrating countries are forming a market. Market relations must have a subordinate status with respect to planning. Hence, there is a need to develop techniques that would enable us to determine, by planning, the exchange rates and prices on the basis of which a planned equilibrium could be reached.

In his paper, Bogomolov rightly states that 'it would be wrong to regard integration through planning as being incompatible with the market and socialist commodity and money relations. Economic planning under socialism implies a development of commodity and money relations both within individual socialist countries and between them. These relations are a necessary element of the planned economy within the national and the international framework.' Bogomolov does not develop this concept further. However, it seems to me important to do so, since this will show how to improve the current efficiency of integration in the short run.

The task of this paper is to present an approach to integration through planning, by using equilibrium models of international trade as a planning tool.

II. THE PROBLEM

The basic problem that we are trying to solve is how to construct a planning
method, for optimisation of an integrated entity composed of sovereign states,
that would guarantee that the solution reached by the central planner of the
integrated entity would be equivalent to the solution reached by individual
countries co-operating within the framework of a competitive simulated market. The planning approach has the advantage of avoiding the real costs of
reaching the solution by trial and error in a real market game.

We are mainly concerned with the first, initial stage of integration – that
is, the current optimisation and equilibrium of foreign trade,[1] leaving aside the
analysis of investment and the transfer on capital or labour, and using linear
models. The main purpose is to propose a quantitative method for the determination of prices for equilibrated intra-CMEA trade. Let us consider the two
possible approaches.

(1) *Competitive equilibrium model.* This approach is based on an equilibrium model encompassing individual sovereign countries. Each co-operating
country formulates its own optimisation model with its own preference function (for instance, minimisation of labour outlays or maximisation of nationa
income of a given structure). There are no conditions imposed by other
countries, nor are there quantitative directives or limits in foreign trade. Price
in foreign trade are treated as parameters. To find equilibrium, international
prices have to be adapted in such a way as to clear the international market
in all commodities. The model reflects integration by market forces.

(2) *Integrated joint optimisation model.* The model encompasses all activities, commodity balances and constraints of individual countries, as well as
balances of exports to, and imports from, the international market. These are
treated as conditions of market clearance. However, the joint model does not
incorporate as conditions the foreign-trade balances of individual countries.
The overall preference function is a weighted sum of the preference functions
of individual countries. In cases where the preference functions are composed
of labour costs expressed in domestic currencies, the coefficients weighting
the preference functions have the dimension of rates of exchange of domestic
currencies in relation to the international currency. This model reflects integration by planning.

We are assuming here a multilateral form of balancing intraregional trade.
The above models can be formulated both for the case of convertibility and
for that of inconvertibility of the joint regional currency. If this currency is
inconvertible, the balances of foreign trade with the outside world market
should be treated as constraints for the models' individual countries.

In general, the above two models are not equivalent. In some cases, when
the coefficients weighting the joint preference function are set on an arbitrary
level, a country may have higher costs than in the case of an autarkic solution.
Hence, by selecting arbitrary coefficients in the joint preference function, an
individual country may worsen its position. This danger does not occur in the

---

[1] The model in its present form can be used also for short-term projections on competitive markets, as a tool for determining new equilibrium prices resulting from sudden
and unexpected changes in supply or demand and disequilibria in international balances
that may develop as a consequence of granting loans.

competitive equilibrium model, as each country always has free choice in selecting the autarkic solution.

It is possible to prove[2] that when the coefficients weighting the joint preference function are fixed at a certain specific level, then the solutions of the integrated joint model and of the competitive equilibrium model will be identical. In such a case, the prices of commodities in the competitive model are equal to dual prices in the joint model; at the same time, marginal rates of exchange (shadow prices of currencies) in the competitive model are equal to coefficients weighting the joint-preference function of the integrated model. In other words, equilibrium is reached by adapting the exchange rates weighting the joint-preference function in such a way as to fulfil the individual balances of foreign trade of each country (that, exports and imports as obtained in the optimal solution multiplied by the shadow prices of commodities obtained from the joint commodity balances).

When these conditions are fulfilled, no country can be worse off than in the autarkic solution.

III. METHODS OF SOLUTION

When using the planning approach we are searching

— in the competitive equilibrium model, for a set of prices assuring the clearance of the market;
— in the integrated joint optimisation model, for a set of rates of exchange assuring the fulfilment of foreign-trade balances of individual countries.

Both of these tasks can be formulated as the problem of finding the fix-point for some multidimensional function. Until recently, these tasks were numerically unsolvable.

The recent findings of H. Scarf,[3] in the domain of constructing an efficient algorithm for the solution of equilibrium prices, make it possible to solve these models numerically. It so happens that the numerical solution of the integrated joint model proves to be easier than that of the competitive-equilibrium model (the number of exchange rates is smaller than the number of commodity prices).

For the sake of illustration, the numerical solution of a problem involving ten countries and some scores of commodities can be reached on a large computer in about an hour of computing time. Hence, it is the problem of collecting data that becomes a major constraint, and not any difficulties of computation. When we are interested in solving practical decisions on an international scale, dealing only with selected particular branches, we can proceed in the following way.

First, we solve the joint integrated model, disaggregating selected basic raw

[2] J. Mycielski and W. Piaszczynski, 'A Mathematical Model of International Economic Cooperation', in *Proceedings of the First Scandinavian—Polish Regional Science Seminar*, Szczecin, 21—23 August 1965, p. 263; *KPZK PAN, Studies, XVII*, PWN, W-wa 1967; and J. Mycielski, 'A Model of Regional Harmonization of National Development Plans', in *Economic Bulletin for Asia and the Far East, XVIII*, no. 2 (1967), p. 44.

[3] H. Scarf (with the collaboration of T. Hansen), *The Computation of Economic Equilibria* (forthcoming).

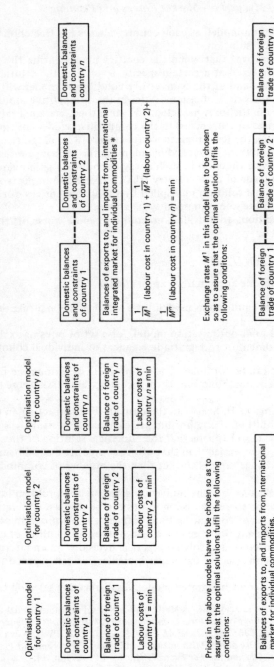

Fig. 1. Comparison of Approaches.

Competitive equilibrium model

Optimisation model for country 1	Optimisation model for country 2		Optimisation model for country n
Domestic balances and constraints of country 1	Domestic balances and constraints of country 2		Domestic balances and constraints of country n
Balance of foreign trade of country 1	Balance of foreign trade of country 2		Balance of foreign trade of country n
Labour costs of country 1 = min	Labour costs of country 2 = min		Labour costs of country n = min

Prices in the above models have to be chosen so as to assure that the optimal solutions fulfil the following conditions:

Balances of exports to, and imports from, international market for individual commodities.

Integrated optimisation model

Domestic balances and constraints of country 1	Domestic balances and constraints of country 2		Domestic balances and constraints country n

Balances of exports to, and imports from, international integrated market for individual commodities *

$$\frac{1}{M^1}\ (\text{labour cost in country 1}) + \frac{1}{M^2}\ (\text{labour country 2}) +$$
$$\frac{1}{M^n}\ (\text{labour cost in country } n) = \min$$

Exchange rates M^1 in this model have to be chosen so as to assure that the optimal solution fulfils the following conditions:

Balance of foreign trade of country 1	Balance of foreign trade of country 2		Balance of foreign trade of country n

Balances in terms of shadow prices.

* Balances in terms of shadow prices.

materials and a few products essential for that branch, while aggregating the rest. From here we get equilibrium exchange rates and equilibrium prices for these basic materials.

Second, the joint problem with the above rates and prices and disaggregated for the branch under consideration can now be treated as an optimisation problem. By decomposing it we get the problem of optimisation of a given branch on an international scale.[4]

This analytical approach can also be applied to the problems of international co-operation between centrally planned economies and market economies (as a domestic market economy can be described as an optimisation model of an analogous type).

[4] J. Mycielski, in *Economic Bulletin for Asia and the Far East*, *XVIII*, no. 2.

Opening Statement for Group Discussion
Harry E. English (Canada)

Since the main paper and discussion papers have been made available in
advance, I shall not endeavour to summarise them. Instead, I shall concentrate
on two purposes. First, I shall highlight the main issues that emerge from the
papers. Second, I shall introduce a few issues that may go beyond the scope
of the main paper, but nevetheless relate to the group's concern with 'integration by market forces and through planning'.

The first major issue raised by Bogomolov and by Haberler is: which of the
schemes is the more discriminatory against nonmembers of the association or
community? This is a matter requiring empirical investigation and, as Haberler
suggests, it cannot be settled easily, because the instruments causing discrimination in the two integration arrangements differ. Those employed in the EEC
are more general and obvious in character (the external tariff and the common
agricultural policy), while discrimination in the CMEA results from priorities
and practices deeply embedded in the planning systems and in the operations
of state-owned enterprises. One cannot begin to compare the overall effect by
looking at total trade flows, because, as Bogomolov emphasises, it all depends
on the characteristics of the time period over which the comparison is made
and what other policy changes have been affecting multilateral or nonmember
trade.

A second major question posed by the two papers is: which approach is
better suited to the achievements of monetary integration and the elements
of the later stages of economic union. Here Bogomolov supports the CMEA
system of joint and unanimous decisions co-ordinating national plans, formulating common principles and solving problems. He cites the limitations of the
EEC approach, quoting Dahrendorf: 'for instance, majority decisions on farm
prices [etc.] may mean for the time being only that those remaining in the
minority will go their own way'. Bogomolov and, in a different way, the paper
by our Polish colleagues argue against the importance of supernational decision making. Haberler's paper is not especially concerned with these issues,
but he does suggest that, if anything, integration among centrally planned
economies is likely to require more co-ordination, and that it is therefore
possible that unanimity imposes a greater constraint on integration among
such countries. The Polish paper suggests that workable models can be developed on either of two assumptions — that centrally planned states are
operating independently, or that they are operating with a central plan for
the integrated entity. The authors suggest that, with a willingness to set
commodity or money exchange rates so as to clear the market and balance
the trade of each member, it should be possible to get an equilibrium system
either way. But it would be a different system, and how economically efficient
each alternative would be is not clear. It does, however, serve to remind us that
national political as well as economic forces must be assessed to determine
how sound and how stable an integration scheme is likely to be.

To deal with these issues we need some clarification of just what is meant
by 'planning' and 'markets'. There is a danger that each side in this debate
will set up a straw man — a stereotype of the other system — and will attack
it. In fact, what are we comparing? We are comparing a system of central

planning in which increasing attention is being paid to the problem of response to consumer needs and preferences, and a system of *decentralised planning* in which increasing attention is being paid to the need for some government intervention. This intervention is to make sure that decisions in the markets do not reflect the concentration of economic power; and where concentration of economic power seems unavoidable (because of structural forces tending to very large units in some industry sectors) that the most effective forms of public regulation be devised.

There is still room for much debate, but this should be concentrated not on the pure, ideological stereotype, but on how to make each system work as effectively as possible, and on the extent to which it is possible, given suitable modifications for each to be as effective as the other in achieving efficient resource use and public welfare.

I should be interested to hear from our East European colleagues how the centrally planned system uses, or hopes to use, pricing or other methods of testing consumer preferences in the markets, domestic and international, in which they operate.

As for the market economy, I think that Western economists must present as clear a picture as they can of the nature of the modern market system. There is a tendency for some Western economists to talk and write as though virtually every industry sector is experiencing a natural tendency toward monopoly. The students of industrial organisation (more are needed here) can help to set the record right on this subject.

Very few industries are natural monopolies (that is, requiring such a large scale that only one enterprise can supply the market efficiently), unless we are talking about small national markets. In the United States, over half the labour force is in services with very unconcentrated markets (except in some local market situations). Manufacturing industries are typically highly concentrated, though not on account of production economies. Some (for instance, the space and defence industries) tend to higher concentration because of research and development costs, but with many more it is because of large marketing operations that generate economic power and pecuniary economies for business, and only few real economies for the final consumer.

Policies for making the market system work better include: (1) promoting international integration on either a multilateral or regional-group basis; (2) national fiscal or other measures for limiting the scale of marketing; and (3) policies limiting restrictive use of technology-transfer agreements, patent and trade-mark licences, and so on. If these things are done, the market system can work tolerably well and can economise bureaucracy while giving it a vital and efficient role in the mixed economy.

There is a very real need to ask some more fundamental questions about the purpose of integration schemes. I believe that the three papers we have heard here, and indeed many of the traditional treatises on international integration, are less clear than they might be on the objectives of integration and, consequently, on the criteria by which the success of particular schemes should be judged. In many discussions it appears to be assumed that integration is a goal in itself. The logic of that view is that all member countries should be merged into one. Clearly, this could not be *generally* supported in either Eastern or Western Europe, and certainly not in the integration schemes of the developing world. Thus the emphasis has been upon full *economic* integration, presumably because this carries with it identifiable benefits in the form of economies of specialisation, scale economies both in production and in the development of industrial technology and management skills, and so on. Many, if not most, of these benefits can be derived from simple free trade – the absence of artificial restrictions upon the exchange of goods. Movement of labour, of capital, and of management skills can also bring benefits, but it would appear from both West and East European experience that the major gains from such movements have very often emerged from relationships between member and nonmember (or associate member) countries of integration schemes, probably because differences in unit cost of labour and capital are likely already to be relatively small among full-member countries of integration groups.

The benefits of stages of integration that go beyond the common market raise a series of questions about the elements of harmonisation that are really necessary. There is a considerable literature on policy harmonisation and a consensus has not emerged. It is clear from both theory and practice that elements of harmonisation of fiscal and monetary policies are desirable. It is not clear, however, what specific institutions are required to achieve this harmonisation, because the crucial point is whether the member countries are all similarly motivated by, for example, a concern for substantially full employment and the avoidance of serious inflation. The particular problem of recent years in macro-policy has been the achievement of optimum flexibility, especially among market economies and notably in exchange relationships. This policy issue changes very little whether one focuses on the relations among members of the EEC or between them and the United States. The fact is that international monetary problems are not really amenable to purely regional solutions unless the regional group has almost prohibitive barriers on the import of goods and capital.

Other national policies posing harmonisation problems are those that affect the competitive position of industry – for instance, commodity taxes, or subsidies to regions or factors of production. These taxes and subsidies occur whether we are speaking of private or of state-owned enterprise. Such policies can affect the competitive position of particular industries relative to those in other member countries. Governments and the countries they represent may have different preferences concerning the distribution of the tax burden, the support of less well-endowed regions, and so on. The effect of many policies of this kind is often to handicap industries in international trade, or to compensate for their inefficiency or high-cost location. Only when government is seen to subsidise an industry enough to undermine a more efficient external supplier is there likely to be direct conflict between trading partners. In any case, countries tend to accept most international differences in social policy and to pay the consequences of their own policy.

All of these comments are meant to illustrate the point that social and political considerations may be important enough to justify a sacrifice of the economic benefits of integration. Only rarely are political and social factors strongly for international integration. The circumstances·of the early post-war decades, during which both of the major European groups were established, witnessed stronger political forces favouring integration than have been typical of more normal, peacetime conditions, under which it could reasonably be expected that, on balance, such forces would operate in the opposite direction. It seems to me to be most reasonable to build the dynamics of integration analysis around an equilibrium conception that there is a degree or level of integration that is optimal for any grouping, and that, when an association of countries moves toward closer integration, such a move will be sustained only if the net social benefits are positive and if it is both possible and practical to compensate any member that may otherwise suffer losses. It seems to me that, if this process results in partial integration, and the degree of integration stabilises at some level, it would be unwise to conclude that integration has failed. If it can be demonstrated that all of the major benefits of integration have been achieved with limited cost by the time an association has achieved a customs union or a common market, why should one expect the momentum toward closer integration to be sustained?

This leads us to the question of what considerations will govern how far a group of related countries will go along the route to complete economic (or political) union.

Among the conditions that will determine the equilibrium level for any given grouping are the size and political importance of the various members. In general, smaller countries will derive much larger relative economic advantages from integration, while larger countries will be interested in strengthening their political influence and in sharing in the economic gains. The political factor is likely to generate some tension between larger and smaller member countries.

The stage of development may also affect attitudes toward the net benefits of integration. Although developing countries, especially smaller ones, may find integration strongly attractive economically, they are also likely to be very hesitant about derogation of sovereignty, as they may overvalue the scope for the exercise of political independence in economic matters, especially if their independence has only just been achieved.

Thus one may conclude that a group of small or medium sized developed countries probably will opt for a higher degree of integration than will a group of countries of very unequal size. A lesser degree of integration may emerge also if the members are at relatively early stages of development. In all cases, of course, major benefits of one kind (notably economic) may overwhelm political costs. But the fundamental point is that the success of integration schemes probably should be judged by their success in achieving the equilibrium level appropriate for them, as broadly defined above. Their success might not be hampered by unrealistic expectations if this approach were more widely taken. To relate these comments directly to the concerns of this working group, I feel that the considerations I have cited are more likely to affect the nature and success of an integration scheme than is the fact of the predominance of either centrally-planned or enterprise-planned economies. An integration scheme forces either type of economy to plan more realistically and to manage more efficiently.

It is tempting to go through the papers before us to point out how this analysis may be affected by the approach here suggested. But to avoid extending this opening statement, I shall leave that task to you. To cite only one illustration, I think my approach takes much of the substance out of the debate about the desirability of supranational institutions. It may well be that that issue is not settled for the EEC in the same way as for the CMEA — not because higher institutional levels of integration should not be taken as superior to lower levels, but perhaps because they are more appropriate for one set of political—economic conditions than for another. All of this indicates that we need to have more empirical work on the magnitude of marginal economic benefits from higher levels of integration, and if possible, on related non-economic costs or benefits.

I have one further brief comment. When I saw the theme given to this Working Group I thought that there might be some discussion of the problems and prospects of integration among countries with different economic systems. I have had some direct experience with one such situation, the East African Community, in which one member is a stronghold of African socialism, another is largely private-enterprise-oriented, and the third is following a somewhat uncertain middle course. I discovered that national political instability is a much greater threat to the success of such a scheme than any ideological difference is likely to be. The EAC is a group in which no individual member is either large enough or rich enough to contemplate self-sufficient development or to be influenced by a motive to maintain part of the integration bequeathed by a colonial power.

I hope that the discussions of this topic will pay some attention to the lessons to be learned from developing-country experiments in integration, which are of great relative importance to the countries involved, even if the absolute impact on the world economy cannot match that of the European schemes.

Report on Group Discussion
Béla Csikós-Nagy (Hungary)

The discussion in Working Group I showed great interest in the problems of regional integration through planning and by market forces. The number of participants varied between 150 and 300, a total of thirty-five speakers asking for the floor. It would be impossible here to report on all the problems raised and opinions expressed in the discussions. I think I can best meet the expectations of the congress if I confine myself to only the most important issues discussed, if I attempt to characterise the discussion from only a few aspects, and if I try to sum up the most important conclusions with respect to future research.

There is, however, one comment to be made in advance. It is regrettable that only a few economists from the developing world participated in the work of our group. They obviously assumed that the group was to deal particularly with European problems: with a comparative analysis of the economic mechanisms of the CMEA and the EEC, respectively. True, this was the predominant theme of the discussions in the group, although the Programme Committee of the congress specified a general subject — namely, to examine what role is being played by planning and by the market in the economic integration process. To have examined this problem on a world level would have been the most desirable way of treating it, because it could have clarified the differentiating effect of the market on economic growth, and it could have clarified to what extent government planning can be an efficient tool for keeping abreast of general economic development. In the discussions, many speakers pointed out that the differences in the stages of development of the European socialist countries co-operating within the CMEA have been greatly reduced in the last twenty-five years, and that this could never have happened if 'market integration' alone had been applied.

As a matter of fact, however, it was to be expected that most economists, at this congress at least, would study the planning and market models on the basis of the two major prototypes of European economic integration. This is how Bogomolov designed his main paper, and Haberler and Hardt their discussion paper. Thus, throughout the discussions the problems of the economic integration attained so far within the CMEA and the EEC were the focal points of attention.

In the work of our group many dealt with a thesis expressed by Balassa in connection with the various types of integration. He had compared 'market integration' and 'production and development integration', and outlined the preconditions under which 'production and development integration' might be transformed into 'market integration'. Many participants shared Bogomolov's opinion that the planning methods of CMEA integration simply cannot be compared with the market techniques of Western integration. Socialist economic planning presumes the development of commodity and money relations both within the individual socialist countries and among them. These elements can be considered, both on a national and on an international level, as indispensable in a planned development of the economy. Similarly, West European integration cannot be interpreted as merely an automatic international system based exclusively on market conditions. In the case of the

EEC, the problem is rather how and what limitations should and could be applied by government intervention in the process of integration.

Many in our group became convinced that the development of economic and political co-ordination in the Western countries and the utilisation of commodity and money relations within the CMEA simply cannot provide a satisfactory or acceptable basis for a convergence of the two different socio-economic systems. These trends will never change or modify the two systems in their essence, which for one is public ownership and for the other is private ownership of the means of production. This difference pervades the economic mechanisms of the two systems.

The discussions in our working group contributed to a better mutual understanding among economists expressing fundamentally different opinions. Economists favouring either a socialist planned economy or a capitalist market economy re-examined their positions rather realistically. They all know that there is quite a difference between any ideal model and the actual situation. They know also that the actual working of any economic mechanism could be improved and, finally, that general socio-economic development will continuously generate new problems, which must be answered with the help of scientific research.

You may wonder what questions the Western and Eastern participants wanted to have answered by their counterparts. Western economists mainly asked questions about economic efficiency in the process of socialist integration based on plan co-ordination. Here the role played by prices in the socialist economy was the focal point of attention. This part of the discussion was largely based on the discussion paper by Trzeciakowski and Mycielski of Poland, who introduced two, alternative models. In one model, the socialist countries carry on their planned activities independently of one another; in the other, joint planning is pursued. Both these models provide for an optimum solution through exchange rates and prices, respectively. In the course of the discussion, the authors emphasised that good use can be made of these models in regulations based on both planned directives and economic instruments. In one case, the exchange rate reflects the average value of the foreign exchange, whereas the price represents the national input. In the other case, the exchange rate is adjusted to the marginal value, whereas the price reflects the relative scarcity of the product concerned.

In connection with this thesis, many pointed out that, although it illustrates feasible alternatives, it surely does not depict the actual situation. Reference was made also to the fact that, instead of working with fixed or frozen prices, the market system has the advantage of price flexibility, so that relative prices are being properly adjusted to structural, technological changes.

In connection with the discussion of the price systems of socialist countries, I should like to call attention to a few important points. It will no doubt be remembered that, immediately after the creation of the Soviet Union, Ludwig Mises published his famous challenge to socialist economists, claiming that socialisation of the means of production would make economic calculation impossible. He wanted to prove that without private ownership of the means of production there would be no free market based on competition, and that without such a free market there would be no price mechanism; as a result, the preconditions of economic rationality would be missing. The Lange—Lerner solution of this problem is well known. In the 1930s Oskar Lange, a Polish economist, showed that there can be economic rationality in socialism, but that it has to be adapted to the framework of government planning. Now, in connection with socialist economic interpretation, similar planning techniques with the use of prices have been introduced, again by Polish economists.

With all this I want to emphasise that in socialism the debates about prices are not debates about plan *versus* market, regarded as alternatives. The essential question is what role prices should play in national planning. On the national level the debate is about state planning, and on the level of the CMEA it is about the criteria that are the basis of planned co-ordination. When, in socialist countries, economists speak about the activation of 'commodity and money relations', they primarily have in mind the strengthening of the scientific basis of national planning and the perfecting of purposeful development.

Economists from the CMEA countries, analysing the problems of integration in the EEC, pointed to various disturbances in the market mechanism. In our working group, their attention was directed to inflation and to the uneven de-development of the different countries. They pointed out that, under inflationary conditions, prices cannot operate as suitable guides for economic decisions and that the development lags or income gaps of certain countries and regions create social tensions. Western economists freely admitted that the controlling role of the free-market mechanism has been diminishing in several countries with market systems. Haberler formulated this by stating that these countries have 'mixed' economies, in which the role of the state and of governmental economic policies is assuming increasing importance.

An urgent question for economists — socialist, capitalist, mixed, or neutral — is whether it is possible to find up-to-date ways of achieving a greater measure of international division of labour between different socio-economic systems. Can we expand international economic relations, even though in one country it is the plan and in another it is the market that plays the dominant role in guiding economic processes? I have the impression, indeed the conviction, that after the discussions in our working group the prospects for a realistic approach to intensive division of labour among countries of different socio-political systems have improved. Let us hope that research will help to develop new ways to achieve this common objective.

I wish to emphasise the great significance of this congress and of our discussions, because in the main paper prepared for our working group and in the first discussion paper we were offered radically different judgements. Bogomolov said that the system of co-operation in the CMEA caused fewer difficulties in the organisation of a European-wide co-operation than does the EEC, with its customs barriers discriminating against nonmember countries. Haberler, on the other hand, pointed out that each and every regional integration is, of necessity, discriminatory against countries outside. He added that the difference in this respect between the EEC and the CMEA is a difference only in the manifest forms, in the institutional character. In his opinion, in a socialist economy the state monopoly of foreign trade is equally a manifestation of discrimination. It is also discrimination in that users of materials, semi-finished goods and final products have no freedom of decision in selecting the alternatives most favourable to them. Among other things, there is no freedom of decision as to where to buy whatever may be needed or wanted from the domestic or the world market and, in the latter case, from which country.

In Europe, both the socialist and the capitalist socio-economic systems are realities. European societies, with respect to their objectives and the instruments used to implement them, differ radically from one another. These are real (objective) differences because the different societies are controlled by intrinsic laws of development. And, if this is so, the economic control system of any society cannot be judged according to alien criteria. The economists of the socialist countries cannot make it a condition of the intensive division of labour with capitalist countries that the latter should abolish private property and introduce planned economy. By the same token, the economists of Western countries must not link up the intensification of the division of labour with socialist countries with the abolition of socialist property and with the introduction of a market economy. If we really strive to achieve co-operation, we must all become acquainted with the intrinsic laws that make these societies operate. Otherwise, the co-operation would be subject to unrealistic conditions and we would ultimately deny the possibility of peaceful coexistence of countries having dissimilar socio-economic systems.

The discussions in working group I have shown that in international negotiations (as, for example, in the GATT) the conceptual framework within which the parties think, reason and argue has failed to adapt to the fact that there is no longer a homogeneous world economy, but that there have evolved different socio-economic systems, the coexistence of which calls for other concepts if our discourse is to make good sense.

We need not, however, give up hope for a better mutual understanding. The members of Working Group I were in substantial agreement on the maxim that regional integrations should not lead to closed blocs. They saw eye to eye in insisting that each regional integration should develop an economic mechanism that will promote the widest possible international division of labour in order to make the economies more efficient. And I believe that this is the essential thing. Thus, I think that the decision of the Executive Committee of International Economic Association was right when it selected the economic relations of countries living under different socio-economic systems as the subject of a future conference. At the present congress it has been possible only to touch on this problem. The planned conference could set itself the task, after the necessary scientific preparation, to make the greatest possible contribution to the evolution of modern forms of rational co-operation among countries living under different social and economic conditions.

13   World Trade and Intraregional Trade: Trends and Structural Changes (Main Paper, Working Group J)

Gunther Kohlmey (GERMAN DEMOCRATIC REPUBLIC)

I.

Problems of international, intraregional, and subregional trade may be approached from three methodological points of view: the sociological, socio-economic method; the method of pure economic theory; and the historical – empirical method, including analyses of international economic policies and institutions. Each of these approaches is useful for specific purposes. In this paper, elements of all three are used to tackle at least some of the main features of our broad subject, the analysis of general aspects of post-war development and future trends in intraregional and international trade. The thesis of this analysis is that in the early 1970s the world economy and world trade entered a new phase of development.

II.

During the last three decades, increasing changes caused by socialism – and working in its favour – have become qualitatively the characteristic feature of international economic relations, though quantitatively these changes have not yet always been sufficiently effective.

This point should be stressed again, because twenty – and even ten or five – years ago several economists were of the opinion that something like an 'Eastern world' existed but that it would not raise new questions for the theory of international trade. Meanwhile, things have changed, as is proved for instance by the topics being discussed at this congress. With the growth of the international socialist system, many new problems have arisen, not only for international economic policies but also for the theory of international trade. Old-fashioned ideas about free-market forces functioning as basic parameters for models of international economic relations are as unsuitable for solving these new problems as they were for solving the old ones.

The part socialist countries play in the world economy has grown swiftly. For example, the CMEA countries' proportion of world industrial output rose

from 18 per cent in 1950 to approximately 33 per cent in 1972.[1] As will be
seen from the following percentages, the CMEA countries also ranked first as
regards the average annual rates of growth of their per capita national income:

	1961–5	1966–70
World	3·2	3·4
Developed market economies	4·2	3·9
Developing market economies	1·5	2·7
CMEA countries	4·7	6·4

The CMEA countries' proportion of world trade (quantum index) rose
from an average of 9·5 per cent over the 1956–60 period to 10·8 per cent in
1961–65 and to nearly 12 per cent in 1973. In that same year, their share in
the value of world exports (current prices) amounted to only 9·5 per cent.
The inflationary increases of market prices in the capitalist world accounts for
the difference. Foreign-trade price changes in intra-CMEA trade and price
changes in the international capitalist markets did not differ very much from
each other from the latter half of the 1950s until 1968, but for 1969 onward
it is necessary, when computing the socialist countries' share in world trade,
to take into account the rates of inflation in capitalist markets.

That commodities worth approximately $70,000 million (at current ex-
change rates) were traded at nearly *stable* prices among all socialist countries
in 1973 is noteworthy in these days of inflation, price instability, monetary
crises, and speculations in capital markets. This trade accounts for about 10
per cent of world trade. The stability of socialist foreign-exchange relations
should also be emphasised.[2]

A few years ago, it became possible for the CMEA countries to make gains
in economic integration in order to obtain greater advantages from a division
of labour among participating countries.[3] Under socialism, social ownership
of the means of production allows partners with equal rights to implement
economic integration in a comprehensive manner on the basis of central planning and long-term agreements. The measures taken generally embrace the
entire reproduction cycle in selected sectors of participating economies –

[1] Unless otherwise indicated, all data in this paper are based on the author's calculations
from information in UN, *Statistical Yearbook* and *Monthly Bulletin of Statistics*;
Sodruzhestvo Sotsialisticheskoe ('Socialist Community'; Moscow, 1973); *Statisticheski
ezhegodnik stran-chlenov S. V.* ('Statistical Yearbook' of CMEA Countries'; Moscow,
several editions); *Narodnoe Khoziaistvo SSSR. Statisticheskii ezhegodnik* ('Economy of
the USSR Statistical Yearbook'; Moscow, several editions).

[2] The gold content of the common currency of CMEA countries, the transferable
rouble, as well as its exchange rates with currencies of member and nonmember countries,
are agreed upon by the partners. Naturally, changes are also agreed upon.

[3] CMEA *Comprehensive Programme for the Further Extension and Improvement of
Cooperation and the Development of Socialist Economic Integration by the CMEA
Member Countries* (Moscow, 1971).

from basic research, through investment and production, to marketing. Bilateral or multilateral centres co-ordinate work on important research subjects. There are also multinational research and production organisations and joint enterprises, with all the advantages of co-ordinated (or unified) planning. In these institutions, scientific–technical councils work out the required scientific, technological, and economic strategies: they plan joint and co-ordinated research projects; they design work and set up common standards; they co-ordinate investments, international specialisation and co-operation in production, purchases, sales and technical services. Thus, joint planning and a common technological policy are developing in selected sectors. The sphere of responsibility of enterprises and other economic organisations is growing within and among the national economies concerned and an economic mechanism adapted to this integration needs to be further developed.

Thanks to their own efforts and to mutual co-operation, the CMEA members have made progress in reducing the originally large disparities among them in terms of level of technological and economic development (see Table 1). If each country's national income per capita in 1960 equals 100, then for 1972 the index for Romania stood at 246, for Bulgaria at 221, for Yugoslavia at 191, for Poland at 190, for the USSR at 189, for Hungary at 183, for the GDR at 171, for Czechoslovakia at 161, and for Mongolia at 106. With the exception of the Mongolian People's Republic, the countries that were originally the least developed have experienced the highest growth rates. In the case of Mongolia, a comprehensive plan aimed at promoting the republic's economic development has been launched within the framework of the CMEA countries' programme of integration.

The changes in the ratios of machinery exports to machinery imports (see Table 2) clearly indicate the levelling processes that have taken place within

TABLE 1

PROGRESS IN REDUCING DISPARITIES AMONG CMEA COUNTRIES
IN TERMS OF PER CAPITA LEVELS OF ECONOMIC DEVELOPMENT
(USSR = 100)

Country	National Income		Industrial Production		Agricultural Production	
	1950	1970	1950	1970	1950	1970
Bulgaria	60	96	43	82	84	113
Hungary	119	81	78	71	165	132
GDR	131	135	136	154	84	106
Poland	114	81	70	73	169	120
Romania	55	70	31	57	78	80
Czechoslovakia	172	109	143	110	120	92

Source: J. N. Beliaiev and L. S. Semionova *Socialist Integration and World Economy* (Moscow, 1972), p. 76, (text in Russian)

TABLE 2

RATIO OF MACHINERY EXPORTS TO MACHINERY IMPORTS OF
EUROPEAN CMEA COUNTRIES 1955–72
(imports = 1)

Country	1955	1960	1965	1970	1972
Bulgaria	0·05	0·28	0·57	0·78	0·77
Czechoslovakia	3·65	2·21	1·63	1·54	1·54
GDR	14·10[a]	3·85	2·98	1·40	1·67
Hungary	2·76	1·23	1·16	0·98	1·01
Poland	0·42	0·92	1·00	1·04	0·93
Romania	0·15	0·57	0·49	0·54	0·54
USSR	0·65	0·68	0·61	0·67	0·65

[a]Metal manufacturing industry.

Souces: Calculations based on data contained in the Statistical Yearbook of the CMEA countries, 1971 and 1972; and *Statistisches Jahrbuch
der DDR,* 1955.

the CMEA region. Corresponding to this development, the percentage of foodstuffs, raw materials and fuels traded among the CMEA countries dropped
from an average of 42 in the 1956–60 period to 27 in 1966–70, while the
machinery percentage rose from 29 to 37.

III.

Post-war intraregional and international trade in the non-socialist sector of the
world economy has been characterised primarily by the following developments.

(1) The anti-colonial liberation struggle and the well-nigh complete elimination of the old colonial empires have led to breaks in and transformations of
economic relations between former colonies and 'mother countries', and the
consequent emergence of several new flows of international trade.

(2) The developing countries have been growing. They have appeared on
the international trade scene and at international conferences with essentially
unified proposals, even though politically and economically they differ considerably from each other and the differences are increasing.

The share of the developing countries in world industrial output (national
shares differ widely) has risen slightly, but for most of these countries economic
relations with the capitalist world have not been a source of growth, development and social welfare.

Foreign capital controls a large part of the output and foreign trade of the
developing countries. The dual-economy system has been extended. It is
estimated that, on average, multinational-corporation exchanges account for

over 30 per cent of the foreign trade of the developing countries,[4] whose share in world trade has dropped steadily. Both their debts and their debt services have increased sharply. Their public and private debts rocketed by an annual average of about 15 per cent during the 1960s, while debt services went up by about 10·5 per cent. On the other hand, their exports increased by approximately only 7 per cent.[5] Regionally and structurally, these aggregate processes were highly disproportionate. Phenomena of a 'decapitalisation' of developing countries are exemplified by the following figures (in millions of US dollars):[6]

	1960	1970
Direct private US investments in developing countries	210	956
Profits	1835	3688
Reinvestments	358	575
Distributed profits	1506	3115

Trade among the developing countries dropped from 4·8 per cent of world exports in 1960 to 3·4 per cent in 1970.[7] Their customs unions, economic communities and attempts at integration met with only a modicum of success. Their share in the foreign trade of developed capitalist countries declined from 29 per cent in 1955 to about 18 per cent in 1970.

Although for historical reasons still small, the share of socialist countries in the foreign trade of the developing countries increased during the 1960s. The average annual growth rate of exports from developing countries to centrally planned economies was higher (8·6 per cent) than the rate of growth of their exports to the United States (5·3 per cent), to the EEC of the Six (8·0 per cent), and to EFTA (4·1 per cent).[8] We can draw the conclusion that the imperialist policy of keeping a large number of peoples and economies underdeveloped was and is one of the strongest impediments to world trade.[9]

(3) The free-trade era during the second half of the nineteenth century was based on the hegemony of Great Britain. Similarly, after the Second World War the capitalist sector of the world economy was dominated by the United States. The Bretton Woods system functioned on this basis. It became possible, to a certain degree, to liberalise international capital movements and (within the framework of the GATT) international trade of capitalist countries. At

---

[4] *International Trade Information Bulletin,* Moscow, 29 Dec 1973.
[5] World Bank–IDA Reports; UN, *Statistical Yearbook.*
[6] *Survey of Current Business,* Aug 1962 and Oct 1971.
[7] UN, *Yearbook of International Trade Statistics and Monthly Bulletin of Statistics.*
[8] Ibid.
[9] Cf. the Political Declaration of the Fourth Summit of Non-Aligned States, Sep 1973. German text in *Asien, Afrika, Lateinamerika,* no. 1, 1974, pp. 45 ff.

the same time, capitalist governments and the giant corporations introduced more and more economic regulations indirectly affecting foreign trade. The growing economic strength of the competitors of the United States was paralleled by the extension of nontariff and exchange regulations. This led to the breakdown of the Bretton Woods mechanism, the international monetary crisis, and speculations on short-term capital movements,[10] which gave rise to well-known deformations and conflicts in the capitalist sector of world trade.

(4) In the post-war era the capitalist sector of the world economy has witnessed the emergence of a new phenomenon in the form of integrated regional blocs of developed capitalist economies. These blocs signal not only a new internationalisation of economies, but also a new linkage between imperialist policies and international economic relations, as is evidenced by the connections between the EEC and NATO.

In contrast to the case with the CMEA region (see Section V.2 below), intra-EE trade showed a conspicuous increase over EEC trade with third countries. Past and present regulations discriminating against socialist states and developing countries are another disturbance factor in international economic relations.[11]

(5) The swift growth and expansion of the sphere of influence of transnational corporations, particularly of the American multinationals, introduced another new form of international economic integration . But it was also another disturbance factor for international economic relations. These corporations are multi- or transnational not through ownership and management, but through their affiliates, spheres of influence, and economic operations.

While the CMEA member countries secured their sphere of integration against infiltration by the transnational corporations, the latter consolidated their positions in many developing countries and brought about a further economic interlocking of the developed capitalist economies. As vertically integrated corporations, they have a disintegrating effect on the horizontal integration of regional groupings such as the EEC. They have created monopolistic and oligopolistic market situations and, at the same time, have sharpened international competition: 'While their operations are often global, their interests are corporate . . . their predominance can often create monopolistic structures which reduce world efficiency and may displace or prevent alternative activities.'[12]

According to UN estimates on multinational corporations, the 1971 output of these concerns was worth approximately $330,000 million and thus topped by about 32 per cent the sum the developed capitalist economies realised through their exports. International trade *within* the multinationals accounts

---

[10] The *Economic Report of the President of the United States* mentions (p. 116) Jan 1973 'short-term capital movements, which recorded a net inflow of $0·09 billion at an annual rate in the first three quarters of 1972 compared to a net outflow of $10·2 billion in 1971'.

[11] Cf. Section XI of the Economic Declaration of the Fourth Summit.

[12] UN, *Multinational Corporations in World Development* (ST/ECA/190; New York, 1973), p. 2.

for over 15 per cent of nonsocialist world trade. (According to other estimates it accounts for 25–30 per cent.) In the capitalist sector of the world economy, a substantial proportion of international trade is therefore *direct* intracorporation trade (and, of course, far more is indirect).

During the 1960s, the multinational corporations intensified their influence on nonsocialist international trade. For example, affiliates of American manufacturing corporations boosted their foreign trade by 225 per cent, from $23,600 million in 1960 to $76,800 million in 1970. Over the same period, the export of American manufactured goods soared by 138 per cent, from $12,300 million to $29,300 million.[13]

The multinationals *exploit* the differences in national laws and regulations (wage and social policy, finance and tax policy, price and currency policy) and at the same time *influence* these policies and laws. Because 'the decision centres of the multinational corporations lie outside the range of possible territorial action',[14] they undermine the economic independence and political sovereignty of other countries, particularly the economically weak ones. The multinationals were, and are, among the main forces of neocolonialism.

(6) Old and new forms of national and international exploitation underlie the economic power of the big capitalist countries and the expansion of their influence on capitalist international trade; in 1955, 58·3 per cent of it was trade of the United States and Western Europe, and this percentage increased to 67·1 in 1972.

The new forms of international exploitation include: (a) the temporary or permanent employment of immigrants, a foreign labour force that enjoys neither equal rights nor equal treatment; (b) the 'Brain Drain', as a special type of this immigration; (c) the waste of natural resources and the purchase of low-priced foodstuffs, raw materials and fuel from developing countries; (d) the employment of cheap labour by foreign enterprises in developing countries (here, the ratio of output to wage is in some cases higher than in developed capitalist countries); and (e) the draining-off of profits from developing countries, with terms of trade and monetary crises aggravating the drain.

(7) Other important factors that have disturbed international trade during the past two or three decades include: imperialist local aggressions; antinational, antidemocratic and antisocialist actions; and a variety of other discriminatory acts. Each of these factors has interfered with the functions of international trade, functions that are peaceful and conducive to social welfare.[15] From this it follows that proposals for more rational international economic relations should be combined with programmes for *détente* and peaceful international co-operation based on equal rights for each partner.

(8) Although imperialist political and socio-economic policies deformed and

[13] P. G. Peterson, *The United States in the Changing World Economy* (Washington, 1972), chart 57.
[14] EEC experts, quoted from *Handelsblatt*, Düsseldorf, 5 July 1973.
[15] Cf. Section A·5 of UN General Assembly Resolution of 24 Oct 1970, document 2626 (XXV) in UN, *Second Decade of Development*.

obstructed the historical trend towards further internationalisation of economic
life, post-war international trade, strengthened by the application of science
and technology to modern large-scale production, developed more quickly than
did national income and industrial output.

Exact and comparable data are not always available, but it can be said that
international capital movements, services, transfers of knowledge (know-how,
technology, licences, and so on), and tourism increased about as quickly as did
international trade.

IV.

A slight generalisation of the outlines presented in sections II and III above
indicates manifold interdependences and contradictions in the current development of international trade.

(1) Marx's formulation of the fundamental economic dialectics of productive forces and production relations is manifested in present-day world trade
in two trends, one toward further general internationalisation of production
and the economy, accompanied by the extension and intensification of an
international division of labour and international trade, and the other toward
socio-economic differentiation and determination of these processes, derived
from given production relations and social structures.

(2) In today's world economy we observe the contradictory process of the
further emergence and consolidation of independent nations with complex
national economies, on the one hand, and of closer connections among peoples
and national economies, on the other.

In CMEA co-operation, the formation and consolidation of *socialist* nations,
states and national economies goes hand in hand with the association of member countries. This implies the gradual reduction of differences in their economic levels and the integration of their national economies.

In many developing countries, the struggle against the neocolonial alienation
of peoples has resulted in the formation of free nations and in the consolidation
of their autonomous, complex national economies. Internationalisation by large
corporations that profit by underdevelopment spells world economic alienation;
internationalisation by equality-based co-operation and mutual assistance spells
the linkage of peoples. Hence, it is untenable to maintain that at the present
time nations and national forms are static, while international corporations are
dynamic.

(3) With the new processes of internationalisation of production, both the
formation and the exchange of international values are given new foundations,
driving forces and forms, and the same holds true for the utilisation of comparative advantages by the international division of labour and foreign trade: In
the absence of international mobility of production factors, comparative advantages are utilised via foreign trade only. When there is international mobility
of one or several production factors, the international transfer of knowledge

is an important aspect.[16] International values are formed by international research institutions and enterprises.

These new processes of formation and realisation of international values give rise to new foreign-trade functions that become operative primarily in integration processes. These include: (a) the exchange not only of raw materials and of final products, but also, and increasingly, of components, modules, parts, subproducts, hardware, and so on, within the framework of international specialisation and co-operation in production; (b) dealings in connection with international movements of production factors, such as granting and payment of credits, participation in investments, and the international transfer of knowledge in various forms; and (c) sales of shares in joint institutions, as well as the purchase and sale of multinational enterprises.

(4) The dialectics of intraregional and international trade *derives* from (1), (2), and (3); that is, it is a *secondary* dialectic. The regional is but an attribute of the socio-economic. The valuation of processes of bilateralism (for example, bilateral co-operation in production), intraregional relations and international trade is entirely dependent on their socio-economic nature and effectiveness, on their functions in the development of equality-based international economic relations, and on the promotion of economic growth and living standards.

V.

To extrapolate developments into the next fifteen or twenty years is impossible in these times of international, socio-economic and political change and of structural transformations of international economic relations. Nevertheless, some future trends in the development of international and intraregional trade can be tentatively mapped out.

(1) Qualitatively and quantitatively, socialist countries will enlarge their share and influence in international economic relations. The technological and economic potential of the CMEA countries will be strengthened by economic integration. The integration functions of the intrasystem trade mentioned in Section IV.3 will be extended and thereby cause improvement in exports of manufactured products. The growth rate of foreign trade, only somewhat higher than that of industry and national income during the second half of the 1960s, increased between 1969 to 1972 and is due to increase still further.

This development is caused by increased industrialisation in hitherto less developed socialist economies and by increased international division of labour. If we formalise the data presented in Table 3, the ratios of changes in exports and imports to changes in production will be seen to cover three phases.

First phase. The introduction of industrialisation causes an intensely growing import demand (investment goods, raw materials, fuels) and a (generally slower) increase in exports to pay for imports (primarily agricultural products, raw materials, and simple manufactured goods).

[16] Harry G. Johnson spoke on this subject at the Third IEA World Congress, Montreal, Sep 1968.

Second phase. Developing industries satisfy an increasing proportion of the domestic demand for investment and consumer goods, but the new industries can compete very little as yet in foreign markets. As a result, the growth rate of foreign trade relative to that of industrial production declines for a time.

Third phase. Industries are effective enough to compete in the international field; international industrial co-operation and specialisation are now possible and necessary; as a corollary, substitutional foreign trade begins to dominate and, consequently, foreign trade again intensifies.

(2) On the basis of socialist economic integration and within the framework of the policy of peaceful coexistence, CMEA trade with nonsocialist economies should at first increase somewhat more quickly than does intra-CMEA trade, and then grow at about the same rate as the latter (quantum index).

TABLE 3

GROWTH RATES OF INDUSTRIAL PRODUCTION AND FOREIGN TRADE OF
EUROPEAN CMEA COUNTRIES, 1951–1972 (per cent)

Period	Industrial production	Exports and imports
1951–5	89	89
1956–60	62	77
1961–5	49	49
1966–70	48	54
1971–2	24	25

Sources: Calculations for 1951–70 are based on *Sodruzhestvo sotsialisticheskoe* 'Socialist Community'; (Moscow 1973), p. 740 and appendix, Table 1. Those for 1971–2 are based on UN statistics.

The percentage share of nonsocialist countries in the total foreign trade of the CMEA states has been as follows: 1956–60, 25·0; 1961–5, 29·5; 1966–70, 34·2; 1970, 35·1; 1971, 35·9; 1972, 33·2.[17] Table 4 lists the annual rates of growth of the foreign trade of the CMEA countries with various other regions.

The concept of *ex ante* (or *ex post*) autarky of the socialist national economy and the CMEA community as a whole[18] already stands corrected by practice and is theoretically untenable.

Activities of the socialist countries in East–West trade could be extended[19] if various Western authorities would give up their insistence

[17] Calculated on the basis of the Statistical Yearbook of CMEA Countries, Moscow, 1973, and the UN, *Monthly Bulletin of Statistics.*

[18] Cf., for instance, the contributions of several American economists in *International Trade and Central Planning*, ed. A. A. Brown and E. Neuberger (Berkeley and Los Angeles, 1968).

[19] If there had been no cold war and no other impediments to East–West trade, export structures of CMEA countries could have been improved earlier. Also, the differences between their level of technological development and that of Western industrial countries could have been reduced more quickly.

that most-favoured nation treatment cannot be applied to socialist states, and if other Western impediments to trade were removed. Exports and imports of centrally planned economies in overall East–West trade could increase from approximately $22·5 billion in 1972 to about $80·0 billion and more in 1985 (assuming unchanged exchange rates and prices). Such a development would also be important for security and *détente* in Europe.[20] Trade between CMEA and capitalist countries should not remain restricted to final products only; the exchange should also serve the expansion of co-operation in scientific, technical and production areas. New institutional forms could be introduced, such as the international economic organisations of the CMEA states that were mentioned in Section II above.[21]

(3) Whereas foreign trade among the CMEA countries rose by an average of 9 per cent per annum from 1961 to 1965 and by an average of 8·2 per cent per annum from 1966 to 1970, trade among CMEA and developing countries rose over the same two periods by 17·4 and 11·2 per cent respectively (see Table 4).

TABLE 4

FOREIGN TRADE FLOWS OF CMEA COUNTRIES, 1956–72:
ANNUAL RATES OF GROWTH OF EXPORTS AND IMPORTS
(PER CENT, CURRENT PRICES)

Period	Total	Between European CMEA countries	With other socialist countries	With developed market economies	With developing market economies
1956–60	10·9	10·9	4·9	13·5	17·6
1961–5	8·4	9·0	−14·0	10·1	17·4
1966–70	8·7	8·2	3·2	11·3	11·2
1968	9·1	10·9	8·5	6·7	5·1
1969	10·4	9·0	3·2	13·3	13·0
1970	11·0	10·7	5·2	11·3	13·3
1971	9·0	9·1	20·6	11·0	2·0
1972	18·4	20·6	3·3	14·6	17·7

Sources: UN, *Yearbook of International Trade Statistics*, and *Monthly Bulletin of Statistics.*
Notes: Trade with People's Republics in Asia and between the GDR and the Federal Republic of Germany is not included.

Percentages for 1956–70 are averages for each of the five-year periods in question.

The UN statistics count Yugoslavia among the developed market economies and Cuba among the developing market economies.

[20] Cf. the draft of a joint statement (by Hungary and the GDR) on the development of co-operation in the fields of economy, trade, science and technology, and in the field of environment protection. This was presented in Helsinki in July 1973 during the first stage of the Conference on Security and Co-operation in Europe.

[21] A different form of organisation was chosen for the Agreement on Co-operation between the CMEA and Finland, dated May 1973. (Cf. *Foreign Trade, Moscow*, no. 10, 1973).

The two rates of growth will continue to differ, although in 1971 trade between CMEA and developing countries rose by only about 1 per cent. In the *First Over-all Review and Appraisal of Progress during the Second United Nations Development Decade,* issued by the UN Department of Economic and Social Affairs, it was assumed that this was a 'a trend for the Eastern European countries'[22] and that in the CMEA and in the EEC there are 'similar uncertainties regarding the prospects for imports from developing countries'.[23] But such an assumption does not correspond with the principles of socialist policy towards the developing countries and ignores the economic co-operation that has been taking place between the CMEA and the developing countries. Furthermore, the growth rate of foreign trade between centrally planned economies and developing countries was nearly 20 per cent in 1972 and 28 per cent in 1973.

In 1970–2, nearly 10 per cent of world exports to developing countries came from socialist economies. The percentage probably will increase to about 15–18 per cent in 1985. In this context, socialist countries, by priority, will continue to step up their imports of semi-manufactured and manufactured products from the developing countries. Scientific– technical co-operation between socialist and developing countries, as well as the joint construction of plants, infrastructure facilities, and so on, are due to play a more important role.[24] Long-term stability in relations is just as necessary as the involvement of new institutions already mentioned.[25]

VI.

The following are some probable development trends of international trade in the nonsocialist sector of the world economy.

(1) Growing trade among developing countries indicates that their share in world trade will slowly increase (value and quantum). Economic co-operation, the forming of economic communities, and so on, by developing countries will bring about new intraregional trade flows. There will be various types of economic communities. Among others, anti-imperialist states with progressive property, social and income structures will co-operate more closely. Moreover, developing economies that

---

[22] 'Implementations of the International Development Strategy', papers for UN, *First Over-all Review and Appraisal of Progress during the Second United Nations Development Decade* (New York, 1973), II, p. 92.

[23] 'The International Development Strategy. First Over-all Review and Appraisal of Issues and Policies', Report of the Secretary-General, ibid., II, p. 46.

[24] Cf. four proposals to improve industrial co-operation between centrally planned economies and developing countries, in 'Implementations of the International Development Strategy', ibid., p. 106.

[25] The founding of a development fund with the CMEA International Investment Bank was decided on in 1973. The fund became effective on 1 Jan 1974.

are already industrialised to a certain extent (including countries that produce important raw materials and fuels and occupy certain monopolistic positions) will probably become regional industrial centres for groups of developing countries. As a consequence, their demand for raw materials and fuel will rise and competition will intensify in the international markets for 'simple' manufactured products.

Differences will become more marked between the least developed and the more industrialised developing countries.[26] International measures will have to be taken in order to reduce hunger, disease and illiteracy in the least developed countries.

Under two conditions, subregional integration of developing countries will be not only successful but also progressive. These conditions are: (a) the improvement of domestic productivity by socially just and growth-promoting structures of property and distribution;[27] and (b) international co-operation with socialist states and with all nonsocialist countries and institutions that guarantee the building of an independent national economy and equal rights in economic co-operation.

(2) The foreign trade of developed capitalist countries will continue to grow more quickly than will their industrial output, because of the further advance of modern large-scale production. However, it seems likely that both the industrial output and foreign trade of these countries will grow more slowly in future, because of (a) the weakening of the basis of international exploitation for the leading capitalist economies (cf. Section III.6 above); (b) the destabilising effects of inflation, of monetary, capital-market, and balance-of-payments crises, and of hectic price fluctuations; (c) increasing social and political conflicts; (d) increasing expenditure on environmental protection; and (e) relative fuel and raw-material shortages – with research on substitutes and *de facto* substitution lagging behind for many years to come.[28]

(3) As a consequence of the trends outlined above in Sections V, VI.1 and VI.2, competition is likely to grow sharper in international capitalist markets. Trends towards regional groupings, protectionism, and bilateralism will increase – with competition among transnational corporations, on the one hand, and among individual countries and regional and subregional groupings, on the other. Among developed capitalist countries and several developing countries (those that are raw-material producers in the process of industrialisation), new regional economic relations (with agreements on investments, production and trade) will probably emerge. More disintegrating factors will be active in the EEC for these and other reasons.

[26] Cf. the relevant reference to present trends in World Bank–IDA, *1973 Annual Report.*
[27] Cf. UN, *Second Decade of Development,* document 2626 (XXV) and UNESCO, Committee for Development and Planning, Tinbergen Report, 1970.
[28] This lag is primarily explained by the fact that the purchase of low-priced fuels and raw materials from the developing countries stimulated the waste of these materials and not their replacement. The so-called 'energy crisis' is not a natural scarcity crisis but a socio-economic process.

(4) Decreasing growth rates (quantum index) in the foreign trade of the developed capitalist economies may be expected for the reasons presented in Sections VI.2 and VI.3. The percentage share (quantum index) of certain groups of developing countries in international trade will increase. Since raw materials and fuel are going to be in steady demand in all sectors of the world economy, an approximately parallel price development of raw materials and manufactured goods can be expected in the long run (and on average). These and other previously mentioned factors make it somewhat improbable that there will be a further drop in the percentage share of the developing countries in world trade.

VII.

I hold that the above-mentioned processes and trends justify the thesis that the world economy and international trade have entered a new phase in their post-war development.

To solve the problems of international economic relations in the new period, we can rely on the Declaration of the Sixth Special Session of the UN General Assembly, which stated, 'The present international economic order is in direct conflict with the current developments in international political and economic relations.'[29]

In the new phase of international economics, progressive forces in conflict with others will try to induce 'a rational, just, and equitable international division of labour' and aim at 'a fundamental restructuring of the world economic system'.[30]

[29] UN General Assembly, 'Declaration on the Establishment of a New International Economic Order'.
[30] Ibid.

Comments
Abba P. Lerner (Israel and USA)

I find Kohlmey's paper much too interesting. It deals with too many topics far beyond the narrow relationships, the complementarities and the rivalries — I almost said the contradictions — between intraregional and extraregional or international trade. His tendency to see more of the good in socialist co-operatively planned economic integration and more of the evils when the integration is planned by multinational corporations seems to me to be a reflection of his concern — which I strongly share — for greater equality of the division of wealth and income among different individuals, for a lessening of the difference between rich men and poor men. But I doubt if the desirability of this kind of equalisation, with its diminution of waste by the rich and of suffering by the poor, is really helped by other equalisations such as equalisation of the ratio of machinery imports to machinery exports of different countries. On the contrary, I would suspect such an equalisation to be the result of all of the countries trying to do all of the same things. They would do better to exploit differences in comparative advantages and differences in needs by letting the countries that are better at making machines specialise in making them, while the others specialise in other products, to the advantage of both. That would also mean more complete economic integration.

Greater economic integration is certainly much to be desired as a potentiality for greater personal incomes. But there is no guarantee that economic integration tends to *equalise* either personal, national or regional per capita incomes. All that it does is to maximise the *total* output of the integrated economy. It may very well increase the inequality at the same time. There is, indeed, no guarantee that it will not even *absolutely* reduce the income of some countries and regions and it is certain to damage some individuals.

Economic integration tends to be confused, by some writers in capitalist countries, with perfect or near-perfect competition. More accurately, it is the maximisation of output by the equalisation of marginal rates of transformation and marginal rates of substitution. This is a mathematical implication of efficiency that is no more respectful of the differences between capitalist competition and socialist planning than is the ratio of the circumference of a circle to its diameter, or the earth's gravitational constant of 32 feet per second. In any case, the equalisations (whether the appropriate ones or not) by socialist economics, and the alleged 'unequalisation' (Kohlmey's 'policy of underdeveloping') by imperialist or colonialist economics can be the result only of actions or policies that *sacrifice* some economic integration for the sake of the achievement of other objectives.

In this connection, one cannot explain the alleged 'unequalisations' as due to the 'vertical integrations' of multinational corporations frustrating potentially more beneficial 'horizontal integration'. Economic integration does not distinguish between verticality and horizontality. Both vertical and horizontal integrations are not economic integration at all. They are administrative combinations that may, perhaps, increase administrative efficiency and yet hamper economic integration if they are used in restrictive, monopolistic ways. And if they are used in these ways, they will *diminish* the amount of trade, whether intraregional or extraregional. It is too easy to say that the growth of socialist trade is *due to* socialist measures, and that the growth of multinational-corporation trade takes place *in spite of* the multinational corporations' activities. We have also been reminded, in many papers in this congress, that more trade does not always mean more gain from economic integration.

I find myself very critical of many points in Kohlmey's paper — and I cannot refrain from commenting on his castigation of capitalist countries for 'exploiting' workers from poorer countries, as if it would be better to refuse to employ them. Yet I want to turn to a more fundamental issue, where I think we may be moving in the same direction. In his repeated references to the superiority of socialist economics I think I see — though possibly I only imagine it — a recognition that economic integration is not really an ultimate. Economic integration is not a good in itself. Indeed, it is in direct conflict with objective that has, perhaps, a slightly stronger claim to be a good in itself. I am thinking of economic independence. Economic integration inevitably involves economic interdependence, which is nothing more than economic dependence — indeed, it is economic dependence doubled. It goes both ways.

Economic *in*dependence is sung in ancient literature — in the Biblical ideal of each man under his own fig tree— in the nineteenth century romanticism of Belloc's and Chesterton's 'Distributism', and in recent science-fiction fantasies of an economy where social organisation has been rendered impossible by the proliferation of atomic weapons, so that human life can go on only in single-family 'force-field' fortresses where ultra-technology permits high-economic-level family autarky — the ultimate in economic independence.

Indeed, economic science — it is, I hope, no longer necessary to call it bourgeois economics — can be conceived of as another model of artificial economic independence. If, as in capitalist perfect competition, or in a perfectly working socialist market economy, each member of society is paid the value of the marginal product of this labour, it makes no difference to all of the other members of the economy whether he works much or little or not at all. Exactly the same total product remains available for all of the other members. It is as if he were enjoying the results of his own labour in his own garden, tending his own fig tree, working much or little or not at all, and earning for himself the large, the small, or the zero harvest. The same logic holds remorselessly if each member is paid the marginal product not only of his labour, but also of any other factors of production that he owns, if his ownership of his factors of production is protected by society just as the ownership of his own labour is protected in a non-slave economy.

Of course, such a system, with its perfect 'economic independence', is compatible with extreme economic inequality, with its social inefficiency — the great waste by the rich and the great suffering by the poor. The same logic also holds inexorably where only labour gets its marginal product. There will still be the efficient, the industrious, the well-connected and those favoured by scarce skills — who will be rich; and the inefficient, the lazy, the unlucky, the weak and the sick — who will be poor. In neither case do we get social justice, although, of course, the wider the range of private property, the greater the scope for inequality and social injustice. Neither economic efficiency, nor economic independence, nor even the economist's model of the trick of extracting economic independence out of the most complete economic interdependence together with the ultimate in economic integration provides the social justice of economic equality.

But we are stuck with economic integration as inevitable for the survival of the burgeoning billions of our populations. We are beginning to realise that our economic progress is no gift from the gods. Our inventiveness is the daughter of necessity. It is the escape from the breakdown of ecological equilibrium. Social justice calls for *equalisation* of income — the elimination of inequality called exploitation. Efficiency — necessary for survival, because it maximises the product available for division — calls for the functional *inequality* that results from paying the value of the marginal product. As usual, one of the main tasks of the economist is to soften ideological calls for extremes in a *quantitative* compromise such as ideologues, who deal only in *qualities*, hate. What we have to aim at is not the most complete economic integration with its maximum profit, irrespective of the inequalities — the 'exploitations' — it would bring with it. Nor can we hope to reach the complete equality that would leave us with much too little to divide. We have to aim at the *optimum degree of integration*, which is, at the same time, also the *optimum degree of equalisation*. Seen from the other side, it is also the *optimum degree of exploitation*. In seeking the good society we thus have to aim at the optimum degree of exploitation just as we have to aim at the optimum degree of pollution or the optimum degree of corruption and even the optimum degree of crime. This is what is meant by striving to make our world a little more like the best of all *possible* worlds.

I should like to turn for a few minutes from these general, rather philosophical themes to the announced topic of this working group: 'World Trade and Intraregional Trade' — though I am afraid I must leave entirely to others the examination of the 'Trends and Structural Changes'.

I take it that our interest here in both kinds of trade is focused on their contribution to economic integration — and, of course, I prefer my own definition out of the vast way at which Machlup has vouchsafed us a peep. For maximising efficiency by equalising the marginal substitutabilities and transformabilities there is no need to choose between intra- and extraregional integration. Both are good. Nevertheless, we are continually faced with the sacrificing of external integration for the sake of furthering the internal integration of a region. I refer to the problem of trade creation and trade diversion.

We are occasionally warned that trade creation is not always good and trade diversion is not always bad. I prefer to put the issue in terms of the combination of the reduction of internal restrictions and the increase of external restrictions. We can expect the reduction of (internal) restrictions to be almost certainly good for efficiency and the increase of (external) restrictions to be bad.

If, for any reason, the two have to be combined, we must estimate the net result of the sum of the good and the bad. The difficulties of so doing are magnified by their interdependence. The reasons for having to combine the two elements are most intriguing to an economist, just because they are not economic reasons and they give him a chance of escaping for a while from the confines of 'the dismal science'.

It may be that the promoters of such projects are really much more interested in disintegration for the protection it would give them from external competition. We then get into the politics of their ability to get their private gain to overcome the social harm. It may be that the promoters are ambitious enthusiasts for politically or emotionally gratifying — but, nevertheless, economically wasteful — 'monuments' for which the integrated area is not as obviously inadequate as are the constituent parts. Or it may be that the internal benefits swamp the external damage, but they cannot be established without consenting to the damage. That the gain is greater than the loss, so that there is a *net gain*, is more likely the larger the integrated area is (economically) in relation to the outside. Machlup brought this out in his *reductio ad tautologicum* envisaging the integrated area as the whole world economy. The economist then finds himself back in his own familiar world.

Comments
Mikhail V. Senin (USSR)

Kohlmcy has given a detailed and profound report on the subject concerning this working group. My comments will not go beyond the questions put forward by him; they will only draw special attention to some of them.

I. THE ROLE OF THE WORLD SOCIALIST SYSTEM IN WORLD TRADE

I agree with what Kohlmey has said about the development of the socialist countries' economic and trade ties on a world scale. But I should like to dwell in more detail on the trends developing within the CMEA countries' economic community.

Statistics show that the CMEA countries' foreign economic ties develop in two main directions from the social—geographic standpoint, as it were: (1) intraregional trade within the CMEA community; and (2) trade with the rest of the world. In assessing the prospects for the future, account must be taken of the fact that the CMEA countries' economic community is a region characterised by very dynamic growth. Between 1949 and 1973 the combined national income of the CMEA member countries increased more than eight-fold and industrial production more than twelvefold. Over the same period agricultural output grew by approximately 150 per cent.

As regards the volume of foreign trade of the CMEA member countries, this grew between 1950 and 1973 more than elevenfold. Specifically, trade among the CMEA countries grew by a multiple of 10·5, trade with industrialised capitalist countries by a multiple of 13·0, and trade with developing countries by a multiple of 22·0.

Over the same period the CMEA countries' foreign trade grew (and continues to grow) faster than their national income, which shows that international relations play an ever-increasing role in their economic development. True, intraregional trade accounts for the bulk of the total foreign trade of the CMEA countries. Yet the rising trends of extraregional trade must be noted, the more so because the CMEA community is an open organisation both actually and legally.

How does the openness of the CMEA countries' economic community show itself, and what are its characteristics?

Undoubtedly, the social and economic similarity between the CMEA countries and other socialist countries makes it possible for the latter eventually to become active participants in the socialist integration. Openness in this sense has been in evidence for some time; it has been confirmed by the entry of the Mongolian People's Republic (1962) and then of Cuba (1972) into the CMEA organisation, by the co-operation between the CMEA and Yugoslavia on the basis of a special agreement, by the participation of observers from the Democratic Republic of Vietnam and the Korean People's Democratic Republic in the work of certain organs of the CMEA, and by relations between the CMEA countries and several other states.

At first the CMEA took shape as a multinational formation of European socialist countries. This was confirmed by the CMEA Charter adopted in 1960. As a result many have the impression that the CMEA is a *regional* formation of adjacent European socialist countries.

However, the entry of Mongolia and then of Cuba proved that this was not so. Considering the trends now in evidence, we are safe in saying that the CMEA countries' economic community has become a *social region* that unites socially homogeneous states and at the same time *does not rule out the possibilities for co-operating with countries of a different social system.*

In the latter case, the crux of the matter is that the nature of the CMEA, though a community of socially homogeneous states, by no means implies autarky; that is, the establishment along social lines of an economically secluded, closed grouping of countries rejecting economic ties with other states. On the contrary, it not only directly presupposes the development of such ties but also *helps augment the CMEA countries' export—import potential and potential for scientific and technical co-operation with countries of a different social system that are willing to develop such co-operation.* Moreover, the CMEA countries' integration has a special significance for the improvement of their economic structures *with a view to their more active participation in world trade.*

There is no need to conceal the fact that within the CMEA community there is still a tendency toward complete self-sufficiency, but this tendency is, in our opinion, of a merely temporary nature. It will unavoidably change in the historical process of integration under the influence of three counterforces:

(1) the objective (inevitable) process of balancing the intersectoral levels of production and eventual saturation of our markets with products now still in short supply;

(2) the unavoidable extension of worldwide division of labour and the gradual acceleration of industrial growth in the developing countries (which now comprise more than a half of mankind);

(3) the peaceful competition of two social systems, in which the CMEA countries' participation in world trade with 'key' industrial products is playing and will continue to play an ever-increasing role.

In considering the CMEA's participation in world trade in the light of these three factors, it is important to ascertain the implications of the community's relations with the industrially developed countries of the West.

Which of the two alternatives will be chosen: intense, competitive and possibly destructive struggle, or reasonable co-operation? I believe it is necessary to intensify the quest for forms of mutually advantageous co-operation; that is, to abide by the law of the inescapable internationalisation of economic life. Mutually advantageous co-operation corresponds to the principle of peaceful coexistence and is a major means of its implementation.

As regards the legal aspect of the CMEA's openness, the CMEA countries' economic community is guaranteed safe from autarky by the right of its members to maintain economic and scientific—technical ties, according to definite principles, with nonmember countries, and by the right of these nonmember countries to participate in the implementation of the measures mapped out in the CMEA's Comprehensive Programme. On this score the Programme says, 'Any country that is not a member of the CMEA may fully or partially participate in the implementation of the Comprehensive Programme. A non-member of the CMEA, sharing the aims and principles of the Programme, may participate fully in its implementation.'[1]

The words 'fully or partially' merit special attention. They refer to a question of principles. To be sure, perhaps not a single capitalist country fully shares the aims and principles of the *socialist* community, which are also its socio-political principles. Yet the principle 'all or nothing' is excluded. Modern productive forces, their technical–economic similarity and common nature in various social systems, and the deepening world division of labour have made it not only possible but also necessary for the socially heterogeneous partners to co-operate in the economic, scientific and technical fields. In this context it is precisely the legal principle 'fully or partially' that offers broad vistas for countries of contrasting social systems to participate, on the basis of mutual advantage, in different economic enterprises outlined in the Comprehensive Programme.

Thus, it is not by chance that the joint document of the CMEA countries states, 'International division of labour among socialist countries is carried out with due account for the division of labour in the world as a whole. In developing their economic ties with all countries of the world, the socialist countries thereby strengthen the material base for the peaceful coexistence of the world's two socio-economic systems.'[2] This idea has been amplified and further developed in the Comprehensive Programme.[3] The incipient co-operation between the CMEA countries and Finland on the basis of a special agreement eloquently illustrates this point.

It would appear that it is through such measures to promote increased international co-operation that the tendency, noted by Kohlmey, towards a slowdown of economic growth can be alleviated.

II. THE DEVELOPING COUNTRIES AND THE TRADE AND ECONOMIC RELATIONS BETWEEN THEM AND THE SOCIALIST STATES

It was not by chance that Kohlmey devoted so much attention to the developing countries, which are on the threshold of an industrial take-off. What attitude should be adopted towards this prospect? Should we impede or promote their industrial development? I believe that promoting these countries' growth is in the interest of all industrially developed countries, regardless of social system. A good clue to the solution of this problem is the principle of international co-operation in production based on mutual advantage and not the principle of imperialist self-interest. If we follow this route, we shall remove many hotbeds of international tension.

The question of mutual economic advantage has to be viewed in the historical perspective. It should be clear that a developing country at the stage of accumulation cannot export commodities that, as regards the degree of their manufacture, are equal to those supplied to the external markets by industrially developed countries. As a supplier of goods to the external market, a developing country passes through three stages in the process of becoming an industrial country: (1) it supplies products of extractive-

[1] *CMEA, Comprehensive Programme*, p. 98.
[2] *Fundamental Principles of the International Socialist Division of Labour* (Moscow: Ekonomika Publishers, 1964), p. 7 (in Russian).
[3] CMEA, *Comprehensive Programme*, p. 10.

industries and agriculture; (2) it supplies finished manufactured goods for mass (personal) consumption; and (3) it develops into a supplier of equipment (machines, components and spare parts) for industrial use. Of course, this is not to say that a country that has achieved a higher stage of economic development will entirely leave off supplying products characteristic of an earlier stage of development.

A distinguishing feature of the CMEA countries' economic policy is that all three stages are regarded as a strictly interdependent single chain, not a single link of which is allowed to loosen and become detached. The CMEA countries do not permit for 'freezing' of economic relations either at the first or at the second stage. This is precisely what constitutes the effort to promote the comprehensive industrial development of the developing countries.

It is quite natural that the industrial countries at present view the developing countries first and foremost in their capacity of suppliers of fuel, raw materials and farm produce. Yet the developing countries' economic importance as suppliers of goods for mass consumption will eventually grow more and more. The possibilities for the supply of these two types of goods are still far from being exhausted, but the logic of development is such that in a historically short period of time the currently developing countries will supply the world market with equipment and tools, machines and their components.

The prospects for the developing countries' transition to the third stage are directly connected with the problem of international economic integration. The developed countries should be ready for the currently developing countries to participate in international trade with their own industrial products, machines and mechanisms, on the basis both of the international division of labour and of their involvement in international co-operation and specialisation in production.

Economic relations with the developing countries are even now taking shape under a strong impact of integrational processes at work both in the socialist and the capitalist systems. Moreover, both socialist and capitalist countries display an increasing trend toward a joint involvement in the market of the developing countries. This involvement vigorously promotes the economic growth of the developing countries, but it must not affect the foundations of their social order. The decades of economic co-operation between countries of the two social systems have convincingly shown that this co-operation can be implemented without the imposition of one country's social order on another country. Social changes are governed by their own laws.

A number of business ventures in developing countries have been undertaken jointly by socialist and capitalist states. It seems that appropriate ways must be found to strengthen this tendency, so that a transition can be made from sporadic joint ventures to the implementation of a broad, long-range programme of co-operation.

Taking into account the criteria outlined above, the tendency toward a decrease in the developing countries' share in world trade seems to be unnatural and temporary, since these countries themselves are objectively in need of expanding trade. The same desire to expand trade is to be observed in the capitalist countries as well. The present overall economic situation is such that both capitalist and socialist countries must face the need to change the current tendency and channel it in a different direction.

The imperialist policy of impediments, noted in the report by Kohlmey, runs into a (by no means dialectical) contradiction with objective expediency and necessity. This necessity will itself contribute to the change in this policy, but it would be better if all this is understood soon and taken into consideration in the formulation of a new policy line.

I am convinced that the 'decapitalisation' of the developing countries and the mass export of profits from them (also noted by Kohlmey) is a phenomenon that runs counter to the interests both of the developing countries and of the countries responsible for it, because it undermines one of the foundations of their future development, which must be approached from the standpoint of the law of economic internationalisation.

Kohlmey underlines the dominance and the impeding exploitative role played by the multinational corporations in the developing countries' economy, and adduces convincing figures to support his view. But why are the corporations in a position to play such a role? Because of the way countries differ from each other with regard to level of development, structure, and economic legislation — differences that the corporations are able onesidedly to exploit and use to their own advantage. Therefore, support of the developing countries and their integration must be aimed at the elimination of these 'loopholes'. Such support would accord with the interests of world progress. I believe that the suggestions Kohlmey makes concerning new forms of international trade and productive co-operation merit close attention from scientists. Economists could be excellent mouthpieces for these ideas, which are consistent with the requirements of our day and age.

In my opinion, some conclusions contained in the report by Kohlmey give rise to further questions. They include: (1) the conclusion that *regional* industrial centres for groups of developing countries will develop, and that, as a result, competition for 'simple' finished products will intensify in the international markets; (2) the conclusion that centrifugal forces and forces of disintegration will begin to operate in the EEC; and (3) the conclusion that the volume of trade among the developing countries will grow only slowly as a proportion of total world trade.

Intensive industrial development will change this last trend. So far as the share of the developing countries in the world trade is concerned, it cannot naturally be reduced to the regional commodity turnover. Statistical data reflect the growth of trade between the socialist and developed capitalist countries on the one hand, and the socialist and the developing countries, on the other hand.

These tentative conclusions suggest that, should these processes make themselves felt, the differences in level of development will be intensified and relations on the world market will worsen. However, we can arrive at different conclusions if we take account (and this is not simple) of a broader range of factors that can simultaneously act in the opposite direction. Indeed, is this process fatally inevitable?

On the one hand, Kohlmey's conclusions are compatible with the law of the unbalanced economic and political development characterising the epoch of modern capitalism. On the other hand, the question arises of whether sufficient account is taken of other objective factors, such as the consolidation of the world socialist system, the cumulative effect of the law of the world division of labour, the nuclear factors, and the greater requirements imposed by recognition of the principle of peaceful coexistence and mutual assistance.

So far as I can see, Kohlmey is far from relying on the spontaneous and fatal processes. It is clear that greater conscious effort must be made to organise international co-operation. It is highly commendable in this context that he points to the need to reallocate huge resources currently devoted to military needs to the organisation of assistance and the development of trade. This is all the more important because disarmament and reduction of military outlays remove 'fetters' from precisely those branches of the economy and types of production that are of primary value for the development of international trade and assistance to the developing countries, especially for the purpose, so necessary for the world, of equalising of levels of economic development within and among different groups of countries.

Opening Statement for Group Discussion
Madan Gopad Mathur (India)

This statement identifies some of the main trends in international trade over the past two decades and looks briefly at some future prospects.[1]

Since the early 1950s, the growth of world trade has continued to accelerate both in value and in volume terms and, especially for mining products and manufactures, has been more rapid than the growth of world production. The ratio of imports to GNP has risen not only in the developed market economy countries, including the United States, where it increased from 4·6 per cent in 1953 to over 7 per cent in 1972, but also in the socialist countries and in the developing areas.

The highest per annum growth has been recorded by the trade of the developed areas, which today account for over 71 per cent of world exports and conduct 77 per cent of their global trade exchanges with one another. The share of the CMEA or Eastern trading area in world trade has remained stable at 10 per cent. The trade of developing countries has not only declined in global terms up to 1970, but also, in spite of the relatively higher rate of increase to the CMEA area, has tended to become increasingly concentrated on the developed market economy countries.

In the trade among developed countries, trade flows inside customs unions and free-trade areas (or under other special arrangements, such as the United States—Canadian Automotive Agreement) have been growing faster than has trade under most-favoured-nation rates. Likewise, trade within regional groups of developing countries, such as the Latin American Free Trade Association and the Central American Common Market, has tended to grow faster than has trade among developing countries in general. Trade among the CMEA countries has grown somewhat less rapidly in recent years than has the external trade of the area, but this is accounted for, in part, by the greater stability of prices within the area.

The movement towards various forms of economic integration, however, has made greater progress among developed than among developing countries. Developing-country markets have thus remained narrow and fragmented. At the same time, due to changes in trade shares, a more balanced multipolar relationship has emerged among the developed countries and, notably, among the United States, the EEC, and Japan.

There is no clear evidence that trade under special arrangements between developed and developing countries, such as those represented by the Commonwealth system of preferences or the EEC association agreements, has been growing faster than has trade between developed and developing countries in general. A significant expansion in the scope of these special arrangements may occur as a result of the negotiations for the association of the Caribbean, African and Pacific countries with the enlarged EEC, as well as from the arrangements worked out with the Mediterranean countries. However, the impact of these arrangements on trade flows will be affected by the Community's trade and development policies towards other countries.

---

[1] The views expressed in this paper are those of the author and not of the organisation to which he belongs.

How development policies of other countries and the formation of trade links among developing countries are affected would also be important.

There has been a remarkable increase (from 49 per cent in 1955 to over 65 per cent in 1972) in the share of manufactures in world trade. This has been influenced, in part, by changes in the relative prices of primary commodities and manufactures, particularly between 1951 and 1962. Trade both in agricultural products and in raw materials has also continued to suffer from a pattern of price instability. However, trade in agriculture, in particular, has been affected by frequent imbalances between supply and demand, and by the insulation of national and regional markets through governmental measures of price and income support and through intervention at the frontier. On the other hand, the sustained economic growth of industrial economies over most of the post-war period has permitted a moderate year-to-year growth in trade in raw materials. This contrasts with the sharp swings experienced in the pre-war years.

Of particular concern is the fact that the agricultural exports of developing countries have grown even more slowly than has global trade in agriculture, thus accentuating the overall decline in the share of these countries in world trade. Exports from developing countries have remained concentrated on a number of agricultural commodities, such as tropical beverages and agricultural raw materials, for which world demand has grown only slowly. The share of these countries in the more dynamic product groups (such as meat, foodgrains and feeding stuffs) has also been declining. While policies of agricultural protectionism have played a role in these developments, the increasing dependence of many developing countries on imports of foodgrains suggests a long-term failure of agricultural productivity to expand in line with rising domestic demand.

Developing country exports of manufactures have expanded at a rate faster than the global growth of manufactured exports and now cover a number of product categories extending far beyond the traditional labour-intensive manufactures. Nevertheless, such exports still constitute only about 7 per cent of the total imports of manufactures into developed countries and about 1 per cent of the domestic consumption in these countries. About 90 per cent originate in some fifteen relatively higher income countries where their high rate of expansion can be said to be the leading factor in the high growth rate of the economy as a whole. A similar percentage of exports to developed countries is concentrated on about 500 tariff lines, or twenty product categories or subcategories, and have, according to estimates made by Mahfuzur Rahman in his 'Exports of Manufactures from Developing Countries', an average capital intensity of less than $1000 per worker, as against a global average of more than $3000.[2] On the other hand, for more sophisticated products such as office machines, television tubes, computer circuits, and the like, the proportion of value-added accounted for by processing in developing countries is relatively small. A more leading role for exports of manufactures in contributing to GNP growth and trade prospects in developing countries would imply an increase in the number of countries participating in this trade, and not only a growth in exports in

[2] In terms of fixed capital per person employed, based on the method used in the Indian Annual Survey of Industries, 1965.

those categories in which these countries already enjoy a comparative advantage, but also an upgrading of the overall export structure.

Trade exchanges among developed countries have been characterised by an increasing concentration within the same narrow industrial branches, the most dynamic of these being in the engineering and chemical industries with a high research and development content. Hufbauer, in Raymond Vernon's *The Technology Factor in International Trade*, has provided a convenient, if catch-all, summary of the explanations provided for this result by contemporary trade theories, which variously emphasise such factors as skill requirements of production and distribution, scale economies, and leads in learning, technology and product innovation. The operation of these factors implies a process of growing intra-industry specialisation that, as pointed out by Béla Belassa and others, has become particularly pronounced in trade among the EEC countries.

The progressive gearing of production to regional or international markets on the basis of scale economies and product and process specialisation has been greatly facilitated by the liberalisation of trade within regional arrangements and, more generally, on a most-favoured-nation basis. It must also be seen against the liberalisation of investment flows and the progressive internationalisation of production that this has helped to bring about, particularly through the special form of transmission of capital, technology and management represented by the multinational or transnational corporation. In 1970, according to the Report to the United States Senate Finance Committee on 'Implications of Multinational Firms for World Trade and Investment and for United States Trade and Labor', multinational firms accounted for only 23 per cent of total world exports and 20 per cent of world exports of manufactures. Outside of Latin America, where the multinationals' 30—40 per cent share of exports of manufactures gives them a special interest in schemes for regional trade liberalisation, the share of multinational corporations in the exports of developing countries is even smaller. However, there are three aspects of the impact of multinational corporations on trade flows that merit particular attention.

(1) As pointed out by Raymond Vernon, in an oligarchic market the balancing of conflicting demands of different sources and supplies by multinational corporations may have more influence in shaping the direction of international commodity transactions than do cost advantages and factor endowments in individual countries. This can be a source of particular concern when a parent company suppresses competition within its network through allocation of markets.

(2) In sales between multinational corporations and their subsidiaries, market flows and prices tend to be replaced by internal flows and prices of international firms. This, again as pointed out by Vernon, raises some important questions about the role of prices in international trade in manufactures. Here, of course, it must be remembered that, even though trade liberalisation in the post-war era has served greatly to reduce market rigidities, the role of prices and of comparative cost advantages in international trade in manufactures has been affected over this period not only by horizontal or vertical integration of the type represented by multinational corporations, but also by product and brand differentiation, dual

pricing practices and governmental measures of tariff and nontariff protection.

(3) The relatively recent growth of so-called runaway industries in developing countries represents a dynamic new extension of the efforts of multinational corporations to locate production facilities in those countries that provide the most favourable conditions for servicing a world market. This phenomenon does bring with it questions about the contribution that subcontracting or assembly operations in developing countries make in terms of linkages with other sectors of the economy and the acquisition of technology or marketing skills. It also stimualtes concern over the export of jobs from the home country. However, it is not clear that either home or host countries would regard as a more desirable alternative the large-scale import of immigrant labour into the industrialised countries in order to sustain certain types of industrial activities.

It seems deep-rooted in the forces underlying the growth of industrial economies that there should be further rapid integration of developed countries through trade exchanges and investment flows, accompanied by an increasing concentration of trade exchanges on manufactures and an increasingly important role for intraindustry and product specialisation and for large multinational agglomerations. Past trends in the shaping of trade flows would also imply that the share of developing countries in imports of manufactures into developed-country markets will increase to considerably above its present level of 7 per cent, accompanied, however, for many of these countries, by an increased dependence on agricultural imports.

While exports from the CMEA area have expanded equally for both the developed market-economy countries and the developing countries, the increase in imports from the former group has been considerably larger than for imports from the latter. The trend towards a particularly rapid increase in East—West exchanges is supported by the emphasis on the multilateralisation of trade relations among the socialist and the developed market-economy countries, the production and trade links being forged on both sides, and the importance attached by CMEA countries to improving productivity through high-technology imports.

However, even prior to the fuel crisis of 1973, both the limitations and the success of existing policies in promoting the interdependence of national economies were beginning to give rise to serious problems of adjustment requiring new initiatives in the monetary and trade field. While trade flows have increased since 1970, they have also been characterised by an increasing fragility and a highly volatile reaction to monetary uncertainty, differences in national rates of inflation, and differential pressures on commodity and factor markets. Future trade patterns for countries outside the CMEA area, in particular, are likely to be influenced both by the unusual process of uncertainty and change to which the international economy has been subject in recent years and by the restructuring of trade policies to take account of the new pressures in the agricultural and primary-commodities sectors. In a harsher economic environment, protectionist pressures against imports of textiles and other labour-intensive manufactures from developing countries are also likely to intensify, so that if past growth trends — which involve, as they do, a process of interindustry, as opposed to intraindustry, specialisation — are to be maintained, more active policies of structural adjustment may be needed than have so far been pursued in developed countries.

In 1973, world trade grew in value terms by nearly 37 per cent and in volume terms by 14 per cent. For the second year in succession, exports of primary products grew more rapidly in value than did those of manufactures. In contrast to a twenty-year trend, exports from developing countries grew at a rate slightly faster than did world trade, most of the increase stemming from the rise in commodity prices. The further continuation of these trends will, however, be influenced by efforts, in nearly all oil-importing countries, to tighten measures against inflation, to absorb oil-induced deficits and to achieve the recycling of oil funds, and to adjust investment patterns to the higher cost of energy. There have already been important changes in trading patterns among the oil-exporting countries and others. To the extent that supply shortages continue to be a dominant factor in spite of shortfalls in industrial demand, the more important role of raw materials in international trade will bring additional gains for a number of developing countries and for some other resource-producing countries. It seems evident, however, that many of the most populous developing countries (which are also important importers of raw materials) may find that, without a breakthrough in agricultural productivity (which has been made even more difficult by the increase in the cost of agricultural inputs), their growth prospects and their participation in international trade have become more meagre than ever.

Report on Group Discussion
Henk C. Bos (Netherlands)[1]

The subject for discussion in Working Group J was 'World Trade and Intraregional Trade: Trends and Structural Changes'. The description still leaves open various approaches to the subject: quantitative assessment of these trends and changes; economic analysis of the factors that have determined the actual developments; and formulation and, preferably, empirical testing of trade theories, or critical evaluation of trade policies. Geographically, the theme of the working group covers the global development of trade by volume and structure; that is, composition by countries and commodities (or groups of these), trade relations among 'developed' and 'developing' countries and between centrally planned economies and developed market economies, and intraregional trade in various regional groupings.

The opening statement by Mathur contained a careful analysis of changes in world trade patterns over the period 1955–72, supported by a wealth of factual information. However, this statement did not set the tone of the discussions. The group heard and, at various points, discussed, not only the invited papers, but also summaries of some seventeen papers contributed on a voluntary basis, mainly by East European economists. These papers covered more or less all of the subjects just mentioned. However, most papers and the discussions that they generated focused on the economic and trade relations between East European and Western countries. The emphasis was on the future and on desirable changes in trade and other economic policies, rather than on statistical and economic analysis. Some of the themes that had emerged during the plenary sessions were reflected also in the deliberations in the group.

One such theme was that international trade is not the only, nor even the most important, aspect of economic integration. Another was that integration within the EEC had unfavourably affected trade flows between the EEC and the rest of the world, whereas integration within the CMEA had had no such negative effects. A third theme was the urgent need to expand East–West trade and economic co-operation.

Four groups of questions were distinguished for the structuring of the discussions. They concerned: (1) general aspects of world trade; (2) trade among developed and developing countries; (3) East–West trade and trade within the CMEA; and (4) trade within other regional groupings. As has already been mentioned, it was the third subject (East–West relations) that attracted most attention.

The most important *general* aspect of world trade discussed concerned the development of prices in the world market, and, in particular, the consequences of the recent price increases for primary commodities. The presentation of estimates of the terms of trade between primary products and manufactures over the long-run period 1896–1973 gave rise to a lively discussion on future price trends and on the methods to be used for forecasting prices. The historical data show the absence of distinct trends

[1] The assistance of Rune Hellberg is gratefully acknowledged.

and the possibility of sudden changes in prices over shorter periods. The difficulties of forecasting price developments were recognised, but the need to have such forecasts as a basis for decision making and long-term policy formulations was equally emphasised. There was agreement that simple extrapolations of historical price trends do not provide reliable results and that, whenever possible, forecasts should be based on the results of an analysis of the causal factors determining the price developments.

Although some speakers from Eastern Europe maintained that the CMEA should adopt its own price structure, independent of the world market, with prices to be derived, where possible, from the application of programming models, the general view was that Eastern Europe could not isolate itself from price developments on the world market.

One theoretical paper discussed the dynamisation of the theory of comparative costs.

On the second subject − trade among developed and developing countries − the importance and urgency of improving the trade opportunities for developing countries were recognised. The complex effects of the increases in the price of oil and of other raw materials for the developing countries, as well as the impact of the transnational corporations on the developing countries, were pointed out. However, and unfortunately, no real 'triologue' involving East, West and South took place.

Several contributions on the third subject, East−West relations, concerned various aspects of the economic and trade relations between the EEC and the CMEA. Statistical data were presented to illustrate the low level of the trade relations between the two groups. The statistical pitfalls in measuring the intensity of these relations were pointed out. There was agreement that there still exists a great potential for increasing trade between the EEC and the CMEA countries. Both economic and institutional factors explain the present relatively low level of such trade.

Several speakers brought out the familiar complaints against the EEC and other market-economy countries, saying that not all of these countries accord most-favoured-nation treatment to imports from Eastern Europe; several impose quantitative restrictions; the EEC agricultural policy has unfavourably affected East European exports of dairy products, livestock (cf. the temporary meat surplus in the EEC), and so on. As there were few speakers from Western countries, the complaints of these countries against the trade policies of East European countries, as evoked in the discussion, were those ascribed to them by the East European speakers!

However, more balanced statements, illustrated by statistical data, expressed the view that integration within the EEC and EFTA had not noticeably hampered the growth of trade between the EEC and EFTA, on the one hand, and the CMEA countries, on the other, and that the still relatively low level of this trade could not be blamed on only one party.

The main emphasis in the discussion was, however, not on the past and present, but on the future growth of trade − in particular, of trade between the EEC and the CMEA. One speaker suggested that this subject should be recommended to the Executive Committee of the International Economic Association for future conferences.

One speaker from Western Europe pointed out that the natural counterparts of the foreign-trade monopolies in the East are the transnational corporations in the West; that, however, special consideration should be given to the interests of small countries and small firms; that trade and industrial co-operation should go hand in hand; and that further efforts should be made to multilateralise East—West economic relations. In addition, examples of positive experiences with industrial co-operation between East and West, with positive side-effects for trade relations, were given by an East European participant.

In the discussion on trade within the CMEA group, it was emphasised that it is not possible to optimise trade on a regional basis. An improvement in the modalities for East—West trade should concern not only the relations between the EEC and the CMEA, but also those between the CMEA and the rest of the world — both other developed market-economy countries and developing countries. This theme was also expressed by others, in terms of the need for developing an international division of labour, not at a regional but at a world level. It was reported that research on this subject is going on both in East European and in Western countries. Attention was drawn to the desirability of co-operation in this research, particularly as concerns the economic relations between the CMEA and the EEC; and it was recommended that the organisation of such scientific co-operation between East and West be brought to the attention of the Executive Committee of the International Economic Association.

For the fourth and final group of questions discussed, the working group listened to a summary of the results of a statistical study on the estimation of changes in trade flows between one specific country (Turkey) and the EEC. Finally, attention was drawn to the importance of including external effects, in particular environmental damage, in the analysis of foreign trade, so as to prevent a deterioration in the stability in world trade.

In summing up the main characteristics of the discussions, it may be said that, although several economists from Eastern Europe expressed strong criticism of Western economic thought and policies, at the same time a more balanced view was expressed. This view stressed that regional integration, although useful, is not sufficient, but that wider economic co-operation is necessary. More East—West co-operation in science and technology, in industrial development and in economic research on the basic trends in world economic development was strongly recommended.

Index

Entries in **bold type** indicate papers contributed by participants; entries in *italics* indicate comments on papers and discussion of papers by participants.